THE STRANGE DEATH OF ARCHITECTURAL CRITICISM
MARTIN PAWLEY
COLLECTED WRITINGS

THE STRANGE DEATH OF ARCHITECTURAL CRITICISM
MARTIN PAWLEY
COLLECTED WRITINGS

Edited by David Jenkins
Foreword by Norman Foster

black dog
publishing

Preface

I thought I knew an awful lot about Martin before we even met. When I arrived at The Architects' Journal in 1987 he was still spoken of with a mixture of awe and horror. He seemed to haunt the newsroom like a poltergeist. A year later when I went to his flat to talk about the Foster books, which he was then editing, I discovered another person entirely: sharp, no doubt, but also witty, kind and unfailingly generous. I came away from that first meeting feeling that I had learned something and I have felt the same way after each subsequent encounter, of which there have been many. When illness forced Martin to announce his retirement as a writer in June 2005, some colleagues wrote encomia that I thought had a premature whiff of the obituary about them. Knowing Martin's dark sense of humour, I suspected that they would have made him chuckle. I sent him a note suggesting that we should have lunch to celebrate the fact that he was still very much alive. From that lunch grew the idea for this book. That was the easy part: deciding which essays to include took some time. We started with a very long list and slowly whittled it down to 100, arguing the various merits and demerits of each piece as we went. In making the final selection I felt it was as important to reveal Martin the man as it was to represent Martin the critic, and I hope we have found a balance. In editing this book I am grateful to the many people whose support and creative contributions have made it possible. In order of appearance, I would like to thank Philippa Morrison for being such an excellent sounding board and a marvellous host; Oliver Pawley for his heroic search through vintage computer files, which recovered lost treasures; Paul Finch and Emap for generously sponsoring the re-keying of Martin's early essays; Bart Pawley for helping to choose the title ("Martin Pawley: the best bits" was briefly considered); Thomas Manss and Joana Niemeyer for developing such an elegant design; Louis Hellman for allowing us to reproduce two of his cartoons; Duncan McCorquodale of Black Dog for having the vision to publish the book; and Norman Foster for agreeing to write the foreword. Most of all I would like to thank Martin: for the many pleasant hours we have spent working together; and, not least, for being so unfailingly enjoyable to read.

David Jenkins
London, May 2007

Contents

10 Foreword—Norman Foster

13 Introduction—David Jenkins

24 The Time House 1968

35 Looking for a sound 1969

40 Meeting Buckminster Fuller 1970

45 A new kind of message in a bottle 1975

48 My lovely student life 1975

59 We shall not bulldoze Westminster Abbey:
Archigram and the retreat from technology 1976

70 Thoughts on the design of houses and banknotes 1978

72 This England—coming home 1980

74 What does vernacular really mean? 1981

76 The defence of modern architecture 1983

85 Sex, violence and design 1983

87 Self-build workstations: a partial history 1983

90 Norman Foster 6.0, 6.0, 6.0 1984

95 Building revisits: Coventry Cathedral 1984

99 Building revisits: Hunstanton School 1984

106 The most important building of the twentieth century 1984

109 Heavy stuff this symbolism 1984

113 Beyond messing about in boats 1984

117 Office design in Eternia 1985

119 Quinlan Terry: beyond the tantrums of modernism 1985

123 Plucky Jim 1985

128 Doubts about Lloyd's 1986

134 Two triumphs of twisted wire 1986

140 Dan Dare: an extremely small step for mankind 1986

143 Welcome to the House of Fun 1986

147 A winter school's tale 1987

149 Objects of our time: the Piccadilly Line train 1987

154 Tower blocks and tourist castles 1987

158 Technology transfer 1987

173 The secret life of the engineers 1989
179 Life in the urban war zone 1989
186 Lost arks of the air 1989
189 Dymaxion: the car that never flew 1989
193 Is ecology all hot air? 1990
198 A precedent for the Prince 1990
208 The footmen of Alexandra Road 1990
211 The best lecture I ever gave 1990
215 In pursuit of the ultimate driving machine 1990
219 Exogenous shock 1990
226 Where the big sheds are 1990
229 Notes on the meaning of trivial things 1991
233 The design origins of royal train syndrome 1991
238 High-tech architecture: history versus the parasites 1991
247 The cost of the new culture of cities 1991
250 Henry Ford and the biospherans 1991
253 What London learned from Las Vegas 1991
257 What's in a name? 1991
260 Stansted and the triumph of big sheds 1991
268 And you thought your car was good for nothing 1992
271 Nigel Coates: from nihilist to planner 1992
275 A full and Frank talk 1992
280 The case for uncreative architecture 1992
283 Lunch with Leon Krier 1992
288 Zaha escapes the pull of gravity 1993
292 Tales of the obsolescent 1993
295 Invasion of the body snatchers 1995
297 Invasion of the vibrators 1996
299 Frank Lloyd Wright fights for his life 1996
301 The rise of the engineer 1996
304 After postmodernism, terrorism 1996
307 Meeting the future everywhere 1997
309 From here to modernity 1997

311 Seat pocket aliens 1997
313 The myth of monumentality 1997
318 So long recycling, here comes secondary use 1997
320 A night to remember 1998
322 Terminal architecture 1998
330 The strange death of architectural criticism 1998
332 When air conditioning meets its match 1999
334 A brace of fins du siècles 1999
336 The new life of Albert Speer 2000
338 Traffic congestion and confusion 2000
340 America: it's 24–7 at mission critical 2001
342 Ordering buildings like hamburgers 2001
344 Rocket science at the AA 2001
346 Shooting at statues 2001
348 Hong Kong's space shuffle 2001
350 Tall buildings: the end of a civilisation 2001
352 How to get famous by not building anything 2002
356 Battleships hold the key to the future of tall buildings 2002
358 Saved by the intelligent toilet 2002
360 Why prefabrication fails 2002
362 Technological jewels in the crown 2003
364 The defining moment of modernism 2003
366 Porsche 911, a genetically modified machine 2003
372 Nonsuch Metropolitan University summer school 2003
374 Return of the phone box 2003
376 Not-so-smart intelligent buildings 2003
380 Henry Ford and the limits of prefabrication 2003
382 The end of an interface 2003
384 It's an ill wind... 2004
386 The nine ages of transport 2004
388 The myth of the urban future 2004
390 Flying antiques 2004
392 Heavy bottles for a picnic 2004

394 The strange world of luxury watches 2004
396 The young dig in their heels 2005
398 How total urbanism will come to grief 2005
400 The answer to an historical conundrum 2005
402 The biggest house sale in history 2005

406 Notes
413 Sources
419 Bibliography
441 Index
448 Credits

Foreword

If you are an architect you might think you need a critic like the proverbial hole in the head. Most times you are probably right. This is perhaps a reflection on the level of criticism as much as the architect's vanity or insularity. Fortunately, there are enlightened exceptions. Sometimes a critic emerges whose perception is so sharp, and whose arrow is so swift and accurate, that it stops you in your tracks. It makes you think.

However, critics of this kind are rare indeed; and writers of Martin Pawley's insight and fluency are rarer still. A conversation with Martin can set your brain buzzing. His depth of knowledge and historical range is astonishing. So too is his grasp of contemporary culture. It gives him an incredible perspective. Allied with that is the ability instantly to see through humbug or challenge accepted wisdom—to bring fresh thinking to bear. This book, therefore, is a cause for celebration under many headings, not least because it reminds us how original and refreshing architectural criticism at its best can be.

Reading him sometimes you detect his frustration with the rest of us mere mortals and our failure to grasp the real issues, especially with fundamentals such as the environment or the future impact of technology. Bucky Fuller, who changed the way we think about such things, was very similar in that regard. Interestingly, reading Martin's 1970 interview with Bucky you see how even he—one of Martin's personal heroes—was not immune from criticism. Bucky's failure, if that is the right word, was that he had not managed to convince the world of the essential 'rightness' of his position.

In other instances, you detect Martin's anger, though it is often disguised beneath a mask of humour. Naming no names, there are people—even princely beings—whose historicism offends him so deeply that as you read you can practically hear the wheels of the tumbril and the thud of the guillotine. In that sense, there is more than a hint of the revolutionary, the anarchist even, in his writing. But like all true revolutionaries he has a deep understanding of history, and how it tends to repeat itself—whether as tragedy or farce. He has spoken about the shortness of the public memory; about the immediacy of the past and the 'old-fashionedness' of the present.

It was Martin who highlighted for me how, despite the awesome machinery of construction at our disposal, the command and control system that we use in Britain to direct development has become so ponderous that it cannot even match its own performance of 150 years ago. Look at our approach to infrastructure and note that in the 50 years to 1888, in the process of building the railways, the Victorians laid 1,000s of miles of track, built 100s of bridges and stations, and prompted the adoption of standardised time across the country. Travel times shrank by margins so vast that we can only marvel at it. A journey that had taken four days at the beginning of the nineteenth century took four hours by the end of it. That it probably still takes us four hours, whether we travel by car, train or plane tells us how, in a sense, we have barely advanced upon the Victorians at all.

Over the years, Martin's perception of history—and mastery of historical detail—has helped to bring many contemporary issues into sharper focus. He urges us to look forward but with a watchful eye on the lessons of the past. He shows us how technology is evolving and how our expectations of what is possible and desirable evolve with it. And perhaps most importantly he offers a reminder for those among us that would turn back the clock —that the only constant is change.

Norman Foster

Introduction

The title of this book—*The strange death of architectural criticism*—is drawn from a piece that Martin Pawley wrote for *The Architects' Journal* in July 1998. There he laments not just the decline of architectural criticism as a discipline —an art even—but the passing of an era in which architects were prepared either to openly embrace criticism or simply take it on the chin. However, a diligent coroner looking at this case might note that even at its most vigorous, architectural criticism was always an arcane discipline kept alive by the efforts of a handful of writers. Among that distinguished group, Pawley himself stands out as a master. This book, therefore, is both a celebration of Pawley's 40 year career as a critic and a reminder of how exhilarating architectural writing at its best can be.

If Pawley is right, and architectural criticism is indeed now finally dead, it is a death long foretold. JM Richards, editor of *The Architectural Review* from 1937 to 1971, bemoaned the lack of architectural criticism in England in the 1930s. He noted that architecture had been wrapped in "professional mystery" to a point where only those from within the profession were thought to be qualified as critics. In that gentler age, most architects, he believed, were "inhibited by the professional man's reluctance to infringe etiquette by criticising his fellow practitioners". Responsibility therefore fell on 'outsiders' or lapsed initiates, like Richards himself—who gave up a career as an architect—who knew exactly how to lift the mysterious veil. Pawley is another initiate turned outsider, though in his case one senses a professional career not so much abandoned as quietly parked and never restarted.

Martin Edward Pawley was born in 1938 in Borehamwood, where his father was a sound engineer at Elstree Studios, working with the celebrated Crown Film Unit. Later, when his father managed a country cinema, the teenage Pawley would spend evenings holed up in the projection room —there is every sign of a misspent youth. His studies took him first to the Oxford School of Architecture, where he edited a subversive but sadly abortive student magazine called D, then to the École Nationale Supérieure des Beaux-Arts in Paris, and finally to the Architectural Association in London. Pawley's AA diploma thesis "The Time House" was published in the September 1968 edition of *Architectural Design*—a rare distinction —and it is included here.

The AA is significant also as the scene of his first period of teaching and his second, albeit gloriously brief, foray into magazine editing. In 1974, he became founding editor of the AA's weekly broadsheet *Ghost Dance Times* —a politically charged and (presciently sex-crazed) tabloid. Memorable headlines include "Dr Charles Jencks on Sex and Communication" with equally memorable accompanying imagery. Sadly in 1975, after little more than 20 issues, AA chairman Alvin Boyarsky pulled the plug. In issue 24, Pawley wrote a suitably sardonic editorial headed "*Morituri Te Salutamus*" ("We who are about to die salute you"—the gladiatorial salutation to the Roman emperor on entering the arena.) As Pawley says, "It is an axiom of the trade that all editors will one day be ex-editors, possibly sooner rather than later." It was an early lesson in the price of principle—that you can't be an irritant as a critic and have too many friends.

By Richards' criterion, Pawley is perfectly cast in the role of critic. But he is far from the donnish figures that Richards might have passed on the stairs of the Architectural Press. He is an altogether more elusive, complex character. He is highly sceptical of environmentalist dogma, yet an early proponent of finding new ways of building using waste materials. He is ever ready to puncture ballooning egos or challenge the absurd, but fiercely loyal to those he admires. He is a lover of the motorcar and mechanical contraptions of all eras, yet happiest in a sailboat with the wind behind him. He is an accomplished historian—an expert in the history of the Second World War—but more comfortable in the role of futurologist.

His earliest 'signature' pieces were written for *Architectural Design* while he was assistant news editor of the rival *The Architects' Journal*, forcing him to go under the cover of 'Rupert Spade'—a character he bracketed somewhere between Sam Spade and Rupert of the Rhine. One imagines a Bohemian boulevardier, full of the turbulent spirit of '68—a hint of the blade in the flash of his pen. Another earlier, but sadly less used, alias was 'Bert Trench', 'war poet'—doubtless a brooding son of toil.

Yet, while the *nom de plume* is a common device in architectural criticism —JM Richards resorted to 'James MacQuedy' to get under the skin of the modernists—Pawley has always preferred to confront his targets in the open. Over the past four decades, he has contributed to, or edited, every major British architectural journal, written for all the leading international magazines, served as London correspondent for the Italian magazine *Casabella* and been the architecture critic of two national newspapers, *The Observer* and *The Guardian*.

On five of those journals he has held the Olympian position of columnist, culminating with an unbroken run of 505 weekly contributions to *The Architects' Journal*, many of which are included here. It is a position that Pawley relishes for the creative freedom it allows. For ten years, from 1980 until 1990, he wrote a monthly column in the *RIBA Journal*, and, from 1990 to 1994, a fortnightly column in *Building* magazine, for which he was voted columnist of the year by the Periodical Publishers' Association in 1991. In 1995, he was voted runner up in the same category for his column in *The Architects' Journal*, and in 1998 was again columnist of the year for his work in the same magazine. It is a measure of his success—to say nothing of his dexterity—that he habitually wrote for several magazines simultaneously, also contributing to *Blueprint* and editing *World Architecture* during this period.

As a critic, Pawley is as engaging on the television screen as he is in print. From 1989 until 1995, he was a consultant and contributor on architecture and design matters to the BBC2 arts programme *The Late Show*. In the process, he consolidated an enviable reputation as one of the most insightful and provocative international commentators on contemporary architecture and design. Nominating the East German Trabant as a 'design classic' was a characteristic highlight; and his 1994 documentary on the effects of the recession on architecture entitled "Architecture Armageddon" attained the highest viewing figures ever recorded for a *Late Show* programme.

Pawley's range as a writer is extraordinary. He can shift from the 'gonzo' style of Hunter S Thompson through the gentle surrealism of the *Daily Telegraph*'s Peter Simple to magisterial sweeps through the contemporary architectural condition that are virtually without rival, both in their depth of study and their sharpness of perception. I add the qualification only because of the inevitable comparison with Reyner Banham, whose energy and erudition as a critic were boundless. Banham tried always, in his own words, "to treat heavy stuff with a light touch". Pawley might be thought of in a similar vein, though his mood is undoubtedly darker.

Banham's dismissal of architecture as merely "a cultural solution to the problem of enclosure" is one of Pawley's springing points for "The Time House" and appears as a leitmotiv in much of his future work. Indeed, *Theory and Design in the Second Machine Age*, which he published in 1990, is in some respects a sequel to Banham's seminal work of 30 years earlier. Yet while Banham is essentially concerned with history, Pawley stands firmly in a troublesome present, which he characterises as "an age without ideology". Prompted by questions about the relationship between technology and architecture that Banham posed in his final chapter, Pawley presents a bleak analysis of architectural thought at a time when the anti-modern reactionaries were gaining ground.

However, it would be quite wrong to try to paint Martin Pawley as a kind of Brahms to Banham's Beethoven. There are essentially two kinds of critic: the messengers, who bring us, second-hand, largely reassuring word of styles and trends as they unfold; and the prognosticators—the seers—who look beyond the known horizon to confront us with often less comfortable truths. In architectural criticism, the 'messengers' abound, but Pawley is one of the very few original thinkers.

For evidence of how penetrating his vision can be, one only needs to look to *The Private Future*, a book of social prophecy, published in 1973. There, he foresees a society with ever greater technical means of communication becoming paradoxically more insular and dysfunctional: "Alone in a centrally heated air conditioned capsule, drugged, fed with music and erotic imagery, the parts of his consciousness separated into components that reach everywhere and nowhere, the private citizen of the future will have become one with the end of effort and the triumph of sensation divorced from action." Reading this description of a twenty-first century iPod-plugged, web surfer you have to remind yourself that it was written more than 30 years ago—on an Olympia typewriter—long before the advent of the word processor or the mobile phone, when most computers were still the size of a small family car.

Allied with this clarity of vision is a willingness to 'tell it like it is'. For early evidence of this, one need look no further than the opening thrust of his 1970 interview with Buckminster Fuller: "Mr Buckminster Fuller, 43 years ago you announced that a world housing industry using advanced technology was the only answer to the crucial problem of human habitation. It seems to me that this judgement applies with even more force today and yet every one of your efforts to bring this industry into existence, before, during and after the Second World War, has been a failure in that it has failed to ignite the enthusiasm of those able to carry out the task." In response, Bucky comes out fighting, but you feel the blow nonetheless. Other less robust interviewees over the years have been left on the ropes.

Reading that extract, it's clear that the root of Pawley's frustration lies not just with Bucky—for whom he professes the greatest admiration—but with a world still failing to pick up the technological baton. This is something he experienced first hand. In 1972, prompted in part by the publication of his book *Architecture versus Housing*, he was invited to Chile by Gonzalo Martner, Minister of Planning, to advise on an emergency low-cost housing programme. His response was to develop a prototype steel housing system using motor vehicle body parts, an episode he describes in *Garbage Housing*. Unfortunately, the assassination of President Salvador Allende and the fall of the Unidad Popular government in September 1973 brought this happy experiment to an abrupt halt.

Following that, he was a consultant to the United Nations Department of Housing, Building and Planning, advising on the use of waste materials in low-cost construction. At the same time he was a visiting professor, first at Cornell University, and later at Rensselaer Polytechnic Institute, in upstate New York. At Rensselaer, as the energy implications of the oil crisis began to hit home, and his colleagues earnestly discussed the coming of log cabins and wood-burning stoves, he remained an ardent technophile. Like Bucky, he maintains that technology is not the problem, but in fact part of the solution. "You don't need log cabins", he argued then: "Why not just use tractors to tow airliners to the end of the runway and save millions of gallons of jet fuel?"

Waste can also be good, if used intelligently, he told his students and, with characteristic elan, constructed the Dora Crouch House using reclaimed glass bottles and steel cans, to prove his point. In 1977, when he joined the faculty of the new school of architecture at Florida A&M University in Tallahassee, he conducted another typically counter-cultural experiment, proving that you could turn the wreck of a Detroit gas guzzler into an efficient 'solar car collector' to supply domestic heating and hot water.

In 1979, he was promoted to full professor with tenure in the Florida State university system. But, ever restless, that same year he moved to Los Angeles to become visiting professor at the School of Urban Planning at UCLA. While there, he took up a consultancy to the city of Los Angeles and continued his research into modes of technology transfer in housing design. (He also ran two lecture courses intriguingly entitled "Housing as the function of great historical events", and "The influence of technology upon communal life".) Anyone tracking his career path at this point might reasonably have assumed that he would stay in America. However, after a year in LA he decided that it was time to give up teaching and go home.

Looking back to his experience in the United States, he believes that it gave him a broader perspective and made it easier to challenge what he found on his return. It might also have served to loosen the straitjacket of his English good manners, which limits the range of most native critics, and to establish him more completely as an 'outsider'.

Coming home, he found a divided and embattled architectural profession in stylistic disarray. The postmodernists were in the ascendancy and modernism had lost its moral compass. It was a fantastic time to be a journalist, especially one with Pawley's nose for a good story—a skill he refined as editor of the London weekly architectural newspaper *Building Design*. Ian Martin, who was news editor on BD when Pawley arrived on the scene in 1981, says he was "quick to grasp the mischief theory of news reporting (rule one: fill the space; rule two: upset someone)". He blazed brilliantly as editor for two years—then he was gone. One row too many with the publisher prompted his resignation and a swansong editorial, "Farewell PKO376W"—the registration plate of his company Cortina. (He has precisely documented details of all 46 cars he has owned over the last 40 years. Significant among these are his first, a 1955 left-hand-drive DKW Sonderklasse, registration XYL33, several Mini Coopers, a Cadillac Coupe de Ville, bought in Albany, New York in 1975, and a BMW 320i, the story of whose purchase he memorably recounted in the pages of *Blueprint*.)

From *Building Design* he moved seamlessly to the newsroom of *The Architects' Journal*, where he had first cut his teeth as a journalist. He is remembered fondly as an anarchic presence. Ian Martin, who also worked with him there, says, "Martin's Wednesday morning editorial meetings were unlike any I'd ever attended. His approach to sifting through the raw material and planning what to write had as its point of departure a series of headlines he'd invent—"What I really want this week is a story with a headline like 'Prince Charles Praises Nazis or Minister Calls for Student Cull'... and we'd all do our best."

While he was news editor at the AJ he was also the architecture correspondent on *The Guardian*—another example of his customary feat of riding two horses simultaneously. But there he was given a much freer rein. It was a post created in the media wake of the now infamous "monstrous carbuncle" speech given by the Prince of Wales to the RIBA at Hampton Court in 1984, in which he launched a personal crusade against modernist architecture. Of *The Guardian* Pawley says, "I felt finally that I had been given a licence to provoke—it was what they wanted. In other cases I had been stretching possibilities—flirting with disaster." He held *The Guardian* post until 1991, when his instinct to get ahead of the news proved his undoing. When a scoop with what looked like impeccable credentials blew up in his face, he resigned with customary aplomb.

His battle against the reactionary forces of the Prince of Wales— conducted throughout the pages of *The Guardian* and elsewhere—is just one manifestation of his frustration with the English tendency to fall back on historicism. For Pawley, it is one of the paradoxes of our time that, while the process of construction has never been so advanced in relation to other industries, architecture has never been so obsessed with its past. And that, in a nutshell, is the issue that has energised him as a writer more than any other over the years.

As a critic, Pawley's critical horizon is entirely uninhibited by art historical clutter. But his vision is stark. In *Theory and Design in the Second Machine Age*, he writes of "the architecture of the information age", offering the first cogent analysis of the impact of electronic information technology on architecture and urban planning—a theme to which he has returned frequently. Invoking Bucky Fuller, he regrets the failure of successive energy crises to transform architecture from "a volatile craft into a science". He also warns of the dangers of a sclerotic urbanism, describing a London where the fate of architecture is diminished in the shadow of a titanic battle "between the future operations of the economy and the intransigent obstruction of a city that is now the sum of all the discarded options of its past". He sees a "state of war", not only "between man and nature, but between the age of science and the accumulated infrastructure of centuries".

In *Terminal Architecture*, published in 1998, he argues that a genuinely innovative architectural future entails a radical shift in values, for which we are entirely unprepared. "Nearly all modern architecture is misconceived", he writes, the importance of buildings today lying "not in their appearance as monuments, but in their role as terminals for information." Again the visionary, in a chapter entitled "From postmodernism to terrorism", he writes chillingly of "the architecture of terror" where a society retreats behind ever more restrictive physical barriers, the end result "an architecture so styleless that it can hardly be imagined".

If these extracts suggest a writer with an apocalyptic vision, that would no doubt be right. But that is not the entire story. For every dark episode there is a countervailing light interlude. He finds mischief in the mundane, and humour in everyday encounters; and he has a highly developed sense of the ridiculous. This shines through in his weekly column for *The Architects' Journal* and in the freewheeling pieces he wrote for *Blueprint* in the mid-1980s. Among the latter is a personal favourite—"In pursuit of the ultimate driving machine"—his story of trying to buy the second-hand BMW 320i referred to above. There, he captures the exquisite social nuances that define the sub-dom relationship between customer and salesman and evokes the 'greed is good' London of the 1980s in a single sentence—"a diamond black two door, a perfect late Big Bang dealers car, still with the original holes where the phone was ripped out when Hazard Brothers sacked 200 staff".

This book brings together 100 of Martin Pawley's most memorable magazine and newspaper essays, some light, some dark. They range from his pithy column pieces to more reflective surveys for journals such as *The Architectural Review* and *Oppositions*; and they represent the entire span of his career, from the first piece—"The Time House"—published in the September 1968 edition of *Architectural Design*, to the last—his final column for *The Architects' Journal*—written in April 2005, shortly before declining health prompted his retirement.

Together, they cover the full range of his concerns and enthusiasms. There are recurring themes and tropes—technology transfer, battleships and big sheds—that he weaves through these pieces with remarkable critical invention. There are interviews with architects of every stripe—from Norman Foster to Leon Krier and Zaha Hadid—in which you sense him teasing and cajoling, if not attacking head on. And then there are biographical pieces —some exquisitely embroidered no doubt—that relate occasionally tragic, more frequently amusing, episodes in the life of Pawley, the man. It is a remarkable body of work, especially so if you consider that what you see here is only the tip of the iceberg in terms of his archive, which contains 1,000s of such pieces. It is architectural criticism at its most compelling —pungent, but full of wit and humour. It is a bravura performance. But above all, it is an insight into a wonderfully original and mercurial mind.

David Jenkins

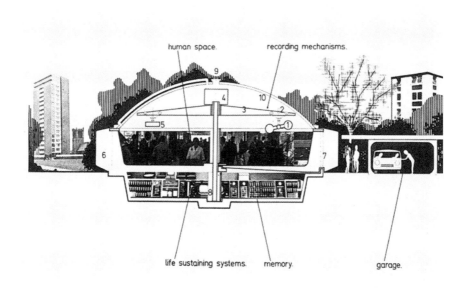

human space.   recording mechanisms.

life sustaining systems.   memory.   garage.

Martin Pawley, The Time House, cross-section, 1967

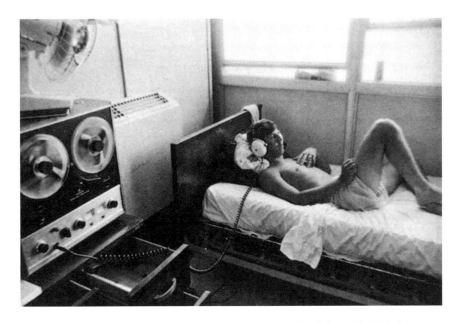

Martin Pawley, The Private Future, 1973

The Time House
1968

Designers often believe that they can produce designs from which subjective factors have been totally excised. In the case of automobiles, for instance, where it is not uncommon for over a million identical units to be produced, it could be assumed that the combination of a ruthlessly objective brief with strictly limited conditions of use would provide a wholly functional product sterilised against subjective infection. The result is far from the case: within a week of purchase the vast majority of automobiles are personalised by one means or another. A vast accessory industry exists for just this purpose with innumerable permutations of gadgetry to differentiate individual means of transport. No sooner is function crowned than myth, image and fantasy usurp the throne. If the designer cannot express his subjectivity the lack is made good by the user: if neither knows how to associate with the object, the seller or advertiser finds a way. Consider the following example.

An old-age pensioner sits in a squalid room; all around him his furniture is arranged, Edwardian veneered cabinets, tortuously carved tables, high backed chairs. Amongst the furniture is further bric-à-brac in the form of vases, prints and photographs in frames. All these possessions represent the 'object evidence' of the pensioner's life, for his relations are all dead and he is alone, using the collection as a barricade against the increasingly cold and hostile world without. His mementoes are living proof of the reality of his former life.

Not far away, in a contract furnished office sits a development architect. He is studying some drawings: on one of the drawings the very house in which the pensioner is huddled is ringed in red. The architect is planning the erection of a multi-storey office building on a site of which a part is at present occupied by the pensioner's tenement; he summons his secretary....

Here is one designer, equipped with technical, legal and economic expertise and a brief drawn from the uncompromising facts of commercial life, marshalling his resources to carry out a clear and ruthless plan. Opposite him is a desperate individual in a shrinking world, staking the very meaning of his existence on the effort of externalisation which has transformed mere furniture into the contents of life. Neither of these characters would acknowledge that they were at opposite ends of a single scale. One would see the other as a threat, the other, if he acknowledged his presence at all, would see his counterpart as a nuisance. They do not see themselves—or each other—as exponents of the binary condition of consciousness, for in effect they are the same person.

Because of this blindness, today's environmental designers are committed for the most part to the obliteration of their subjectivities in becoming the agents of an authoritarian, organisational technology that refuses responsibility for the violence done to human consciousness by its mechanisms. They are utopians in the tradition of More, Fourier and Verne.[1]

This utopianism is exactly what separates designer object from the designer subject—the development architect from the pensioner. The designer's idea of the dwelling is a mélange of functional fabrications; the more closely he looks into it the larger mirror image he sees. Until he can move beyond this convention into a deeper acceptance of the experience of environment, he must remain incapable of moving the act of dwelling back into the realms of action and meaning where it really belongs. The conception of the meaning and purpose of environment in the minds of most contemporary designers is a convention unrelated to their experience of it: a convention which enables them to see the world in a different way to the way in which they *feel* it.

Naked figures watching TV

"The smiling credit manager you spoke to this morning is a piece of company apparatus like the filing cabinet from which he extracts the card that is you; his human appearance is a disguise and his real name isn't Brown but Agent F-362."

In these terms Harold Rosenberg summarises the Jeremiads of contemporary prophets of the American social scene.[2] Their fears of dehumanisation, role absorption and 'other-directed' behaviour, which are by now part of the intellectual currency of the Western world, are closely related to reification—the objectivisation of living things.

In this connection the contemporary designer occupies a curious position: he is the mixer of traditional prejudice with untested theory. The environments which are his creation were born of the marriage between the undigested, unintegrated body of experience that is the presence of the past, and the organisational concepts of production and distribution which are the presence of the future. The outcome of this marriage is an environment in which the roles of function, action and consciousness are hopelessly confused.

This is because contemporary designers do not know how to integrate the vast museum of stone, iron and yellowed paper into a world whose meanings must all be expressed functionally, in the applied scientific sense of tending towards the optimisation of technique in some field or other.

For this reason we still build houses with room for servants when our real servants are electronic mechanisms. We call rooms after functions which once produced sweat but now rarely occasion a broken finger nail. In industry men serve and circle round assembly line monsters that will shortly operate far better without them. In this sense the operators, with their human demands, have become an embarrassment to production.

Along with them most of the environmental spaces in our man-made world have become temples to the dynamism of functions long since reduced to anachronistic double talk. Libraries have become micro-film, cinemas have become television, corridors telephones; travel arrival and departure with a shortening limbo between. All the functions of a house have imploded into a service core the diameter of a telegraph pole. Even the physical space required by its human occupants has been miniaturised to the point where the 'essential' capsule could be sunk to the bottom of the sea or shot to the moon.

A surprisingly large number of design-theorists are prepared to follow this kind of logic to its bitter conclusion. The architectural avant-garde prepare to live in ergonomically designed plastic 'living pods', shifted periodically by crane from megastructure to megastructure, while future-oriented writers like Reyner Banham actually portray naked figures hunkering round television sets in small, collapsible plastic domes.[3] These latter-day nomads have long since abandoned the 'cultural wardrobe', and as their sun-bronzed fingers twitch from channel to channel, their possible reflections on the monumental architectural environment from which they sprang are summarised for them in advance. "It was", says Banham, "a cultural solution to the problem of enclosure—apart from that it became obsolete."[4]

The fantastic notion underlying this attitude—that electronic media are in some way interchangeable with history—springs from two basic origins.

First, that as a result of the Industrial Revolution, nuclear weapons, antibiotics and technology, the historical continuum is broken and consequently 1968 man is utterly different from 1868 man or 1768 man. Second, that man is no greater than his role—which today is the satisfaction of his physical needs and desires by collaboration in the productive organisation of his society.

The image of humanity which results from a ruthless application of these two determinants can be clearly seen every week on television. The puppet characters of *Thunderbirds*, *Rocketship XL5* and *Captain Scarlet* are all perfect prototypes for the nubile, role-imprisoned futurists eagerly awaiting Banham's command to leap from the highest peaks of the present into the bottomless future—without their cultural parachutes. Curiously such delusory flights from place and history often end in the Portobello Road or the antique supermarket.

The limitations of function

Functionalism was originally a morality for environment in that it sought to establish *correct conditions* for use rather than usefulness itself. In doing so, it had the effect of reducing action to configuration and consciousness to objective physical presence.

The manner in which this arcane doctrine—a relic of the positivism which, in science, crumbled long before the Second World War, and in philosophy collapsed shortly after it—has maintained itself in the face of daily proof of its inadequacy, is little short of miraculous. Faced with the constant modification of structures whose 'immutable' function changed overnight, the functional theorist was obliged to don an ill-fitting suit of clothes called flexibility. Every functional environment today is obliged to be able to become anything else —or nothing—instantly. Otherwise it is useless.

Despite this implicit acknowledgement of the relatively short life of any functional organisation pattern, the method is still the basic design tool used for shaping our environment.

In the organisation world—in office blocks, industrial facilities, military and scientific complexes, the presence of individuals is acknowledged only by reference to their functional roles. They are incorporated as elements in planning according to their administrative or productive place in the organisation. They are provided with desks, chairs, typewriters, telephones, paper and pencils —a mass of impersonal, objective equipment within which they can only express their subjectivity by stealth and fantasy—by keeping novels in their desk drawers, or making personal calls in the lunch hour.

Functions at basis are objectivisations of human needs, and because human beings are more than object-entities, these objectivisations are at best simplifications, at worst distortions of the possibilities of real men. The environmental designers' recognition of function or role, instead of consciousness, as the basis of such 'human engineering' as he attempts, is a contributory cause of the anxiety of meaninglessness which is a well documented neurosis of our time.

It is in the realm of the dwelling that functionalism becomes pernicious in the extreme. Primarily because it is impossible to functionally define the *act* of dwelling, which is a continuously evolving drama not a pattern conferred once and retained forever.

A man can 'function' in a certain sense 600 feet beneath the surface of the sea in total blackness. He can 'survive' in a prison cell six feet square, an underground train, a space capsule or a pothole, but he cannot live there—not unless he drastically truncates the possibilities of action and thought that consciousness confers upon him. To 'live' in such situations a man must accept the status of an object, as though the world were always in a state of warfare, famine or pestilence; as though life were a job.

Sociological techniques can never indicate more than that human beings survive in a relatively sociable form in certain environments. The outer limits of those environments must be determined by the sometimes 'unfunctional' demands of action and consciousness—demands which the functional mode is committed to either castrate or ignore.

A measure of our loss of awareness of the importance of these demands is our endless obsession with the kind of environment we construct, instead of with the act of environmental creation itself. It is the creative act, whether carried out with pick and shovel or highly sensitive electronic system, which is of overriding importance.

The importance of context

Territoriality can today be considered as a primary instinctual drive, alongside sexual desire or the will to power. Recent research in the behavioural sciences suggests in fact that individual distance and private territory are invariables in all societies of living things, ensuring that internecine strife never overcomes the basic cohesion of any group.

The Best-Rubinstein experiment with Planarian worms, which are among the most primitive forms of life still extant in the world, indicates that psychological characteristics normally associated only with higher animals and humans are already present in a highly developed form demanding the identity, stimulation and security which proceeds from the ownership of territory.[5] While on the same theme, from an anthropological standpoint, TGH Strehlow describes the fanatical devotion of the Aranda people of the Australian interior to birthplace and ancestral home-site.[6]

Territoriality is thus a significant element in the relationship between being and environment from the bottom of the evolutionary scale to the top. Psychology and animal physiology also supply impressive proof of the significance of context, particularly in those areas where mental and behavioural disturbance can be related to environmental deprivation.

One particular scientific *idée fixe*, which greatly influenced Sigmund Freud, was that primates were obsessed with sex and it was this sexual attraction which held troops together. This conclusion was drawn entirely from extended observation of captive specimens and it was not until the field studies of the late 1930s that it could be conclusively proved that the role of sexuality had been greatly exaggerated by unnatural living conditions.

In human terms, Goffman has shown that, in the context of the mental hospital, deprivation of meaningful context can make rational, though desperate, human behaviour seem to confirm insanity, when in reality it merely confirms deprivation.[7]

Searles cites many examples of schizophrenics whose loss of orientation stems in their own eyes from excessive movement and loss of personal possessions.[8] The movement of the family from one town to another, the movement of the individual from one room to another in the family house, even the reallocation of desks at a school or the seizure of a favourite chair. In all these cases, Searles affirms that "... for such patients... the loss of various elements of the non-human environment, elements which have become part of the person's body image, may be experienced as a mutilation of the body itself".

The entire body of this scientific and clinical evidence suggests that in animals as well as humans, behaviour can only be understood in the context of the environment in which it takes place. This is because environment confers its own movements, contortions and vistas on to those who use it, becoming in the process effectively a part of the personality.

The social implications of this contention are readily visible in the stratification of status in terms of possessions, type and location of dwelling, and personal appearance. Also in the more intangible benefits which the long genealogy of an aristocratic family confers upon its descendants. The family home, in the case of many aristocratic families in Europe occupied for 200 or 300 years by successive generations, offers a unique basis of stability as well as evidence of experience which is ordered in space and time. The human need for this sense of identification is illustrated most pathetically by institutional recidivism—the tendency for long hospitalised or imprisoned persons to be unable to establish themselves in the outside world and instead to seek re-entry to the cell or bed they know.

The deep-seated nature of the contextual impression and its presence as a major motivation in contemporary resistance to change and the rejection of 'consumer product' housing, has not been specifically recognised in architectural circles. Burnham Kelly points out that, "The largest marketing problem is found in the fact that houses are not mere consumer goods, to be used and thrown away when they fall apart. They are the focus of the basic unit in our society."[9] This he explains by a discussion of current systems of house finance, all of which require the dwelling to be an asset whose durability is supposed to at least match, if not exceed, the term of the loan with which it is purchased. This explanation only partially touches on the true value of the dwelling as "the focus of the basic unit of our society". Apart from its viability as a product, which is attested by its steadily appreciating value and potentially infinite life span, the traditional house represents territory in a way that its wheeled or prefabricated counterpart can never do. The language alone in which these rival concepts of dwelling are discussed leaves little doubt as to their relative value in this regard.

The house is 'a castle', 'security', 'a home of our own'. The caravan or prefabricated dwelling is 'accommodation', 'emergency housing', 'temporary' or 'mobile'. The key factor in this comparison is the permanent status accorded a house in its relation to the ownership of land, and the non-status accorded the owner of a caravan who buys something to live in but nowhere to live.

This desire for permanence underlies the general hostility to redevelopment plans exhibited by the inhabitants of the area to which they refer, the relatively large numbers of persons implacably opposed to even the surface appearance of the newer forms of environment, the plethora of organisations devoted to the preservation and reclamation of historic buildings and towns, and the large numbers of technologically aware individuals who prefer to live in the rehabilitated dwellings of a century or more ago. To these persons redevelopment is as destructive as it is creative. The old environments blotted out by the bulldozers are the physical context of human experience. What replaces them is generally pure form, unrelated to persons or to history.

The hostility that the public exhibits to consumer housing is thus as rationally based as its hostility to demolition and redevelopment. Neither of these concepts recognises the importance of identification with place or known objects, and neither comprehends the significance of the kind of behavioural history that accompanies and stabilises successive generational occupations of the same dwelling.

In a relatively little known book published in 1961, NJ Habraken outlined these defects in both the redevelopment programme and the short-life dwelling.[10] He also clearly enunciated the principle stated earlier—that it is in the action of changing and creating it that the individual confers meaning on his environment. Habraken saw the redevelopment process not only destroy existing environments to replace them with memoryless novelties, but also remove individual responsibility for the ordering of environmental space by rigidly establishing identical equipment and layout for hundreds of thousands of dwellings at a time.

The overriding factor with Habraken is an acute consciousness of the importance of continuity in time and place, which he attempts to achieve by means of support structures with a useful life of the order of bridges or dams; thus guaranteeing an unchanging overall environmental pattern in spite of changes in dwelling units.

Because he does not examine any means of retaining the evidence of the past within the dwelling unit itself, Habraken is committed to achieving continuity in the public realm. Consequently his major arguments are directed against the massive increase in bureaucratic environmental control that has taken place in this century under the guise of planning and organisation, for it is from this direction that the greatest threat to formal stability comes.

For some reason he does not see any hope of a solution to this creeping paralysis of the creative will in the process of privatisation with which the mass populations of Western societies have greeted it. For him, just as the problems of efficient communication, distribution of resources and maintenance of public order have called forth a massive volume of environmental legislation, so has the political progress of this century —towards equal distribution of wealth, higher living standards, social security and administrative populism—worked against the freedom of individuals to express their subjectivity in the outside world. The result has been an ingrowing privatisation, facilitated by media and overpopulation, whereby individuals withdraw into their homes as a refuge from the dangerous exposure of public life.

This process, variously castigated as 'apathy', 'lack of initiative' and 'ignorance', is in fact a perfectly rational response to the confusing and destructive demands of an uncomprehending and largely unsuccessful environmental administration. Habraken's efforts to stabilise the rapidly evolving world of life-sustaining systems are doomed before they begin. In this context change cannot be arrested—though this is the desperate dream of preservationists. All that can be done is to equip human space with mechanisms capable of absorbing the evidence of time and change in order to mitigate the horror of change itself. By incorporating into each successive configuration the elements of all its predecessors, change could be separated from destruction, and loss and a continuum achieved in the private realm which is still to some extent legally and economically protected.

Recognition of the violence done to the concept of a continuous tradition of human identification with place by contemporary notions of mobility and obsolescence, is vital to the idea of context as a part of personality which was developed earlier. George Kubler suggests that to treat the dwelling as a finite object, subject to obsolescence, corresponds to a lifelong sequence of violent and discontinuous changes in time: alternate destruction and creation so complete as to resemble conditions reigning under bombardment, evacuation or earthquake.[11]

Historical evidence seems to indicate that the design, use and retention of objects is an ACCUMULATIVE process like learning or growth. The design doctrine of functionalism on the other hand implies that it is a SELECTIVE process, whereby different conditions demand successive and radically different personality orientations.

The arrangement of objects
An individual populates his own dwelling with objects and information, some of iconic value, some purely functional, some sharing the characteristics of both. No outside observer could ever estimate the subjective value of these objects and messages according to an external scale of values, although in the least inventive and most conventional surroundings he might roughly approximate them. The *subjective* value of these objects resides not in themselves but in their interrelation, their sequence and their significance as extensions of the personality of their owner. In other words, they are not really isolated objects but connected molecules in the atomic structure of the individual's own consciousness. This factor alone is sufficient to demonstrate the absurdity of the separation between user and designer, and designer-object and designer-subject that we observe today. It has been calculated that although a very high percentage of the perceived urban or suburban environment is man-made, only about five per cent is planned in terms of its juxtapositions and sequences. The rest is a confusion of object-disorder, conforming to either random or subjective patterns.

The ideas and images of his own life that the individual entertains are for the most part expressed in this latter world of subjective 'content', where the value system which links the object-evidence of these ideas and images is locked inside the sequential code of behaviour that first gave them meaning. This circuit is unbreakable, it can only be *simulated* by media, for in the human situation *ideas and images derive from and create content—even when external considerations totally determine form.* Thus value systems as well as ideas and images are expressed in the object world.

In a sense, each individual lives in the same world as his fellows only by virtue of his, and their, relationships with the same objects. Either through their universality, as in the case of a cup of tea, or through their uniqueness, as in the case of their own bodies. Proof of this can be seen in any war situation when questions of identification and allegiance are settled by interrogation on matters of national or provincial shibboleth; or in art or entertainment where success often depends on the close observation and reproduction of key associations which link the performer to his or her audience. The 'situation' of these relationships, destined to be forever insoluble to the objective designer, is centred in the fate of the individual to feel and to observe simultaneously. His 'situation' is the relationship between the experience of being and the evidence of being: the relationship between behaviour, objects and time. It is here that Kubler's theory of replication is of vital importance, for he demonstrates that behaviour can only be understood as experience when it is *repeated*, and that only varied *repetitions* can create a consciousness of time and change. "Without change there is no history, without regularity there is no time."[12]

Looking for a sound
1969

At the dawn of my architectural experience I worked for a small rural practice in Berkshire. The senior partner carried a shooting stick, wore a pork-pie hat, and had recently taken on a dashing young associate from London who had all sorts of new ideas like 'exposed agg' finishes and flush doors instead of drawing boards. Our offices consisted of two small rooms at the top of a very small terraced house, one room for the draughtsmen and the other for the partner and associate. As a consequence of this juxtaposition, their conferences (which were frequent as there was little work) could be easily overheard, and during one of my spells pressed against the communicating door I heard a remarkable exchange.

The young associate had apparently seen *The Glenn Miller Story* the night before and had been much impressed by James Stewart's single-minded pursuit of 'a sound'. He recounted to his sceptical senior the tribulations of the young Miller—trombone pawned, mud on trousers, marital problems—ending with a description of his eventual triumph and an explanatory humming of "In the Mood". This last seemed to kindle a spark in the mind of the elder, who then inquired as to the point of this exposition. The associate replied that he thought their current difficulties could be compared to those of the great popular musician, but that eventually they too would discover the architectural equivalent of 'a sound' and move on to fame and fortune. The young associate did in fact usurp his colleague's position within months and shortly afterwards set up in practice on his own account, but that is not the moral of the story.

The point is: are architects (some eager in wild shirts and bell-bottomed trousers—others cautious in 21s with cuffs) talking about *Bullitt* in the same way?

Bullitt is an extraordinarily relevant film to the would-be designers of the "second, organised surface of the earth" (love that phrase) because it is about machine-paced people: people immersed in technology so that their motivations are split, modulated and amplified into signals that only engineers can decipher, only cameras record. The characters are all subconsciously committed to playing for keeps with technology—one false move and you're dead; carbonised because you lost control of your car, or shot because you tried to go the wrong way through an automatic door. The action of *machines* paces the whole picture; the characters watch an oscilloscope which tells them if a man lives or dies, wait patiently in traffic jams, wait impatiently around a facsimile transmitter, wait for planes to arrive at gates, wait for autopsy reports. When they try to act at a human level the result is like some death-defying dance of flies on the whirling blades of a combine harvester. The terminal sequence shot on the airside of San Francisco airport shows hunter and hunted running with painful slowness across the path of blind, screaming jetliners on a gigantic electronic chessboard.

This integration or submersion of men into huge machine patterns is not confined to the *action* of the film, but was also a characteristic of the *process* of its production. The celebrated car chase, for example, illustrates a straight feedback from reality through script and production technique to filmed action. It was obviously impossible to film it realistically in crowded mid-week San Francisco—the only conceivable real-time was early on a Sunday morning. But the realism of the story prevented Sunday morning being passed off as Wednesday afternoon. Result, Sunday morning has to be Sunday morning and the story, production and action modified accordingly.

It is important to realise that this is not merely a question of changing the script to suit the exigencies of the conditions of production. Rather it is a matter of turning the script into a record drawing instead of a sketch design, so that what happens on film on half a dozen Sunday mornings becomes the primary reality. The preconceptions taken on location in the first place are thrown away.

Now it should be possible to admit that this is what happens in most environmental design. The synthetic art forms of the twentieth century only succeed when their internal logic—that is the *process of their production* —overtakes the sketch in the mind of the creator and liberates him from it. The recording manager, for example, sets up the levels on his eight-track mixer before the first take, but thereafter trial and error, post-synchronisation and happy chance bring into existence something which could not possibly have been pre-identified, let alone brought into the studio to start with. The same thing is true of the role of the darkroom in photography, the rearrangeable texts of Burroughs and others, and numerous experiments with kinetic, auto-destructive and computerised art.

It is also, of course, true of architectural design. Amendments, revisions and variation orders vie with newly discovered regulations, obstructive officials, second thoughts and simple errors in the toll they take on the original conception. In no other creative field would such Acts of God be so consistently thrust under the carpet of omniscient foresight. Whatever happens to a building during the course of planning or construction—the extension that never comes off, the ten storeys excised at the last moment, the embarrassingly sudden change of use—all must be presented by the architect as foreseen, irrelevant to his true purpose, or (in particularly severe cases), the catastrophic result of the intervention of others. This syndrome, as others have pointed out, applies with even greater force in the field of planning proper: unmasked it is the pretence that one day there will be a *final configuration* so perfect that, as Cedric Price has said, all we will have to do is polish it up now and then.

There will be no such configuration ever. In reality, the process rather than the plan is the generator. Once we realise this we can start to construct events instead of pretending that what it looks like is the unique sound we heard in the first place.

Richard Buckminster Fuller, Wichita House, USA, 1941–1946

Richard Buckminster Fuller (centre) with his Dymaxion car, 1933–1934

Meeting Buckminster Fuller
1970

Richard Buckminster Fuller was staying at the Stafford Hotel in St James'
Place, a quiet cul-de-sac near Piccadilly. He had not yet returned from lunch
at the time of my appointment and I was shown into a television lounge
where the assembled staff were watching horse racing in the company
of a solitary guest. Shortly after a much disputed finish he appeared in
the company of a partner from Boston and apologised for being late.
We were led up to his room on the fifth floor which was small and modestly
furnished. Once inside, Buckminster Fuller ordered a fruit salad and a large
pot of tea. He is now 75 years old and has some difficulty hearing, but his
energy is undiminished and this fact alone is occasionally surprising—as
when he opens doors, pulls up chairs and indulges in elaborate mimicry
to make a particular point. His behaviour is in no sense that of a man used
to servants or a retinue of admirers.

"Mr Buckminster Fuller, 43 years ago you announced that a world
housing industry using advanced technology was the only answer to the
crucial problem of human habitation. It seems to me that this judgement
applies with even more force today and yet every one of your efforts to bring
this industry into existence, before, during and after the Second World War,
has been a failure in that it has failed to ignite the enthusiasm of those able
to carry out the task."

"I would contradict that completely. In the first place the world housing
industry is an industry not a thing. It is not a thing that people can *buy*, it's
a whole process... if people had to go to the market to buy all their own guts,
with them hanging up all around, nobody would buy them. There's not any
part of a human being that anyone would buy if they didn't have it anyway."

"Wouldn't they buy brains?"

"What that awful thing? (laughter). OK that's where you start. Now one
of the first things I remember in my home when I was a child was the
telephone, we had one of the very first telephones, the number was Milton
10. Of all the things in my home that was the only one the family didn't own.
Now it is a well known argument that in the capitalist world you have to have
competition for things to improve, that is not correct because the telephone
was a complete monopoly from the very beginning. They didn't sell the
telephone, they sold a *service*, and they found that every time they improved
the telephone more people used it: they saw that it paid them to go on

increasing the distances it could operate over and generally improving the service. Without you asking for it, they continually replaced your telephone with a better one, increasing frequency of use and generally improving things.

Now, if they had *sold* these early telephones there would have been a Christopher Wren telephone, a Louis XIV telephone.... In the First World War there would have been a Trench Type telephone, then an alligator... all this horrible equipment you would have paid a fantastic price for would have stopped development of the service itself.

The lesson of the telephone taught me back in 1927 that housing was going to have to be a service industry, a truly logical complement to life embodying the principles of nature, recognising entropy and the inevitability of change... (arrival of salad and tea) Put it on the bed. Anyone want to change their mind and order a salad like this? No, okay. A bird picking up twigs to make a nest turns the action into a complement of its life, a spider makes a web, a mole makes his hole. They alter their environment in preferred ways. Human beings do that too, they are not unusual in that... only the extent to which they do it. So you see it is not arbitrary that we make tools, it's part of the design of you and me. Man has always been technology, he is nothing but technology. External technology that goes on and on by itself is no more surprising than a child born from the womb going on and on by itself. All the principles of our technology are used by the universe over and over again from the bat flying to the worm's chemistry."

"I see what you mean in relation to housing. If you try and sell it, you demonstrate that you cannot understand it."

"I say it's a service... should be. When you use it—as we have—as a castle... to say you're supposed to die, you stay outside the walls (rises to feet with menacing gesture) just look at my shield, see what I got on it? A lion. I can roar like a lion! By this time you're supposed to be scared to death. Housing as an advertisement for how great you are is not what we are talking about at all.

Now I said earlier that I would contradict you completely and I will. After the First World War I was horrified by the course of the automobile industry in America. There were 125 companies... it was the most immoral thing I ever saw, all these automobile companies going bust, and yet it was

the most successful period in automobile development—the price of Fords
dropped by 30 per cent. That success should be accounted by bankruptcy
after bankruptcy seemed to me to mean that society just didn't know how to
account for what it was doing. I looked into it and found that the accounting
system we were using was invented solely for agriculture—the main business
of man for centuries. Now crops are an annual thing—either they come in or
they don't. So you get annual accounting. Speaking of economies, we always
say the 'fiscal' year: the 'fiscus' was the basket with which the man came
round to collect the tithe annually. I realised that the gestation rates of
industrial undertakings were not annual, but that everybody was betting
on them as if they were... if they didn't come in that year all the stocks went
down and so on. I saw that we were not thinking in the right brackets and
I began to work out the gestatic rates for different industries taking this
basic failure into account. Would it be a thousand years before man's
thinking could be catalysed in better ways—in which case I couldn't have
much effect at all—or would it be much shorter? Well, by cataloguing all
the known inventions and scientific events, logging the rate at which
scrap metal came back on the market as a raw material, I found that in
electronics—then a very new industry, an invisible world in which you
couldn't see the waves and they were handled mathematically, so that you
could prove them mathematically without too much argument—things
happened quite fast: the gestation lag between invention and use was
about two years. I found in the airplane industry there was a five year lag.
In the home dwelling the lag was between 40 and 50 years. Much as I was
interested in developing a new housing concept, I had to count on half a
century between invention and industrial production. If I wasn't ready to
wait 40 or 50 years—don't tackle it. I knew then that anything I did en
route would be premature for production.

Since then everything has been coming in on schedule and the
industrialised dwelling will be coming in too—right on the nose, between
1972 and 1975. They'll look an awful lot like the Dymaxion house too....
Old style housing is just about stopping—it is in the United States anyway."

"Do you mean the terrible difficulties under which housing operates?
I mean here too interest rates, land values, maintenance costs, manpower
costs—everything is spiralling steeper and steeper...."

"Look, in 1927 I wrote a book pointing out that the government was getting involved in housing because private industry had dropped it—not just because it was unprofitable but because it was completely obsolete. Since that time all the Western governments have got in deeper and deeper: in the United States they have had to take over all the mortgages... we have been underwriting obsolescence for 40 years. We've been trying to revive a dead man, we've got a corpse on our hands and it's taken nearly 50 years for anyone to realise it's dead!"

"But the connection between houses and land—how will it be broken?"

"I am talking about a scientific dwelling service industry. It's no good having a revolution, saying 'I'm going to take the land away from you.' If you do that you start all over again with new land owners—the government —it's still land. What I'm doing is *making land owning obsolete*... absolutely onerous... nobody will want it, not even the government. It will become very hard to get anyone to look after it."

"But this change over from land...."

"You don't have to own the ocean to have a boat. You don't have to own the sky to have an airplane: you're not really going to have to own anything to have a really good dwelling service around our universe. My revolution is to make the old thing obsolete, not to attack it. The old method of housing will soon be too expensive, too slow, too cumbersome... land ownership will become a liability... these things are already happening. In the United States people buy houses with loans over 40 years and then leave town every four years. They buy cars over two or three years and then trade them in as soon as they finally own them. Ownership is already out of date."

"But I'm concerned about the political changes...."

"And I'm concerned that you started off by calling me a failure. Failure is a word invented by men, there is no failure in nature. Man's confidence in his judgement has failed—nature never fails. Don't talk to me about failure, it's a word, like pollution, invented by ignorant men. There is no such thing as pollution. Nature invented beautiful chemistry and men pull out some and leave in some. All we do when we pollute is to make recovery and recycling difficult by spraying the waste products from one process into the air or the sea where it's difficult to get them back again... that's all. All the young people are going wild today because they know the old people have been asleep at the switch! The whole housing mess we're in comes from the ignorance and fear of financiers. The governments of the world have had 50 years to prepare for a *housing service industry* and they have done nothing at all!"

"One basic question. If we lose this idea of possession, ownership of land, all these things, is there a loss in human terms? Do we lose something forever?"

"You never did own so you didn't lose a thing... you're losing a notion that's all. You don't own anything or anybody, ownership is absolutely fallacious."

A new kind of message in a bottle
1974

In a recent book about the tragic involvement of the United States in Vietnam, Frances Fitzgerald wrote that enormous differences in culture and perception separated the Americans from the native populations of South East Asia.[1] "For the Americans in Vietnam", she pointed out, "it would be difficult to make this leap of perspective, difficult to understand that while they saw themselves as building world order, many Vietnamese saw them merely as the producers of garbage from which they could build houses."

In a way the "leap of perspective" necessary to see garbage as a potential building material is difficult for all Western peoples—even though in Europe a bare 30 years has passed since the last time this was done on any scale. We in the West have come to identify the termination of one use with the termination of all usefulness, a lacuna in our thinking which we carry through ruthlessly, in our treatment of the aged as much as our treatment of the waste products our culture generates in such profusion.

Even when shortages of certain materials force us to reconsider the value of this enormous waste, we still think only in terms of 'recycling' it; of consuming yet more energy in a war of attrition against the entropic energy losses of single-purpose distribution. By this means we may perhaps return a proportion of the glass, steel, aluminium and wood fibre that mass consumption requires to the factories where it is stamped, cut, extruded or forged into the products that we use; but in the process we do not so much bring about an increase in the *value* of waste, as an increase in the price of the product. While waste remains valueless it will be wasted: and this valuelessness is a consequence of the tunnel vision from which we in the West all suffer.

Were we to learn to share the perception of the Vietnamese or any other Third World citizen, we would come to see a value in much of what we waste quite distinct from its industrial scrap value. We would note, for example, the structural properties of a steel can or a bottle; the ingenuity of the wind-up window incorporated into the door of a car, the durability of an aluminium can, the rigidity of a cardboard packing case, the precision of a foamed urethane moulding. If we not only shared this perception but were also of a practical bent we might also see ways in which some slight alteration to the design of such objects would fit them admirably for an alternative, quite unrelated use. We live all our lives in close proximity to machines, but we seldom think even of the interchangeability of our domestic energy slaves. Of how the vacuum cleaner motor might—at a pinch—power the washing machine, or the refrigerator pump be used to produce warmth as well as cold.

Since we seldom make such connections, even in small ways, it is hardly surprising that we should fail to make them in larger ones. Whereas the Vietnamese people might see the immense detritus of the war so tragically visited upon them as a veritable mine of building materials, we on our part have grown almost incapable of connecting the sight of a bottle full (with some consumer product) with the sight of a bottle empty (to be disposed of immediately). The first has value, the second has none. We do not think of containers in terms of strength any more than we think of steel in terms of cans, or glass in terms of bottles. In our minds all these identical elements are separated by us: the only new thing we have invented to replace the retrieval systems of the older economy of scarcity where bottles are concerned, is the idea of smashing them so that their fragments can serve as aggregate for tarmac.

How many of us even know how strong a bottle is? How great its pressure resistance has to be simply to withstand the process of pasteurisation and the impact of capping? How many of us know how close that strength comes to the strength of the bricks and concrete blocks the world's construction industries use in their billions to build houses? Yet we produce almost ten times as many bottles as we do bricks, and if it were possible to replace one with the other we might so increase the value of the empty bottle that retrieval on a pre-industrial scale would become possible again. Even in Third World countries where containers such as bottles and cans still have a scarcity value, the idea that consumer industries might play a part in the execution of housing programmes and other infrastructural developments—instead of, as at present, absorbing much needed hard currency to little long term benefit—already makes economic sense. The history of adaptation and skilful modification in such matters is more illustrious in the Developing World than in any Western country. Surely it is better, therefore, to make intelligent use of unavoidable consumer expenditure than it is to endeavour to suppress the desire for higher living standards that motivates economic growth itself.

Garbage Housing is about the application of a very primitive and ancient idea to a very complex and modern problem. There is nothing original about the idea of secondary use (except its application to the design of industrial products), and nothing simple about the housing problem (except that in part it stems from an anomalous failure of industrial production). Nonetheless, there are elements of originality in the fusion of these two areas of thought: if Western consumer goods, from cars to cans of Coca Cola, were *designed* for secondary use, then their presently redundant properties might be pressed into the same efficient service as their more obvious attributes. The extraordinary strength of the bottle for instance would not be wasted just because its contents had been consumed. The phenomenal corrosion resistance of the aluminium can would become a virtue instead of an embarrassment. The sophisticated subsystems incorporated into every automobile—junked as soon as its primary function is over—might find a second life. Even the cheap pressed steel body parts from which all cars are made might be put to alternative uses if assembled in a different way.

The theoretical advantages of a secondary use technology do not end with the examples cited above. In economic terms, for example, design for secondary use would amount to a merging of hitherto discrete sectors of the economy. If houses came to be built from retrieved containers, then the process of retrieval and collection would itself become a form of savings programme. Products whose initial purchase today contributes to the inflationary spiral would, by way of secondary use, be converted into the equivalent of capital goods. The simple process of saving whilst spending, popularised by the stamp trading companies, might be developed into an unprecedented programme of *deflationary consumption.*

My lovely student life
1975

There is tendency, perhaps less pronounced nowadays than once upon
a time, to regard one's schooldays as carefree and happy. Wicked masters,
bullying prefects, acts of flagrant injustice, whole days of blind terror—all
dissolve with time into a contented vision of *overall* happiness, poetic justice,
a benign wisdom and, above all, a sense of effortless community. Most of
this is the product of nostalgia, although wits warn us that even that is not
as good as it used to be. The truth, of course, is very different: the injustice
and misery of school was real, only there was less of it and it was simpler
than what was to follow.

   Student life is similarly regarded in retrospect—the longer the interval,
the greater the enthusiasm. Thus, in celebrating the 125th anniversary of the
Architectural Association the sheer longevity of the establishment becomes
its own justification. The activities of those students of the last century who
founded the school become invested with revolutionary political meanings
utterly obscure to those who took part in them; the activities of the school
in aiding the London Association of Masterbuilders to prevent the birth
of unions in the building industry at the turn of the century are forgotten.
The AA is a revolutionary place; it always was. Why? Because it has been here
for 125 years, that's why! To the graduates and dropouts of the establishment
who never return, who do not lunch in the members dining room or sprawl
in armchairs above it, who do not talk loudly in the bar or present memoranda
to the school community; this memorial is dedicated. It is the story of my
own student life, which on recollection was neither as amusing nor as
adventurous as it might seem. It was not all spent at the AA—in fact only
one-sixth was—but people who have been through the swirling fog
of architectural education anywhere will recognise part of it. It is not for
nothing that our beloved discipline has the highest dropout rate of any
subject studied at university.[1]

   My lovely student life began on 17 September, 1956, at the Oxford School
of Architecture and ended on 12 March, 1959, in La Santé prison, Paris.
It began again in Oxford on 23 May, 1959, and this time lasted until 24 July,
1960. It began again at the Architectural Association on 19 September, 1961,
and ended again the following July. Its final flowering took place at the AA
between September 1966 and July 1967. I received my AA Diploma in July
1968 when I was 30 years old. I had studied architecture for 12 years.

Not 12 academic years: six of them were spent in architects' offices, the average time in each working out to less than six months. I only ever supervised the construction of one of the large number of buildings I drew —and on that occasion was sacked whilst in hospital because the contract was dragging behind time.

At the time I entered the Oxford School of Architecture I was awaiting a summons to commence my National Service. Thrilling to the pleasures of command whilst in the cadet force at school, I had suffered a rude shock at my army medical examination when the coarse jokes of the orderlies and the spectacle of grown men desperately running on the spot in order to display heart murmurs they did not possess convinced me that whatever did lie inside the wire it almost certainly was not the skilful deployment of tank divisions or the comradely clink of glasses amidst the ruins of some conquered town. I chose architecture.

The first year at Oxford was "a time of creative preparation" whose aims were an "understanding of the basic principles of design in its widest sense".What design in its narrowest sense was we never discovered, as we learned how to stretch Whatman sheets, execute Roman lettering and plot the shadows cast by objects on the ground. During my first year I designed a tool shed, a harbour light, a chapel at Nomlas (which someone worked out spelt 'Salmon' backwards), a bicycle shelter and a pair of gazebos for a stately home. I also drew Corinthian columns according to Scamozzi and designed a Georgian facade. One of the rules of the establishment was that there should be no discussion of politics in the studios—everybody worked in the studios in those days—but it didn't matter because nobody knew what politics was.

Second year work at Oxford was "an expanding synthesis of first year experience". That phrase "expanding synthesis" has haunted me ever since; apparently it meant designing a shop "for T Winterbottom Esq," a transport cafe, a sailing club, a small art gallery and a house on Boars Hill. During the summer vacation preceding my third year I negotiated two terms exchange to be spent in Paris, in the Atelier Faugeron, École Nationale Supérieure des Beaux-Arts.

On my arrival in Paris I moved my solid English drawing board and expensive German instruments into the Gorbals-like atelier in the Rue

Jacques Gallot. The French students found my equipment amusing but obviously useful too—because they stole it all the first night after I went home. Thereafter I learned the virtues of working at my digs, as indeed did most of us. Work at the Beaux-Arts differed greatly from work at Oxford. I did three projects, each of which lasted six weeks. The first, a barracks for a motorised regiment, was placed *hors de concours* because it was drawn to the wrong scale. "*Un metre, qu'est que c'est un metre?*" I had jeered at them, "*mais un pied, c'est un pied!*" How wrong I was. The second project was admitted but failed because it was not "geometrical". The third, a cinema, was not submitted because my extramural life had by then led me away from the Beaux-Arts altogether.

My recollections of the Atelier Faugeron have been through several moral climates since 1959. At the time I found the monstrous plagiarism clear evidence of decadence such as the late war had revealed. I wrote: "A number of the students in the 'Classe Seconde' are married, their wives are students also and they all help each other. In fact everybody helps everybody. There are two really good designers in the atelier, Orzoni and Brochard, they design everything, not just the projects of the 'Classe Seconde'. Other people are good at selecting colours, rendering washes, composing sheets, even just going out to buy sandwiches or cigarettes or beer; they respectively do all this 'specialist' work for everybody else. Czato, a Hungarian, has the largest collection of architectural magazines, he is generous with them and they are ironically called the 'bibliothèque'. Schemes are copied down to the smallest detail from this library and it is normal to see aspiring architects at work with tracing paper and dividers upon plans of the American Embassy at New Delhi, or the Governor's Palace at Brasilia. This last, as a matter of interest, recently gained the Prix des Anciens as a 'Maison des Avocats'."

To me this smacked of a corrupt attitude to 'original design' which was, of course, a sacred creative struggle. I worked on my designs alone and all night and would have none of the 'teamwork' so beautifully worked out in the atelier. In later years I came to realise how practical and entirely reasonable their approach was. If the professors of the institute were so stupid as to award prizes for plagiarisms any third year architectural student could recognise, what on earth was the prospect for 'original design' in the world outside? In any case, being at the Beaux-Arts might be one thing, but living in Paris was another. I stayed in a small hotel near the Place St Michel, I breakfasted in cafes, read Hemingway, Scott Fitzgerald and Elliot Paul. For the first three months I spent most of my grant getting drunk with Americans. Then I started trying to steal cars and eventually stole a typewriter instead in order to write a novel entitled *The Middle Distance*. Another thing I discovered in later years was to beware of things that started with a title. After a time I moved onto a yacht, moored opposite the Eiffel Tower, that belonged to a one-legged American colonel from SHAPE. He used to give me a carton of Marlboros every week and I lived off the supplies he was amassing aboard against his projected summertime cruise of the Norwegian fjords. I thought about going with him as his deckhand.

Back in Oxford that May everything was different. The school had moved into a new office block in Headington and was now an integral part of the Oxford College of Technology, Art and Commerce. I only had three weeks to work for my Intermediate examinations but that didn't matter because cheating in structures and construction was easy as well as widespread. When we had all passed our Intermediate, except for a few who didn't deserve to pass anyway, we all went to The Trout at Godstow for a celebration drink. A student named Proudman jumped into the river with his clothes on and we all laughed and threw beer mugs at him.

The fourth year—1959–1960—was a struggle. I only got my grant back after my escapades in Paris by breaking down in front of the Berkshire County Council Education Committee and threatening to commit suicide. The chairman of the committee took me outside and I confessed to non-existent gambling debts. "When a young fellow tells me how much he owes I usually double it", he said with a twinkle in his eye. I nodded miserably. He was an old army officer and I got my grant back.

The autumn term I went to live in a pub. I could get drinks sent up from the bar and borrow the landlord's car. At the school I began a series of gigantic projects entitled "Symphony Number One", "Symphony Number Two", etc.. "Symphony Number Two" was a vast circular casino of Neoclassic aspect. For a time a sketch of it was pinned up in the staff room. The one thing I had learned in Paris was technique.

That year I fell under the influence of Biltin Toker, a Turk who was in the second year. He was a revolutionary and had produced a design for a workshop that looked like some kind of crumpled up cardboard: the staff were in a wild surmise about him because he had read a few books. He had read Sartre, Camus, Jaspers; he listened to Webern, Schoenberg and Stockhausen. He and I became joint editors for an issue of the Oxford Architectural Students Society magazine D. The issue was to consist of a long article by each of us with a photograph of the face of a popular girl in the fifth year on the cover. My article was about student despair at the meaninglessness of the course of study; this extract deals with the mythical student Schomberg burning the contents of his portfolio.

"Slowly the heavy Whatman sheets began to take fire. Architecture took longer to burn than poems or prose works, and it made a different kind of smoke, thick and yellow. Schomberg coughed happily and screwed up some more large sheets. It was raining so heavily outside that he could still hear it over the furnace like roar of the blazing masterworks.

After a bit the sheets of card he added seemed to block the flames so he got some paraffin from the store room and sloshed it all over the fireplace and the torn portfolio. There was a big sort of 'whoomp' noise and huge flames played up and down the full height of the wall. Lurid shadows flashed about him and he began to laugh out loud. With a croaking shout he threw his Nobel Prize winning gasometer drawings on to the blaze and climbed fully clothed into bed coughing and spitting. 'Roll on death', he mumbled brokenly."

Toker's article was somewhat more optimistic but it was at least 20,000 words long. It dealt with architectural theory as it had been presented to us by the leading theoreticians of the Oxford school. He made nonsense out of all of it, but his own theories were a kind of nonsense too because he was totally ignorant of the real conditions of architectural practice, as were all of us at the time. He cast his article in the form of a dialogue between "A progressive architect" (himself) and "A conventional architect" (also, for the unfair purposes of his exercise, himself). The incredulous conventional architect begins: "But what if the architect creates a form that is completely out of scale, suppose the height in some places is three feet and in others 87 feet. Is this architecture?"

The progressive architect replies: "An architect with new ideas is not a fool, he is not mad either. If he designs a space three feet high there will be a good reason for it. He must have thought of that space as something useful for his design. Whether he is right or wrong will be proved by the people who are to use the building. If society rejects it, it is bad. It is not up to us to decide. I cannot see any reason why such a design should not be called architecture. It is architecture. It is architecture even if it has no roof and no foundations, or just three walls and a column in the middle. Whether it is good architecture or not is beside the point. Nowadays everyone seems to go to an architect and describe exactly what they want. Some of them interested in art even draw perspectives and give actual measurements. Architects lacking social responsibility prostrate themselves by accepting such limitations. So in practice many buildings are designed by the clients themselves."

"What do you do after you create the form?"

"The form created under subconscious restrictions to satisfy certain requirements becomes the plan."

"Suppose it doesn't work?"

"A form is an entity. Any alteration will destroy its unity. Therefore the only alternative is to create another form."

Toker kicked down the ramshackle theories of Modernism but was totally unable to erect an alterative structure—I mean quite simply a building—to put in their place. Because he could think of no other way to finance what he called progressive or "four-dimensional" buildings apart from seizing political power, he wasted a lot of time. He went to Berkeley in the end and was deported from the United States after his visa expired. He runs a tourist magazine in Turkey now.

The issue of D magazine was destined never to appear. The student committee got to hear of the contents of the articles and withdrew the proofs from the printers. They described the cover as "pornographic". Toker declared war on them and was expelled from the school. He organised an exhibition in Lincoln College, distributed pamphlets attacking Pier Luigi Nervi when he spoke at Oxford and gave a lecture himself at the Ashmolean Museum where he was barracked by fifth year students and pelted with eggs.

At the end of my fourth year I took only three of the seven examinations for admission to the fifth. The first question in the Theory of Architecture paper ran as follows: "What form of building should be sited a) on a flat plain, b) in a hilly or mountainous country, c) amongst the trees?" I answered by drawing some mountains and writing underneath, "Guess what should go here?" I drew a flat plain and wrote underneath, "Guess what should go here?" Finally I drew a wastepaper basket and wrote beneath it, "Guess what should go here?"

I spent the next academic year working in the offices of an architect in Berkshire who had contrived the job of designing three council houses for the rural district council. He parlayed this windfall into a whole estate of 40 houses. I went on to design a whole suburb with six-storey balcony-access flats, a dual carriageway road, new bridges over the Thames and the railway, and a Le Corbusier-style sports ground. In the summer of 1961, there was a credit squeeze and when the architect presented his bill for fees for the new Brasilia, he was told that an architect's department could have been established for less. The partnership folded shortly afterwards and the architect went away to work for a builder. Two years later he found an unqualified draughtsman masquerading as an architect and exposed him.

Throughout this year of 'practical experience' I fell more and more completely into Biltin's way of thinking. I wrote a play which was performed by members of the Progressive Architecture Movement (as we were then called) to a packed house in the Northgate Hall, Oxford. The action was supposed to take place in the Temple of Forms, a vault to be found beneath the RIBA building in Portland Place. The play ended with a mob sacking the building and executing all the officials—a theme which was to occupy my mind for several years.

In the summer of 1961, I endeavoured to retake the examinations I had spurned the year before but was refused re-admission to the school. I applied to American universities but without success. Toker and I wrote to the cultural attaché of the Soviet Embassy asking for political asylum to continue our revolutionary work in the USSR. We got no reply and were too frightened to pursue the matter. Toker wrote to the principal of the Oxford School, denouncing him for sacking four members of the Progressive Architecture Movement (two of whom were later to qualify at the AA), and we all got ourselves into the papers. I appealed to the RIBA but was told I richly deserved my fate. Here is an extract from Toker's letter, it reveals the rich vein of paranoia we were mining at the time.

"... I have seen you reading Rudolph Arnheim, I have seen the books you have read, you are up to date, interested in architecture. But I have never heard you committing yourself, making positive suggestions to people. Is this wise? I am not going to dispute it. But your passivity influences your staff and thus becomes an active negativism. Why pretend? There is no neutral state. We all commit ourselves 1,000 times a day through our behaviour.

I think you have completely misunderstood Progressive Architecture and by dismissing its members you have only demonstrated that you yourself are a total failure striving to exist in a world which you consider to be hostile. This is a pity for if you faced yourself you would be much more useful to architecture and thus to humanity. At this time in history people of your intellectual power are needed. Perhaps as a result of not committing yourself for 20 years you really have lost your power of intellectual judgement. I don't know.

Yes, what you have just read, whether you wish to face it or not, is the simple truth which you have been looking for all your life. It is a truth which you will never find in the students you are keeping in your school as opposed to the ones you have dismissed. This comedy of meaningless statements, lack of knowledge and bearded faces must end. For your sake. For society's sake. Your mask has fallen. You can no longer afford to take refuge in the future. The present will judge you. You and your staff."

Inexplicably the principal ignored this letter and continued as principal of the Oxford School of Architecture for a number of years. We of the Progressive Architecture Movement believed that the whole architectural establishment was victimising us because we saw through their sawdust and tinsel to a golden future. The more misfortunes befell us, the more convinced we became of our rectitude. If power was not almost within our grasp, why was everyone so frightened?

In September 1961, I enrolled for the fourth year at the AA on money loaned to me by my mother-in-law. Toker, as I have explained, went to Berkeley. The others went to London and got jobs. September 1961 was William Allen's debut as principal at the AA, which was lucky for me both then and later because I started right in with 'progressive' schemes.

The first was 'a colliery workshop' which bore a strong generic resemblance to Toker's Kidlington Library project of two years before. The second was an office block for the site presently occupied by St George's Hospital; here workers, families and computers alike were to tread the sloping floors and use the lifts, which rose at different angles to the vertical. Finally, I designed a National Film Theatre which consisted of 700 single viewing cubicles fed by video tape so that anyone could see any film he chose at whatever time he chose. In deference to my wife, I later modified the design of the cubicles so that two persons could use them. Later, when I was desperately designing the massive megastructure into which the National Film Theatre would fit like a needle in a haystack, she exercised a further humanising influence. "What about Kitty and Tomkins?" she enquired, after I had explained my plastic Piranesian vision. She went on to claim that people should have the right to own cats (like the aforenamed) and potted plants too if they chose. "No room for that." I gritted, and drew on, but the seed was sown.... Doubt, dreadful doubt.

At one crit during my fourth year at the AA a student collapsed whilst his project was being energetically ridiculed by a visiting critic. The critic did not notice this event until a dreadful silence caused him to turn round some moments later. At Oxford, girl students had sometimes burst into tears and locked themselves in the lavatories under similar circumstances. "Come out, Miss Barrett, please come out!" At the Beaux-Arts some students had committed suicide. My own route, as you have gathered, was to go mad.

At the end of my fourth year I left without taking any examinations and without paying my last term's fees—then £102. I went to work for Enthoven and Mock and then several other places. During dull moments in offices I wrote plays about architecture and planning and design methodology. I particularly hated Manikins and fictionalised their use as follows.

"It is some time later in the same day. A and B are hard at work on the human specification. This vital and secret document is of course A's responsibility as job architect but lacking any real confidence in himself he is weak on authority and B has recently discovered his extreme suggestibility. Their target for this phase of the design work is to reduce the volume required by 16 science students by three per cent and A is perceptibly wavering. 'Years ago' he says helplessly, "'people all used to have to be able to stand up.' B cuts deftly back.

'Look A, surely if we graft two six year old arms onto this student in the corner by the ventilation trunking, his face need only be five mm away from the sloping sides of the gas showers when he is working.' Obsessed with carrying his point B thinks nothing of the agonies of the student, with truncated arms and condensation-laden metal sheeting before his face.

'Well', struggles A. But the coffee comes in and with it the morning question. Relievedly he replies. 'Oh, I think I'll have BS 1057 this morning please Mulbriel, with perhaps a touch of brown sugar to bring out the grey.'

'OK then A', cuts in B 'I'll ring up Jones and see if we can't get his head to lean back another 2 degrees....'

'No, not yet.... Perhaps his arms could be a bit shorter....'

'I'll ask him about that too.'

'You can't, I've just remembered, Jones is in Greenland, won't be back until Thursday.'

'Eight-year-arms would give you....'

'At least 12 mm.'

'Yes, you're right, wouldn't gain anything. What about sevens?'

'No good. He couldn't reach his genitals.'

'Yes. Of course. He'd need to do that. Hygiene.'"

By the end of 1965 the impending action "The Architectural Association versus Myself in the matter of Tuition Fees" had finally been settled out of court. By then I had a son and my wife had been killed in a car crash. For a time I managed a pop group called "The Heretics" who made a film for BBC2 about pop groups that didn't make it—the best of their three singles sold 372 copies in spite of being a Radio Luxemburg Hit Pick so they were well qualified. I was also one of the people who started the London School of Pop, a big operation intended to handle planeloads of American teenagers on a six week residential course in swinging London—somewhat like IID. Press agency interviewers told us that we would be millionaires by the new year but we weren't. I couldn't escape from architecture, from my wound. I kept scratching it. In 1966, I finally took the examinations I should have taken in 1962 and by the time-honoured method of cheating passed all but one. In 1966, I re-entered the school for the fifth year.

This time I knew exactly what I wanted. I knew architectural theory was a farce and 'design' simply didn't matter; I'd worked in offices, you see.

What I did was to embark on a project for a dwelling where 'the individual' (me) could hide—away from planners, architects, bank managers, other creditors, journalists, local authorities, codes of practice and social utopians: all the disjointed horrors of the world I had inhabited for the last decade. "The Time House" was to be a means of escape—to use a phrase with which I had become familiar in another context. I worked on this apotheosis of private life, this machine to shelter my own madness, for the whole year. I wrote it, designed it and lived it. In July 1967, I was given an extension for a year instead of a Diploma. I cried inconsolably. A few days later I received a report from the school which claimed that my portfolio had not even been submitted to the RIBA external examiners for Part Two. This was not the case and I became so incensed at my wasted year that I rang Peter Cook up at two o'clock in the morning to complain about it.

After a brief return to the architect's office where I was born I got a job on *The Architects' Journal*—largely, I believe, as a result of a recommendation by William Allen, the long-gone principal. That worked out well for a time. Thanks to Charles Jencks I got to publish "The Time House" and, thanks to Robin Middleton, to write for *Architectural Design*. In June 1968 I resubmitted "The Time House" and it passed. My madness, if not over, was at least internalised.

Architectural education today seems to me to be a trick, or rather a series of tricks. Not the sort that people play on you—although it seemed like that sometimes—but the sort you win at whist and other games. After 12 years of madness, I learned to win tricks at architectural education but at the very moment I learned to win, the whole game became worthless, like currency devalued overnight. The whole trip from status to paranoia, from paranoia to status now lies in two dust-covered portfolios under my bed at home. What it really meant I don't know; but I do know that when I chose the title for this piece some weeks before writing it I thought it would turn out to be a bundle of jokes and reminiscences—"My lovely student life". When I finally came to go through my papers and my memories I realised what an enormous part of my life was bound up in them. I realised that whatever else it was, my student life was not a joke—unless it was a joke on me.

We shall not bulldoze Westminter Abbey: Archigram and the retreat from technology
1976

The love is gone.
The poetry of bricks is lost.
We want to drag into building some of the poetry of
countdown,
orbital helmets,
Discord of mechanical body transportation methods
and leg walking.
LOVE GONE.
Archigram Paper 1, May 1961

Remember Archigram the name, because one afternoon of heat the express train (of technology) drew up there unwontedly; it was late spring. 8 May, 1975, to be exact, and the biggest audience at the Architectural Association for a year or two packed in to see the revised tenth anniversary performance of the Archigram Opera, despite the warm weather and manifold distractions of the metropolis beyond the lecture hall door. Lecture Hall No One— formerly called 'the dining room'—has a strange configuration which I can liken only to a now-defunct cinema in Queen Street, Oxford, which was similarly divided, like trousers. Imagine short trousers seen from the front, the wearer's legs astride: convert this elevation into a plan and figure the stage as an old-fashioned trouser pocket—not a patch pocket or a hip pocket. In the pocket at the opening of the show stood Warren Chalk, with two packs of cigarettes and a box of matches in his hand fully 14 years (perhaps to the day) after the publication of the original "mettlesome broadsheet", *Archigram 1*. Behind him a long, curved paper screen running from the lowest point of the pocket to the opposite side of the waistband. In the area of the trousers reserved for genitalia, on tables piled upon tables, stood a battery of slide projectors, tape decks, and king-sized speaker cabinets: behind them sat Dennis Crompton. Deep in one trouser leg, wearing a polka-dot shirt and rapping with admirers, was Peter Cook. Ron Herron was somewhere about too as the lights dimmed. There must have been 200 people in the trousers, maybe 300. "I suppose I am the oldest member of the group", began Warren, "and I'm going to introduce all this stuff because it will take hours...."

Part One

Loud funky music broke in, louder and with better quality reproduction
than ten years ago. Then, with the stage bare, the slides opened up exploding
on alternate sides of the screen. Pictures of the wild bunch: Warren himself,
Peter Cook, Ron Herron, David Greene, Mike Webb, and Dennis Crompton;
then the junior team, Colin Fournier, Ken Allinson, Tony Rickaby, and others
I could not recognise; then the precursors and chroniclers, Buckminster
Fuller, Cedric Price, and Reyner Banham. Pictures of them spanning 1,000
years in the memory; some hanging loose in California, some uptight with
short hair and urgent conversation (about what to do before they realised
this was it?) at the dawn of real time. How sentimental. How tragic the
atmosphere. The music changed to Richard Strauss as the slides dug deep
into the roots of the Modern Movement, to the images that launched
1,000 careers (even those that floated)—Mendelsohn, Scharoun,
the Taut brothers, the Constructivists, de Stijl.... Back, back to the
Ashmolean Museum in 1960, to Northgate Hall, Oxford, to Folkestone,
to the old ICA, to the time when they bought leather coats to celebrate
winning a competition. A slide flashed, BUT WE TURNED ELSEWHERE.

"Almost without realising it, we have absorbed into our lives the first
generation of expendables.... Foodbags, paper tissues, polythene wrappers,
ballpens, EPs.... So many things about which we don't have to think.
We throw them away almost as soon as we acquire them. Also with us are
the items that are bigger and last longer, but are nevertheless planned for
obsolescence.... Our basic message?.... That the home, the whole city,
and the frozen pea pack are all the same...."
Archigram 3, Autumn 1963

And now came the real sources of their inspiration; pictures from magazines
of zeppelins, submarines, spacecraft, molecules, transistors, and girls. Pages
from the various issues of *Archigram* flashed on and off (now it was steel bands
and grand funk again) until the real stuff came pouring through—the rich,
unbelievable schemes, the effortless translation of technology into architecture.
"Machine-monster worry?" said a slide. "Then package it!" What did that
mean? Too late now to find out. It always was too late. *They* know or at least

they *knew*—but now it is buried beneath projects for motorised tents. "Capsules become pods", explained a slide knowingly, whilst another exclaimed "In Oxford Street the architecture is no more important than the rain!" In five years they envisioned an entire landscape of super-humanist equipment; an existential technology for individuals that the world will, in time, come to regard with the same awe as is presently accorded to the prescience of Jules Verne, HG Wells, or the Marquis de Sade. Futile to complain (as many do), "but they never *build* anything". Verne never *built* the *Nautilus*, Wells could hardly drive a car, and the Marquis de Sade? Well, he was in prison for most of his life.

Debate
It was impossible to take many notes that day. I sank into a reverie, filled with shame at my failure to recognise genius all those years ago. Now I understood the meaning of the stream of visitors to Aberdare Gardens over the years; those backpacking Brazilians, translucent BBC men, uncomfortable professors (all too aware that those new luminaries were exactly like the students they feared at home): all of them had been more honest and more grateful than I, who had been merely picayune, jeering at the interstices in Peter Cook's net of words whilst mighty fish slipped away to Germany, to Italy, to Japan. Now, I reflected, he has his revenge. Svengali-like impresario bestriding the London art scene like a colossus, welding drawing board and palette into a sacrifice to be laid at the feet of hobgoblins who have themselves parlayed Palgrave's *Golden Treasury* and a little antiquated music hall technique into influential careers....

"The building has been designed large enough to include its own component production units. These manufacture moulded reinforced plastic panels, which are conveyed, folded up, to their positions in the structure, and then opened out to form usable floor space.... Transport consists of raw materials arriving at one of the ports and being pumped through pipelines to the site production units. Plant 1 produces main supporting structure components (prob. based on Bucky Fuller's "Aspersion Tensegrity" whereby a standard tensegrity structure will erect itself in the air by tensioning its outer edges). This would form the transparent, weather-resistant skin."
Archigram 4, 1964

Reading this extract from Michael Webb's account of his House Project, one relives the wonderment of discovery. The Archigram group, in their heyday, dismissed the limited capabilities of the construction industry with the same impatience as Jacques Maisonrouge (Chairman of IBM) displayed in his famous announcement that "The world's political structures are completely obsolete. They have not changed in at least 100 years and are woefully out of tune with technological progress." At one time Archigram and the multi-national corporations were made for one another; there is perhaps a hint of panic in Webb's "prob. based on Bucky Fuller..." but compared to the absurd posturing of Archigram's detractors, inured as they were in "the world's political structures", this is trivial indeed. Of housing, Archigram said in 1966, "housing is a crust of capsules hung on the diagonal tubes"—who would have the nerve to define it thus now? Their past is still our future, the triumph of reaction can be but temporary. Indeed we can still only deal with their already ten year old vision by way of jokes reminiscent of the kind of futile opposition offered by literati to the coming of the railways. Defensible crust? Vandalism in the diagonal tubes? When Instant City really camps in Death Valley who will be churlish enough to mention Charles Manson? When the Archigram dirigible *Rupert* greets the citizens of Bournemouth who will be as tasteless as to breathe the name Hindenburg?

"Walls, ceiling, floors—in this living area—are wall, ceiling, and floor conditions which adjust according to our needs. The enclosures of the living area are no longer rigid, but adjustable, programmed to move up and down, in and out. The floor state too is variable. At particular points the floor can be made hard enough to dance on or soft enough to sit on. Textures and colours depend on the user's taste at any moment.

Seating and sleeping arrangements are inflatable, and details such as weight of bed-covers and number of cushioned elements are controlled by the user. Bed-covers are not really necessary, as the living area, which is air conditioned, can have special warm air areas—but some people might like a token cover.

The old concept of a movable chair has become a travelling chair/car. The model in the living area is designed on the hovercraft principle, and can also be used outside for driving around the megastructure city. The bed-capsule (not included in this display) can also change to a hovercraft and run outside. The crucial issue of privacy versus general communication—which dogged designers of the open plan—is effectively resolved in Archigram's design. The robots can shoot out screens which enclose a required area of space. The ceiling lowers at this point, and whoever requires it has a private area. The robots are movable—on wheels. They do most of the work.

Refreshments can be drawn from them. They contain a compressor for blowing up the inflatable furniture. They also have an element for retracting dust from the living area. The robots also incorporate radio and television —including favourite movies and educational programmes—which can be switched on when you want them. The television is, at the present stage of development, seen on wide screens, and can be programmed so that viewers are surrounded by realistic sound, colour, and scent effects. The controls can be worked by a gesture as delicate as that of batting an eyelid. Every day the robots must be taken to the service wall end of the living room to refill with water, air, and the rest, and to deposit dust and rubbish. This service wall connects with a vast service truck, shared with the megastructure city, which is one of the key facilities of Archigram's structure. Items such as clothing (which is envisaged as disposable), food, and milk are piped into individual living areas, and can be changed or returned by the same system, or disposed of when finished with by a pipe leading to the shared disposal system.

Each living area is fitted with ultrasonic cooking equipment for the cleanest, quickest cooking, but otherwise arrangements will depend on the interest of the cook. Cooks will be able to simulate the physical conditions needed for perfect open-fire cooking, slow-oven baking, barbecuing and spit-roasting.

The design of the living area goes some way towards allaying the widely-held fears that the future points inevitably to standardisation and conformity of living accommodation. The purpose of the Archigram scheme is to give people a level of personal choice and personal service which as in past decades has only been approached by the richest members of society."
Catalogue for Harrods 1990 room set, designed by Archigram, 1967

Their certainty in those years was unbounded. Verging occasionally on the Monty Pythonesque (as with the hovercraft bed that can "run outside"), it nonetheless cut through the nostalgia of that May evening in 1975 like a knife. I made a note in the darkness punctuated by the bright flash of slides: they did their best work at one of those times when visionaries believed that what they had drawn and described had really happened. They were, of course, aided in this belief by critics who—lacking any faith in the 'invisible hand' of the marketplace—believed equally strongly that only their opposition stood between the Archigram blueprint and its realisation. Critics always believe that, it is at once the force and the futility of their craft. The only real antidote is the enlargement of experience.

The resemblance of EXPO '70 at Osaka to an Archigram metropolis in the flesh has been noted more than once. Indeed, the only thing at Osaka that was not Archigram-like was the tiny Archigram Dissolving City exhibit tucked away in the roof of Kenzo Tange's gigantic Theme Pavilion. There, surrounded by pods and capsules, gloops and nodes and robots that were not mock-ups made of painted blockboard, the intended question and answer tunnel stood silent, none of its complex electronics installed. No foreign visitor ever asked a question or obtained an answer from it —a fact never mentioned in published versions of the Dissolving City scheme. When first confronted with the Japanese version of what Archigram had been drawing for so long, one could only gasp at its enormous scale and technical completeness. I remember wondering what the Archigram team themselves thought whilst being led by Japanese hosts along the moving ways of Instant City EXPO to the conference centre where Dennis Crompton spoke. The impact must have been as shattering as Cavour's first conversation with the Selenites, or Professor Arronax's introduction to Captain Nemo aboard the Nautilus.

"The government of Monaco have asked the Archigram group of London to proceed with their design for the new entertainments centre on the sea front at Monte Carlo. This project was recently the subject of an international competition and the winning project by the Archigram group was judged by Pierre Vago, René Sarger, Michel Ragon, and Ove Arup. It was the only English entry invited into the final stage together with 12 other projects

(by architects from France, Spain, Poland, America, Finland, Norway, and Germany). The building will be totally underground with a large uninterrupted circular space 250 feet in diameter. Almost any show can be provided including ice hockey, the circus, large banquets, theatre, audio-visual exhibits, go-karting and sports. To make this possible, Archigram are designing a series of approximately 20 different robot-type machines which plug-in to a service grid above and below. Everything, including the seating, lavatories, stages, and walls will be movable and the 'architecture' of the building will depend upon the wishes of the producer of the show. There are six entrances—so the layout of the building can be constantly changed. The entire building is seen as a giant cybernetic toy in which the architecture plays a similar role to the equipment in a television studio. Total cost of the scheme is estimated at $6,000,000 and building work is expected to start late in 1971."
Archigram Press Release, 1970

The projected Features-Monte Carlo structure would have been—had it been carried out—the largest underground dome in Europe since the German rocket launching silo built at Wizernes in Northern France in 1943 was destroyed by bombing. Archigram did not think of it like that: to them it was the basement of a "plug-in land beach" wired up to enable you to "dial for drinks from anywhere in the park". I remember a brief conversation with an acoustics architect about it. "Hmmm", he said, "20 robots, that's eight miles of integrated circuits… say $16,000,000."

Intermission
After a solid hour of bright images and good music, an intermission was called on 8 May. The lights came up, curtains were pulled, and Peter Cook, a bunch of magic markers in his hand, came over for a chat. There had been a rumour about for a week or so that—owing to the adverse economic climate—the Archigram office was to close down: I taxed him with it. "Well, we thought about it, but we decided what the hell, we've been going this long, might as well keep going", he explained.

If Archigram nearly made the big time with Features-Monte Carlo, there was still just enough steam left that night to keep Jacques Maisonrouge hovering at the back of the hall with a contract in his hand. That intermission was remarkable; there must have been 300 people in the trouser-hall with a temperature not far short of 90 degrees fahrenheit, but few of them left, even to get a drink from the bar. Cook (who is generally private in public and public in private) described a lecture tour from which he had recently returned; Copenhagen, Aarhus, New York, and the East Coast. No flak anywhere, not even at MIT. "They really hated us there in the old days."

Part Two

Instead of music and slides, Part Two offered a speaker—Peter Cook himself—more slides, and the strains of Delius. "Yes, Delius", he began, "it never has a theme that develops anywhere: it just goes on and on. Perhaps sickening. Who knows?" Jacques Maisonrouge does, he slips the un-signed contract back into his pocket and returns to his black chauffeur-driven Cadillac. "The heliport", he grits. And just in time, for it is *conceptual architecture* at last. As ART NET is to ARCHIGRAM, so is CONCEPTUAL ARCHITECTURE to ZOOM. It is what architects (and would-be architects) do when they finally *believe* that the drawings will have no building, that intercourse with the drawing machine will produce no pregnancy, that the distance separating Captain Nemo from the USS *Nautilus* (SSN 571) is so immense that it is not even worth attempting.

"MAYBE ARCHITECTURE IS JUST A GAME? Maybe the historical back-and-forth of morals and symbols dressed in architectonic styles is a game being played out? So what's different about today? What's new? Every so often our frontiers are so greatly extended by science and invention that the way to live takes a leap. Sometimes architecture is there waiting to help, or sometimes playing in its own corner. Technology? No let's see, hear, breathe, feel worlds outside our own world...."
Peter Cook
"Control and Choice", reprinted in *A Continuing Experiment*, Architectural Press, 1975

"This is a bland piece of land", Cook continued as the strains of Delius began to fade, "but sneakily something happens (next slide), and it is interrupted

by a *crevice*, then the land continues (next slide).... Such paradoxes are
the milk from which one draws."

An orchard. "The orchard became (next slide), dare one suggest it,
a kind of megastructure *manqué* (next slide), in this case, mechanical trees."
A structure. "One couldn't resist quirking the plan even before one began
(next slide) cancerously adding the lumpen stuff to it. The tactile quality of
satin.... The cream as it folds. This is beyond architecture, honestly it is."
There is a strange interjection from the audience in Italian, a slight flicker
of terror in Cook's voice, but he continues: "I found myself in Edinburgh at
an oil conference. Most of it was moralistic.... What I call the Celtic fringe
which includes Norway, Canada, and certain parts of Alaska." A second
spontaneiro from the audience offers "Anchor an ocean liner up there!" But he
too is ignored as the speaker pushes on into broad comedy with deliberately
Scottish pronunciations of "burns" and "bairns". Cook conceptualises
rapidly; he illustrates and evaluates architectural manifestations such as
THE LUMP (Mont St Michel), THE HEAP (a mound of wrecked cars), THE
MOUND (One of the parts of *Archigram 5* was the discussion of the molehill),
and finally THE SPONGE with orifices.

By eight o'clock the opera has been running for three hours, there
are still 40 or 50 people standing. Cook has been speaking for two hours
and shows no sign of exhaustion; the paper screen is covered with multi-
coloured drawings made with magic markers and still the slides are coming.
"Archigram", he says, "went through two stages of development. First the
mechanisms, and second *this architecture of the thing to be so far beyond one's
experience of other objects as to be something else again.*" While he draws there
are intervals of Haydn.

Dear Sirs, We looked at Peter Cook talk on the TV programme and
thoroughly enjoyed his talk. He talks a load of plain common sense.
Let's hear more from him. Now we think that the Royal Institute of British
Architects should have a surgesttion box (sic) for the public to give their
ideas to. We think it should give the address outside the post office where
the public could write if they wish to. Here some ideas to help the architects:

1. Never build to many houses in a turning for the public to walk to the next
    road the most should be ten houses never 200.

2. Have more slidding doors in the homes. They better in every way. No banging like the Japan have. Never have open DOORS.

3. Make the Bathroom the Best place for health and cleaness. Have the toilet in a separate room with the bath incace a person is in the bath or shower and people cannot get to the toilet.

4. Do away with dirty old cellars. Some people full them up with old junk.

5. Bring sunlight into Homes. Never Hide with Great Big Walls. Have slidding walls.

6. Schouls built with plenty of sport rooms for children to get rid of energy if they wish. 14, 15 and 16 years old. and so on with more new idears to help. So from our surgesttion box idears to yours.

Letter to the RIBA Journal, 1972
(Some spelling corrected)

The opera ends at last on the same note of funky music as it began. There were no questions and the trouser-legged hall slowly emptied as the roadies packed up projectors and tape decks. "I don't mind", Cook had once confessed, "what they do as long as they don't start chanting." He has had audiences of all kinds since he started, at first they were speechless; then they got angry. At the Folkestone International Dialogue of Experimental Architecture in 1966 he was slow-handclapped off the stage. In Amsterdam, in 1970, dull-witted ideologues tried to prove that he *had* signed a contract with Maisonrouge—if not with the Green Berets. In Paris, in 1971, a whole audience walked out. But like any performer, and of the Archigram group he is the *only* performer, he has had good times too—especially lately. Now the audiences are speechless again; they turn up in droves but they no longer heckle or question as much as they used to. They sit (or stand) and listen and applaud and go home and read in the papers that hopes for nuclear power have dimmed; that gas prices will rise again; that inflation has reached 15, or 20, or 25 per cent; that public housing starts are the lowest for 18, or 20, or 25 years; that unemployment is still rising; that food is poisoned; that cars are smaller than ever; that former astronauts are working as evangelists; that mad people keep on trying to kill the president; that—and this is only if they search hard in the most obscure papers—brilliant young architects are selling their drawings of the brave new world to the galleries and museums of the craven old in order to make a living.

"Machine-monster worry? Too bad. No one's going to package it now. The idea of an expendable environment is still somehow regarded as akin to anarchy.... As if, in order to make it work, we would bulldoze Westminster Abbey."
WE SHALL NOT BULLDOZE WESTMINSTER ABBEY.
Archigram 3, Autumn 1963

Thoughts on the design of
housing and banknotes
1978

The other day a curious letter arrived addressed "To our friends at" followed by the correct number, street, city and zip. Through the windowed envelope could be seen "credit to the order of" and then, in the exciting fuzzy red numerals of a cheque-writing machine, "$25,000 and 00cts". I looked at the return address and saw that it came from a mortgage and investment company. Cautiously I slid the blade of my Swiss army knife across the top seam and withdrew the contents. Sure enough, it was a come-on, with an ornately designed "cash availability certificate" and a form letter beginning "Dear___ Your house is a kind of savings bank."

When I first started out in architecture I was told, and I suppose believed, that my house was a machine for living in. Designing a machine for living in was a tricky task, but rewarding, for a fine private residence could establish a reputation and go on reinforcing it on glossy pages long after it had been irretrievably mutilated by its occupants. The problem with machines for living in was to make them good but cheap, so everybody could have one.

This led to dymaxion dwelling units, industrialised building, the mobile home industry and other matters of interest to architects. Indeed the most important role any architect could perform was often characterised as the matchmaking of the productive capacity of machines to the global and growing need for housing. Of course, this is passé stuff nowadays, as my mortgage and investment company explains: the real thing is home ownership and its encyclopedia of economic benefits.

Today it is difficult to open a newspaper without being advised to buy a house. People apparently do still write to columnists asking if they should do it now or wait until next year, but they always get the same answer. Perhaps the letters are written by realtors. In the last ten years the value of the average American home has risen from $26,000 to $65,000, such a colossal increase that property taxes, once a trivial adjunct to home ownership, are now so high that some skilful traders-up, having parlayed early purchase into small fortunes using their $12,000 or $14,000 incomes mainly for interest payments, are now faced with ruin.

Such investors are to be found all over the United States camping in smart suburban neighbourhoods, converting carports and garages, excavating swimming pools, multiplying floor area with never a thought for furniture or comfort or permanence, only for resale and the replacement rule. The much touted 'taxpayers revolt' is of course the response of these individuals to the injustice of being taxed as though they were millionaires when in fact they are only gamblers.

If these are the facts of the housing market, how should the architect relate to it? Clearly it is futile to fiddle with energy or the five points of architecture when the real issues are points of interest. Futile, too, to harmonise with historical styles when all the sporting investor wants is to combine *all* the historical imagery he has ever seen or heard about. The mobile home industry is way ahead of the architectural profession in this matter; the speed with which manufacturers switched from streamform to log cabin was wonderful to behold. No accident that double- and triple-wides can now be financed over 20 or 30 years, just like 'real' houses.

The successful designer of houses today can no longer study briar pipes, steam ships or automobiles, nor can he profitably dwell on the bottomless excesses of postmodernism. Better by far to immerse himself in investment imagery; to study the semiology of banknotes, share certificates, stocks, bonds and debentures. Gothic lettering, pyramids, eyes, scrolls and Latin inscriptions, these are the elements of the new domestic architecture. The world would surely beat a pathway to the office of the architect who actually made houses look like the units of trading they have become.

This England—coming home
1980

Returning to England from Los Angeles concentrates the mind wonderfully. The salesman in the garage where you buy your Japanese pickup truck (trucks are a good American habit) expresses genuine sympathy when you tell him where you have been. When you drive the truck away it takes an hour to do 17 miles—a distance you commuted in 20 minutes on the freeways. A good part of the hour is taken up with being overtaken by cows and brought to a halt by horsemen in leisurely conversation with the occupants of stationary Range Rovers. In England the social hierarchy is shockingly evident, but then so is the future.

As far as the architectural profession is concerned it falls into three phases. In the first, conservationists gain such power that the practice of architecture actually becomes illegal; in the second, the urgent need for hundreds of thousands of modern high-performance buildings becomes so obvious that conservation becomes illegal; and in the third, machines that make buildings out of drawings can be bought over the counter at Boots —by which time the practice of architecture as we know it will be viewed with the kind of suspicion now directed towards freelance exorcism.

Having just returned from the future I can fix an unwavering gaze upon all these stages. To take the last first, the wafer-thin-pocket-building-calculator age will begin with the development of articulated lorry-sized machines based on present-day micro-processor technology. Miniaturisation will be rapid and within a few years an LED version of the old sketch on the back of an envelope will simply be placed on a sheet of silicone at the centre of the site and bombarded with ultra-violet rays.

The resultant building will be ready for use within minutes. By this time the president of the RIBA, using the Institute's own equipment in his chauffeur-driven car, will have the power to re-erect all the buildings in the country three times over. This *force de frappe* will, however, only be used under extreme provocation.

In the preceding phase, the spectacle of half-forgotten skills applied to overwhelming need will fill the country with fiascos and disasters. Huge half-completed housing projects will be dynamited because the stairs cannot be made to fit and the windows pop out like champagne corks. The universities will be scoured for antiquaries able to interpret specifications, and copies of Mitchell's *Building Construction* will change hands for 1,000s of pounds. In the end, experts will be imported at great expense from Zaire and Papua New Guinea.

In the very first phase, which will start soon, the delicate peace now reigning between gold-medalled modernist knights and the preservationist lynch-mob will explode into a latter-day revocation of the Edict of Nantes. Witch hunts and kangaroo courts will mete out savage punishments. Some practicing architects who tonight sleep soundly in their beds will live to hear themselves sentenced to community service, spending up to six hours a week in the compulsory restoration of country houses. All this is very clear when you first arrive.

What does vernacular really mean?
1981

According to Thorndike and Barnhart's excellent *High School Dictionary* the word vernacular means "a native language used by the people of a certain country or place". According to the *Concise Oxford* it means "indigenous, not of foreign origin or learned formation". According to planners it means the way most building used to be done in any definable locality. By adopting the local vernacular a homogeneity can be created out of ingredients separated by hundreds of years. The pool house can resemble the cow byre, itself recently converted into a studio after being a garage, and the passive solar house can blend in with the centuries-old cottage without south-facing windows for fear of the plague. The simple concept of formal similarity enables those utterly lacking in aesthetic sensibility to pronounce at length on taste and style.

In fact, of course, the vernacular image is much less important than the vernacular reality. It is astonishing that all planners, most writers on architectural subjects and far too many architects should grasp the first and remain resolutely ignorant of the second. The reason most pre-industrial buildings in a given region of the country look like one another is a matter of economics, not aesthetics, and the economics of that homogeneity are still ruthlessly apparent to those prepared to understand them. Take the picture postcard country cottage, today fetching £50,000 or more in synthetic thatched, sandtexed, plastic guttered, double-glazed and damp-proofed form. When it was built it was a marginal enterprise in every sense. It owned no land, but stood instead on the edge of a productive field against a useful road. It was built from waste or salvaged materials: straw gleanings for thatch and lathing, mud for mortar, dead trees for timber, broken barrels for windows, mud and cow dung beaten into a floor, field stones piled up for walls. Even the labour that built it was waste labour, time off rather than time on.

All this was efficiency as much as it was poverty, for while traditional agriculture achieved poor productivity by modern standards, it left no waste that could not be absorbed by the land itself or the rural built environment. The dwellings of the poor were part of a complex system of waste consumption with even the bones of the slaughtered animals used in paving, the hair from their hides used in plaster, the dung they produced while alive burned in fires to make heat.

From the richness and sophistication of this sustainable economy, with all its lessons in the use of renewable resources and the exploitation of waste, we have seized upon one totally irrelevant detail to promote to the level of dogma. We want our buildings to look like their predecessors and we call this emulation "vernacular", even though our present efforts have not one syllable of systematic thought in common with them.

The vernacular demanded by planners is not a language used by the people of a certain country or place. It is of foreign origin and it is a 'learned formation'. Our craving for a seamless join between old and new is really evidence that we are unable to face the light years separating our global consumer economy from the parochial autarchy of the pre-industrial world: unable in fact to think clearly enough about the relationship of building to economic activity to develop a vernacular of our own.

It is undeniable that the architectural vernacular exists only in the relationship of building technique to local resources. When that relationship is broken, we forfeit all right to use the term and there is logically no more reason to assume the guise of a sixteenth century cottage than a lunar landing module.

The defence of modern architecture
1983

Bernard Levin, Angela Rippon, Roger Scruton, Robert Hughes, Christopher
Booker, Conrad Jameson, the son (or was it the grandson?) of Gunnar
Asplund, Robert Stern, Charles Jencks, Bryan Appleyard, Kevin Woodcock
(and 100 other cartoonists), Jimmy Young, Lord Carrington, Keith
Waterhouse, Tom Wolfe... everyone from Dangermouse to the Duke of
Edinburgh attacks modern architecture. The less they know about it the
more they attack it: the more they attack it the less likely they are to receive
a rebuttal. They can say it is more dangerous than nuclear weapons, they can
demand that its perpetrators be shot. Welfare spokespersons can stand up
at conferences and announce with all the visual evidence of a sincerely held
belief that "architecture brought that family through our door"—referring
to the fact that pulling the plug on their all-electric council house drove
them into care.

There is no limit to the number of persons who will attack modern
architecture to find yet more pernicious evils for which it can be held
responsible. They come from all walks of life; from belted earls who
complain about drinking gin and tonic in high-rise hotels looking down
on the parish church, to dishevelled winos who rise from bottle-strewn
concrete benches in windswept plazas to utter one final curse on those who
made all this happen.

Given as I am to hyperbole as a way of life, even I cannot mount
the foothills of exaggeration that the most untutored critic of modern
architecture takes at a run. There is no limit to the numbers of the critics
of modern architecture, no system of O levels or A levels to say who is
or who is not qualified to join this national, nay international army.
Unlike the schools of architecture themselves, the schools of criticism
practise a genuine policy of open entry; indeed they practise in the matter
of technical qualification a reverse discrimination that must be the envy
of avant-garde educationists everywhere. For every professor of
architecture or well-known playwright who enters the lists, space will
be cleared for ten genuine single parent families compelled to live in a
tower block. I have seen conferences brought to a halt by the appearance
of just one exponent of real world living prepared to stand there looking
forlorn, mute testimony to the evil work of the practitioners who form
the audience.

Critics of modern architecture use two basic arguments to legitimise their attacks. They always say that architecture is inescapable, indeed architects themselves say this. Owen Luder in his inaugural address said it: "You don't have to listen to music, you don't have to read a book..."—I am sure that all of you could complete the triad. They also say that because they are all building users they have an inalienable right to speak. Everyone from Mira Bar-Hillel to architecture's current mad scientist, Peter Smith, says it at the beginning of every diatribe. "We are all consumers of buildings and therefore entitled to search for meaning in them", says Smith—before finding them deficient in meaning. One can imagine a corresponding dialogue in the casualty ward of any hospital: "It's my body and I've got a right to decide what's wrong with it."

What is involved here is a denial of expert status, and there may be some justice in it. The sleepless doctor in the casualty ward may indeed be one of those who faked his qualifications and has been winging it for the last three or five years with remarkable success. The architect may be one of those who submits a competition entry showing a cable-braced double cantilever structure with the offset tension pylon hinged top and bottom—and this with an engineer's endorsement.

Ignorance is a vital component in every attack on modern architecture; not merely of what modern architecture is or was—I shall come to that in a moment—but of what *everything* is or was. During my years spent teaching university students in America, I began dimly to perceive the vast continent of ignorance that is the sum of the lacunae in every human brain. In 1976, a survey of 14,000 High School Seniors in Virginia showed that 40 per cent believed that Columbus had discovered America in 1776 (so much for the publicity surrounding bicentennial year); that half believed it was illegal to start a new political party in America; that only four per cent could correctly identify three presidents before Gerald Ford. One year later, a questionnaire given to 400 students at the University of British Columbia showed "an extraordinary lack of recognition of historical figures".

No less than 70 per cent confused the philosopher Jean-Jacques Rousseau with deep sea diver Jacques Yves Cousteau; 60 per cent could identify neither Karl Marx nor Friedrich Engels; and a canny 60 per cent identified Adolf Eichmann as "an aide to President Nixon". I do not share the conceited belief that our schoolchildren or university students are better than theirs. I think, *mutatis mutandis*, that you would get the same kind of result in this country. And if that is the case, it has profound implications both for the level of debate surrounding the good or evil of architecture and, perhaps more importantly, it explains the lamentable failure of those who do know history to make a historical defence of the architecture of our century.

How, for instance, is anyone ignorant of the scale of the European catastrophe of the Great War, with its 25 million casualties, its ruined empires, its colossal accumulated debt and its cataclysmic physical and moral damage, to make sense of this passage from Berthold Lubetkin's 1982 RIBA Gold Medal Address? "Modern architecture acquired its impetus, its cutting edge and vigour, as a result of the 1914 war. The old society embarked on an unprecedented festival of carnage and squandered a generation."

What possible sense can a non-historical multitude—amongst whom I would include most, if not all, so-called architectural historians—make of the same author's description of the policy of the architect-led 'Disurbanists' in Soviet Russia during the 1920s? "Through the disurbanisation of towns and the urbanisation of the country we shall achieve an abolition of the contradictions between the urban and agricultural proletariat. We must not have concentrated and unhealthy habitations, but throughout the country endless streams of human dwellings along the big arteries of contemporary life joining our centres of industry and agriculture. Existing towns are doomed to quick extinction; only the art monuments must remain surrounded by vast parks. Thus in a socialist state the whole population must be more or less uniformly distributed along arteries of transport of power and goods. To this end a multitude of small villages have been abolished and very large state farms have been created in their place. The areas they occupy are sometimes so large that it takes seven or eight hours' car journey to cross them from one side to the other." (Quoted by Berthold Lubetkin in *Town and Landscape Planning in Soviet Russia*, 1932.) And what can this same multitude make of the anti-modern architectural statements of Adolf Hitler, many of which are unconsciously parroted by conservationists today, as Robert Goodman gleefully discovered in *After the Planners*?

Few critics of modern architecture would bother to disagree with Alexander von Senger's 1931 claim that Le Corbusier was the Lenin of architecture, hurling Moscow's blazing torch into a tranquil, unsuspecting Europe, destroying and proletarianising 100s and 1000s of self-employed building tradesmen, liquidating the heart of the *petite bourgeoisie*. But the other side of the coin might give them a little trouble. *The Architect and Building News* of 4 August 1939 reveals that Sir Oswald Mosley lived in a house designed by Giles Gilbert Scott, Number 129 Grosvenor Road.

A measure of what ignorance and the passage of time have wrought with the identity of architecture can be gained from a comparison of two more quotations. The first is from Berthold Lubetkin's famous letter of resignation to the Peterlee Development corporation in 1947. "Architecture is a statement of the social aims of the age. Its compelling geometrical regularities affirm man's hope to understand, to explain and control his surroundings. By asserting itself against subjectivity and equivocation, it discloses a universal, purposeful order and clarity in what often appears to be a mental wilderness. It can be a potent weapon, a committed driving force on the side of enlightenment, aiming, however indirectly, at the transformation of our preset make-believe society, where images outstrip reality, and rewards outspace achievement."

The second quotation is taken from the tale of an architect taking the train to London to attend the 1981 RIBA Conference on New Opportunities which formed the subject of the conference's introductory paper. After "shooting an admiring glance at the neoprene gasket detailing of the windows of his carriage", our hero finds himself in conversation with businessmen. He conducts himself with becoming modesty but propagandises for the recent code changes nonetheless. "I think the new relaxations in our Code of Conduct will put architects in a better position to take the initiative in the production of buildings. They will be able to operate at a broader policy level." At a broader policy level? Broader than that of the 'Disurbanists' in Russia? Broader than that of the architects of public housing in Britain in the 1950s and 60s? Broader than the designers of New Towns, new cities, new capital cities? In 1964, in Britain, architects' commissions amounted to ten per cent of the Gross Domestic Product. By 1982, they controlled less than two per cent. The entire value of their work today is less than most estimates of the size of the black economy. So much for ignorance.

The world upheavals of the first half of our century created work for architects on an unprecedented scale. Construction work was centralised, licensed and under strict control, but it took place in conditions of immense design freedom. The vast housing programmes that followed the Second World War created, correspondingly, vast opportunities for architects, not merely to do what they were told, but to be asked what to do. In a very simple sense the centralisation of architectural work confirmed its importance. Whenever any activity is brought under central control that means it is important: when talk of local initiatives and decentralisation proceeds unchecked, we can be sure that the activity in question has ceased to matter. The important agencies are always centralised, like defence. Calls to centralise control of the police force today merely reflect the increased importance of law enforcement in a society where people are redundant, superfluous, unnecessary. A society utterly different from that which raised the planning, design and construction of buildings for the masses to the level of a principal government activity, the heart of every political programme. Now that the health of our population has ceased to matter, because we do not need workers or soldiers, our National Health Service is to be dismantled.

The historical defence of modern architecture requires a knowledge of a historical period, a knowledge of a world that has passed away. Even participants cannot describe this world or summon up this knowledge. Patrick Dunleavy's book on high-rise housing, *The Politics of Mass Housing in Britain 1945–75*, notes that 500,000 tower flats were built by local authorities during this period and he records an interview with a politician directly responsible for a large programme in Birmingham. Why were they built? The man replies, "I don't know, perhaps we just woke up one day and found we were surrounded by them."

As Nietzsche said, one must have a good memory to be able to keep the promises one makes. And Berthold Lubetkin, a man whose intellectual and architectural achievements, as much as his longevity, entitle him to be considered the most powerful defender of modern architecture alive, can simultaneously equate attacks upon it with an attack upon thought itself: "An attack upon systematic thought is a treason against civilisation.... Let us remember this when we hear the drumbeat and rollcall to return to vernacular tradition." But he can also admit: "I abandoned architecture because it had lost its line. It was the harbinger of a better world and it turned out to be like... miniskirts."

The honest defenders of modern architecture must now be social and political historians and, alas, as Marshall McLuhan said, "Classification is not the beginning of the study of a problem—it is the end." So are we to conclude that the ravages of time and the functional utility of ignorance will between them write *finis* to the story of modern architecture by simultaneously forgetting and misrepresenting it? Will it thus be finally delivered into the hands of architectural historians as a style like all the others, to become just one more item in the postmodern bag of tricks?

This dead end would indeed come to pass if the essence of modern architecture were not something other than its glorious social and political history, its glamorous place in our century's turmoil and reconstruction. This essence has something timeless in its thought that speaks both of the political instrumentality of architectural practice and of the now questioned 'expert status' that I mentioned at the beginning.

In addition to being an adventure, modern architecture was a drastic solution to the conflict, that was never resolved in the nineteenth century, of reconciling new materials and new techniques with the reigning cultural notion of what architecture ought to be. When Roger Scruton recently made the fantastic statement that "We must get back to the three principles of vertical posture, articulation through detail, and light and shade", he was not merely flexing his muscles as a popular obscurantist, but addressing, in however bizarre a fashion, the unresolved problem left by modern architecture. The Modern Movement *did* have a way with technology, with economics, with contract deadlines and thermal performance, with environmental controls, with government and with all the neat stuff that comes out of research laboratories all the time.

The earliest Modern pioneers wanted their architecture to be related to the phenomenon of machine production, to "think out afresh", as Frank Pick said 50 years ago, "all the problems of building in terms of current materials and current tools". The most discriminating and knowledgeable opponents of Modern architecture, like Sir Edwin Lutyens, knew that this was, and always will be, the acid test of all architecture, when he wrote in 1931: "The Modern impersonal architecture of so-called functionalism does not seem to me to be replacing the inherited lore of centuries with anything of comparable excellence or to show yet a genuine sense of style—*a style rooted in feeling for the right use of materials.*"

Max Fry understood it when he wrote in 1944—in a quotation that I often and unashamedly use—"If the structural developments which have led to our present technical skill were to continue at the same pace into this century... then our hopes of establishing a workable architecture would be slight." Semi-apologetically, Herbert Ohl, an apostle of industrialised building, enunciated the same thought in 1966 when he wrote: "Our task seems to be crude, simple and trite beside the accomplishments of architectural history, but to build monuments is one of the least important tasks of our time. The true monuments of our time are the anonymous, innumerable, infinite, unflagging and objective tools of production."

And the masters of High-Tech today, notwithstanding their dismissal by certain postmodernists as practitioners of a baroque and degenerate terminal phase, see it too when they enumerate the masters who have influenced them, as did Norman Foster when he said recently, "Philip Johnson? Just a kind of hucksterism. I was influenced by Bucky, Prouvé, Eames, Mies...." All these are men who took the technical task seriously, almost to the exclusion of everything else, men whose durability of reputation stands on their incontrovertible achievements in the world of technique, of technology transfer, of literally doing more with less and better than has ever been done before.

The intellectual and cultural climate is such that *The Times* may editorialise with as much truth as with that, "Broadly speaking the thing a building most needs to secure public affection is to have been standing a very long time. This is a quality hard to achieve in new construction." The instructions to the sons and daughters and the grandsons and grand-daughters of the Modern pioneers may have swung from invitation to command from "Build us a new society" to "There should be only one staircase, one exit from the building, and one exit from the grounds to the street. No more than six dwellings should be accessible from the same entrance, and entrances should face the street. One block of flats of three storeys maximum is infinitely preferable to interconnected complexes of tower blocks, and short landings should replace long corridors."

But even at this level the question remains. Who is to design it? How should it be built? How long will it take? How much will it cost?

The critics of architecture do not know the answers to these questions. As Elting Morrison, author of *Men, Machines and Modern Times*, wrote in 1973, "It is impossible to understand technological tools without working with them. Artists, poets, critics cannot solve the problems—they do not even know what the problems are." The lost sociology of modern architecture does not mean the loss of its methodology, nor the end of its power to impose order on chaos, or reason on the kind of madness that creates half a million listed buildings to be maintained, regardless of expense, for the rest of recorded time.

Today's architect lives in a different world from the Modern pioneer. He may respond to, rather than create, events. He may have no meaningful past, he may be so many things to so many people that he appears to belong to the future rather than to the present, to be subsumed by deciding rather than doing. But his technical mastery, such as it is, is his only hope of immortality. Compared to this, the matter of style and historicism is unimportant, though we each have our taste in these matters, and mine, I think, is known. I do not mind if Teflon-coated woven glass is used above farcical Tuscan columns, or if the intake ducts to a sophisticated environmental control system are found in the reveal of an immense Norman arch. These are after all, as their projectors repeatedly tell us, only jokes. But the jokes must be made by architects, for if they ever lose the technical ability to make them they are doomed.

Thus the non-historical defence of modern architecture is not so much retrospective as predictive, both a promise and a warning. The modernists of the first half of the present century made technological innovation socially acceptable in building. To be sure it was not as guiltlessly assimilated as it is in the design of cars, aircraft or rockets, video games or computers, but thanks to them it is on the table as an option.

I believe the process must be continued if architects are to continue as independent professionals who are approached by people or organisations who want buildings. Technology transfer as an art is the living legacy of a period whose alarums and excursions have died away and whose history no longer carried social or political weight. As a punkish Mies van der Rohe might say: "We are concerned today with questions of a personal nature. The group is losing significance; its destiny is no longer what interests us. The decisive achievements in all fields are individual and their authors are for the most part world famous celebrities."

The collective social organisation that was a survival function in the era of the Great Wars and in their aftermath is now disintegrating under hammer blows. If we represent the 3,000 years of literate history as a clock face, the human race has enjoyed the printed word for nine minutes, the telephone for three minutes, radio for two minutes, talking pictures for one minute, television for 30 seconds and computers for six seconds. And which one is everyone talking about now?

I think that the tale of the Air Traffic Controllers in America has a cautionary value for architects uncertain of their future. On 3 August 1981, 11,000 of these highly trained men and women were dismissed after a short strike. In less than two years they had been replaced by newly trained substitutes graduating at the rate of 300 a month from newly created academies and delivered direct into the job training schemes.

I would like to deal with some architectural critics in this way but, by the same token, I am sure there are those in positions of power and authority in our society who would like to do the same to architects themselves. Now what was that list of names again? Bernard Levin, Angela Rippon, Roger Scruton....

Sex, violence and design
1983

Just before the M4 off-ramp, about level with Aztec West, lost in the darkness his twinkling rear lights grow and separate. Nearly 6000 rpm, an indicated 180 kph and he corkscrews wildly through a convoy of articulated lorries. Brakes down to 4th, tacho whirling into the red, seat belts straining, his lights stretch wide across the bar of the EZ 42 automatic sight. No need to brake again, one long burst at point blank range, boot lid flies off, black smoke, then he is gone, cartwheeling over the armco in a ball of fire.

Yes, it's true. The gun-nuts are coming out of the armoury and on to the typewriter. My toes swim in my boots. It's TA 152 time and Hummer time and you-know-it-was-originally-designed-by-the-Bantam-car-company time and 37,000 feet-a-minute time, with all the test pilots killed. When design becomes so arcane and so ornate and so esoteric and done up with Tuscan columns and pediments and the arguments of Roger Scruton there is only one thing to do. As Herman Goering might well have said, "When I hear the phrase postmodernism I reach for my revolver."

A fascination with weapons is the sign of a good designer, because weapons represent design shorn of all sell-functions. It used to be racing cars. I like the way my silver GTI has a thin red rim around its grille, the same colour scheme as Bernd Rosemeyer's Auto-Union *Rennwagen* that went over the armco in a ball of fire at 320 kph on May 21 1938 on the Dessau record strip only a stone's throw from the Junckers factory and the Bauhaus, where they were fitting a pitched roof at the time, Mies being busy in Jackson Hole thinking about big sheets of plate glass.

Yes, the cowards always pretend it's something to do with art, with Futurism, with the Paris-Madrid race of 1901. Nozzo! It is the sheer perfection of military equipment. Racing cars had it once, lost it, had it again. Now they are about as fascinating as hovercraft, or worse still, vacuum cleaners. The real stuff is the Becker system (wherein the impetus of the returning breechblock compensates for its lack of weight and enables a light weapon to throw a heavy shell), or the liquid fuel rocket in a plywood airframe that *without the consumption of so much as a pint of oil* hurtled its pilot into the air like a living shotgun shell to fire his 24 rockets at the bomber and descend by parachute.

High technology, desperate urgency and unlimited resources make for hot-shot design. That is why the weapons of the losing side are always the most interesting. Take the Confederate submarines: hand-crank operated, eight men in a streamlined wooden tube with an artillery shell on a long pole sticking out of the bow. Barroom! Down goes the Federal steam sloop *Housatonic*. Down goes the crew of the CSS *HL Hunley* too. There was even one before that, the *Nautilus* designed by Robert Fulton in 1800 and offered to Napoleon to beat the British blockade, and before that, Bushnell's *Turtle*, the one-man boat used to attack HMS *Eagle* in 1776.

Later stuff is better. Britain's contribution was the original boffin Pyke, who in 1940 designed *Habbakuk*, an aircraft carrier to be made of frozen wood chips; in 1941 the original *Snowcat* (for raids on occupied Norway); in 1943 a pipeline through which *soldiers* could be pumped, and in 1944 planned an attack on the Ploesti oil wells using fake Romanian fire engines landed by glider. After the war he designed a pedal-powered tractor, then he died.

Honestly, how can the Hampton Competition compare with Air Ministry Specification F28/34—the one that produced the Hurricane and the Spitfire? How can the Hayward Gallery match the Maus tank (strange similarity though)? How can Bean Hill, of which all photographs appear to have been destroyed, be compared to a row of Anderson shelters.... Wait a minute, didn't I see a Centurion bridging tank somewhere in the design references section of the Hongkong Bank?

Of course, not all military hardware is well designed. This is no place for rewrites of old American *Harper's* stories about the shortcomings of the M-16, or the supposed 'inferior' helmets issued to Allied troops, but it is true that weapons failure plays a part. Sometimes the Mk-108s just will not fire. Sometimes too much peace has produced unworkable weapons (Bren carrier, two-pounder anti-tank gun, virtually defenceless frigate, hopelessly expensive tank), but more often than not the design of weapons is better, tighter and more ruthless than the design of anything else.

Self-build workstations, a partial history
1983

According to my calculations, I have constructed and used no less than 16 domestic workstations since I was a lad. Some were good, some were bad, some were indifferent, and five were in America. This is their story.

In the mid-1950s, studying for my A levels in a country town in Berkshire, I built my first bench. It consisted of five 6 x 1 inch planed boards with an insufficient number of cross pieces. One end stood on a piece of 4 x 2, plugged with matchsticks (that was the way in those days) to an external wall of my bedroom. The other end stood on part of the bench itself, verticalised after having been cut off with a saw. Immediately above it was a wooden bookcase, also plugged to the wall. On the lower shelf of the bookcase was a presentation brandy box that slid out to throw a pool of light on the black-painted surface before it: it contained a 100w bulb. I was proud of that detail, but it got very hot. I left it on one night and the box caught fire—luckily I slept in the same room. This prototype workstation, number one, lacked both refinement and concentration. In retrospect, the best thing about it was my chair, a Duralumin recliner from a de Havilland Dragon Rapide.

During my student life, domestic workstations two to five were dominated by the problems of the drawing board; mine was an antiquarian one, bought for £3 from a retired Oxford architect. This giant required substantial underpinning, which it did not always get. Once I constructed a Warren truss for it; another time, a frame that slipped over my bed.

It was not until I went to the Ecole des Beaux-Arts in Paris that I glimpsed a model for all my subsequent constructions—the tiny *en loge* cubicles which we were locked up in for eight hours at a time to do our sketch designs. From the point of view of a writer, these bald chambers had only two drawbacks: nowhere to store books or papers, and everything at too high a level, based on the use of draughting stools. I finally settled the latter question by adopting a low-level compromise, which led to wide, thin drawings.

As I drew less and less and wrote more and more I hit upon a magic combination—desk at 673 mm, chair at 482 mm—and this I have stuck to ever since workstation nine. For sheer effort, workstation 13 in Florida had no peer. Its desk consisted of two 2,500 x 1,000 mm solid core doors arranged at right angles, as big as an aircraft carrier. It had an IBM typewriter, digital clock, separate telephone line and a short-wave radio

(I followed "The story of the Bee Gees" on the BBC World Service). I built it into one end of a car-port, with a plywood covered timber frame, wall-mounted air conditioner unit, Pontiac Grand Prix fender as sculpture and a floor-to-ceiling 'window' of bottles set in mortar. I poured the concrete floor, too, using numerous beverage cans to reduce the amount of mix necessary. Unfortunately, the cans floated to the top of the concrete and even though I stayed up all night pushing them down, the carpet was structural from then on. This study adjoined the utility room of the house, where the hot water tank, washing machine and dryer were located. In the summer, terrific thermal battles took place between the air conditioner and high humidity with 100 degrees fahrenheit temperatures. When the air conditioner was off, books grew mould and sheets of typing paper disintegrated like tissues; it took an hour's cooling before the room was habitable.

The immense effort that went into this sub-tropical den was largely wasted, for a bare six months after finishing it I moved to Los Angeles. There, conscious of an intentionally short stay, I took the opposite approach, and workstation 14 consisted of nothing but a large dissecting room table, bought from Ralph the Recycler, purveyor of disused equipment from the UCLA campus. This table was a study in itself, weighing more than a Dymaxion house and held together by just four bolts. It had deep, downstand pressed metal beams that, coupled with the deep-piled shaggy carpet in our split-level ranchero, left much to be desired in the way of comfort.

Back in England I used brain power to reduce quantum effort and cost. Workstation 15 was located in a timber-framed chalet overlooking the sea. Ruthlessly, I chose the only corner with no view of the lighthouse and set two flush doors at right angles resting on bearers screwed to the walls. The two ends were supported by filing cabinets. Thus only four metres of wood, two doors, plus a few screws, held three square metres of white laminated desk top exactly 673 mm above the carpet. In terms of value engineering this structure represented the apogee of my workstation building life. But 16 was ideologically better.

Returning for inspiration to the old Beaux-Arts cubicle, I bought a large supply of Office Equipment Company B204 closed-sided metal shelves. By running a flush door between two banks of them I recreated the *loge*, but with shelves instead of side walls. To stop the two supporting banks of shelves from breaking, I screwed a second door vertically between them, leaving a neat gap for flex, coaxial cable and telephone cord, and creating a natural pin-board and slide projector screen. The only problem with this one is that the desk top deflects, but there is a solution. I reverse it from time to time... like turning a mattress.

Norman Foster 6.0 6.0 6.0
1984

Foster Associates is grey and white and empty—like a museum of technology dotted about with large, complicated exhibits. In the distance twinkles the odd red anglepoise. Invented by Horstmann, derived from a tank suspension system actually. Horstmann's great-nephew—probably the only other person in the world who knows this—runs a fresh food restaurant in Dartmouth. Donald Sutherland ate there for seven straight weeks while he was making *Ordeal by Innocence*. The rest of the furniture is strange lightweight stuff, straight off the *Graf Zeppelin*, the legs look as though they might be filled with helium.

I am embarrassed by the fact that the cassettes I have brought do not fit my tape recorder. While I wait I try to borrow some of the right kind from the helpful teenager in reception. Hers don't fit either. It is a disgrace to arrive at the heartland of high technology with all this obsolete junk. Perhaps I should wrap a towel around my head and blow my brains out. At this point a charming young person who has been working away behind the scenes comes up with the news that Norman will lend me his own tape recorder and I am led to where he sits, with associate Richard Horden, poring over plans of the Whitworth exhibition. Behind them is lunch, laid out buffet-style on a white credenza. I take a chair and the new tape recorder appears. "One, two, three, four, testing", says Norman. The machine obediently repeats this back to him and he places it on the table.

"Whitworth have been pressing for some time for an exhibition of our work", begins Norman. "We had cold feet at one time but by then they really had the bit between their teeth." And they said "Oh no, a promise is a promise. There isn't much more to it than that is there Richard?"

"No, except they haven't done an architectural exhibition before so in that way we have had a bit more experience than they have. We are doing the layout work for them." The description goes on and my eyes wander round the cavernous space, filled with an oppressive electronic emptiness like the hiss of high fidelity before the music starts. The absence of the Hong Kong team is almost palpable, a bomber crew away on a raid. How many will come back?

The loneliness of high command.

While we are talking about the exhibition far away at the end of long and vulnerable lines of communication destiny is unfolding in the East. Even here, hidden somewhere, there must be really big stuff. Plans for the

BBC building in Portland Place, maybe even the first pregnant visuals of the third London airport.

"You come in here and there is a big image which might be just a simple sketch of the Bank." I look at the inscrutable doodle Horden has exposed. It is a surprise. I had been expecting holograms or lasers.

"It looks... Corbusian." I venture.

"Really", says Norman evenly. "Is that good or bad?"

"It's just a reaction. He used his own sketches like that."

"Yes."

In the vast white and grey aircraft carrier nothing stirs. No typewriters clicking, no telephones ringing, not another person in sight. Just these giant models, each with its own bundle of historic associations. There is the large, partly completed model of the Buckminster Fuller house—abandoned with the death of the master nearly a year ago. There are sketches of the Humana project, the commission lost to Michael Graves, the man who embodies the approach to architecture most foreign and most deadly to Norman's own. There are vast sections of the structure of that Brinks Job of architecture the Hongkong Bank; pods, modules, nodes, most of which will find their way up to the Whitworth for the exhibition. And now, like the ghost of Christmas yet to come, there is an immense model of Portland Place with a vast but enigmatic assembly of Perspex and polystyrene emerging from the place where the Langham Hotel now stands. It looks enormous but it is less than half the size of the mighty Bank. There is Foster's own house, untouched for three years. And finally there are the ghosts of the people who used to work for him and no longer do.

He starts to talk about the BBC job. "A tremendous amount of research on that. Not abstract, but movement and observation. Where we visited with the BBC.... From Canada to the West Coast of America, Eastern seaboard, Germany, Scandinavia, France. The length and breadth of the UK in terms of broadcasting facilities... Japan. Anything and everything from specialist drama to studio complexes... Switzerland...."

"What do they actually want you to do on the Langham site?"

"Something that will bring them together and take them through to the next century.... It's pretty aggressive in its posture, a very tightly postured problem. It's unbelievably complex, by far the most complex problem we have ever tackled, far, far more complex than the Bank, socially, politically, technologically...."

"Given the pressures involved, are you going to do something behind a facade?"

"It will make very real urban gestures to the site, it will have to. But that doesn't mean we will have to resort to pastiche. I don't see why we should."

But he does see the pressure that will remorselessly push in that direction. At such moments, looking at this slim casually dressed man, neither old nor young, neither arrogant nor ingratiating, keeping an interviewer at arms length as he must, one dimly senses the enormous burden that he bears. It is impossible to be Norman Foster *sans complexe* because of all Norman Foster has done and still has to do.

Outside in Great Portland Street the stone-age traffic grinds its way through the ancient carcass of the city. The very people who abandon their stationary taxis in despair are those who 20 years ago opposed the motorway box that might have prevented it all. They are the people who fight for old piers, plot to prop up old buildings, favour above all things the old, the old, the old. They use our oil to keep things old and incompetent and mediocre and disorganised. In the middle of all this we have Norman Foster. He designed the world of Torvill and Dean, where you can still win 6.0 6.0 6.0. So far he has outrun the bureaucracy, served the conservationists as a stick to beat lesser mortals with, eluded the opinionated nonsense of the Scrutons and stonewalled the latter day flat-earthers like Gradidge and Terry. Perhaps because they have only to take up their blunderbusses to hit a dozen easier targets, the historians—who are working day and night to take the future off the agenda forever—have yet to get him in their sights.

Time for lunch.

"I'm flying tonight, I'll just have Perrier." The Niersteiner bottle hovers over Norman's glass and moves on. Lunch is like refuelling, a snack taken at a run. This is the food of a general with the fate of armies on his mind; fresh salad, wholemeal bread, smoked salmon, cheese and fruit. We eat it at the plan table amongst the drawings and sketches for the exhibition. A week earlier, over another bottle of wine from which he did drink because he was not flying that night—or even planning to drive fast—Terry Farrell had told me Norman was a Futurist.

"He likes aeroplanes, helicopters, turbo-charged racing cars. He is just like Marinetti." What he meant was that Foster was somehow *old fashioned* in this taste for Porsche 911s, Bell Jet Rangers and slim pod gliders with wings of enormous aspect ratio. Old fashioned and perhaps just a little totalitarian as well.

"I think we are all like mountaineers", says Richard Horden. "Michael Graves is the kind of eccentric chap who goes up alone with a walking stick. We use crampons, pitons and oxygen... and we go higher."

"We are everything that is unfashionable—but we have a track record." Says Norman, and he smiles because it is true.

"The Sainsbury Centre is about space and light never achieved before." Says Horden, who has worked with Norman for a decade but still dresses like a chartered accountant. "Graves could never do it in a million years, he simply doesn't know enough about materials."

In the gathering shades of the seamless web of townscape does Norman not fear outrunning all possible clients? After all Graves got the Humana job, Farrell nearly got the Langham job. How many patrons are there left who can keep pace with the kind of technological evolution that leads from Fred Olsen to IBM to Willis Faber & Dumas, to Sainsbury, Renault and the Bank?

"We haven't even scratched the surface. People think we are always on the leading edge, using untried technology. It's not true. We are a belt and braces outfit but nobody believes it. On Willis Faber & Dumas we had a complete alternative glazing system ready to go if the one we used had not prototyped out. On Sainsbury we had a plastic, recessed-gutter roof we could have used if quality control on the superplastic aluminium panels had turned out to be too much of a risk!"

But supposing the steady drip of anti-modern propaganda from the architectural critics of the media finally and irrevocably led the zeitgeist away from the right stuff into a maze of historicism? Norman Foster did not get where he is today by succumbing to the pale cast of thought and losing the name of action. Only the week before he had been talking to Stuart Lipton the property tycoon, a man who had suffered the deadly attrition of community groups and public inquiries at Coin Street. Lipton wasn't put off, in fact he suggested that he and Foster should do something together before long. The critics and the patrons operate on different strata of the earth's crust; the former can stop things working out, but only the latter can make things happen. Would the Renault people have consulted Gavin Stamp or Marcus Binney? Of course not, but that was Swindon and the Bank was Hong Kong. In London, in Portland Place, it might be different.

When he says that Foster Associates haven't even scratched the surface, he is laying down a challenge to himself. When he says he has a track record it is nothing less than the sober truth. When he says, "We are everything that is unfashionable", he is saying something that might only just be beginning to be true. A great architect, like Wright or Corbusier can move through periods of popularity and periods of something not far short of contempt. His weapons are experience and longevity and patience, for even with fast cars and jet-copters the progress of architecture is glacially slow.

Throughout the post-cultural void of Norman Foster's architecture, through the rustling perforated blinds, the modulated lighting, the neoprene, the superplastic and the crinkly metallised fabric with its two-hour fire resistance, shines the quintessentially modern phenomenon of winning —which alone gives meaning to our actions. It is the world of Torvill and Dean because his use of the obsolete culture of architecture is like their use of Rimsky Korsakov. In one sense it is sacrilege, or simply a waste. In another it assembles elements into moments, like the first visit to the Sainsbury Centre. It doesn't matter if you like it or not. It is about light and space and, be honest, nobody else even comes close.

My interview is over. I take the tapes I have hardly used and return in a taxi to Castle Greyskull. Everything is getting worse except ice-dancing and architecture, and in both I see the triumphant reversal of what Hannah Arendt called the banality of evil. I see—as Torvill and Dean sprawl ecstatically across the ice-floored sports hall of Norman Foster's architecture 6.0 6.0 6.0 in a roar of applause—a burst of excitement made up by genius out of the bits that are left when pomp and circumstance and history are flattened like pennies on a railway line.

Building revisits: Coventry Cathedral 1984

The stairwell leading down from the body of the Cathedral Church of St Michael into the gift shop and visitors' centre—once the refectory and verger's flat—is decorated with a series of messages painted on panels and fixed to the walls. "Hits just the right note", says one, attributed to a Coventry schoolteacher; "A powerful experience", says another, culled from the thoughts of Lorraine Peters of Waterloo, Ontario; "Very moving and encouraging", says a third, contributed by Teddy Milne ("for the Quakers"). All of these notices refer not to the cathedral itself but to something else.

At the bottom of the steps all is explained. An enlarged telex message from Orlando, Florida, reads: "Congratulations. The show has won a top award at the 1983 Association of Multi-image Festival!" "The show" is an audio-visual history of the Cathedral running continuously in the circular basement of the Chapel of Christ the Servant. In more ways than one it is what the building is all about: 20 years after consecration and 25 years after its design beat 218 others in open competition, the marketing of the myth of Coventry has taken over from the controversy about its architecture.

For a visitor today it is not so much carping as honest to note first and foremost the Coventry Cathedral T-shirts and sweat-shirts, the little crosses of nails (made in Sweden) and the powerful presence of Fraters coffee-shop and bistro. These things make a profound impression, more profound by far than the architecture of what was, in its time, the fastest cathedral ever built. All over the building there are odd things tucked away that launch a frisson. Not just the regular strains of Vera Lynn wafting up from the award-winning *son et lumière* blitz going on downstairs, or even the photographs of comedian Nat Jackley clowning with the mayor, or model Vicki Harris demonstrating a bath specially designed for the disabled, but also the bust of Christ crucified by Helen Huntington Jennings of Norman, Oklahoma, which is made from the metal of crashed cars and bears the inscription: "The crucifixions of man by man, in careless driving as in war, are only redeemed by love."

Uncertain taste is printed throughout the most famous modern building in Britain, and was from the very beginning. When Sir Basil Spence's design was first illustrated it burst through the hard carapace of popular indifference to art as nothing else ever has.

In the press furore of 1950 everybody became an authority on Coventry Cathedral. Hundreds wrote anonymously to Spence, denouncing him and his works, so much so that his wife was obliged to intercept the letters and keep them from him to preserve his peace of mind. Hundreds more wrote to the newspapers, to their MP and even to the King. In the end the opposition killed itself off with apoplexy, and all before so much as a foundation stone had been laid. Nowadays in the summer more than 2,000 people visit the building every day and it has come to share the heritage status of Jimmy Young or Winston Churchill's grave. Uncritical pilgrimage is its lot, and the guides pander to it with a factitious litany: "The screen of glass weighs eight tonnes and is supported by a steel frame also weighing eight tonnes.... The font was transported from the Holy Land.... The coins set in the floor show the choirboys where to stand."

Because of this distraction the design, with all its faults and virtues, has become invisible. It requires an act of will to concentrate on it, like keeping one's footing on a heaving deck. Despite materials proudly specified to last 500 years, the structure is already ephemeral, a media event from beginning to end. Ironically its architect, knighted for his work, foresaw this fate for his own career—which had been in exhibition design before the Cathedral commission came along. He thought so substantial a work would save him from what he once described as "a form of architectural journalism".

Coventry Cathedral hovers at the beginning of the electronic age. It passes from cinema to television with its chancel an auditorium, its great tapestry a screen, and its stained glass windows stone prophets of the coming video arcade. What will the future make of John Piper's magnificent baptistery window except to see it as a brilliant guess by pre-electronic man at what colour computer graphics might be like! After only a quarter of a century its first impact is derivative of the electronic present, a gigantic frozen image of the explosion of the death star in a video game. Looked at closely, each stained glass section shocks because of its utter, informationless abstraction; its composite image disintegrates into dots and lines like a magnified TV picture. Between the lines there is no history and John Piper joins with Richard Hamilton in a world better described by Marshall McLuhan than the Holy Bible.

It is the crucial abstraction of the glass that makes Spence's building modern and destroys the link with the Medieval past he was so determined to retain in other ways. Tiny fragments of the original windows that are preserved on the other side of the chancel show recognisable images: parts of faces, Gothic script. You cannot look through them to an electronic future—they became obsolete in the age of high-explosive on the night of 14 November 1940 when the Coventry myth was born. As the audio-visual display is to the offertory box, so is the abstract stained glass of Coventry to its ancient precursor. A whole world dies between them.

About the design of the building itself, nothing said today can add to what was so honestly written by Robert Furneaux Jordan in *The Architectural Review* in July 1962—and it, too, though in a different way, refers to the use of glass. "One of the great delusions of the Modern Movement", he said, "has been that glass is transparent. It is transparent in one direction only. In the other direction, according to the light, it is either black or reflective. At Coventry the architect spent 12 years looking into his model from the outside; what a pity he was never able to get inside and look out."

What Jordan meant by this was the tragedy of the eight tonne, clear-glazed wall so beloved of the guides and their clusters of schoolchildren standing on the steps, linking the bomb-blasted ruins of the old cathedral with the edifice of the new. This vast window, four times the size of Piper's masterpiece and almost single-handedly the destroyer of its visual impact, is an utter failure. Looking towards the altar, the colossal volume of light it admits obliterates the effect not only of the baptistery window, but also that of the sawtooth windows running down the sides of the internal space and intended to illuminate the giant tapestry at the end. Looking back from the altar, from which a view of the stained glass of the sawteeth should be inescapable, it is instead dulled by glare, even on an overcast day. The glass west wall leaves the visitor with only a growing consciousness of the austerity of the chancel, its unpleasantly inappropriate enclosure of maximum volume with minimum structure—not soaring vertically as in Gothic times, but spreading usefully as in a warehouse. At Coventry glare destroys the colour separation of the interior—put bluntly, it ruins the building.

Spence understood the myth of Coventry better than the building he designed there. It was the myth of the terror raid with 600 dead, of the old carpenter erecting a cross of burnt roof timbers the morning after, of the soldier/architect watching helpless as Medieval churches were shelled to pieces before his eyes during the Normandy invasion. It was the myth of the lone creator with no consultants who won the great competition. The self-taught politician who convinced committee after committee and cleric after cleric that one grotesque error after another was as nothing compared to the ultimate image in his mind's eye. It was the myth that gave Graham Sutherland the commission to design—and boldly *sign* the largest and most abominable tapestry in Christendom. The myth that gave the ancient Epstein strength to complete the impaled and expressionless statue of St Michael.

The myth let Spence go on when the money ran out and rendered block had to be used instead of Staffordshire stone and plain glass instead of stained, when the solid link with the Chapel of Unity was replaced with glass—clear again—and the colossal initial effect of the models and sketches evaporated under the arc-light of the west wall. Even after he was dead, the myth that Spence embodied paved the way for the gift shops, the mini-Imperial War Museum in the basement and the remorseless marketing of itself.

Inside the Cathedral photographs are not allowed. No photographs of the outside can be published without the provost's approval, and even then they must be taken before 9.00 am. According to the vergers on duty, nothing can even be written about the Cathedral without the provost seeing it first. Coventry Cathedral does not belong to the history of architecture but to the history of the twentieth century.

Building revisits: Hunstanton School 1984

Hunstanton School is now twice as large as it was when the Smithsons won the 1949 competition commission, with 1,000 pupils and 60 staff instead of 480 and 30. This factor is important because it explains why the original welded steel frame and brick panel Mies van der Rohe Illinois Institute of Technology campus lookalike is now all but engulfed by later additions. Most of these bear a passing resemblance to the gaunt brick and black-painted steel original. But one—a swimming pool added in 1974—boasts an absurd green GRP roof modelled on a seafront entertainments structure a mile or two away on the coast. Some of the starkness of the original photographs—by which most architects would seek to recognise this out-of-the-way but influential building—is lost, too, by the addition of tall chain-link ball-screens and row upon row of parked cars, lacking —apparently—a car park.

But the eeriest difference of all is to be found in the unaccountable opacity of many of the floor-to-ceiling windows. It is this unexpected deadness that draws a visitor close to the buildings—only to discover that black-painted sheets of plywood have replaced sheets of glass at random all over the famous elevations. Furthermore, many still-glazed openings are marked with a painted cross, like trees destined for felling. Right now, 180 windows out of 1,000 are in the process of being replaced; one because a pheasant flew into it, one because two men carrying rugby posts had an accident and two more because of pupil horse-play—but all the rest because they simply could not stand the stresses placed upon them by this revolutionary building.

It comes as a shock to discover that windows have popped and doors dropped at Hunstanton ever since September 1954 when, after a 15 month delay caused by steel rationing, the school opened up for business. Since then it has led a kind of Dorian Gray existence: externally youthful in the pages of architectural literature but ageing horribly in its strange isolation on the windswept Norfolk coast. As with Oscar Wilde's creation, the two sides of Hunstanton never coincide. While a famous architectural critic shows slides of it in the air conditioned lecture theatres of the University of California, children faint and whole classes are evacuated from heat exhaustion in England. While 100 graduate students type the words "New Brutalism" into their dissertations, condensation drowns photocopiers and freezing children dare not trust their feet to the tile-bubbling, resistance-heated floors.

New Brutalism—a critical phrase that brought great fame to the architects of our tiny kingdom—is inextricably bound up with images of Hunstanton School. It reaches back to the modest achievements of the Hertfordshire schools and forward to the birth of High-Tech at Reliance Controls, by way of the famous Braithwaite water tank (now lined with concrete because it has rusted, been replaced, rusted, been replaced and so on forever). But New Brutalism is not just a style, it means the staff taking turns to climb into the heating boiler to clean it so there will be some protection against the bitter cold. On the one hand we have photographs of the building on completion, lacking not only people but furniture, too—by the wish of the architects. A school that founded a school, with architects and critics whirling together in a mad dance, faster and faster, from impoverished England to the West Coast. On the other hand we have certain practical problems.

In the prize-winning design as constructed there are four window conditions: direct single glazing to wall frame, direct double glazing to wall frame, vertical sliding in subframe and horizontal sliding in subframe. Improbably, the fixed glazing has been more troublesome than the windows that open, and now it has reached a point of no return. Direct glazing to site-welded frames calls for fine tolerances and, at the very beginning, 50 of the 1,000 panes had to be retrimmed to get them in. Since the wall frames themselves are welded to the structural frame and the whole armature of the building expands and contracts integrally, getting the windows in was only the beginning.

Today, Douglas Little, head teacher at the school, sits at his desk in his ground floor office and watches the changing reflections in the windows as the sun moves round the building. The panes become concave or convex and then flatten again. After a few years of this they crack and grind their edges against the glazing frames until they fall out. Corrosion of the glazing beads and the frames themselves has, in the last decade, greatly exacerbated the problem, applying additional pressure to intact panes and reducing the support to them. In 1981, an inspection of the windows, demanded by Little, resulted in 180 being condemned and 60 more being removed immediately. This heralded the era of the black-painted plywood sheets.

It is worth considering the question of corrosion, especially in coastal areas. Hunstanton School is 60 metres above sea level and only 400 metres from the sea. Onshore winds are so high that a neighbouring site was specially chosen by the CEGB, one of two in the British Isles, for aerogenerator experiments. The windows at the school are perpetually covered with salt. Direct glazing into painted steel wall frames never stood a chance.

The high exposure of the building correlates with its high heat loss. Equipped from the start with a slow-response underfloor heating system, the light, quick-response building envelope is perpetually at war with it. Under a cloudless sky, south-facing classrooms can leap to 104 degrees fahrenheit in February, with the heating full on trying to maintain 65 degrees fahrenheit on the north side. The heating system takes six hours to warm the building after a weekend shutdown, but to run it flat out risks curling the vinyl floor tiles. Because there are no absorbent surfaces, condensation runs down the glass walls and forms puddles on the floor until it evaporates or is mopped up. Textbooks swell and their bindings warp; paper for photocopiers has to be kept at home by members of staff and brought in a few sheets at a time.

Noise is another critical factor, like glazing and heat. The main building is 200 metres long with just one expansion joint. On both sides of that joint everything is welded to everything else and the sound of maintenance work reverberates 100 metres away. The special planning of the school, with multiple staircases and no corridors at the first floor teaching level, means that every class change is accompanied by the thunder of an approaching tube train. Going from one side of the school to the other involves passing in and out of doors many times, and each time some heat is lost. Where the heavy steel doors have dropped on their hinges they stay open, permanently.

Head teacher Little has been at six other schools, old and new. "This one" he says, "is in a class by itself for maintenance. And then there's the Warnock report. This school could never be adapted for handicapped children because with its population doubled even the downstairs corridors are not wide enough."

But Hunstanton is not only in a class of its own for glazing failure, heat loss, acoustic reverberation and maintenance—it has world influence to contend with as well. To Americans, it is a poor copy of Mies, but to the English it represents 20 years of hegemony in design and criticism. The Smithsons, of course, disowned it, or, more correctly (in all senses), moved on to better things, but its image still has unaccountable power. Norfolk County Architect's Department, for instance, continues to respect its low ground floor headroom—just over two metres from floor to ceiling in the woodwork shop—when adding extensions, and suffers agonies of guilt over the fatuous swimming pool roof. Even the Queen allegedly complained about the clumsily whitewashed gymnasium windows—floor to ceiling glazing facing on to the main road, of course—and this led to their speedy replacement by black glass sandwich panels which are to be installed everywhere up to dado height.

"Old Smithson would have used them, I'm sure", says Little, "if they had been around when he designed it. You can't blame him for everything. The roof lasted 30 years—not bad for felt. And the rewiring, well, all old buildings have to be rewired."

Old Smithson figures prominently in the head teacher's well rehearsed summary of the building's defects. He has never met the architect but says he feels as though he has. He has heard of Brutalism, too: "It was sociological as much as architectural. A kind of insensitivity to people's needs. Christian socialist ideals in education had come and gone when this building was designed."

The tragedy of Hunstanton is that it is an experiment perpetualised. Old Smithson should have built 50 schools, not one. Then he could have learned enough, and building technology could have developed so that photochromatic gasket glazing, improved thermal performance and acoustic isolation could all have come to play a part in something manageable and better. If there had been the money in 1950 for a full-scale mock-up, the kind of thing Mies or SOM insisted on, then things might have been different. But there wasn't, and there was no sequel to Hunstanton. Over the last 30 years, 5,000 children have spent five years in the experiment, instead of viewing it for five minutes in some museum of technology. Little thinks he knows what they feel about it. "These are country children here. Some of them complain of claustrophobia. You can see when they light up their fags in the lavatories, a little flash and off you go. There is nowhere to hide. Nowhere is private. That's what they say, and in my own heart I feel it, too."

Curiously enough the glass-expanding experience—described by Little as happening every time the sun sweeps across the courtyards—is a duplicate of what happened behind the south-facing facade of Le Corbusier's Salvation Army building in Paris, designed and built only two years before Hunstanton. But for this lesson to be learned, the two worlds of architectural criticism and user feedback would have had to acknowledge one another's existence—and such a thing would be as fatal as was Dorian Gray's own terminal meeting with the old and distorted image of his apparently youthful self.

Basil Spence, Coventry Cathedral, England, 1950–1962

Peter and Alison Smithson, Hunstanton School, England, 1950–1954

The most important building
of the twentieth century
1984

In December 1944 Richard Buckminster Fuller, the American inventor, engineer and architectural guru, was invited by the Beech Aircraft Corporation of Wichita, Kansas, to consider the problem of designing a low-cost house that could be assembled using the materials and methods then employed by the company to make communications aircraft for the United States Air Force. Mindful of the progress of the war and the massive housing shortage that was sure to follow it, the company had decided to plan for a progressive diversification away from airframe assembly into the construction of prefabricated houses, and Fuller's design task was to open the way with a prototype for evaluation.

What Fuller came up with and was finally built in 1946 looks like no other house ever designed, partly because it was devoid of what later came to be called "sell functions"—those ornate pieces of Georgian tomfoolery that building societies confuse with value—and partly because it was designed to be light in weight, a function that has historically played little or no part in the design of the house that you and I live in. The Wichita House, as it came to be called, was intended to be assembled at a rate of 1,000 units a week from January 1947, with a selling price of about £1,200. A controlled ventilation aluminium bungalow with a floor area of 80 square metres (one-third larger than the contemporaneous prefabs being built in Britain), the Wichita House was a circular dwelling suspended from a stainless-steel central mast without internal struts or bracing of any kind. It derived its strength from its double-curvature metal roof and circular form, and required only a central pad foundation. Complete with fitted kitchen, two bathrooms, cupboards, curtains and sliding doors, the entire 200 component house could be packed into a reusable stainless-steel shipping cylinder with an all-up weight of only four tonnes—and this at a time when the average American timber frame house weighed something like 150 tonnes. Why was the weight difference important? Because Fuller, alone among the pioneers of prefabrication in housing, of whom there were many, understood that low weight was the answer to low cost. In 1946, when heavy concrete prefabrication systems were under development all over the world, Fuller said; "A house requires a 98 per cent reduction in its present weight just to bring it within the possible range of units that industry can mass produce." Despite this insight and the visionary advantages of the dwelling system he proposed, Fuller's house was never put into production. The prototype, like the smaller (and heavier) AIROH prefabs that were built on bomber production lines in Britain at the same time, remains an isolated signpost pointing to a future as relevant to the massive redundant production capacity of the car industry today, as it was to the idle warplane production lines of 40 years ago.

As the American architectural critic Peter Blake once said, it is as impossible to think of modern architecture without prefabricated building as it is to think of Christianity without the cross. What he did not add was that it is also impossible to think of prefabrication without thinking of the two World Wars of the present century and all their manifold effects. It is true that Modern Architecture as an art movement did begin before 1914, but as a vital tool of social reconstruction it only began to come into its own in the aftermath of the wrecked and impoverished Empires and the 25 million casualties of the Great War. There were many reasons for this; the loss of skilled craftsmen, the great need for rapid building, the threat of civil unrest, the massive development of machine production during the war itself. Together these macro-causes elevated Modern Architecture from an avant-garde parlour game to the status of a blueprint for a new and better world. The pioneers of the art rose with it through this dizzy transformation, just as the computer pioneers of the 1950s rose from playing with what were little more than toys to a virtual command of information technology today.

The advent of the Second World War so soon after the First, with even more destruction, more casualties, and even more diverse and wonderful developments of industrial production, made modern architecture in the years after 1945 inevitable. It was the only framework of ideas that could possibly synthesise these chaotic ingredients into a building programme. The importance of modern ideas about materials and prefabrication under these conditions is impossible to exaggerate. Modern architectural thought, at the forefront of which Fuller stood until his death in 1983, achieved its greatest ascendancy in the reconciliation of massive social needs with new resources in conditions of absolute urgency. There could no more have been a 'Victorian', 'Classical Revival' or 'vernacular' architecture at mid-century than there could have been a cavalry defence against the Luftwaffe.

There are critics of modern architecture who will concede all this but still consign it to the dustbin of history along with gas masks and ration books. It is here that they make their most crucial mistake, for the idea of a built environment derived from industrial production and exploiting the materials and methods of advanced technology never really died. The conservationist injecting silicon into St Paul's against the ravages of acid rain, like the classical revivalist with his glass-fibre Doric columns and the postmodern innovator with his Teflon-coated pavement awnings, still depends on the transfer of technology from the laboratory to the production plant to the building site that began with modern architecture. What has been lost is the underlying theory that Fuller and some of his contemporaries so clearly understood. With the exception of a very few architects, who are still allowed to pursue this inner logic under the name of High-Tech, the profession now practices a kind of voluntary schizophrenia in which space-age materials masquerade as their pre-industrial equivalents. Today, light, timber framed houses are deliberately skinned in brick—even though this brings time-consuming wet-trades back on to structures where there is no need for them. In the same way, apparently traditional stone buildings in our cities now actually consist of wafer-thin slivers of stone glued to synthetics set between steel or alloy beams and stanchions. All this is said to be culturally necessary in order to perpetuate a seamless, fake Ruritanian townscape—but in fact it is no more vital than the wood trim and real leather upholstery in a Rolls Royce.

What Buckminster Fuller showed with his single Wichita House 40 years ago was that the kind of product design found today in a Citroën BX or a Macintosh microcomputer, could have been developed in the built environment as well, making every kind of building envelope just as beautiful, efficient and expendable. Alone among the architectural 'styles' modern architecture held the promise of such "ephemeralisation", as Fuller called it. Making buildings as 'invisible' through their cheapness and availability as a ballpoint pen or digital watch.

Heavy stuff this symbolism
1984

On a bright, short day in early winter, Charles Jencks' house looks much like any other in the discreetly expensive West London residential street where it is to be found. Rows of parked cars—not double-parked to suggest multiple occupancy—rows of mature plane trees, subtle traffic diodes that ensure the peace and quiet of the occupants. This is a world of walled gardens and white stuccoed walls, with only the bright yellow of the burglar alarm to spoil the early Victorian scene. In such surroundings, the eccentric can merge and disappear, so it requires unaccustomed attention to rooflines and front doors to pick it out. On Jencks' house the chimneys are capped-off and joined together at the top like Siamese twins; there is a strange arrangement of fretwork around a small terrace between them, itself topping an ogival lead roof flanked by funny stepped window sills with another fretwork shrouded slot of window descending the side wall. This is unusual.

Approaching the front door there are other hints of craziness within. A narrow stripe rises from the pavement gate to the door and, cutting through the porch above it, leaves a strange mushroom-shaped peep-hole in the door itself. There are two door handles for the single door and two door bells. It looks like the home of a cult; Scientology and Werner Erhard must live like this. In fact the man responsible is the most successful architectural critic alive—Charles Jencks of whose 30 books one alone —*The Language of Post-Modern Architecture*—has sold more copies than any work of architectural criticism published since the War and brought him a worldwide reputation. Jencks is an American in his mid-40s who has lived in London for more than 20 years. The house is not his first foray into architecture, nor will it be his last, for collaboration with architects and craftsmen, builders and sub-contractors, and most of all with clients, has given him a taste for the work. Indeed, his strange, amphitheatric study is littered with sketches on yellow tracing paper and the kind of formal models that Renaissance figures have strewed about them in murals.

The key to Jencks' new home is symbolism. Where any old architect or interior designer can give you a stylistically integrated backdrop to your life, Jencks can put together an entire mythology in which everything *means* something. It is, as he says, "slow food architecture, customised by a team of willing collaborators". What you get is something you can explain to all your friends as you take them on a tour of the house. You have to explain it because, Jencks believes, all the *agreed* meanings of architectural and decorative details have been lost like babies in the bathwater of tradition that was unceremoniously thrown out by the moderns. "To design a symbolic house in an agnostic age may seem folly", he says. "What is there to celebrate by decoration in the age of economic man?" He decided to find out by converting "at about one-twentieth the cost of a good Picasso" a straightforward end of terrace house he bought in 1978 into the bizarre creation in which he and his wife and children live with evident pleasure today.

Does this new symbolism work? Well, the open planned kitchen has a frieze of spoons around it, which seems clear enough, and the downstairs loo has a gallery of postcards from all over the world that can be changed at will. More obscurely, the same loo has two flushing levers—only one of which is a dummy. Furthermore it opens off an elliptical hallway formed of mirrored doors, all of which also have round knobs on both sides and concealed hinges. According to Jencks there are two main symbolic themes in the house. The first concerns 'cosmic time' which he explains as the four seasons and the passage of the sun, the moon and the galaxies—and the second concerning 'cultural time'—for which there are representations of Egypt, China, India and several periods of Western art. Above the elliptical hall is a mural which he modestly describes as "showing the evolution of the galaxies after the Big Bang and several exemplars of cultural pluralism who I admire, starting with the Egyptian architect and healer Imhotep and ending with Thomas Jefferson in conversation with Hannah Arendt".

As the visitor moves from the street front to the garden back of the house, the alterations to its original nineteenth century structure become more radical, culminating in a grand double escalier descending to the garden beyond a sheet of motorised glass that opens up the entire south side of the house to the elements by dropping into a concealed slot—in the same manner as Hitler's famous glass wall at Berchtesgaten. The pivot around which the thematic transformations of the house revolve is the hollow-centred, reinforced concrete circular staircase, with its spiralling stainless steel handrail worked with globes representing whirling planets. To anyone accustomed to the kind of utilitarian structure that admits cultural references only by way of Channel 4, Jencks' house has the complexity and dangerous richness of a Viennese cake. And yet the overall effect—at least in the main ground floor rooms—is of a cosy brownish kind of luxury that would be evident whether the inventor's patient litany of references, themes and contributions by this or that famous architect or sculptor, was understood or not. The massive sawing-apart of rooms and spaces that has been undertaken is all but invisible, so utterly has the original axial regularity of the house been converted into something continuous and bewildering but also strangely ordinary—with the latter impression reinforced by the Jencks' family's own cheerful telephone answering, going-off-to-school and message carrying, demonstrating to all the world that living in the midst of a veritable operating theatre of buried symbols is no more demanding than riding a BMX.

One way of illuminating the subdued strangeness of the Jencks house is by way of its strange lack of identifiable finishes. In a conventional building, particularly a modern one, you are continually confronted with building materials whose factitious identity can be in no possible doubt. "This is brick", says the white-painted junior common room wall; "This is concrete", says the towering, undecorated side of the apartment escape stair. Users of this sort of building often hate modern architecture precisely because they need a pneumatic drill to hang a picture—a result of the 'truth to materials' of which the architect was once no doubt proud.

In the Jencks world of symbolism this entire situation is reversed because it is impossible to determine what anything is made of. In the main living space, the two giant armchairs, the rising steps of the study floor, the window seats in the astronomically engraved 'sun room', the breasts of the multiple unused fireplaces, the kitchen table, the floor itself: all appear to be made out of the same glistening and magical kryptonite painted in a variety of tasteful colours and glissading effortlessly from unenclosed space to unenclosed space so that everywhere can be seen from everywhere else and there is no such thing as a square room with a door, or a simple piece of wood anywhere. This material and spatial endlessness is reinforced by Jencks' own seamless and well rehearsed symbolical analysis; "This level is labelled 'cosmopolite'—lover of the world—and the ceiling is labelled 'cosmos'—order of the world. There are 15 other word themes including 'cosmotecture'—world envelope."

Under this multivalent barrage it takes real concentration to remember to ask what all this stuff is actually made of. When the answer finally comes, it is as anticlimactic as the comfortable sort of aspect of the house itself —medium density fibreboard or MDF. All this fantastic symbolism is really a composite, grainless twentieth century material that can be cut and glued into any shape and assembled in any way on top of a higgledy-piggledy armature of structural supports that it renders invisible under an all-over sheen.

As an experiment, I try to move one of the titanic velour upholstered MDF armchairs next to the fireplace designed for Jencks by Michael Graves—it is impossible. The apparently casual angle is no accident, for symbolism in the late twentieth century—like symbolism in the Renaissance—is built to last.

Beyond messing about in boats
1984

I can distinctly remember the day that I transferred my product fantasy life from cars to boats. It was late on a summer's evening and I was seated on the terrace at Torcross staring out to sea through powerful U-boat commander binoculars—the kind you have to use a tripod for otherwise you cannot keep a distant object in view. Three chaps in wet suits were out in a Dart catamaran, zooming back and forth across the bay to the North of Start Point. The sun had already set, the wind had sprung up and they were making phenomenal speeds up on one hull and then the other in clouds of spray. Suddenly the Dart tripped over its lee float and went over on its side, the black, wet-suited figures whirling in all directions. They spent the rest of daylight righting it. Every time they swung its masthead into the wind and levered it over, it went through 180 degrees and down the other side. At last they got it to stand up and sailed swiftly back to the beach at Beesands. I never saw them out in it again—and was in due course to find out why.

That night I read JG Lockhart's account of the wreck of the *Rothsay Castle*. Shipwreck yarns take some beating at the best of times, but this one is a Victorian classic, with cowardly crew, indignant passengers and a spectacularly drunken Captain Atkinson: "Captain, there seems to be a great deal of danger. I wish you would turn back."

"There's a... deal of *fear*", retorted the Captain, "but no *danger*."

Yet already the water was forcing its way in through the axles of the paddles, the seams of the ship had begun to open, the cabin floors were awash, and in the furnace room the fires were being kept up with increasing difficulty.

The *Rothsay Castle* went aground off Great Ormes Head in 1830 with great loss of life—tidily including that of the fearless Captain. Such tales anchor in the mind, like the wreck of the *Khyber*, driven by storms for seven days onto the rocks at Lands End at the conclusion of a four month voyage from Australia; or the *Thomas W Lawson*, a steel seven-masted schooner of 4,000 tonnes (at the time the largest and most modern sailing vessel afloat) that went down off the Scillies two years later in 1907. It is difficult at first sight to relate these gothic horrors to messing about in Start Bay on a fibreglass trampoline catamaran, but let me explain what happened next.

The following year I crewed for a friend with a Spark—a smaller version of the Dart I had seen through the binoculars. On our fourth trip out, in a fresh off-shore breeze, we were reaching along at what seemed phenomenal speeds. I was trapezing and he was at the helm. Faster and faster we went, and wetter and wetter we got as the lee float dug in. Suddenly she cartwheeled and I whirled through the air on the end of my wire rope. Within seconds the Spark was on its side, the masthead dipping into the sea about a mile off Slapton Sands. I disconnected myself and, when my friend had surfaced, we kicked and splashed the masthead round into the wind, tightened the sails fore and aft, and got the wind beneath them to lift her over. Up she came... and then down she went, just like the Dart the previous year. Only this time I was a room's length away from the twin hulls and the trampoline, vertical to the water and acting like a sail, was carrying the boat away from me faster than I could swim. My colleague was astride the upper float. "Come on you can do it", he cried as he sped fast towards the horizon. It was at this point that, in my own mind at least, I joined the doomed heroes of JG Lockhart. There certainly was a... deal of fear about.

Then, with a suddenness equal to the speed of the capsize, the tone of my friend's cries changed from exhortation to horror. The Spark, its enormous mast filled with sea water, was turning through another 90 degrees so that it floated upside-down. Though bad news for the owner, who now knew he would never get it up again unaided, this was my salvation, for I was able to catch up with it and struggle on to a float. There we sat for six hours, my friend almost dead with cold because he had no wet suit, until we were towed in and forced to tie up to a buoy so close to the beach that the waterlogged mast bumped on the bottom at low tide.

It was three days before the Spark was righted and, when it was, the mast had to be within five degrees of the vertical before it would stand up and slowly drain the gallons of water it contained. My friend contacted the makers after this drama and was told that it was my fault because I should have eased up on the jib to prevent the cartwheel, and that if he went to their yard they would show him how to right it themselves. Alas he did not avail himself of their offer and the Spark has rested in a garage ever since.

This tale is small beer compared to the fate of *Beefeater* II off Cape Horn, or indeed of the gallant *Twiggy*, a 31 foot trimaran that capsized in the 1982 Round Britain race after sailing (like the luckless Khyber) all the way from Australia without incident. *Twiggy* was righted at sea, repaired and renamed *Rennie* as a result of sponsorship, and promptly went over for good on its next race. What one learns about multihulls, from real life as opposed to the newspapers and such amazing books as Nicolas Angel's *Capsize in a Trimaran*—the boat's sponsors failed to announce the yacht was overdue, for fear of bad publicity—is the ancient design virtue of heeling with the wind, which enables monohulls to resolve the stresses laid upon them automatically by simply laying flatter and flatter and eventually coming head up to the wind. Multihulls will not do this because they sail nearly vertical and can only resolve the forces laid upon them into forward motion. This means, in grossly oversimplified terms that, when they are pressed, they either go faster and faster and faster, or break up, or—like the Spark—sort it all out by turning upside down. The fascination of multihulls is speed, which no monohull except a planing sailboard can ever match, and this is why their design and construction is a fascinating study in itself as any visitor to the annual Portsmouth Speed Week will testify. But I digress.

My own first boat was a 21 foot wooden cabin cruiser, as old as it was long and powered by a marinised Morris Minor engine. About as far from such high-tech creations as a guaranteed 18 knot inflatable catamaran as it is possible to get. But even with this lumbering antique there was still a... deal of fear about, largely through the high incidence of engine failure, which invariably occurred off Start Point in failing light or in the summer congestion of Salcombe harbour, surrounded by £100,000 yachts. Once my auxiliary Seagull outboard broke its connecting rod and the inboard Morris blew its head gasket on the same voyage. This unreliable craft taught me a great deal about messing about in—as opposed to sailing—boats. It was bombastically named *Sea Hawk* because it is an invariable rule that all tiny estuarial cruisers are named after Errol Flynn films, while ocean racers are called things like *Carling Black Label Lager* or *Photocopier III*. What it had in common with these monsters was the fact that working on it was like working on a car turned upside down with its doors, windows, bonnet and boot welded shut. For obvious reasons there are no holes of any consequence in a hull.

Sea Hawk spent six months out of the water being 'worked on', months filled with the gloomy certainty that she would never go back in. When she finally did—at a cost of £72 plus VAT and numerous gouges in its newly antifouled hull (its beam and the width of the gateway it had to pass through were identical), the engine promptly failed again; £200 later I sold it for £300 and considered myself very lucky. *Sea Hawk's* new owner has never put to sea, though he is to be observed 'working on it' most weekends.

My next and current boat was a 20 foot bilge-keel sloop called a Signet. This vessel, I was gleefully told by the brokerage lady on the delivery voyage, had belonged to a choleric middle aged individual, not dissimilar to myself, who had died of a heart attack after going aground in the Dart estuary on a falling tide. His body had been dragged ashore through the mud wrapped in the mainsail. There were some stains on the sail which could, in the imagination, be assembled into something like the Turin Shroud, but the matter has never preyed on my mind. Curiously, I put the *Storm Bird*, as she is characteristically named, on the mud myself soon after buying it. After desperate attempts to drag it off I threw out the anchor and ferried my 70 year old mother, six year old son and his six year old friend to safety in the ten foot tender with a huge six hp outboard on the back. We had an inch of freeboard all round and bailed continuously all the way home. I collected *Storm Bird* alone at high tide the following day by the ingenious expedient of locking the outboard straight ahead in the stern of the tender and crouching in the bows. This way I found I could run it at full-throttle and steer it in wide-radius curves by leaning from side to side.

Apart from the financial issues that dog the boat-owner at all levels of the market, sailing and talking about disasters; quarrelling about who should give way when tacking; shouting at the unwilling crew; making a mess of picking up the buoy; getting in the way of trawlers or ferries and just plain missing the tide make messing about in boats much better than good books or fast cars. There *is* a wonderful absence of regulation that extends from the design of the boats themselves to the absence of any real rule of the road. You need no licence to start and anyone who has a boat is always eager to sell it. Like any business, it is harder to get out of than to get into.

Office design in Eternia
1985

Apart from the ever-thrilling spectacle of massive efflorescence on the walls of Blake Carrington's mansion in the weekly title sequences of *Dynasty*, there is little for a discriminating architectural TV viewer at this time of year. Of course, there are programmes about architecture, but these are monopolised by individuals chosen for their rustic regional accents and uncritical enthusiasm for anything built before 1914 and thus lack any credibility. Architects are dynamic, thrusting individuals thinking always of the Third Millennium and the newest milium-coated cladding material; it must be purgatory for them to sit and watch cameras zoom down boring streets in Taunton and hover lovingly over spires recently repaired regardless of expense. Fortunately flexitime and underemployment (architects are seldom *unemployed*) have between them liberated whole sectors of television watching normally denied the working population; roughly speaking the great scad of time that stretches between *Postman Pat* and *John Craven's Newsround* now lies within the grasp of much of the profession.

Take *He-Man and the Masters of the Universe* (Monday afternoons at 4.20 pm—but check for local variations). This animated saga is set in a strange world called "Eternia", which is nominally ruled by a king and queen but in practice is regularly saved from destruction and slavery by their son, the apparently inadequate Prince Adam, by holding his sword aloft and crying, "By the power of Grayskull!" and "I have the power!"—cries which can be heard echoing across school playgrounds everywhere by those with ears to hear.

The interesting thing about Eternia is not so much its Roman football team social structure as its unusual built environment. The Royal Palace is a fine postmodern assemblage reminiscent of an aircraft carrier-sized Staatsgalerie incorporating all the ghastly architectural jokes Stirling thought of but did not incorporate in the original. In close up it appears to consist of large slabs of stone, cut and fit with Incan precision but cantilevering with such abandon that space-age adhesives must have been employed as well. Information technology slots into this environment as effortlessly as a Herman Miller workstation would fit into the Parthenon—which is to say not at all well. For a time I thought this was a major weakness, with Airbus flightdeck-style 'laboratories' never sharing a shot with the stone bastions supposed to house them; but that was before an episode called "Castle of

Heroes". In this 15 minute epic, the operations centre of the arch-villain Skeletor was seen in more than usual detail and much became clear.

Skeletor has a magnificent throne—a Biedermeier of bones—with a rough stone desk in front of it carrying a hologram hemisphere fed by surface conduits like claws. He apparently has no data storage but, instead, is perpetually aware of what is going on in Eternia. Thus, living in a paperless office in an eternal present, he does not need a flat desk surface and has pioneered a new departure in office furniture design. Skeletor's 'new electronic rough-desk' could be marketed tomorrow. It would fit into any environment of pre-Columbian simplicity.

Quinlan Terry: beyond the tantrums of Modernism
1985

A visit to the office of Quinlan Terry, architect, is an amazing experience. It would be trite to say that it is like walking back into history, and misleading too, for the phrase suggests something like a return to the world of Jane Austen and white Georgian houses. Terry's modest shop on the main street of a tiny Essex village is actually reminiscent of the post-war era evoked by *Dance with a Stranger* or *A Private Function*.

Nowadays one does not often see a radiant bar electric fire in an architect's office, let alone one in every room; or antiquarian drawing boards with tee-squares covered with large pencil drawings and a total absence of designer furniture—or 15 assistants wearing ties who work a six day week. All these things belong to the 1950s, a time when the direction; "Just across the street from the post office, you can't miss it", seemed part of the common, unhurried parlance of a rural utopia now forgotten even by the Archers of Ambridge —who are deep into agribusiness.

And yet behind the tiny polished brass plate that says "Quinlan Terry Architect" is the powerhouse of Classical Revival in British architecture. Inside this low-ceilinged, Spartan rabbit-warren of a village house are production drawings for current projects worth £30 million, for clients as hard-nosed and established as Haslemere Estates, the London developers, and Downing College, Cambridge. Quinlan Terry's office may resemble a set from *Dr Finlay's Casebook*, but his workload could buy up the whole village and for that reason alone he cannot be dismissed as an eccentric working in an obsolete architectural tradition. The whole phenomenon of Classical Revival—the literal return, with such modest improvements as air conditioning and double-glazing, to Georgian architecture—is as coming a thing as community architecture or High-Tech futurism. Indeed, encounters with its leading exponents such as Terry himself, or the younger Robert Adam who recently designed a classical building for Amdahl Computers, is a chastening experience; far from coming on like Jerry Lewis in *The Nutty Professor* they are so relaxed and sure of themselves that one immediately thinks of half a dozen better known London practitioners of different persuasions whose chances of even reaching the Third Millennium ahead of cardiac arrest must be immeasurably poorer. The Classical Revivalists face the twenty-first century with unimpeachable calm, and why should they not? 15 years to another century is as the twinkling of an eye to those whose art is founded on a tradition that stretches back more than two millennia.

Quinlan Terry himself is a tall, properly dressed country gentleman who wears, when he is not in town, a tastefully distressed three-piece suit. He has piercing blue eyes and a slow but precise way of saying things that no one who reads the newspapers or watches television ever expected to hear said again—except perhaps in a funny voice designed to show that they are not meant to be taken seriously. He sits at a highly polished eighteenth century wooden desk on a chair of similar age and value and describes the vast tumult of the Modern Movement in architecture as "a kind of tantrum" for which Raymond Erith, the now dead Classicist whose practice he acceded to, predicted disaster even in its heyday. He would sit here, towards the end of his life and say, "It's all going to fall down and I shall split my sides laughing." Now, with all these defects in those massive high-rise council schemes, we can all see that he was right. Terry is no kinder to the High-Tech tours de force of his own time. "If they will insist on exposing all their structure instead of protecting it with a good slate roof they must expect trouble before long. Yes, it is definitely headed for disaster."

One of many surprises about the man is the way in which he does not allow his essential sympathy with conservation to lead him into the conventional path of opposing growth and expansion. His own tiny village, with a population of 1,800 could double in size if development were unrestrained, but he sees nothing intrinsically wrong in this. "The Georgians knew how to deal with growth, their century was a period of enormous population expansion. In Edinburgh in the eighteenth century they built a new town and it is the best part of the city. Growth is a problem when the architectural styles and the values that people have at the moment are so Mammon-orientated that everything is reduced to a financial equation. All the Georgian squares in London, plenty of growth, but allied to common sense and a good way of building. If we can return to that tradition, as a matter of principle, then we will get the results that we all seem to accept. Today you have a lot of very talented architects around but, working in the Modern tradition, they produce an environment that everybody hates."

Terry has very clear ideas about what architects can and cannot do. Although he stops short at saying that the post-war generation should never have got involved in the major prefabrication programmes, he does stress the limited control they had over them—a fact that most critics of modern building refuse to admit. "It depends on what the architect's instructions are. If he has to house a quarter of a million people a year and that is what he is told to do and in order to do it he has to use factory-made units, he is not really being an architect at all, he is being an industrial designer. You don't need an architect to clap those things together because they won't last very long. But if you tell him; 'We want to build as many houses as we can, we want to build permanent houses for people that won't have to be serviced and maintained every five minutes and won't fall down in 20 years, how many houses can you build?' Then I think the architect can advise the politicians. But that isn't what happened. And it still isn't happening. A lot of this package building involves architects simply because they haven't got enough work and they need a job. Refurbishment is the same. You don't need architects for that."

The largest scheme on the drawings boards in Terry's office is a £20 million mixed development incorporating some existing buildings that has just gone on site in Richmond. The project, for Pension and Property Unit Trust with Haslemere Estates as the developer, will be the largest Classical Revival construction in the country on completion and shows the remarkable elasticity of the concept in the face of modern commercial requirements. Although he affects to be unsurprised by the ease with which he has been able to adapt the architecture of the Renaissance to the needs of developers in the past—notably at Dufours Place, in London's Soho, where he recently completed another Haslemere scheme—Terry candidly admits that the popularity of his approach with conservationists and planning authorities plays a part in the arrival of such commissions. This is what he calls "an element of fashion" in the popularity of his work; but he is sure that the tried and trusted methods of classical architecture, the old working details and the crack-resistant flexibility of load-bearing brickwork will soon overtake it in an era of mounting defects liability claims against architects. "Classical architecture is really accumulated common sense, and eventually the people who pay for buildings must come to understand that."

There is in Terry's personality and work a fruitful amalgam of principle and adaptability. When told that the American postmodern architect Philip

Johnson plans a $300 million complex in Boston with "more Palladian windows than there are in the whole of Vicenza", he finds the notion absurd. For him evolution is a falsehood and exaggeration the product of greed. Reason and sound principles of construction will render tractable the greatest problems, even those of success. He cheerfully admits to producing 100 drawings for a tiny summer house he designed for Michael Heseltine when the Conservative politician was Secretary of State for the Environment. The notion that such an output is "uneconomical" or "could be done by a computer" has no reality. He has already proved—to his own satisfaction at least—that innovations like lifts, air conditioning, modern fire regulations and electronic technology can be accommodated in symmetrically planned, Georgian windowed, brick walled and pitched roofed buildings.

His office employs few qualified architects; at one time he employed none because he believed that the ravages of a conventional school of architecture education made them "the most useless people in the office". Since then, with the coming of fame and success, he has found it easier to attract like-minded individuals, four of whom at present are qualified, although this was not a condition of their engagement. Nor does the gravitation of his work towards London make him wish to set up an office there. One suspects that he shares Cobden's view of the metropolis when he explains that he has so arranged his affairs that "I will not have to go up at all this week."

Plucky Jim
1985

On page 162 of the new book *James Stirling, Buildings and Projects* there occurs the surprising sentence, "I was conceived in a bunk on board ship, lying in New York harbour in the roaring 20s." It reads like the first line of an autobiography or a swashbuckling novel. An uncompleted work alas, in part no doubt because so Hemingway a beginning requires a second sentence of equal power, then more and more stretching to at least 40,000 words. In short, it needs *writing*—and that is not what 'Plucky Jim' (as Reyner Banham christened him) does for a living. Instead, he designs, and looks inscrutable, a vast shambling heap of a man with a reputation in the land of *Vorsprung durch Technik* as well as the New World.

When Stirling arrived at *The Architectural Press* launch of *Buildings and Projects* last month he looked distinctly ill at ease. In the squalidly baroque surroundings of the Bride of Denmark—a rendezvous haunted by the ghosts of the gin-swilling giants of yesteryear, whose successors sip Perrier and converse in whispers—lest their post-utopian drivel be overheard—Big Jim's arrival was like that of a great Victorian actor. There he stood, sweating profusely in a straw hat, Guernsey sweater, ragged trousers and desert boots, while the colourless crew of hacks, flacks and hangers-on who had previously populated the shiny brown cellar pressed themselves back against the walls to give him room. There was a moment when he could have given a blood-curdling scream, a booming laugh, mocked them as scum, or simply snatched up the circulating jug of Pimms No 1 and drained it at a draught. Instead he coughed nervously and said, to no one in particular; "I've just come back from Venice", followed by "It beats Newhaven." And then, as though sensing this was not enough; "I thought the students would be all Rossi...." At this point polite conversation finally began. The giant of English architecture, the greatest practitioner since Sir Edwin Lutyens and the greatest survivor of the post-war utopia had arrived.

One week later, in the gracious surroundings of his London office Stirling is hunched over a low drawing board set before a curved window facing west into the setting sun. Classical music emerges from a modest-sized ghetto blaster. The room is large but stylelessly furnished, like a house master's study with a large table set against one wall for laying out drawings. There is an atmosphere of calm and order, you could hear the sound of a cricket bat if we were not in central London.

"Jim Stirling, I have come to ask you some questions."

"You will get lots of 'No comments'."

"That's OK. You can pass on ones you don't like. Number one. Has Peter Palumbo spoken to you about taking on Mansion House Square?"

"No comment."

"If he did ask you, would you refuse out of respect for the wonderful buildings on the site?" (Gavin Stamp et al, passim, etc.)

"Whatever happens there is bound to be a tremendous focus of attention. Nobody's going to leave it alone. They will pick it to death."

"Why did you support the Mies scheme?"

"Because it would have been a better building than anything else in the City. I really thought it would go through in the end."

"Would it have been better than anything that could go there now?"

"No comment."

"Are you a famous architect?"

"Famous, infamous, it's the same thing really. I don't particularly like it."

"You don't like being a Gold Medallist, a Pritzker Prize winner?"

"I feel proud—no proud is not the right word—I feel pleased about having got those sorts of things, but it leads to embarrassment. It is impossible for me to walk down Fifth Avenue or across the Piazza San Marco without a little old man coming out of the shadows and plucking my sleeve and saying, 'Mr Stirling, you remember me, I was in your class in '59!' And I look at this guy, and he is quite ancient actually, and there is no way I can relate his face to the very beautiful young man he must have been in '59. He knows me because my ancient face keeps coming up in magazines, but I have no way of recognising him. It never happens to me in London of course, or in England, ha ha. But very much so in America and Italy. In Venice last week someone grabbed me and I pretended not to be myself. 'You're Mister Stirling!' he said. 'You're Mister Stirling the architect.' I said 'Who? No. You've got the wrong person.' No point in having a conversation: he knows who I am but he doesn't know me and I don't know him."

"Do you consider yourself a Modern architect?"

"Well I sincerely hope I am. That was how I grew up, believing that Modern Architecture was a beautiful kind of fairy story about revolutionary forces overthrowing Victorian ugliness. And I still believe that story."

"Is it connected in your mind with the Labour landslide of 1945, the forces vote and we are the masters now?"

"It's certainly connected with Sigmund Freud and Modern Art and Socialist building programmes—in that order."

"Did it fail?"

"Yes, it did, largely because Modern architects hadn't got much talent. The language itself was so reductive that only exceptionally talented people could design modern buildings in a way that was interesting. Lesser architects, when they do it.... It's somehow just too simple. Anyway, fail may be the wrong word. In a sense it got, what's the word, stuck. It got stuck and it will have to unstick itself to move on. When I came on to the scene after the war Modern Architecture had been a matter of villas for millionaires, at least in England. I saw it as something that could be grafted on to big building programmes, schools, housing. I saw it as the same thing as pre-war but with the clientele changing. Now of course it has all dissolved away. For me it started dissolving in the mid-50s. I think if you look at that project for houses for Basil Mavrolean; if that had been built you would have seen the beginning of postmodern jokes. The houses were much too large, it was all very Charles Addams, they had a slightly creepy character."

"Is having built things in Germany as rewarding as having a German car?"

"I do have a German car. I drive a BMW. But yes, I am very pleased with the Staatsgalerie. I did not think it would be a colossal popular success. I assumed it would be a critical success. As to building in Germany, yes again. Their building regulations are to an incredibly high standard, far higher than here. Everything from roof drainage to insulation to structure, contract management, workmanship, everything. It's not the same in England, or in America. It's a marvellous basis for building. It may have been like that here in Edwardian times. Architects have enormous status in Germany, especially if they have the word 'Professor' in front of their names, which most of them do. Whenever the architect opens his mouth in the building trade in Germany, people stop talking. It must be the contractual documents or something; the initiative is entirely with the architect. You don't get the terrible legal hassle you get over here."

"Is it true that the contractor on the Tate Gallery site here couldn't fit the German windows in and that's why the building is a year late?"

"No comment. No, that is completely untrue. It's completely wrong. Maybe the English builders couldn't build what was on the drawings. Not the windows but what was *supporting* the windows. Maybe it's all very elementary.... Don't quote me!"

"Do you think architectural jokes are funny?"

"There have always been architectural jokes, you can find them in Borromini. The trouble today is that people only talk about the jokes as if that was all the building is... a collection of jokes. In that issue of *The Architectural Review* about the Staatsgalerie where they had four people write about it, the only one that made any sense was Emilio Ambasz because he looked right through the jokes and out the other side and talked about the relationship of the central space to the German soul."

"What do you think of Albert Speer?"

"Ha ha. Well, I'm one of those unusual people who thinks that Albert Speer was a terrible architect. I look at the plans and the drawings and, considering his background, Tessenow and that tradition, it's not very good architecture. Maybe that's why he moved on quickly to that other management job. The only interesting thing he ever did was that temple of light, you know, with searchlights. Very ingenious, but not typical of him. No, I think he was a very poor architect."

"Which living architects do you admire?"

"Whose work would I go out of my way to look at you mean? Well, I always go—expecting to be disappointed—to anything by Venturi. I would always look at anything by Michael Graves. Then there is Hans Scharoun of course, the post-war work, verging on the arbitrary and the pretentious.... The Philharmonie... I don't know. Most architects are a disappointment."

"Do you admire any architectural critics?"

"I admire quite a lot of critics, sometimes, you know. I admire Colin Rowe, of course...."

"And he admires you."

"Yes, but that is because we grew up together. Really, I like reading historical criticism, about Palladio by Ackerman, that sort of stuff."

"What about theorists like Tafuri?"

"I have a lot of trouble reading those Italians. I can never make much sense out of it."

"Frampton?"

"I was very disappointed in that Critical History book about modern architecture. It seems to be an old story.... Somewhat boring really."

"Quinlan Terry and Leon Krier both worked for you in the past. Did you influence them.... Or did they, subsequently influence you?"

"Ha ha. Well... they were both splendid draughtsmen and that's what they did when they were here. I think working here helped them both make up their minds about things. That's all I can say really."

"Was your 1972 Southgate housing, with the overhead service lines, based on Gropius' Siedlung Torten?"

"No, we had to link with services that had already been laid, using a completely different type of housing, that was why we did it."

Three days later. "I was conceived in a bunk on board ship, lying in New York harbour in the roaring 20s" is a wonderful sentence. The kind a man could carry around with him for the rest of his life, unable to follow it with another and thus condemned to proceed to the grave with a whole branch of his personality undeveloped. It may seem strange to say this of a man whose life in architecture has touched peaks and troughs inaccessible to the vast majority, and whose reputation extends farther and deeper than that of any other British architect, but James Stirling really wants to write. His admiration for Colin Rowe, the old vaudeville trouper, stems from this—for Rowe is no more comprehensible than Tafuri or Frampton and—growing up with Stirling aside—the only real bond between them is their mutual difficulty in writing. It took Rowe ten years to put together a kind of appreciation of his friend in *Buildings and Projects*. Stirling values that, just as he values the memories of Sam Stevens Rowe evokes, and the memory of a motor trip to look at the Leicester Engineering building when the world was young and he was not 59 years old.

Doubts about Lloyd's
1986

One sunny morning a couple of weeks ago 53 year old architect Richard Rogers and his partner of 20 years, John Young, were standing on the crowded floor of 'the room' at the base of the soaring atrium of the new Lloyd's building. They were positioned only a few yards from the tall, columnated wooden frame that supports the Lutine Bell itself, now incongruously boasting a large colour TV monitor and a microphone as well as the dangling white rope attached to the clapper traditionally used to announce a shipwreck.

Among the milling throng of underwriters with their security badges the two stand out in their baggy pastel summer suits. It is not long before a middle aged, pinstripe figure approaches.

"Excuse me, but are you Richard Rogers the architect?"

"Yes. I am."

"My name is Stevens and I am an underwriter here. I was hoping that you were the architect because there is something that I want to tell you."

"Go ahead."

"Look, I don't care what you have done to this building on the outside, but some of us have to physically work inside here and let me tell you it really is bad news. All this concrete, it's like a car park, it's atrocious. Can't you paint it or something—surely it's not too late for that?"

Rogers, whose demeanour shows that he had expected praise from the tone of the initial enquiries only to suffer a nasty shock, replies at last: "There is an underwriters' committee that has approved every step of the design.... Perhaps you should...."

"The committee!" ejaculates Mr Stevens, sudden anger replacing the tone of pleading in his voice. "I am appealing to you as an individual human being who has to work day after day in this monstrosity. Is there nothing you can do to make conditions here more tolerable?"

Before the plainly disconcerted Rogers can answer, another figure, this time much younger, detaches himself from the throng of underwriters milling round their strangely prep-school-looking wooden booths.

"I heard that Mr Rogers, and I would just like to say that I completely disassociate myself from my colleague's remarks. I think this building is a work of genius. I work here every day too and I think the whole conception is brilliant! I would like to shake the hand of the man who designed this modern miracle."

Rogers complies with a bewildered grin. The two underwriters smile confidently at one another, as experts in invisible exports should, whatever their opinions. After a few moments they both politely take their leave.

Since its opening two months ago the £180 million Lloyd's building with its most prominent facade on to Leadenhall Street opposite the Commercial Union Plaza in the City of London, has become the first high-profile symbol of high-technology architecture in England. There have been high-technology buildings before, and there are even more impressive ones overseas, but all previous English examples have been either too small, too cheap, or too provincial to arouse strong feelings.

Lloyd's is different. The people who hate it do so because they know it is the product of new and dangerous principles against which their own innate conservatism is as powerless as the helpless rage of Mr Stevens the underwriter.

To the surprise of the planning authorities who permitted it as a curiosity in 1978, Lloyd's has come to represent the real beginning of a new finite architecture. In the same way as the oil price crash and Chernobyl can be said to foreshadow the end of the last energy subsidy for the old traditions of English life, Lloyd's can now be seen as the first real harbinger of a traditionless future, sharing only the word 'architecture' with such infinite and eternal structures as Salisbury Cathedral, Blenheim Palace, and even James Stirling's brand new, but utterly obsolete, proposals for Mansion House Square.

The essentially pre-industrial role of buildings like these was to remain the same from generation to generation by way of eternal repair regardless of expense. But the new finite architecture is post-industrial, something designed to last for 50 years at the most; and that only if technological and market trends run as predicted.

No viewing of Lloyd's prior to its opening could prepare anyone for the amazing density of occupation of its underwriting floors, where more than 5,000 people now gather in a space that, under the Offices, Shops and Factories Acts, should only contain one fifth that number.

Standing in what is intended to be the visitors' viewing gallery on the fourth floor (except that some underwriters are bidding for space already) and staring down into this gigantic pit, through three floors of criss-crossing transparent escalators, is an unnerving experience. Directly below, the seething mass of underwriters is so dense it almost obscures the acres of blue carpet. To the side, the streams of people on the escalators become invisible against the greyness of the concrete, the steelwork and the specially developed bubble-finish glass walls and only the whirling yellow bogey wheels inside the moving stairways catch the eye.

The immense ground floor is like the cargo hold of a huge ship taken over by troops who have parked their kit in every available corner.

"Excuse me sir, may I ask what are you doin' up 'ere?" A character from Dickens dressed in red and black forces open a plate glass door and advances upon me.

"Let's see your pass then."

I show the Lloyd's man my pass and his manner changes. Even so he escorts me from my vantage point to somewhere less convenient. I ask him what he thinks of the new building.

"It's been...'ot in 'ere the last two weeks sir", he begins, as I look at his thick woollen cloak, hat and leather boots—designed no doubt to be struck by lightning. "And they don't like it at all."

Alas the new car park style is even less classy than those pranksters who heave files across the void from one level to another imagine. For one of the most important calculations made as soon as Lloyd's accepted that the new building was to take the form of a vast multi-storey cube with all its ancillary accommodation—"the 15 year parts", as Rogers calls them—bolted on around the outside, was the precise number of lavatories needed to accommodate the distended bladders of the underwriters at 2.30 in the afternoon.

The answer came as close to giving the exterior of the car park its distinctive configuration as any other single feature—except perhaps for the escape stairs.

Richard Rogers is completely straightforward about this approach, as well he might be in the knowledge that nothing else can remotely come to terms with the 20 per cent a year growth of the financial services industry, or the microtechnology boom that increased power consumption at Lloyd's by six times in as many years.

He got the Lloyd's commission because the great insurance conglomerate was bursting at the seams and needed an architectural concept that would hold it together more than it needed a traditional corporate headquarters.

Standing in the Commercial Union Plaza, facing this shiny, uncompromising structure, I asked Richard Rogers: "If you put the 50 year part on the inside—and the 15 year parts on the outside—where is the architecture?"

"It is like modern poetry", he said. "It doesn't rhyme like a limerick any more, but the beat is still there."

When I first saw Lloyd's I was sure that Rogers had lost control of it; that the heating, cooling, power, lifts, escalators and ventilators were running riot round a vast empty core. Now I have seen how crowded the 'empty core' can get, and how extensively the service towers might be changed around without really altering the concept at all—I am not so sure.

Richard Rogers Partnership, Lloyd's Building, London, England 1978–1986

Foster Associates, Hongkong and Shanghai Bank, Hong Kong, 1979–1986

Two triumphs of twisted wire
1986

It is a truth universally acknowledged that inconsequentiality is the enemy of good design. If the parts of which any design is composed cannot be shown to relate to the logical needs of the whole, and the whole does not appear to represent the sum of its parts, then the design can be unravelled by criticism until it stands bereft of all justification; revealed as the product of whim or impulse, or the creation of a series of expedient decisions within no framework of intelligence. It was a developed critique of this order that enabled the Modern Movement to sweep away the massive agglomeration of historical styles that dominated nineteenth century architecture; and the abandonment of this rationality that led to the resurgence of historicism in the last 15 years.

During the heyday of the Modern Movement functionality in architectural design was virtually unquestioned. Today, as the huge investment in such epic structures as Richard Rogers' £157 million Lloyd's building and Norman Foster's £600 million Hongkong and Shanghai Bank has confirmed, function is on the move again; in key economic areas from science parks to financial service buildings, the primacy of the operational purpose of buildings has become as unassailable as it was when nine figure budgets were considered beyond the reach of any architect. This resurgence is the result, not of new architectural thinking, but the fusion of information technology with financial management that is creating a new kind of building and providing the massive economic resources to develop it. Like the revolutionary new techniques of construction that launched the Modern Movement, the new technology of economics is aesthetically blind; it knows no architectural history; has no social goals; observes no formal shibboleths. Instead, it forces its way forward by infiltration; penetrating at the weakest point, widening the breach, shouldering aside the opposition. Guided only by the need for conditions in which its complex machinery can work.

The economic engine works by advanced electronic technology but it uses advanced construction technology only when it must. The Adam Room at Lloyd's is a case in point, carelessly transplanted from its ground floor eighteenth century origins to one new location after another; most recently to a glass arcade on the eleventh floor of the new building. Similarly, the ancient talismans of the Hongkong and Shanghai Bank; Persian rugs, over-stuffed Chesterfields, Opium War relics and ancestral portraits, are hoisted into the bizarre environment of aluminium-encased steel beams at the top of One Queen's Road Central. Architecture is instrumental to the economy, not an end in itself. Even apparent exceptions really conform to the same philistine rule; we can see this through the way that economic rationality works lower down the fee scale. In the case of Quinlan Terry's £20 million Richmond development, or James Stirling's new £60 million Mappin & Webb triangle, the ruthless requirements of economic logic may be less obvious to the observer, but we can be sure they were crucial to the client. Why are both schemes clothed in historical facades? Because this is a camouflage to enable them to make their way through the planning bureaucracy that each has encountered in a city where many layers of the power structure are still dominated by romantic and illogical ideas that would otherwise obstruct the forward march of the machines of the new economy. It is more rational to advance under camouflage in such circumstances than it would be to invite the trench warfare of conservationist lobbying and public inquiry. This does not mean that either Quinlan Terry or James Stirling is cynical in his use of classical or postmodern architecture: it means something far more fundamental—that it does not matter whether they are or not. Those who believe that in the nooks and corners ruled by heritage thinking an alternative kind of rationality prevails, mistake the weight of the changes that are to come, and ignore the fact that designing to navigate through the received ideas of the building control bureaucracy is part of the same functional process as designing so that you can double your cable runs and replace the lifts and toilets without tearing the building apart. Whether it produces better buildings when it is dominant will, in the last analysis, be evaluated by economists indifferent to style. As recent history has shown, where the economic force deployed is overwhelming—as in the case of the £1.5 billion Canary Wharf project—all such subterfuge disappears and the opposition is overwhelmed by frontal attack.

In this context, the case of Lloyd's and the Hongkong and Shanghai Bank is doubly interesting because each is an example not only of massive economic force, but of phenomenal design talent. Not only was relatively little navigation of the bureaucratic world of received ideas carried out in either case—perhaps because both clients were institutions of such political and economic power that a degree of compliance with their wishes at the bureaucratic level could be assumed—but neither architect was asked to do anything other than to produce an urgently needed state-of-the-art high-technology financial services building. The popular mythology is that Norman Foster was asked to build "the best bank in the world", and Richard Rogers to "make the new Lloyd's building work for 50 years". Because the design of each building was dominated by the needs of an unprecedented boom in global money markets predicated on the demands of an explosively developing electronic technology that ten years before had barely existed, even these cryptic instructions embodied an enormous task. It can be argued that it was one that barely admitted consideration of obsolete aesthetic issues, but this is a judgement hinging on the choice of architect rather than the circumstances of each commission. Whatever the outcome in other hands, it is indisputable that the technological imperative in both cases made the buildings authentically modern—rather than postmodern—design problems: perhaps the first to emerge on such a scale since the high-rise housing era. Because the two architects specialised in engineering-led advanced construction design, the likelihood of a synergetic advance in form and performance was strong from the outset. A best-case formulation for both might have been; advanced electronic technology + advanced construction technology = the architecture of the third millennium.

The gestation of Lloyd's and the Hongkong Bank can best be seen not as a conventional process of building design, but as a variant of the prototype development process routinely undergone in the more advanced production engineering departments of the automobile or aircraft industry. In fact, the combined cost of the two buildings—both erected on freehold sites—is comparable to the development cost of a new airliner, while the radical advances in building performance embodied in each entitle them to the same 'new generation' status. Even if it cannot be said that after Hongkong and Shanghai and Lloyd's there will be no retreat by the £200 billion financial services industry from advanced technology precision construction, even perhaps from building costs ranging between £4,000 and £8,000 a square metre; it must be accepted that both buildings are already harbingers of the acceptance of a new scale and complexity in twenty-first century construction. Two decades later than their airborne predecessors, they are the architectural equivalents of the Boeing 747 wide-body jet and the Concorde supersonic airliner. And between them they raise the same kind of questions about the obsolescence of the rest of the built environment—not just through their own existence, but as a consequence of their emulation in the future.

Seen purely from the standpoint of their economic function as multi-screen electronic terminals in the financial wiring of two large cities, separated by half the surface of the earth but connected by symbiotic electronic ties, there are strong similarities between Lloyd's and the Hongkong and Shanghai Bank. Indeed, representatives of the global economic institutions that commissioned them probably find them as similar as two Grand Prix racing cars. But seen as objects in an urban landscape the differences are more obvious, and ultimately reveal much about the driving force of the new technology that both buildings house.

The 14-storey, 360,000 square foot Lloyd's building emerges from a tangle of tiny streets flanked by tall buildings with only one major elevation—to Leadenhall Street—that is not so foreshortened that its skyline profile is invisible. The Hongkong and Shanghai Bank, three times the net area and by far the taller at 52 storeys, actually looks smaller and flimsier in context, its delicate tracery of construction elements weaving in and out of what appears to be a series of thin cards set on end and rising to different heights. While Lloyd's, despite its squatness, still masters the buildings in its immediate vicinity, the Hongkong Bank is partially obscured from many views and only dominates the horizon from its magnificent harbour approach to the north.

The most powerful visual elements on the exterior of the Lloyd's building are the tightly wound stainless steel staircase towers, even though they do not connect directly with the three-storey metal-clad plant rooms and maintenance cranes built above the stacked toilet modules projecting far above the level of the barrel vaulted glass roof. Where the huge rectangle of the office and underwriting floors is visible between its satellite servicing towers, it is an anticlimax, dogged by the severity of opaque glass and concrete. The appearance of the Hongkong building is different, not only because it is transparent, but because its total form, rather than one or other of its peripheral elements, is what is seen first. Its equally ubiquitous escape stair towers and toilet modules are never perceived in isolation, but identified later, securely held within the building's profile by uniform glazing and cladding and the firm grasp of the aluminium-clad steel suspension structure.

The best way to pin down this fundamental difference is by way of a computer analogy. Despite its complex outline, the Hongkong and Shanghai Bank is a 'bundled' machine, with its peripherals incorporated into a single casing; while Lloyd's is 'unbundled'—its disc drives, printer and monitor (as it were) all packaged separately from its central processor. Both these approaches have advantages and disadvantages that are analogous in architecture and microcomputer design—ready access to components for replacement or modification versus simplicity of enclosure—and both involve a fundamentally different design emphasis. The Apple Macintosh micro, for example, is 'bundled' (disc drive, computer and monitor in one housing), while the Atari 520ST—which was originally marketed as the 'Jacintosh' because it was alleged to possess the same capabilities at one-third of the price is an 'unbundled' machine with four separate components, all of which required connection by cable.[1] The development of both machines has followed an interestingly convergent pattern, with the upgraded Atari 1040 incorporating a disc-drive into its keyboard housing, thus becoming more 'bundled' than it was, while the Macintosh upgrades have all taken place within the monitor housing as originally designed.

With the two micros, as with the two buildings, the 'unbundled' machine is cheaper—but it is undeniable that the design evolution of the Atari has been towards 'bundled' status. Unfortunately, this analogy does not produce as clear an argument for the superiority of the Hongkong and Shanghai Bank as might at first appear, for the Lloyd's building is designed for a peak population of 5,000 persons in only 360,000 square feet of floorspace; while the Hongkong and Shanghai Bank at present holds only 3,000 in nearly one million square feet. In computer terms, this could be related to the RAM power of each machine, with the Atari's 512K comfortably higher than the Macintosh's 128K (at the time of its introduction), and thus produce a suggestion that the Lloyd's building offers—as Atari's advertising ingeniously puts it; "the power without the price". Proceeding from this analogical data we can conclude that Lloyd's is either obsolete or inherently cheaper; and that the Hongkong and Shanghai Bank is either more advanced or inherently more expensive than it needed to be. In the latter case, elaborate 'bundling' might be a way of identifying the high design effort, high cost area in the Hongkong and Shanghai Bank—which is its aluminium-clad inboard/outboard structural system—as the proper target for development in future.

In the end, the enveloping and servicing of electronic technology is the raison d'être of both buildings, and from this point of view there is a want of simplicity in both. Pure function, as interpreted by Foster in Hong Kong, included the complex re-entrant profile of floor areas to allow for regulation shadow angles and the incorporation of double-storey height refuge terraces at intervals above ground. There can be no disputing the grandeur of the architectural expression achieved by these means, but the absolute necessity of at least one of them must be in some doubt.[2]

Certainly, the often remarked difference between European High-Tech buildings and their United States counterparts can be drawn down to a contrasting approach to envelope design—the most basic form of 'bundling'. Only a few 100 metres from the new Hongkong and Shanghai Bank is a classic example of the American approach, the twin towers of the recently completed £120 million Hong Kong stock exchange by Palmer & Turner, the firm of architects responsible for the 1935 Hongkong and Shanghai Bank. This concrete framed structure encloses one million square feet of office floor area behind a sleek German curtain walling system obviating both the complicated re-entrant structural elements that visibly hold the bank together, and the 'unbundled' peripherals that surround Lloyd's. Foster's complicated shadow angles played no part here; nor did the supposedly mandatory refuge terraces, which are not present. Unfortunately, this triumph of simplicity in 'bundling' conceals a serious technological obsolescence, for the stock exchange has inadequate floor-to-floor heights with no raised floors for cabling. It does, on the other hand, have maintenance cranes that retract into housings below its roofline (so as to be typhoon-proof without having to be strong enough to be typhoon resistant); an instance of sophisticated 'bundling' absent in both buildings under consideration, and perhaps an indication of the extent to which the pursuit of the ultimate form of the twenty-first century financial services building has only just begun.

Dan Dare: an extremely small step for mankind
1986

One of the last remaining myths of Empire is the stubborn belief among otherwise intelligent English people that we invent things first, but unscrupulous foreigners take them up and develop them. Britons yet unborn will no doubt end their days believing that Fox Talbot invented photography, John Logie Baird the television set and Frank Whittle the jet engine.

It is a consoling thought with strong historical antecedents; after all, the Greeks felt like that about the Romans. When it comes to space travel, the myth is particularly poignant, for we no longer even have the prospect of being the first dozen nations to send emissaries beyond the atmosphere; Russians, Americans, Czechs, Poles, Arabs and Indians have already—or soon will beat us to it. This is terribly humiliating, especially when—at a distance of 35 years—you read: Sir Hubert Gascoigne Guest KCB, OM, OUN, DSO, DFC, born 1943. Ex-RAF controller of the interplanetary space fleet, a pioneer of space travel, he was in the crew of the first manned rocket to the moon and commanded a ship in Admiral Grosvenor's first expedition to Mars. Although long over age for active service he also accompanied the 1996 expedition to Venus. Hobbies: swimming, riding, chess. Writing a technical history of fleet organisation and structure.

But when it comes to the Americans all you read is: Pilot Captain Henry Brennan Hogan. A very efficient pilot with a hatred of red tape. Born in Houston, Texas of an Irish family. Hobbies: boxing, car racing, photography, baseball.

Terribly good at *physical* things these Americans, but not much up top. Not like Dan Dare, who was awarded the Order of the United Nations for leadership in the 1996 Venus expedition and was born in Manchester in 1967. His hobbies included cricket, fencing, riding, painting and model making.

All this stuff is from *Eagle* of course. The comic that was written by the Church of England to dupe a generation of English schoolboys into reading a comic strip version of the Bible. *Eagle* first appeared in 1950 with a weekly circulation of one million copies. It was a roaring success until 1962 and then languished dismally until it folded in 1970.

Recently, two books have been published that nostalgically chart the comic's rise and fall. First there was *The Best of Eagle* edited by Marcus Morris—the Christian who persuaded the caring parents of long ago to allow a comic other than the execrable *Children's Newspaper* into their homes.

This appeared in 1977 and was re-printed in 1982.

Now there is Alastair Crompton's *The Man Who Drew Tomorrow*, a gushing biography of Frank Hampson, the exceedingly modest creator of Dan Dare, pilot of the future. Crompton's book is devoted at inordinate length to recounting the very suburban beginnings of Britain's only convincing attempt to enter the space race. Not Admiral Grosvenor's heroic expedition to Mars, but the 1966 Venus expedition, with Dan Dare "cosmic knight errant", racing to the rescue of Rocket Ship No One trapped by the silicon mass on the fringe of the flamelands.

The Venus expedition, under Captain Hunter, involves the dispatch of the mother-ship *Ranger* to within 3,000 miles of the planet and the launch of three small spacecraft to explore its surface for food supplies that can be transported back to earth, where starvation is imminent.

Captain Hunter "tired and worried looking" returns to Earth with no news of the small craft on the same day as food riots break out in Peking and an entire company of the Egyptian army swims the English Channel (honest, it's in the issue, 29 September 1950). Meanwhile on Venus, Dan Dare and Digby have fallen into the hands of the Treens—"Boffins run wild, sir—and quite inhuman—they seem to have no emotions at all"—while Sir Hubert and Miss Peabody—as a result of an unseemly fight over the controls—have crashed into the flame belt that divides the planet in two. Hank and Pierre, in the remaining ship, have landed in what looks like a Florida resort village, occupied by Therons—"They're swell guys, all of them", says Hank.

The rest of the story concerns the escape of the entire party from the Treens, a potted history of the planet, and the revelation that warfare between Therons and the Treens 1,000s of years ago was responsible for the destruction of Atlantis. The urgently needed food supplies are eventually arranged and the danger of starvation is averted. That is how Dan gets his Order of the United Nations.

Into this, and subsequent stories, Hampson inserted his images of the future, drawn from an admixture of Frank Lloyd Wright architecture; George Adamski's deranged ideas about flying saucers; proto-Erich von Daniken space archaeology based on the early visits of extra-terrestrials to earth; and much dexterous application of Sound Barrier vintage technology to the deeply misunderstood problems of space flight.

While the architecture of the Treens and Therons could readily have included North Sea oil rigs, the Hongkong and Shanghai Bank, Lloyd's of London, and even selected bits of Milton Keynes, it seldom progresses beyond Disney World or EPCOT in its sun-drenched contemporaneity. There are visionary concepts—all the Therons eat fruit, don't smoke and have flying houses—but these are invariably let down by what seem now to be curiously anachronistic details. The Theron flying houses, for instance, look as though they were designed by Hans Scharoun and made out of concrete. Blockbusters like the Treen food bath—"30 seconds immersion will give you all the nutriment you need"—are unaccountably never applied to the mission's central purpose of solving the hunger problem on earth.

But the real weakness in Hampson's vision of the future lies in his use of it as a background to Rockfist Regan-style adventure. Necessary, perhaps, in view of the age of his readership, but destructive of any real sense of other-worldness. It is clearer now than it was in 1950 that Dan Dare's fleece-lined flying jacket and uniform are simply Battle of Britain derivatives; that the Treens are Nazis, and the food crisis on earth is a reflection of the grinding austerity of the ration-book years that preceded the arrival of *Eagle*. Quaintly, the space fleet craft are piloted from a forward-prone position, instead of the supine posture adopted by the Russians and Americans only a few years later. Nowhere is the utterly futuristic flair that the actual NASA Lunar Excursion Module, with its wrapping of metal foil and completely unstreamlined appearance, demonstrated in the Apollo missions that took place before *Eagle*'s demise.

In retrospect, it must have been the arrival of real space flight, and the palpable exclusion of Britain from it, that sped the famous comic on its way to oblivion. Admiral Grosvenor must have died of a broken heart.

Welcome to the House of Fun
1986

"The Queen's House by Inigo Jones and the Royal Observatory by Christopher Wren. That's an architectural equivalent to having Elvis Presley and The Beatles on the same bill!" enthuses the Greenwich car card on the Piccadilly Line. But what is it like to have Cedric Price on the bill?

Just past his first half century, Cedric is a hard man to interview. Delightful to talk to, yes, because that is what he wants to do—he is already waiting at his trestle table in his white room at Alfred Place when you arrive, with the coffee piping hot. But he doesn't want to be *interviewed*. "Who reads these bloody articles anyway?" he says at one tense moment. "Only people who are hungry for themselves. My idea for containing oil spills was pinched after somebody explained it too clearly in a *Guardian* article. I don't want to talk about my work. Whenever one of these articles is published somewhere it fucks me up somewhere else! Besides, I hate that magazine *Blueprint*. They published a grotesque photograph of me once, taken with a fish-eye lens. It looked like one of those remote control television pictures of the *Titanic*. I wouldn't be surprised if they don't use it again."

After a while the interview is on a knife edge. He doesn't like the tape recorder: I switch it off. He starts saying that he wants this and that off the record until I don't know what is on and what isn't. He talks animatedly about anything, except what he just started saying in answer to the question I just asked. He wants to stop the interview, I think because he thinks he can't control it without an outburst here and there. Cedric Price is not a reconstructed personality: when he is hurt it shows, and when he is upset he doesn't bother to try to make you think it is not your fault because you are not like all the others. Apart from the overwhelming temptation just to have a heartlessly amusing conversation with a man of iron nerve—which he is—it ends up not being as much fun as you might suppose.

Why does he think all the heavy-duty ideas he and others talked about in the 60s have given way to frothy Royal Fine Art Commission nonsense? "I've found that it's very interesting where, where my peers pop up." (You don't notice the stammer except on the tape.) "And then pop down again. And I think, think unless they have a propensity to deal with my ideas, then they lose their peerage."

Cedric's ideas are deadly serious when you think about them. It is a mistake to drone on about his 25 year unchanged appearance, or to damn him with faint praise for just *going on all this time* as an architect, apparently without work but with his jolly principles intact. For a start, he isn't an architect without work. How do you suppose he has stayed out of the clutches of teaching, selling framed drawings to galleries, getting into journalism or just being a kind of environmental bureaucrat like the RFAC clowns he mercilessly lampoons in *Building Design* from time to time if he has had no work? And for another start, his principles are not jolly. The Fun Palace—perhaps the most successful architectural idea of the postmodern era—is actually a ruthless bull's-eye on mindless, cultureless consumption. Perhaps he didn't actually design one himself, but his name is forever linked to the concept. All the others, Joan Littlewood, Banham, Peter Hall (no, not that one)... where are they today? Cedric is the sole survivor. Cedric is still *influential*, which is what he always has been for as long as anyone can remember.

Take housing. Remember the housing he designed as part of the Potteries Thinkbelt, and the names he gave to the different types: "Sprawl", "Capsule", "Crate", "Battery". Incredible names! Rebarbative. Nothing could be further removed from Barratts' "Premier Range", the "Balmoral", the "Cheviot" and all the other nonsense that brainless equity feeders produce for the traders up and losers out. "Yes, all those names", he remembers. "Like Fun Palace itself. Stomach-turning, sick-making names. They were intended to be remembered, to make people look again."

Cedric really knows about housing. He remembers and laughs cruelly about 'generic house plans', the last throe of the institutional profession before it was kicked out of housing altogether. "They always showed a bicycle and a space for the pram on their 'generic house plans', long after everyone stopped using a pram or a bike." Why, I ask, don't architects talk about mass housing any more? "Because the chill of obvious failure has got into their bones. It's like Northern Ireland now, one of the subjects you just don't talk about in polite society." What was the last good housing idea? He thinks for a second or two. "The 'Louisiana'. It was a house designed by an ambitious Midlands housebuilder just before the energy crisis. The plan had words on it like 'rumpus room' and 'den', all American words that the designer hadn't the faintest idea of the meaning of. It simply meant you could use the spaces for anything. That was the last good idea."

Cedric's own "Battery Houses" were supposed to be in sausages a quarter of a mile long. The "Crate" and "Capsule" houses were to stand on triangulated frames in disused quarries and up the sides of slag heaps. The whole railway university idea was a kind of Punkish deculturalised mass-education system, shorn of traditions and status, very suitable for today in fact—and he thought of it 20 years ago when everybody else was so stupid they thought it was a joke. But it wasn't funny. It wasn't even just serious. It was visionary, and he is still waiting for it to happen, deep down quite confident that it will. Somehow it all connects with the later works of the GLC and the future works of a radical Labour government. The gestation period of a good idea is 30 years—as, he reminds you, Bucky said. And Cedric bought Bucky his last meal in England before the greatest design thinker of the century went back to San Francisco to die.

People think Bucky's legacy is something like Lloyd's or the Hongkong Bank, but it isn't. Thinking about Cedric, you realise that those people never understood a word that Bucky said. For a start, they didn't know the meaning of the word patience.

Asking Cedric about his work, as a way of implying that he hasn't any, is like accusing Richard Buckminster Fuller of being a failure. I have done both and I know. "Failure is a word invented by idiots, nothing fails in nature", Bucky told me in 1970. Now Cedric refuses to talk about his work in the same way. He starts: "I have two railway stations to look at.... No forget it." The last with a touch of asperity. Then a quick canter into irrelevancies; parables about painting only one side of dockyard cranes. There is a reference to his long-running South Bank revitalisation scheme —"No you bloody well can't see it." When will it be finished? "I have no idea, but when it is I will make sure it doesn't get into the hands of the London Residuary Body without a lot of people seeing it first."

Actually, Cedric has remarkable connections: with the government of China; with the older generation of Royals; with the TUC. He says, and I believe him, that he lives entirely off fees for architectural work, whatever scurrilous rumours are put about to the contrary. He has consultancies dealing with submarine environments, industrial islands, all-purpose market stalls, fish farms. In 1978, he actually put in a planning application to Westminster City Council for Buckingham Palace, for a change of use to a youth hostel on grounds of underuse. It was refused, but the council did send him the forms so he could appeal.

This year, Cedric attacked the RIBA's fatuous City Wise conference for actually trying to stem the disintegration of cities. He believes there is a strong case for evacuation because that is what people clearly want. "Isn't it strange that while half the Cabinet exhorts people to 'get on their bikes', the other half applauds those who, having been provided with a few coats of paint and a caring policeman, stay where they are? I think it is not gullibility but laziness that gives credence to the silliness of Alice Coleman."

Cedric is right not to want to be interviewed. He should talk and you should listen. If you try to push him with questions you start to get scared.

A winter school's tale
1987

A long time ago, just before Christmas, I got a telephone call inviting me to run a project at the Plymouth Winter School. Because it is nice to be wanted; because Plymouth is only 27 miles away from where I live; and because the head of the school, Adrian Gale, once took me into a bank to draw out some money, asked the teller, "What do you have that is crisp?", received the answer, "Only 50s, Sir", and then said; "Right, I'll have one of those"—I accepted. Some days later I received a poster and an information pack from the student organisers listing the 430 other people who had been invited. But by then the die was cast.

My previous teaching experience had been limited but varied. I taught in the Diploma School at the AA in the early 70s; did a stint at the Technische Hogeschool in Eindhoven under John Habraken; did a semester at Cornell; three semesters at Rensselaer; two years at Florida A&M under Dick Chalmers, and a year at UCLA. In June 1980, I left America and left teaching—I thought forever. The Plymouth Winter School marked my first appearance in a design studio for seven years. Like many people who escape from teaching into real life, I had passed the intervening years denouncing it. In various capacities on various magazines I welcomed the Esher Report; called for the closure of at least 12 schools of architecture, and once argued that there should only be one school of architecture in the whole country—with competitive entry like Sandhurst or the old Imperial Japanese naval academy. Fortunately when I met my 11 Winter School students on Monday 19 January, they were all too young to have read any of this.

The project I had set for them was to design a house that could be self-built for the price of a car, in this case a Ford Sierra 2.0GL at £8,838 —according to *Autocar*. To avoid 'unreality' I had decided that all the materials and components to be used in the house should be obtainable from the cluster of DIY superstores that had recently opened in Plymouth, and costed at their consumer prices. In pursuit of this aim, all of us spent the first afternoon sauntering through the aisles at Bulk, Payless and Texas Homecare, gazing in wonderment at the shrink-wrapped sticks of timber and tiny bags of ballast that rubbed shoulders with bathroom suites and giant rolls of insulation. It was during this odyssey that a Japanese student got lost and subsequently became the first defector from the group.

Back in the studio my gang started designing A frames. Well, not so much designing them as *assuming* them and costing out all the timber they would need. The only students who departed from the pattern at this stage subsequently defected too. One tried to make a house out of four £800 conservatories; another photocopied several articles about Walter Segal—but unfortunately failed to get enough sleep to enable him to understand them; a third founded a new architectural movement called "The new disinterested"; and a fourth, whose father was a builder, proceeded to draw up a spec estate house and price it expertly from Spon's. This latter student did not exactly defect, indeed he was never absent from the studio during office hours, but he did no actual *designing* at all.

The A frame people were the first to discover that you could easily build a house for a material cost of £8,838—indeed, you could buy enough materials to push well over 100 square metres in floor area and have a double garage and an electrical generator as well. The trouble was that, with only one exception, they refused to move on from this discovery to the thrilling task of designing the best possible house you could get for the money. Several actually spent four-fifths of the week cleverly coming in at £8,837.99 and only the last morning drawing up very primitive and detail-free A frames.

The exception, a truly gifted designer from Newcastle, produced a kind of wooden Farnsworth House with glass walls, a Trocal roof, and marble on the floor, for which he claimed a material cost of only £80 per square metre—but he left early on Friday and besides, like everyone else except the builder's son, there were numerous provisional sums supplied by me amongst his figures.

I do not know what my inscrutable students gained from this exercise, but my own reaction was a definite "don't know". Of course, a Winter School is not the place for serious studio exercises—if indeed my 'realistic' project can be so described. Even so I detected a certain cynicism and defeatism from the beginning. "What's the point?" said one brightly on the second day. "None of this would ever get past planning anyway." In fact not much of it would have got past regs, simply because no detailing was ever explored. As a lad I always enjoyed detailing, but the current generation of students clearly don't.

What they do enjoy is exploring the structural potential of eggs with Sam Webb and building "Medieval machines of destruction" with John Thornton. As a teacher would say, there is a lesson in all this.

Objects of our time:
the Piccadilly Line train
1987

"You'll feel the pressure wave coming down to Barons Court", advised the driver as he winds the cab ventilator shut. Sure enough you do, and it is more violent than you expect. There is nowhere to sit and only one grab rail to hold on to. At 45 mph the feeling is like hitting the water from the side of the pool.

Once inside the narrow tunnel all consciousness of the train behind disappears. The tunnel is pitch black and coated with 50 years of brake dust; the headlights on the front of the lurching Driving Motor (DM) car seem hardly to penetrate the gloom until your eyes adjust. When they do, the large wrap-around windscreens make the sensation more like a video game than a train ride, with the cab deftly twisting and turning, rising and falling, in response to the changes in direction of the tunnel. "The driver's reflexes must be like a racing driver's", you think, and then you remember that the rails do the steering. All the driver does is hold the deadman's handle down and remember where he is. Even so, riding the cab in a Piccadilly Line train is light years away from riding in one of the cars.

Like a car, a tube train measures its life in cycles of acceleration and braking. 1973 Tube Stock, so called because 1973 was its intended year of introduction, is the fastest on the London Underground network, with its short, aluminium-finish trains taking only 90 minutes to run the 40 miles from Cockfosters to Heathrow. But unlike cars, which can apply almost 90 per cent of the force of gravity for acceleration or braking because of their high rubber-to-road adhesion, even the fastest train can only use 13 per cent because of the frictional limitations of steel-on-steel wheel and rail contact. For this reason, the power transmission and braking systems on underground trains are far more elaborate than those found on most motor vehicles.

No less than 32 of a 1973 Tube Stock's 48 wheels are driven, and all are braked by one or more of three onboard systems. The 16 88 bhp electric motors, with their fixed-gear drive, could accelerate the train's 147 tonne self-weight and 76 tonnes of passengers from 0 to 60 mph in 14 seconds —if the power they deliver to the wheels was not governed to stop the standing passengers being flung to the rear like skittles.

On the braking side, the two primary systems (in addition to the hydraulic handbrake) work together under the same automatic load control. Between

20 and 50 mph the train relies on rheostatic braking, a system that uses the momentum of the train itself to drive the motors as electrical generators and dumps the awesome 800 kw of power produced into huge fan-cooled resistance grids under the motor cars. Above 50 mph, 'rheo braking' would produce too much heat for the fans to control: below 20 mph the second system—45 psi compressed air actuated friction braking—drives composition blocks hard against the wheels to bring the train to a complete stop. As originally designed, both braking systems worked through an automatic anti-lock device that prevented any pair of wheels from skidding and was introduced ten years before anti-lock braking systems became common on cars. Even more sophisticated are the sleet brushes and de-icing sprays fitted to the DM and some trailer cars—something that road vehicles have yet to see.

These ingenious features, commonplace or even superseded on later rolling stock, are the tip of an iceberg of engineering that made 1973 Tube Stock—like 1938 Tube Stock before it—a breakthrough in the design of underground railways. Designed by a team led by chief mechanical engineer (railways) William Graff-Baker, 1938 Tube Stock was the first to bury all its mechanical equipment beneath the floor of the car so as to consume no usable passenger space. After several intermediate developments, 1973 Tube Stock, which was designed between 1967 and 1970 by a team led by chief mechanical engineer, the late Alan 'Joe' Manser, consolidated various subsequent advances including aluminium coachwork that was first experimented with in 1956, into the next great leap forward. The detailed engineering design and body styling of the new stock was carried out by the London Underground design office headed by chief draughtsman Stanley Driver, who has since retired.

Intended from the outset to operate only on the Piccadilly Line, the new stock was designed specifically for the link to Heathrow airport which was opened in 1977. To accommodate the new airline traffic, the trains were to be equipped with baggage space in every car in the shape of extra wide doorway standbacks. But more importantly they were the first tube trains ever designed according to a life-cycle costed specification, with a planned operational life of 35 years ending in the year 2008, during which time their maintenance and repair requirements were to be minimal. Understressed, proven components, pain-free finishes and a unique built-in electronic train fault indicator were designed to enable the new stock to extend the major service interval for Piccadilly Line trains from five to nine years, and the depot inspection interval from six to 18 weeks.

At the time of its introduction, not the least of the distinctions of 1973 Tube Stock was that it was the most expensive stock ever ordered, at over £12 million for each of 87 trains. Today there are more 1973 Piccadilly Line trains on the London Underground network than any other type.

The overall size of all tube stock is controlled by the diameter of the tunnels and the tightness of the bends that link their straight sections. Opened originally by David Lloyd George in 1906 as the Great Northern, Piccadilly and Brompton Railway, with a total length of only nine miles, what was to become the central section of the Piccadilly Line was less constricting than some earlier underground railways in the metropolis, but still consisted partly of narrow 3.6 metre tunnels, sharply curved to follow the line of the streets above. 60 years later these unchanging dimensions, coupled with those of the original 106 metre platforms, created the gauge within which the cars of the new Heathrow trains, including their permitted suspension movement, had to fit. The design called for a nominal clearance of 76 mm all round, but London Underground personnel today concede that the rivet heads on the roofs of the cars are occasionally 'polished' by contact with unwanted projections in the tunnel.

The first and most obvious effect of the gauge on the design of the trains was on the length of the cars themselves, and finally the length of the whole train. In the case of 1973 Tube Stock a car length of 17.8 metres was finally arrived at—1.8 metres longer than any of the cars used elsewhere on the tube network—but the trains themselves were shortened from seven to six cars giving an overall length of 107 metres, some six metres shorter than their predecessors. Each car is tapered over the last metre of its length, where the end door is situated, in order to accommodate the tight track curves. In plan the taper is achieved by an elegant 'lost' rebate detail that also accommodates the termination of the hollow sections of the car side wall which form the door retraction recesses.

In order to achieve the maximum headroom above the 770 mm separating the maple-wood floor from the top of the rails, the designers allowed the tops of the wheels to project 100 mm into each car, concealed by the longitudinal seating. But a consequence of this ingenuity was the impossibility of placing the door openings in their most structurally logical place, above the bogies. To complicate matters even further, the door system itself was very advanced, with innovative, top-hung doors with extra wide vestibules (part of the Heathrow specification); selective closing to reduce heat loss during winter waits at surface stations, and a compressed air rapid open and close actuating system (1.4 seconds to close, instead of four seconds on older stock) that needed a complete double car wall with unsealed double glazing to accommodate full retraction. Furthermore, the double door openings cut deep into either side of the compression section of the car roof, leaving very little to maintain stiffness.

As a result, the proposed semi-monocoque structure—finally to be introduced with 1986 Tube Stock—was limited to the riveted aluminium car structure above the floorline, with a steel underframe below the floor of each car. Even so the lightness of the resulting assembly, which incorporates loadbearing angled grab poles to maintain the rigidity of the aluminium car above the underframe, still permits some deflection under fully loaded conditions, a phenomenon which is occasionally visible at the doorline.

1973 Tube Stock has another distinction apart from its advanced engineering. Notwithstanding design parameters as rigorous in their way as those applied to 12 metre yachts and jet airliners—and an operating environment only a little less punishing—the Piccadilly Line train is a tremendous and timeless styling success. The full beauty of the design can best be seen on the long surface run to Heathrow, where the trains touch 60 mph and their big automobile-style wrap-around windscreens, long cars, low tunnel-fitting profile and natural aluminium finish still lend them the electric excitement of a secret prototype—a decade after the line was opened. It is a quality never attained by any of the less numerous tunnel models, and certainly not by the various types of surface stock, whose cars are one metre taller.

Earlier tube stock featured clumsy hopper ventilation windows, projecting window-head rainwater drips, recessed front driver doors, truncated ventilator slots, thick door retraction reveals, or some other stylistic imperfection. All later models, despite their technical advances, are marred by essentially postmodern features, like smaller windscreens made of missile-proof glass, externally fitted doors, or the return of exterior painted finishes to fight off the threat of steadily increasing graffiti.

While 1973 Tube Stock arguably represents the highest achievement of functional modern design in the underground, its perfection is not the unalloyed result of rational technology. Indeed, if that were the sole criterion it would be difficult to fault the claim of 1960 Tube Stock (the first to be adapted for automatic train operation, ATO), or the new 1986 Tube Stock with its continuously welded aluminium monocoque construction. The true design merit of 1973 Tube Stock resides in the tiny acts of artifice that accompany its first class engineering, enabling that which is already simplified to appear to be even simpler than it is. For an architect, this quality of apparent simplicity inevitably suggests the ethos of Mies van der Rohe, of whose famous cryptic utterance, "Simplicity is not simple", perfectly sums up the labour of its achievement.

In the case of 1973 Tube Stock the most subtle example of enhanced simplicity is the 'lost' reveal that accommodates the decreased width of the ends of the cars. Another, even more crucial to the appearance of the whole train, is the dummy ventilator extension above the car windows. On the two preceding tube stock designs—the Victoria Line's 1967 ATO trains, and the Northern Line's 1972 Marks One and Two—the ventilator slit above the car windows stops short at the commencement of the door retraction reveal.

On 1973 Stock, not only does the double wall of the car and the redesigned door retraction mechanism remove the need for an internal reveal, but the black slit of the ventilator on the outside is carried across the retracted door position in the form of a black-painted recess in the aluminium outer skin. The result is a visual logic that enhances the engineering and operating logic of the cars themselves. It may pass unnoticed by the million people a day who travel on the Piccadilly Line, but once you become aware of it you can never fail to appreciate the subtlety of the design of underground trains again.

Tower blocks and tourist castles
1987

"The medium of one age becomes the message of its successor", said Marshall McLuhan in a long forgotten issue of *Playboy* magazine. An opaque statement, but one that is called to mind by a recent visit to Germany and the revelation that the state of Bavaria earns no less than 20 million Deutschmarks a year in tourist revenues from visitors to the three spectacular castles built by King Ludwig II before he was declared insane. Of course, an even greater figure could probably be calculated as the earning capacity of Shakespeare's long-expired copyright. But Mad Ludwig is different, not only was his contribution much more recent, but it was financed by bank loans raised on the international money market in the same way as some big spending local authorities in England do today. Between 1874 and 1886 the Wittelsbach monarch borrowed 21 million marks (approximately £60 million at present day values) to finance the construction of the famous castles of Linderhof, Neuschwanstein and Herrenchiemsee. Since then, all three structures have travelled full circle, from notoriety as examples of certifiable royal profligacy, to the status of key elements in the emerging post-industrial Bavarian economy of tourism. Today they earn as much every three years as they cost to build—a performance most developers would regard as something akin to a licence to print money, and a return on investment that must put those other Bavarian enterprises BMW and Mercedes Benz to shame.

In this sense, whatever he thought he was doing at the time, Ludwig turned out to be a theme-park pioneer: a title irrevocably bestowed by Walt Disney when he copied the design for Neuschwanstein for the centrepiece of the Magic Kingdom at Disney World. Ludwig's medium, the construction of castles, became the message that 100 years later draws tourists down the romantic road from Würzburg to the foothills of the Alps.

Compared to writing plays and building single-bedroom castles, planned construction in the modern manner looks destined to make a poor showing in the eyes of history—except perhaps by accident. Clearly, if Ludwig II had been working in Bavaria in 1974 instead of 1874 he might not have been certified, but he would certainly have been prevented from building much sooner than he was. And where would tourism be then?

The logical conclusion of this train of thought is West Berlin, a spectacular case not only because this year represents the culmination of IBA, the city's International Building Exhibition, but because planning held sway there from *Jahr null*, as the Germans truthfully describe 1945, to the present. The result of planning in Berlin has been vast tracts of levelled bomb sites in the centre—held clear in the hope of eventual reunification —and the profligate consumption of the small amount of peripheral green space inside the wall by such monsters as the 18,000 apartment Gropiusstadt and the 17,000 apartment Märkische Viertel. Today, the conventional wisdom is to regard these and other Berlin high-rise housing settlements as the products of a delinquent episode best forgotten, because attention has swung back to repopulating the centre with a patchwork of mini tours de force by architects from all over the world. Indeed, if some Berlin planners had their way, even ten year old structures like René Gage's 900 metre long, eighteen-storey slab block, locally known as the *Langenjammer* (long misery), would be demolished forthwith and replaced by postmodern maisonettes à la Rob Krier or Matthias Ungers.

This, in my view, would be a mistake. It might seem bizarre to compare the *Langenjammer* with the fairytale Neuschwanstein, but in fact both represent extremes of architecture capable of arousing public curiosity to a far greater extent than any modest collection of IBA villas. Even if they were a planning failure, the towers of the Märkische Viertel, built to house 40,000 persons far from the nearest tube or S-Bahn station on the perimeter of a city within a city, are in fact as bizarre and expensive an experiment as Mad Ludwig's castles and, if they are there in 100 years time, they will be recognised as such by the descendants of the tourists who congregate today around the undistinguished coffee bars and souvenir shops of Checkpoint Charlie. Planners should remember that, even if planning no longer works, history still does. It is the medium that has become the message of the post-industrial economy—and history didn't end in 1914.

Piano and Rogers, Centre Georges Pompidou, Paris, France, 1971–1977

Ford Capri with external 'plumbing', 1986

Technology transfer

1987

Whenever the principles of architecture become unclear, the rudder
of history is moved until they can be understood again. In periods of
uncertainty these movements often describe a circle, as they are doing
today, until the past once again falls into place. That is what happened
when the theorists of the ancient world convinced themselves that Classical
architecture was the progressive refinement of prehistoric construction;
when the theorists of the Renaissance claimed the rediscovery of the
Classical past; and when the Gothic revivalists of the nineteenth century
claimed the patrimony of the Dark Ages. More recently, in a gyration
apparently so drastic as to have no remembered precedent, it happened
when the Modernists of the twentieth century claimed—like mutineers
—that science, technology and socialism had entirely changed the cosmos
so that the whole of architectural history could be compressed into a single
category called the past, and cast adrift in an open boat.[1]

The architects of the generation of 1914, the monocled mutineers
who lived through the invention of the automobile and aeroplane, were
the first to embrace science and technology as a substitute for their
accumulated cultural legacy, bringing these matters into the mainstream
of architectural thought for the first time. They took this step as artists,
licensed to find inspiration where they chose, but they soon found that
immersion in science and technology threatened their old identity. Before
they died, the mutineers came to realise that their art had been summoned
by the machine, and not the other way around. As the twentieth century
progressed, advances in materials engineering, environmental controls
and information technology meant that buildings served up as homage
to the industry of 1914 were soon as hopelessly obsolete as their Victorian
predecessors. Peter and Alison Smithson might naïvely write in the report
that accompanied their 1951 Coventry Cathedral competition design:
"Modern architecture has at its disposal means of expression which
would have sent Brunelleschi wild with joy"—but more insightfully
Maxwell Fry had written seven years earlier: "If the developments that
had led to our present technical skill were to continue at the same pace
into this century, at a pace that is exceeding our capacity as artists to
assimilate them, then our hopes of establishing a workable architecture
would be slight."[2]

Seizing upon the means of expression that would have sent Brunelleschi wild, and yet at the same time assimilating them as artists, proved to be impossible. The logic of their position urged the mutineer architects to make another quantum forward leap, and then another, and another, until a breathless race to keep up with the materials and methods of science and industry became the identity of architecture itself. But chiefly because they chose to remain a collection of individual artists instead of becoming an industry, the architects of the generation of 1914 never did initiate an architecture of continuous technological revolution.[3] Instead, the mutineers fell out, and in what can now be seen as something like the restoration of a monarchy, a large part of their number reverted to the concept of a building technology chained to the limitations of artistic assimilation.

As a result we live today in an age of Restoration architecture, a period populated by frightened practitioners who, in Charles Jencks' felicitous phrase, know just how far too far they can go; and theorists who believe that their task is to heal the gigantic breach caused by the Modern mutiny. Where once the break with tradition was seen as thrilling and final, now creeping tendrils of sentiment are encouraged to grow over it, concealing it from view like a crack in a wall. Long-lived practitioners, veterans of the exciting days of the mutiny, now face career prospects like those of French army officers after the defeat of Napoleon. Venerable surviving Modernists are urged, as by priests at their deathbed, to give their blessing to the Restoration—the triumph of the voyage in the open boat.[4] Who can blame them when they consent? "No memory of having starred atones for later disregard" wrote Robert Frost. In return for denying their golden dawn they receive a moment of brief media attention and the fickle adulation of young architects. And if they refuse? Edmund Burke truly wrote of those who find themselves at odds with the fashion of the times in which they live: "They seem deserted by mankind, overpowered by a conspiracy of their whole species."

The great weakness of Restoration architecture is its lack of ideology. It has no unifying theory—"a supposition explaining something, based on principles independent of the phenomenon to be explained"—as the *Concise Oxford Dictionary* puts it. This is despite a veritable explosion of writing about architecture that has taken place since the collapse of consensus support for modern design some 15 years ago, much of it glorying in the present state of wild opportunism.

A few short years of creeping incorporation and stylistic anarchy has been enough to sink the once clinically lucid language of modern architecture to the level of banality of the fashion page.[5] Fuelled by the unromantic threat of insurance claims; incorporation with shareholders' control; the growth of circumscribed 'design consultancy' work; the consumerisation of minor works, and the migration of so much architectural terminology that the word architecture may be found under 'computer' in the dictionaries of the twenty-first century, a terminal demystification of the profession seems entirely possible. Perhaps the darkest portent of all is the fact that it is now widely believed that there is no longer any need for expert judgement where the design of buildings is concerned. "I know that what I feel in spirit about a building is just as valid a criticism as any professional or technical point of view", the Prince of Wales wrote to Peter Palumbo at the height of the battle for Mansion House Square. And in this, as in so many other matters, there is no reason to suppose that his opinion differs greatly from those of his future subjects.

Restoration architecture combines a superficial glorification of variety and ornament with a concealed convergence of identity between buildings that can be compared to the process of homogenisation that began in the motor industry 20 years ago. With or without regard to the pace at which 'artists' can assimilate it, global product distribution is overwhelming the construction industry, and with it the architectural profession. Just as today the removal of the badge from the nose or tail of a car can reveal its shared parentage with a different make, so can the peeling away of a decorated facade reveal the homogenisation of serviced floor space beneath the skin.

Restoration architects have conceded creative hegemony everywhere except in this 'badge engineering' of buildings, the so-called 'signature building' of American architecture. Carbon-copy engineering—in terms of the names of the consultants responsible as well as the structural and environmental control systems used—is now accepted as the norm. From penetrating deep into the genesis of the building, as it did during the modern mutiny, the power of the architect over construction has shrunk to the literally superficial: a thin skin on the front of a new building, like the badge on the nose of a car; a small feature on the outside of a refurbished building; a bureaucratic role in the filing of applications and the authorisation of payments. An architect's 'capacity as an artist', still offers him this role, but today only inertia saves him from the modified cry of the small boy: "The Emperor is as expendable as a light bulb."

Compared to the great days of the mutiny, when heads of state appealed to architects to replan capital cities, design satellite towns and solve the global housing problem, the role of the architect is tragically diminished. In engineering terms he is hardly a designer at all, his work oscillating uneasily between envelopment by a burgeoning design profession and surrender to the reactionary forces of conservation and historicism. For him there is no future apart from button-down slavery as a corporate executive,
or the thankless task of acting unpaid advisor to community enterprise.

No future, that is, unless something that research scientists call a reordering of the data takes place. For in architecture as well as politics the quickest and most effective way of overcoming humiliation and loss of power is a revised perception of the events that brought it about.

Technology transfer is a term that is used in different ways, but a generally agreed definition might be any process whereby the techniques and materials developed in one field or industry are applied to other fields and industries. A process with a vast unwritten history, technology transfer either results from serendipitous curiosity on the part of individuals, or from a serious marketing effort by corporations intent on developing new outlets for materials or techniques. Modern examples of the second category in building include the use of insulation material as roofing, various spin-offs from aerospace research—like the Teflon coatings and flat wiring now used in a vast range of product applications—and the use of motor industry-developed cold rolled steel structural members for lightweight construction. Perhaps the neatest illustration of the first category comes from one tiny but crucial component in the elaborate NASA unmanned Mars landing programme, where the problem of designing a simple lightweight soil-sampling scoop was brilliantly solved by the adaptation of a coiled steel carpenter's rule, whose dished, semi-rigid extending arm provided the model for the light, retractable scoop that was eventually used.[6]

Few architectural historians have concerned themselves with the role of technology transfer in architectural design, even though its implications can be of the first importance. In fact the only critical assessment of the phenomenon in recent years occurs in Reyner Banham's *Theory and Design in the First Machine Age*, which was first published in the heyday of the Modern mutiny in 1961.[7] While Banham himself takes the view that architecture and technology may have different evolutionary patterns, so that he stands aside from the suggestion that the collapse of Modernism resulted from its failure to keep pace with technology, he alone among historians writing at the time foresaw that collapse. In *Theory and Design* he drew attention to the already worrying obsolescence of the 'new technologies' annexed by Modern architecture from nineteenth century engineering, and identified this area as the one in which its greatest weakness lay.

In the final chapter of *Theory and Design*, he quotes from Richard Buckminster Fuller's 1938 book *Nine Chains to the Moon*, to show that the failure of Modern architects to grasp the *endlessness* of technological evolution had sowed the seeds of their decline as early as 1927, when Fuller's revolutionary light metal, air-deliverable Dymaxion House adumbrated the frame-hung component structures that were to dominate most other fields of engineering design within 20 years. "The International Style brought to America by the Bauhaus", wrote Fuller in 1938, "demonstrated fashion-inoculation without the necessary knowledge of the scientific fundamentals of structural mechanics and chemistry."[8] Or as Banham interpretatively puts it, Modern architecture "produced machine-age architecture only in the sense that its monuments were built in a machine age, and expressed an attitude to machinery—in the sense that one might stand on French soil and discuss French politics, and still be speaking English".

As we now know from developments in related fields, the next step in advanced construction technology after glass, steel and concrete should have been light-frame and monocoque enclosures using the laminated wood, aluminium alloys and plastics developed during the Second World War, ("Enter alloy—exist rust" as Fuller put it in 1949).[9] But whether a handful of avant-garde architects could have dragged the construction industry into a pattern of continuous technological evolution at that time, even with the help of the massive development of light engineering that the war brought about, must remain an open question. Light-frame and monocoque enclosures flowered briefly in the post-war emergency schools and housing programmes, but in the 50 years from Fuller's Dymaxion House to the end of the collapse of the Modern Movement, only a small number of architects published or carried out work based on this method.

Mindful of Fry's wartime dictum, it is tempting to say that failure to keep up with science was the price Modern architecture paid for artistic integrity. Banham is more cautious in suggesting that "What we have hitherto understood as architecture, and what we are beginning to understand of technology may be incompatible disciplines." But either way the fact remains that one generation—however much it may have misunderstood what it was doing—seized the initiative in technology transfer, and the next let it slip away. For the generation of Le Corbusier, Walter Gropius, Mies van der Rohe and Richard Neutra—steel, glass and concrete were revolutionary new materials that cried out to be used in buildings as different from their brick, stone and timber predecessors as a motor car was different from a horse-drawn wagon. With varying degrees of single-mindedness they spent their lives developing new ways to build using these same materials. But when it transpired that steel, glass and concrete were merely the forerunners of high-strength alloys and composites grown from a science and technology leaping daily further ahead, the ingenuity of their followers was overwhelmed.

Tragically, it was assumed by the politicians who elevated modern architecture to global supremacy in the 30 years after 1945 that architects held technological mastery in their hands like an Olympic torch that could be passed on from generation to generation. Seldom can faith in expertise have been more naïvely placed. Not only did the generation of 1914 misunderstand the process of technology transfer, as Banham suggests, but the majority of them did not even think it was a matter of much importance. Taking the permanent architecture of antiquity as their model, the Modern masters expected, rightly, that it might take a century to learn to build properly with concrete and steel. They did not expect, within their lifetimes, to be called upon to explore construction using synthetic materials like nylon, carbon fibre, Kevlar, mylar, nomex, or Teflon; or to have to contend with a massive explosion of information technology within buildings, let alone electronic intelligence itself. Only a very few, like Maxwell Fry, even understood how difficult such a task might be.

For a complex of reasons, Modern architecture tried to ignore the demands of technological assimilation in an age of science. Like surgeons operating without anaesthetic in a modern teaching hospital, the architects of the great mutiny became dangerously obsolete in their own environment. Towards the end of their lives this became evident in their work, just as Fuller had predicted. Despite the spectacular output of synthetic materials and new structural technologies that marked the post-war period, their palette remained limited, as did that of their immediate successors. In spite of the spirited defence of their design studio methodology that is still occasionally advanced, notably by Schon, who still speaks of architects "knowing how to act correctly in conditions of information overflow", it was precisely because the sons of the pioneers concentrated on formal inventiveness rather than exploring the process of technology transfer that had given them their new ways to build, that modern architecture died of ignorance while new information was exploding all around it.[10]

The idea that the collapse of Modern architecture was an information failure throws new light on the nature of the great mutiny. Seen as the result of a temporary coincidence of science and building, the equally temporary success of the Moderns assumes less mythological proportions. What Howard Roark, the composite modern architect hero of the first half of the century, really did was not so much triumph over critics and philistines to bring a new enlightenment, as specify new products and enlarge the market for new materials. Indeed, the financial and political support without which he could never have displaced the entrenched forces of traditional construction, came precisely from these materials producers. Two World Wars created massive production capacity in the cement and concrete industry—likewise steel, light metals, plywood, plastics and synthetic fibres; Modern architects created an outlet for them in the civilian economy by rendering their use culturally acceptable in building. That at any rate was the irreversible effect of their work, however far removed it may be from Ayn Rand's conception of their existential struggle.[11] With the hindsight of 40 years it is possible to re-order the data of the Modern era so as to see the careers of its great individualists simply as the dramatic, populist elements in an essentially undramatic process—the adaptation of industrial and engineering materials and methods to the design of commercial, cultural and domestic buildings.

What we know about the techniques employed by the most successful of the Modern pioneers is entirely consistent with this view. We know that they literally copied the design and construction of grain silos; stripped the masonry cladding from structural steelwork and put in glass instead; and borrowed from the 'look' of the design of ships and aeroplanes to create "a new aesthetic".[12] All these processes involved artistic controversy and public debate but their cultural significance was far less than their economic consequence. In essence they were a resource-shift in building technology, part of the historic process of technology transfer whose aesthetic effects have always been better documented than its substance. While sudden and traumatic, the Modern episode can still be shown to take its place in a long line of technology transfers in building whose very antiquity throws doubt on the idea that architecture and technology are incompatible. For if they are, is it not strange that their encounters against the vast backdrop of history have been so frequent and so one-sided in their results?

Architectural culture is a vast shock absorber against change; like the boom on a gybing yacht it comes over last and it comes over hard, but the driving force, the sail itself, has already taken up its new position by the time the swing occurs.

Perhaps the conversion of timber-frame construction into stone decoration in the ancient world was attended by dramas to match the frustrations endured by Modern architects in the 1920s and 1930s, when their work was as fanatically opposed as is the demolition of historic buildings today. Perhaps the use of lightweight earthenware pots in the construction of the dome of S Vitale of Ravenna over 1,500 years ago had to be fought through the Medieval equivalent of a series of public inquiries. More plausibly the outrage caused by the generation of 1914 came from the pent-up surge of innovation that it directed into building. After the mainsail of industrial production had already swung over on to a new tack, the boom of avant-garde architecture finally smashed the head of academic revivalism—making it possible (as it were) to turn the entire technological legacy of the nineteenth century into architecture in an afternoon. The whole process was an architectural transplant of the great nineteenth century engineering boom in which iron shipbuilding took to the land. Camouflaged as an artistic revolution, the Modern Movement in architecture did no more than break free from the technical suppression of nineteenth century revivalism and restore building construction to its correct relationship with the new production industries. In this sense the 'mutiny' was a sudden change in the 'genetic frequency' of technology transfer in building.

Seen in this way, as a largely unrecognised logistical process, the history of technology transfer in architecture assumes a new importance. But so too do the difficulties that must be overcome in any attempt to bring it, undisguised, to the forefront of design. For not only must the trappings of 'artistic assimilation' be abandoned, but even the idea that the process of building design is 'creative' in the fine art, as opposed to the engineering sense.

As the failure of the Archigram group proves, problems of credibility dog all attempts to separate architecture from permanence. Between 1961 and 1967, this loose alliance of five principal partners produced a dazzling array of projects based on contemporary technology transfer, freely drawing on the materials and methods of the Apollo programme. Ultimately none of it came to fruition except in the contest of the market for architectural drawings, where the original designs were subsequently sold. Comparable in their predictive authority with the 1914 drawings of Sant'Elia and Chiattone, these projects for an indeterminate, intermediate architecture of lightweight mobile enclosure connected with the briefly flowering youth movement of the late 1960s, but failed to enlist the kind of industrial marketing support that once underpinned concrete construction or the idea of prefabrication. With the collapse of the youth movement and the growth of a reactionary investment market in housing after the energy crisis of 1973, the group abandoned its search for real clients to concentrate exclusively on the art market.

The lesson of Archigram's failure to attract investment was that technology transfer, even when based on a considerable knowledge of the products of advanced technology, cannot succeed without the support of an industrial base. In the 1960s, the nascent aerospace industry itself survived on public funding and lacked anything that might be described as surplus production capacity. What Archigram tried to do was to swing the cultural boom over, against the wind of construction investment. In doing so, it found itself opposed by the full force of the heavyweight permanent construction industry and its attendant architectural value system.

The contrast between Archigram's lightweight, transitional architecture and the heavyweight, High-Tech, late modern architecture of, say, Norman Foster or Richard Rogers is instructive. Conceived ten years later than the best-known Archigram projects, Richard Rogers' Lloyd's building, for example, was designed as a permanent, flexibly serviced enclosure which promised a 50 year capability to withstand developments in information technology—an absurd claim as events since its opening in 1986 have already shown.[13] But a truer diagnosis, that only radical flexibility could cope with the space needs of the mushrooming financial services industry, would have produced no £150 million masterpiece. Without a driving mainsail—like the resources of the cement and concrete industry—the case was hopeless. Archigram offered temporary, flexible enclosure and failed: Rogers offered flexible servicing for a heavy concrete-frame structure squarely in a tradition of permanence, and succeeded.

The obstacle presented by permanence is as great ten years after the design of the Lloyd's building as it was ten years before it but the means to overcome it remain the same. Buckminster Fuller was the first to grasp that weight was not irrelevant to building, but ultimately controlled its cost. He saw that true flexibility or continuous replacement could supplant the concept of permanence, but only with the support of industries with surplus production capacity. Thus it had been with the evolution of machine production under the impact of continual technological innovation, and thus it would be *mutatis mutandis* with architecture. What was needed to establish an architecture of technology transfer was neither more nor less than a real time engineering value base. Unlike the 'historic' contribution of permanent architecture, the architecture of the future must be in continual transition. To make itself financially viable it must draw its value from its performance, which in turn must be as exactly measurable as that of a car or an aeroplane, and be calculated like any other engineering system.

Architects who successfully use technology transfer against the background of a Restoration culture do so by compromise with the fine art tradition of permanence. Norman Foster is well known for his ingenious use of components and materials that have their origin in industries far removed from construction: solvent-welded PVC roofing derived originally from swimming-pool liners; flexible neoprene gaskets using a material developed originally for cable-jacketing; adhesive-fixed glazing transferred from the automobile industry; superplastic aluminium panels and metalised fabric fireproofing from aerospace; tensioning devices from trailer sidescreens; raised-floor systems from jetliners; photochromic glazing from jet bombers. All these and more, including techniques of presentation and colour schemes drawn from aviation magazines, are to be found in his projects and his buildings. But Norman Foster will not agree that his work is a more or less organised search for technology that can be transferred. In his view there is a conflict between this 'redneck' definition of design and the prior claims of the fine art tradition and the role of engineering. As Peter Rice has commented: "High-Tech architects have concluded that the discipline provided by the engineer is the best framework in which to conduct architecture." Or, as Michael Hopkins puts it: "Our architecture comes out of our engineering and our engineering comes out of our engineers." Perhaps underlying this faith in engineering is a doubt that technology transfer can stand on its own as a creative process; a reciprocal of the doubt expressed by some critics that the construction of 108 concept models for a major commission (Foster's abandoned BBC Radio Centre at Langham Place) is either intellectual or creative in the traditional fine art sense.[14]

To find total acceptance of the priority of technology transfer in architecture today it is necessary to study the work of a former Foster associate Richard Horden, the designer of the purest technology-transfer building yet constructed in Britain. Horden's 1984 Yacht House in Hampshire embodies the principles of technology transfer that have been sporadically applied by Norman Foster, but concentrated into the generating structural frame of a small domestic building. Horden finds his materials and methods in the high-performance components produced by the yacht spar and standing rigging industry. His unique structure, intended to form the basis of an omni-functional enclosure system, shows not only that architectural design developed from the central principle of multi-sourced industrial component combination is feasible, but that its results can still be culturally acceptable within a fine art design tradition. With it, Horden has gone further than any living architect to show that a true architecture of technology transfer need neither be impoverished nor primitive.

Like Horden, the London and Los Angeles practice of Future Systems Inc, with its two partners Jan Kaplicky and David Nixon, has striven for nearly ten years to develop an architecture of technology transfer. Future Systems has as yet no completed building to mark the achievement of commercial viability, but it does have the distinction of being the only British firm of architects involved in the design of the 1992 NASA manned space station. Future Systems projects, like the seminal projects of Archigram, lean clearly on technology transplanted from aerospace design, but they reach further into the emulation of organic structures and the inclusion of flexibility in the form of articulated movement.

Recently, the deliberate presentation of their advanced structural system projects in the context of conventional Restoration architectural competitions—such as the 1985 Grand Buildings contest for Trafalgar Square, which Horden also entered—has begun to enable them to quantify the benefits of monocoque construction in commercial terms. Exoskeletal construction enabled their Grand Buildings entry to achieve a far higher net-to-gross ratio of serviced floor space than any other competitor, as well as providing a capacity for rapid internal reconfiguration to deal with information technology changes that would put both Lloyd's and the Hongkong and Shanghai Bank to shame.[15]

Today it is only such acts of stealth as Foster's carefully metred inclusions of alien technology within a fine art dominated culture, Future Systems' competition entries, and Horden's unique house design, that the architecture of technology transfer remains visible under the obsolete heritage value system that has ruled architecture since the Restoration. In reality, because it is a theory of architecture as economic, multi-sourced element combination, it belongs to a different and more appropriate value system alongside production engineering, automobile, marine and aerospace design. Eventually, Horden believes, the entire spectrum of manufactured components, from the smallest rigging screw to the largest offshore oil-rig assembly, will become a hunting ground for transferable technology. He tends to draw elements for his designs from the smaller end of the component size continuum, but sees the vast—as yet uncompiled —database of all products as the proper area of search for the architect of the future.

None of this can be done without the construction of a bridge from the rotting hulk of contemporary Restoration architecture to this new conception of building as the product of cross-industry component and material combination. At present such a bridge can only be built upon the ability of architects like Foster, Horden, Kaplicky and Nixon to make its results culturally acceptable. But by itself this ability is not enough. It needs the support of expanding industries and, most important of all, an ideological certainty equal to that which enabled the Modern Movement to temporarily overcome obsolete heritage values.

To begin the process of developing an ideology for this new architecture the best starting point would be a substantial study of its history. Such a document could become the first reference work of the architecture of the information age; a technological and methodological—rather than an art historical—study of technology transfer in architecture. A partial model is to be found in Marian Bowley's 1960 *Innovations in Building Materials*, the last authoritative study of technology transfer in construction.[16] But this volume has, characteristically, little reference to the actual or possible role of architects. Unlike the historians of construction, architectural historians (with the exception of Banham) have only recognised technology transfer as a peripheral matter, remarked in such ancient events as the conversion of the form of decorated tree trunks into stone columns, or the transfer of plant-derived decoration into carving. No-one, Banham included, has ever treated it as a unitary phenomenon, a continuous process whose evolution can be traced through centuries of craft-construction until, with the coming of the Industrial Revolution, it begins to accelerate out of control.

It is one of the many serious consequences of the crucial cultural gap that has separated historians and theorists of architecture from the reality of practice, that no such architectural history on the model of Bowley's has ever been written. Even though a pattern of well-documented examples shows this quickening wave-motion with the clarity of an evolutionary diagram.

The adaptation of wooden boat building into roof construction in the Middle Ages, for example, took place over hundreds of years: the development of reinforced-concrete boat construction into reinforced-concrete building took 50 years; but the adaptation of offshore oil-rig technology to building types in the present century was achieved in less than a decade.[17] The process is clearly identical and clearly important; only the wave frequency of the transfer has speeded up.

There is a clear relationship between the absence of this crucial field of study and the present predicament of technology transfer in the age of Restoration architecture. Without it the delusions of significance that still append to the obsolete categorisation of architecture by style instead of content cannot be swept away, and the progressive marginalisation of architecture will continue.

Compared to the trivial works of style-history that presently crowd out genuine theory in the body of architectural knowledge, a serious analysis of technology transfer in buildings would have the immediate authority of a stock-market analysis coupled with the direct applicability of a consumer report. It would unravel mysteries and explode myths with the clarity and force of the early writings of Adolf Loos or Le Corbusier. From the outset it would provide a quantifiable base from which to compare the evolutionary and economic significance of pre-Modern, Modern and postmodern architecture. Placed in a material historical context some postmodern buildings, for example, might show themselves to be more fertile in technology transfers than their High-Tech counterparts—consider Terry Farrell's temporary Clifton Nurseries building in Covent Garden, with its Teflon-coated fibreglass roof membrane and its Proctor mast roof beams. Classical Revival envelopes executed in profiled composite panels might be more impressive still, representing an ingenious way of 'culturalising' the architectural use of such advanced boat building composites as Kevlar, epoxy and carbon fibre.

By setting aside the obfuscating camouflage of style, a deep study of the architecture of technology transfer would expose the massive material similarity that characterises contemporary architecture, and show more clearly than ever before what are the deep structures and what are the surface structures in the design of buildings.

By opening such a revolutionary field of study the Byzantine world of Restoration architecture would suddenly become accessible to the quantitative analytical techniques that rule the late twentieth century world of engineering design and manufacture. Architecture, which is now an occult world of ignorance and obsolete mystery, shot through with individual acts of achievement, could become an open-access field of competition. The mighty ocean of product information that presently relies on fragmented, peripheral awareness could be given accessibility with the simplicity and directness of a video game. Architects freed of the tyranny of history for the second time in a century could concentrate on design by assembly, identifying the availability of new materials and techniques, and "specifying them into culture" with a squeeze on the joystick button. Like bees, architects would be seen to have been carrying out an evolutionary as well as a productive task. Their genetic role: the cross-pollination of materials and methods from a one-world product economy to a new architecture.

Those who doubt that the emergence of this new field of studying architecture could create its own ideology should consider the power of history, which is not only the story of the past but the ultimate proof of the present. When such a record is absent, our actions become as cyclical and unchanging as those of plants and animals, whose history endlessly repeats itself, and our adaptability is forfeit. Nor would such a change in the story of architecture make it untrue—it would make it true again and again for successive generations—just as the movements of the rudder of a ship, in response to changing winds, changing seas or changing orders, enable it to keep a true course.

The secret life of the engineers
1989

What is it like to be a structural engineer? Like being the director of a film best remembered for its actors? Or the unsung adaptor of an unknown novel into a TV classic? Perhaps it is really most like being the man who designed the engine of Nigel Mansell's car. Most engineers who have worked with architects on famous and expensive buildings are quiet, undemonstrative men. In this way Peter Rice is typical. He is a director of Ove Arup & Partners and his office is in Fitzroy Square, but in the best tradition of the Arup archipelago, even though he has a glass box of his own he still drinks his coffee out of the same plastic cups as all the other staff. Frank Newby, senior partner at Felix Samuely, is similarly unassuming. He sends any member of staff who completes 25 years with the firm on a world cruise. Tony Hunt, and his firm Anthony Hunt Associates, has now been acquired by YRM, but he insists that he is "only going there for the Intergraph CAD equipment". None of the three drives an extravagant car, like Ted Happold's Porsche. You could pass any one of them in the street and not notice. It is not like seeing Richard Rogers or Max Hutchinson on TV.

Le Corbusier once wrote, "an engineer should stay fixed and remain a calculator, for his particular justification is to remain within the confines of pure reason". But that was in 1925, before High-Tech architecture was even thought of. Today, engineers—and architects—see each other differently. Peter Rice, site engineer for the Sydney Opera House, chief design engineer for the Pompidou Centre, Lloyd's, the glass wall at La Villette, the Menil Gallery and many more is in such demand that, in addition to his work for Ove Arup and Rice Francis Ritchie, he gets an average of two pitches a week from architects with projects or competition entries that would gain credibility if they could only say, "Peter Rice says he will do it." Rice knows that most of these cold callers are simply after his name. But the phenomenon is significant anyhow. "It has reached the point where, if the phone isn't ringing all the time, I begin to think I must be losing my touch", he says. That doesn't sound like engineering, it sounds like showbusiness, and though Rice is the first among equals of the golden boys of engineering, it also applies to Tony Hunt, Frank Newby, Ted Happold and other high-profile engineers as well. Hunt even goes so far as to say that he has never turned a competition applicant down.

How did structural engineers, the backroom boys of the construction process, ever attain such crucial status? Rice is adamant that it all started with Sir Ove Arup, who came to London in the 1920s as the representative of a Danish firm of engineering contractors called Christiani & Nielsen. In addition to being a fine engineer, Arup was a cultured person who moved in Modern art circles devoted to Modern architecture. In London he met the patron Jack Pritchard and worked with the brilliant architect Berthold Lubetkin. By 1938, he was the natural choice to structurally engineer Lubetkin's famous Highpoint Flats. But though mythology has it that Tecton, the pioneer firm of Modern architects in which Lubetkin was a partner, invented the revolutionary structural wall and concrete slab system that Arup used to eliminate columns and beams, actually it was the other way around. According to Sir Ove, Tecton submitted a conventional reinforced concrete design which he then drastically simplified as a result of his years of experience with docks, harbours and industrial building. The famous sliding shuttering system too was Ove Arup's own invention. As he wrote to the author of an article about Tecton three years before his death; "I could only work with Lubetkin because as an engineer I had the last say which Lubetkin had to respect."

Some 40 years later, when the functional theories of Modern architecture had collapsed in a heap, the engineers' functional tradition of 'pure reason' established in Britain by Ove Arup, not only survived intact, but burgeoned into the secret stardom of the present. In the High-Tech era as in the Modern, despite always being the first to be left off the credit list, the name of the engineer was always at least as important as the name of the architect. In the case of Reliance Controls, the Swindon light industrial building by Team 4 (Norman Foster and Richard Rogers) that was designed in 1967—and is cited in Colin Davies new book (with no credit for the engineer) as the first ever High-Tech building—history repeats itself. According to engineer Tony Hunt it was not Foster or Rogers who designed Reliance Controls, but him—and he drew the working drawings himself as well. As Hunt remembers it now, Norman Foster's contribution was the idea of continuing diagonal bracing along the side walls (where it was not necessary) as well as along the glazed cross walls, where it was. Richard Rogers thought of putting a water tank outside, like Hunstanton School. All together this was the beginning of a famous English style, like New Brutalism. But who invented it? Hunt sits at his desk in the glass office that he is about to evacuate forever wondering whether to claim it all. He engineered Willis Faber Dumas, the Sainsbury Centre and Inmos, as well as Reliance Controls. "I don't know", he says, suddenly cautious. "It might well have been me. It's difficult to say who had the first idea."

Frank Newby, perhaps ten years older than Hunt and Rice, who are both in their 50s, ponders the same starting point just as carefully. He was the engineer for the Price/Snowdon birdcage and Jim Stirling's earlier tours de force at Leicester and Cambridge. "I wouldn't disagree about Reliance Controls being the first", he says at length, "It was one of the first to be overstructured. When they wanted to put in a window they had to cut some of the structure out. But it depends how you define High-Tech architecture. If you mean 'high-technology' architecture then I would put the 1962 Regent's Park birdcage before it." And who designed the birdcage? "I did. Snowdon and Cedric came round to see me and said, 'Frank, what would you most like to do?' And I said, 'something with tension structures', so I designed that triangular thing and Snowdon, or Cedric, or both of them said; 'Why not have two of them, one at each end?' So we did."

As Peter Rice said a few years ago, "High-Tech architects have concluded that the discipline provided by the engineer is the best framework in which to conduct architecture." That is pretty safe. Another way of putting it is the way Frank Newby phrased it in his 1984 RIBA lecture "Hi-tech or Mys-tech". "High-Tech", he said, "is the use of redundant structure for decorative purposes." Couldn't you just call that decoration? Someone asked him. "No", he replied. "Because it is still structure, however tortured, it must still be architecture. Hector Guimard's art nouveau cast iron was like that. It was decorative but it still carried load."

And if it carries load, unless it is a bathroom extension less than three storeys high, there has to be an engineer involved—and he still has the last say—as Sir Ove Arup wrote. Even the congenitally modest Peter Rice stands firm here. "On the design of the Centre Pompidou there was one crucial decision that could not have been taken by Renzo Piano or Richard Rogers, it had to be taken by an engineer. The whole concept of getting into the building through a tension net, the appearance of the building, depended on the so-called 'gerberettes'—each one a ten tonne steel casting. That was a technology that had not been used in building since the mid-nineteenth century, and Pompidou was an application so vast that only one German foundry could cast them. Only an engineer could have taken the decision to authorise the use of those because public safety was involved." Who was that engineer? "I was."

Nowadays most engineers are not all that enthusiastic about High-Tech architecture. Tony Hunt thinks it used to be alright until it went "over the top" and he cites three buildings where the structure is, as he puts it, "most excessive". The first is Norman Foster's Renault Centre, engineered by Arups' John Thornton; "It is not a readable structure. No one could understand from inside or from outside, you would have to draw a section." The second is Nick Grimshaw's Brentford Homebase, where the engineer was Ernest Green; "That's more readable but it still doesn't make sense." And the third is Grimshaw's latest Camden Town superstore engineered by Kenchington Little. About this Hunt will only say; "Nick should have been an engineer himself, his father was."

Architects both confirm and illuminate this concept of the cruciality of engineering. They never actually say it was the engineer who designed their building, but they come very close. Consider Michael Hopkins in 1985, when he said; "Our architecture comes out of our engineering and our engineering comes out of our engineers." At the time nobody saw that sort of statement as another confession of theoretical bankruptcy in architecture, but in a way that is just what it was. Think of the difference between the Schlumberger Research Laboratories—where Hopkins was assisted by two firms of engineers, Arups and Tony Hunt—and the half-new Bracken House, where Arups are hard at work enabling him to enclose High-Tech office space behind a re-creation of Guarino Guarini. Or even think of Fitzroy Robinson, burrowing away behind the four walls of St Martin's le Grand, where the engineering achievements are crucial but totally invisible—and no engineers credit is given in the practice's own news sheet.

The hypothesis that architects ran out of functional ideas in about 1970 and started to plagiarise engineering has a circumstantial truth. Rice, Hunt and Newby all agree that it was about then that, as Rice puts it; "Architects started to allow the way a building was made to be part of its image."

And from there they went on to "misunderstand the role of technology in the image of building". Right now Rice thinks that things have got so bad that, "No public or private client in Britain would commission a High-Tech building of any size or importance." The present position is a kind of paralysis. He cites Lloyd's and St Martin's le Grand as polar opposites and thinks that each one is as 'isolated' as the other.

Does Peter Rice think then that there will be no 'next step in High-Tech'? No leap forward into space-age monocoque structures of the kind proposed by Jan Kaplicky and David Nixon. "The reason nothing like that has ever been built is simple", he replies. "There is no industry here to do it. The building industry is completely incapable of it, and it is no good citing the aircraft industry because it is completely differently organised. So is the motor industry. Cars and aeroplanes are *not designed*, they are *improved*. The first 2,000 examples of any new car introduced are always bought by the company's competitors. They take them apart to find out what is wrong with them. We found that working with FIAT on the 1978 VSS project, some of the results of which can now be seen in the Tipo. These car people are not brilliant designers, they are very ordinary. It is just that they break all the problems down into detailed manageable tasks and slowly improve their product. The only thing that is remotely like that in construction is the American curtain walling industry, and that is a long way behind. Yes, there will be a 'next step in High-Tech' but I would guess it will happen first in Japan, where there is an industry that can do it, not in Britain, and probably not in Europe or America."

Frank Newby sighs deeply when the same question is put to him. "I don't think High-Tech has made any contribution to the development of engineering structures at all", he says. "You talk about monocoque structures. They are not new. The Nissen hut was a monocoque structure and that was built in thousands 70 years ago. High-Tech architecture is not leading edge technology. It is not challenging for engineers to be asked to multiply redundant structural elements. Nothing like as much as the concrete shells and the hyperbolic parabaloids of the 1950s. If you are talking about 'High-Technology' structures, then in my opinion we have been standing still since the 1950s."

So does Frank Newby think that engineers have been led up the garden path for 20 years by High-Tech architects? "Yes, oh yes! Architects just started using structure as decoration and, because it carried load, we had to deal with it. It made a lot of extra work. But if you are asking me whether High-Tech architecture advanced technology in any way, I would have to say no. It made no contribution at all. There was nothing in all of it half as testing as a long span bridge or a decent sized stadium."

Life in the urban war zone
1989

Ten years off the turn of the century, London offers a lesson that is fraught with serious consequences for all industrial societies. Even as its massive new satellite-communicating developments of London Wall, London Bridge City, Canary Wharf and King's Cross crawl towards completion, 124 mile traffic jams between London and Bristol and complete stoppages of the M25 orbital motorway become a repeated occurrence. Two new rail-heads and two new motorways are lancing across northern France towards three pitifully narrow tubes that will link them beneath the Channel to an ancient railway network and an inadequate motorway system on the British side. Beyond this jumble the city lies inert behind its barrage of fine art and conservationist propaganda.

A vast junkpile of all the building materials of history, London's intellectual infrastructure is scarcely less vital than its physical form. Proposals to punch beneath this vast sprawl of impenetrable built entanglements with tunnelled roadways and subterranean parking garages are fought off with academic 'theories' that scarcely deserve the name. "Building more roads will mean more cars and more congestion" is the unhelpful verdict of a London University professor who allegedly specialises in transport studies. Meanwhile the congested city sets more and more into the pattern of life of the trenches in the Great War: a life of movable but unremovable obstructions through which even motorcycle despatch riders can move no faster than foot soldiers through mud and machine gun fire.

No one is in control of this city—although many have titles that imply that they have responsibility for it. As far as physical planning and building are concerned, it is already too late to do anything about London that will have any measurable effect within any politically useful timescale. No responsible person in architecture, planning or politics any longer believes either that planning in the manner of the Ville Radieuse or Broadacre City is the answer, or that the guiding intelligence, executive power and popular obedience exist within the body politic to make it happen.

The fate of architecture diminishes in the colossal shadow of this battle between the future operations of the economy and the intransigent obstruction of a city that is now the sum of all the discarded options of its past. A state of war exists not only between man and nature, but between the age of science and the accumulated infrastructure of centuries as well. To say that planning is impossible in modern conditions—and this is often said—is itself virtually an admission of the existence of this state of war. In war you take things as you find them and do the best you can to get through—which is what information technology (the new philosophy) already does with the intractable architecture of the past. The economy of the city today requires its citizens to fight: they fight its obstructive physical structure and overloaded systems as though it were a vast wasteland of natural or man-made obstacles.

It is as the war zone that it is today, not the conservationist paradise of new yesterday, or the utopian paradise of old tomorrow, that we must learn to look at the city in order to understand the failure of theory and design in the Second Machine Age. This city is not planned or designed, it is chaotic and out of control: its streets are like trenches; its traffic is armour; its forests of signs are military rendezvous points. Its street life is like life in no man's land. Its crime is combat. Its drugs are chemical weapons. Its policemen are military policemen.

All the major redevelopment projects of this city, the immense commercial developments that boggle the minds of property correspondents, stir the anxieties of the trimmers of the Royal Fine Art Commission, drive in the pickets of the voluntary conservation organisation and alert the great mother ship English Heritage; all these projects have two faces. In one way, they are simply proposals for millions of square feet of serviced floor space, scheduled to be available in three, five or seven years' time; in another they are solemn promises of urban disruption for three, five or seven years ahead. Taking the second way first, we can see these monsters—Broadgate, London Bridge, City, Canary Wharf, London Wall—as bids in a galactic game of roulette. Each bid may not be a winner, but it is a guarantee of uncertainty and a long period of obstruction, inconvenience, pollution and incidental environmental damage. Take a dozen of these big bids whirling at once on the vast money wheel of any city centre and you have the third way of looking at a city: as a heaving, slow-motion battleground. Take three dozen of these bids, staggered in time, and you have 70 years of built-in obsolescence; a lifetime lived in the shadow of destruction and reconstruction with the hope of a finished, perfect city of the future perpetually deferred. Architecture, whatever its surface style, is not important in this slow-motion battle: it is not part of the answer, it is part of the problem.

The role of information technology in this urban war game of the Second Machine Age is exactly the same as its role in any war—it compensates for the impenetrability of the war zone that the built environment has become and thus drives fear of it from our consciousness. One of the most instructive things about signs, images and all electronic media is the way in which they effortlessly keep pace with this slide into environmental war. In part this is because information technology originated as military technology—the telephone-equipped four-wheel drive company car is only a civilian version of the Second World War mobile command headquarters. In part, too, it is because the indirect geography and unpredictable obstructions of the erupting city have made our dependence upon information in the urban environment complete. We are lost in the metropolis without information. In the urban war, as in any war, we only know what we are told. If a war zone is where thought is impossible, then thought must be supplied from outside, by information.

What this means is that the real city of the Second Machine Age—the city perceived in our consciousness—is a binary phenomenon. One part of our brain knows that the information part of the city is *assembling*, despite all this physical chaos and congestion; it is slowly knitting itself together like a vast computer image behind which is a stupendous octopus of electronic awareness whose head is a satellite in outer space and whose tentacles reach into and between all other cities everywhere. At the same time, the other part of our brain knows that the physical city of immobile architecture is disassembling, becoming a semiologically homogenised warren of temporary facades, fronting on to free fire zones populated by muggers, clampers, beggars and the paralysed armoured divisions of traffic.

Put together, these two images create a stereoscopic picture in which what was once the public realm—the civic vistas and spaces, the now clogged and useless streets, the crime-prone squares and parks—has been engulfed by the war zone and converted into an exhausting topography of obstructions. At the same time, the inner information world, including the media, is busy miniaturising the job that all that public space used to do. Part of the crisis of architecture in the Second Machine Age is that it must learn to face the fact that information does not need the public realm—which was the progenitor of historic architecture. Until it learns that lesson it will have no more significance than a man-made range of mountains.

It is popular nowadays to speculate on the possibility of the electronic octopus of information 'breaking the stalemate' of the urban war by leaping over the physical barriers of streets and buildings—just as the tanks of 1916 were supposed to enable the army to break out of the deadlock of trench warfare. This can happen, indeed it already has, but as the task of information ceases to be to direct the war of urban development but to evade it instead, the new configuration reveals itself to be 'dispersal'.

This dispersal does not put an end to the urban war; it converts it instead into a war of movement. And under these conditions the military operations of the economy—raging like a Blitzkrieg unchecked by the discredited defence of decayed and corrupt local planning legislation—turn out to demand an appropriately revolutionary transformation in the use of land, such as: 'prairie farming' over large areas; light industry and commerce dispersed along 'motorway corridors'; the blurring of the distinction between the urban and the rural workforce. Notwithstanding political differences, parallels to all of these can be found in the Soviet Five Year Plans of the First Machine Age. As Berthold Lubetkin wrote in 1932: "We must not have concentrated and unhealthy habitations but throughout the country endless streams of human dwellings along the big arteries of contemporary life joining our centres of industry and agriculture. Existing towns are doomed to quick extinction, only the art monuments must remain, surrounded by vast parks." This, too, is a battle plan, a plan for an endless environmental war. So endless, in fact, that, incredible as it may seem, we can set Josef Stalin's Collectivisation Programme beside the Enterprise Culture of Margaret Thatcher and the join is invisible.

The Second Machine Age began with the awareness of the power of information and the birth of cybernetic control. At the end of it, all human beings, formerly protagonists in the schemes of conquest and rule that we call civilisations and cultures, have been left in a state of unprecedented redundancy. Philosophically we confront the most radical position of all, which is to accept that there are forces of organisation far beyond our control that have removed the initiative from the hands of the creators and the protectors of the built environment. These are instantaneous, inexhaustible forces of energy, communication and production that have no territorial goals or objectives. They are inanimate but invincible; they are intelligent but they have no ideas; they lack ambition but they conquer all; they need neither leaders nor followers. They are objects that need no subject. Moral interventions; value judgements; saying that this is good or that is bad —all of that merely disrupts the process by which they are assembling the future. The search for meaning, the protection of the past, individual creativity, the proof of being right—all that is now merely a needless risk.

In the Second Machine Age, our society has become so vulnerable in its dependence on these forces, so hard-wired in its reliance on their goalless energy, that expecting the unexpected from the exercise of individual genius borders on naivety. The most radical thing that any of us can do now is to do nothing; to wait while the instantaneous forces of the Second Machine Age work out how to construct a future upon the relics of the past that we built but no longer have the time or the authority to change. In this vacuum, those architects who are content to remain "conscientious objectors in the war against nature" may find their time is running out.

Foster Associates, Sainsbury Centre for Visual Arts, Norwich, England, 1974–1978

German airship *Graf Zeppelin*, designed by Hugo Eckener, 1928

Lost arks of the air
1989

All that is left of the great age of the rigid airships is the giant buildings they left behind them. Most have been demolished, but the survivors of these once numerous structures still reach from Bedfordshire to California like the footprints of an extinct species. They were laid out as way-stations for a system of international air travel that turned out to be one of the great might-have-beens of technological history. In Britain, the great sheds at Cardington are relics of the Imperial Airship Scheme that was one of the second Labour government's public works projects designed to beat the Great Depression. They were built as part of a strategy to link the colonies with the mother country. Instead, after the loss of the R-101 and the dismantling of the R-100, they saw no airships for 50 years, until the first tiny blimp of Airship Industries arrived in 1979.

The Cardington sheds, like their counterparts in Germany (East and West), the Soviet Union, France, Italy and the United States, were the most ambitious structures to be built since the Gothic cathedrals. Like the cathedrals too, they sprang into existence with an amazingly sudden access of skill. Of enormous size and bewilderingly different designs, sometimes rotatable or demountable, always technologically demanding, they were the leading edge of construction engineering technology from the turn of the century until the *Hindenburg* disaster of 1937.

Of the extinct dinosaurs the largest sheds were built to serve almost nothing is left. The survivors of the airship species are pigmies dedicated to tourism and advertising: their real history now no more than the flickering nitrate film stock and the quavering voices of ancient survivors you see on an occasional TV documentary. Here and there in a museum there is an odd relic, as of an extinct civilisation. The felt overshoe of one of the crew of a Zeppelin that bombed London (worn to avoid sparks in the presence of millions of cubic feet of hydrogen); bits of duralumin girder looking surprisingly modern; the charred lump of an engine too large for any aeroplane of the time.

Nothing physical or conceptual adequately conveys the strangeness and immensity of the rigid airships. Not the fact that their pre-synthetic fabric gas cells were made from the stitched together stomach linings of 1,000s of cows. Nor the fact that even the smallest German Zeppelin was four times the length of a Boeing 747—which is itself longer than the distance Orville Wright flew when he made history by flying heavier than air in 1903.

Although millions of people in the first three decades of this century saw airships, only a tiny number flew in them. Some of these experienced air travel of a grandeur that has never since been equalled. When the *Graf Zeppelin* and the *Hindenburg* made scheduled flights from Frankfurt across the North and South Atlantic in the 1930s, their passengers were not belted up in tiny seats and force-fed frozen food like today's air travellers: each one enjoyed a private cabin with opening windows, room service, freshly baked bread every day and a morning newspaper printed on board. A pianist, seated at a specially made aluminium piano, played tunes in the spacious restaurant at dinner. Even the doomed English rigids were grand. Lord Thompson thought nothing of taking one tonne of personal luggage with him when the R-101 set out for India in 1930.

In part, genuine public affection and the conviction of ultimate success explains why such elaborate and expensive ground support facilities were built for airships, including masts and hangars in Egypt, India and Japan that were destined never to be used. These vast and expensive installations were seen as the docks and harbours of the future ships of the air, as natural and necessary as the dry docks and basins of the great seaports of the world. More appositely today they can be compared to the massive ground support facilities that have been built for the space re-entry vehicle programmes of the United States and the USSR that have also suffered airship-style catastrophes.

This parallel can be taken further. After the Great War, the Americans took the Zeppelin structural engineer Karl Arnstein to the United States to work for the Goodyear Corporation in exactly the same way as they took Werner von Braun (eventually) to work for NASA 20 years later. The Zeppelins captured from Germany in 1918 were shared between the Allies in the same way as the aerodynamic and rocket secrets of Nazi Germany were seized in 1945. Indeed, in Germany the last rigid airship operations overlapped with the early stages of the development of the V-2 rocket, and thus with the space programme itself. In August 1939, the *Graf Zeppelin II*, the last to fly of the 158 large rigid airships built by all nations in the preceding 40 years, cruised around the British coastline analysing radar transmissions before returning to Frankfurt to be broken up.

But for architecture, it was the technology of the airship age that was the valuable legacy. The requirement for strength and lightness posed by the rigid airships themselves forced the development of tensile wood, fabric and light alloy structures that were the forerunners of all the ground-born geodesic and space-frame buildings that have been designed or erected since. Even the computations involved—300 human 'calculators' worked with the novelist Neville Shute on the pre-computer design of the framework of the R-100 in 1929—had a lasting influence on engineering. Enclosing and protecting rigid airships up to 850 feet long and 170 feet in diameter on the ground was a formidable task that single handedly converted one branch of turn-of-the-century building construction into a modern engineering technology as advanced as aeronautics itself. It is not too much to say that the engineering achievement of the enormous airship sheds paved the way for the primacy of the structural engineer in the constellation of construction professionals that rules the built environment today. When all the great rigid ships were gone, the buildings designed to contain them remained as objects of wonder and achievement. In the end their existence alone is proof of the possibility of the return of the giant airship itself.

Dymaxion: the car that never flew
1989

The aeroplane ancestry of the Dymaxion cars was plain from the beginning. In his 1928 4-D Auto-Airplane sketches, Buckminster Fuller had shown little more than a 'teardrop' aircraft fuselage with recessed front wheels and a combined rear steering wheel and aerodynamic rudder. This vehicle was intended to use the roads under the power of two of three 'liquid air turbines', each driving one of the front wheels. A third 'turbine' would drive the nose-mounted propeller for flight. The transport would take to the air by using its forward motion to inflate pneumatic wings, with the pressure topped up by an air pump.

By 1932, this 4-D Auto-Airplane had developed into the 4-D Transport with twin four cylinder petrol engines, no propeller and no wings. This vehicle still resembled an aeroplane but was intended only to 'plane' with its tail lifted off the ground so as to develop "infinite wheelbase" for comfort and smoothness. We know a lot about the thinking behind this vehicle because it is described—"weight unloaded approx 400 lbs, exquisite acceleration and deceleration as with outboard motorboat racers"—in a long and fascinatingly illustrated article entitled "Streamlining" that Fuller wrote for the November 1932 issue of his magazine *Shelter*. Here the inventor explained that his conception of the car of the future hinged upon weight reduction and streamlining. He was still advocating the unique '4-D' hull form of an inverted V to achieve aerodynamic stability, but leaned more towards contemporary examples like the Granville brothers' "Gee Bee" racing monoplanes with their short, stubby fuselages and wire-braced wings. In the article, his last 4-D Transport drawing before the construction of the real thing showed a twin-engined tricycle frame with rear wheel steering and a retractable aerofoil steering rudder. The dogged adherence to steering from the rear was explained by the exemplary manoeuvrability of yachts, fish, birds and aeroplanes—as well as being a step towards the eventual possibility of flight.

Despite their failure to hover or fly, the appearance of the Dymaxion cars was revolutionary, and must remain a subject of fascination for anyone who has ever seen a photograph of one, let alone the sole physical survivor in the Harrah Collection, Reno, Nevada. Fuller's collaborator, Starling Burgess, had designed two successful Americas Cup defenders and it showed in the beautiful lines of the first vehicle in particular, whose single headlamp and non-opening Perspex windows made for cleaner lines. Between them, Fuller and Burgess had created one of the most startlingly beautiful motor vehicles ever built. A dramatic contrast with all its contemporaries, it was not until the advent of the Porsche 356 15 years later that such a drastic adherence to the principles of streamlining would again be accompanied by breathtaking aesthetic success.

FV 453, the Connecticut registered prototype, looked like the wingless, tailless fuselage of the 1928 drawings, only better. Although it was finished in hand-beaten natural aluminium on an ash frame, it looked like an all-metal monocoque aircraft, its near-perfect teardrop shape was broken only by a broad roof-mounted air intake for the engine behind the passenger cabin. Its 5.7 metre 11-seat body had a Perspex-glazed 'cockpit cover' and doors only on the left hand side. Sections of the glazing and the canvas roof had to be removed to provide ventilation.

At rest, the car stood nose-high, like a tailwheel aircraft of the period. Inside it boasted aircraft seats, with seat belts, and aircraft-style controls and equipment, including an airspeed indicator and a radio. The body was carried on a chrome-molybdenum aircraft steel ladder chassis articulated into two scissors-like sections hinged at the front axle. The forward ladder frame carried the weight of the passengers and the 80 hp V8 rear-mounted engine driving the front pair of wheels, and a long A-frame of perforated steel passing either side of the engine carried the 160 degree-turning rear steering wheel. The engine, gearbox, transmission and running gear were all taken from the contemporary Ford V-8. One of the most serious limitations of the Ford legacy was the archaic formerly rear, now front, beam axle and transverse leaf spring suspension with its friction dampers.

The radically unorthodox layout of the Dymaxion car—Fuller simply turned the Ford differential and back axle upside down to make it drive the right way—possessed some advantages over the front engine-rear drive arrangement then universal in the motor industry but, as it emerged, many disadvantages too. Its principal gain was low-speed manoeuvrability, with a parking distance only 75 mm longer than the length of the car, and a turning circle only 300 mm greater. Fuller frequently boasted that at 15 mph the car could make a 180 degree turn in a matter of seconds.

The negative side of these achievements emerged at higher speeds. All three of the Dymaxion cars built suffered from control problems above 50 miles per hour. In part this resulted from precisely those design analogies with birds and fish that had spurred their inventor on. The implications of this arrangement for a car were clearly appreciated by Fuller—his 1928 drawings of the 4-D Auto-Airplane showed aerodynamic rudder and elevator controls—but it is clear from the 1932 *Shelter* drawings that Fuller believed he had dealt with this problem by deleting the tailplane and elevators altogether and providing only a "retractable air rudder" to take over the steering when the tail rose. But not only was none of the Dymaxion cars ever fitted with such a rudder, the inventor greatly underestimated the tail-lifting effect as well. As the Dymaxion cars accelerated, their tails tended to rise, just like those of aircraft. The effect of uneven road surfaces and the absence of elevator downforce meant there was no way of controlling this tendency except by reducing speed, for whenever the 'tailwheel' left the ground there was an immediate loss of steering control.

The more this phenomenon is examined, the more remarkable Fuller's thinking can be seen to be. Clearly, he expected the Dymaxion to run at a high speed, perhaps over 100 miles an hour. Given a long clear road the loss of ground-contact steering might have been offset by the use of an air rudder, but normal road conditions clearly required the ability to slow down rapidly, as well as run straight and negotiate broad radius turns at high speed. In the early trials of the first Dymaxion car, Fuller discovered that braking at high speed through the narrow footprint of two wheels led to a skid. Even when stationary, the weight distribution of the car was 75 per cent front: 25 per cent rear. This meant that rear-wheel braking was ineffective, and in fact rear-wheel brakes were not fitted to any of the cars. Burgess and Fuller had placed the mass of the engine as far aft and as low down as they could to counteract weight-transfer at speed, but this alone was not sufficient.

Over the years, a legend has grown up about the performance of the Dymaxion cars. Fuller himself claimed to have broken the lap record "by more than 50 per cent" at an unspecified 'midget car stadium in the Bronx' in a Dymaxion. In an appearance at the Roosevelt Raceway, Long Island on 11 August 1933, FV 453 claimed 120 miles an hour, but no official timings were released. As late as July 1988, *Automobile Magazine* in the United States claimed that the car could reach 120 miles an hour with fuel consumption in the 25–30 miles per gallon range.

In fact, despite Fuller's understanding of the importance of power to weight ratios, the kerb weight of the Dymaxions was never revealed or, possibly, never even calculated. It must, however, have been well in excess of 2,000 kilograms and, at such a weight, with a slow-revving side-valve 85 bhp V8 driving through a three-speed gearbox and standard 3.57:1 Ford rear axle, it can safely be said that the claimed figures are impossible.

Is ecology all hot air?
1990

There was once a story about Buddha in which the master asked one of
his followers what in the world he would most like. The follower, hoping
perhaps for advancement, replied that above all things he would prize
wisdom. At this, the sage seized him by the throat and made as if to strangle
him. But just before his unfortunate follower lost consciousness, Buddha
released his grip and, keeping his hands loosely around his neck, asked him
the same question again. This time the chastened man replied; "To be able
to breathe master, to be able to breathe."

When I was a professor in America I used to tell that story in seminars.
Eventually it was joined by a more topical yarn about a friend who was asked
to write an article for *Playboy* on the subject "Ten Ways to Female Orgasm".
Long after the article had been written, published and well received she got
another phone call from an editor at *Playboy* saying the magazine would pay
even more for another article called "Ten More Ways to Female Orgasm".
The friend expostulated that all her ideas had been used up in the first
article. "Yeah", said the editor, "but do you want the money or don't you?"

The purpose of these two dubious tales is to introduce the subject of the
limits of conventional wisdom, which in all areas of human endeavour are
surprisingly rapidly reached. Buddha's alarming lesson notwithstanding, what
human beings really prize above all other things is agreement, and they appear
not to care how much nonsense has to be swallowed to get it. An American
professor once researched this so called "Delphi effect" by quizzing
individuals on different subjects and then putting them in groups and quizzing
the groups. In every case, the answers agreed by the groups after discussion
were less accurate than the results produced by the individual members
of the groups on their own. So remember, while it may be good to be wise,
you have to be able to breathe first. And while it may be impossible to think
of 20 ways to female orgasm, that is only the case if you don't need the money.

One person who continually patrols the frontiers between Delphic 'Great
Bores of Today' wisdom and 'Believe it or not' paradox, is architect Geoffrey
Hodgson of Leeds. Mr Hodgson, whom I have never met, has written to me
twice on the subject of carbon dioxide emissions and the greenhouse effect.
A complex of issues thrust by recent events in the Middle East into something
of the predicament of Buddha's disciple's desire for wisdom, but one certain to
re-emerge before long.

Hodgson's first letter began by congratulating me upon my sagacity for having predicted a new golden age of private motoring because the assembled professors of transport planning of England and Wales had decreed that our current £15 billion road building programme was a waste of money, that no more roads should be built, that cars should be phased out because of their toxic emissions, and that only public transport should be permitted. This conclusion was, I had said, certain to be false and he agreed. But he went on to give an example of the limitations of conventional wisdom that I have never seen mentioned anywhere else.

Hodgson is a student of, unaccountably forgotten, world-threatening disasters extending back into the nineteenth century. He recalls a novel called *The Poison Belt*, a kind of Victorian radiation cloud, which he thinks started off the genre. From there, he could have gone on to the 'heat death of the universe' threatened by turn of the century scientists; or the 1910 prediction of a vile end for humanity in the year 1950 under 140 billion tonnes of solid waste generated by transport animals, a fate lugubriously recalled by Cy Adler in his 1973 book *Ecological Fantasies*. Instead, he poured scorn on the idea that the melting of the polar ice cap would raise seawater levels—"Arctic ice at sea level is mainly floating, it displaces its own mass so it cannot alter the water level if it melts. The really thick ice is at high altitude, at minus 20 or 30 degrees centigrade!" After this, he turned to carbon dioxide emissions.

Hodgson believes that carbon dioxide freaks, or "Greenhouse fans" as he calls them, in order to scare themselves and everyone else, simply count man-made sources of carbon dioxide and ignore natural ones. To prove the futility of this he has obtained from the Ford Motor Company figures which show that his own Ford Escort 1.3 running in urban cycle emits 2.78 kilograms of CO_2 per hour, while he himself, like every other human adult, only gives off about three kilograms of CO_2 over a whole day. That is what the Greens say, but Hodgson then points out that while he is breathing every hour of every day, his car is only in use for about one hour a day. Thus, in a year his car will only give off about the same 1,000 kilograms of CO_2 travelling over 10,000 miles, as he does talking on the telephone or lying in bed. More significantly, if he carries a passenger with him they can drive ten miles sitting in his car (humans give off less carbon dioxide if they do not exert themselves) and emit less carbon dioxide (car and passengers combined) than they would manufacture organically if they walked the same distance!

Given the statistic that there are 310 cars per 1,000 persons in this country, the significance of these comparisons is easy to see. The human population of the United Kingdom manufactures about 60 billion kilograms of CO_2 every year, while the automobile population manages less than half that. Taking the population of the world as a whole as something like six billion persons, the disparity between human and automobile sources of CO_2 is enormous. In fact the car hardly counts in the big picture.

Careless of the warning of the Delphi experiments, I was unwise enough to deliver an oration on the subject of Hodgson's calculations at dinner one night. Present were a scientific farmer, a TV production manager, a geographer and others, all graduates. After an animated discussion, the Delphic consensus was that Hodgson was wrong. His Ford Escort was guilty as hell. Humans did not actually *make* CO_2 so much as breathe atmospheric CO_2 in and out. Thus the conventional wisdom about the evils of the motor car lived to fight another day.

I wrestled with the result of this discussion for some time before writing to Hodgson to tell him about it. This time his reply, which arrived by return of post, was clearly disappointed. "If you believe we only breathe out what we breathe in, and produce no carbon dioxide, we could breathe the same air over and over again in a sealed space. I do not advise you to try it! All animal life uses oxygen to convert food to energy in a process similar to burning. The calories in a diet are the same ones a heating engineer uses in his calculations. Plant life converts CO_2 back into oxygen but there is now evidence that tiny sea creatures do more of this than plants on land do. In any case 4.2 per cent of expelled air is CO_2 but only 0.4 per cent of the air we breathe is. It is true that CO_2 in the atmosphere is increasing, but so is the world's population. The proportion due to fossil fuels is impossible to calculate. Fight ridicule with ridicule by all means, but make sure your facts are right first. PS I don't expect a reply to this letter."

Buddha couldn't have put it better himself.

Nazi caricature of the Weissenhofsiedlung, Stuttgart, Germany, 1927

Völkische housing at Danzig, Germany, 1940

A precedent for the Prince
1990

In the last decade, the Prince of Wales has expressed forceful views on a large number of subjects, but nowhere has his impact been more keenly felt than in the world of architecture.[1] There, a trio of set-piece speeches, a television programme, an exhibition, a book—and his celebrity status as heir to the throne—have combined to make him not only the most widely quoted architectural critic of his generation, but the most powerful opponent of modern architecture in Britain.

A good measure of the Prince's authority in architectural matters today is his standing in public opinion polls. When in October 1988 a popular Sunday newspaper commissioned a poll on its readers' response to Charles' television programme *A Vision of Britain*, no less than 75.5 per cent of respondents answered yes to the question "Do you agree with Prince Charles' view of modern architecture?" To the question; "Should the Prince be appointed to a planning committee to review all major designs?" More than half (51.2 per cent) said yes.[2] A wider based poll held one year later showed a hardening of this popular support. Fully 85 per cent of respondents were in favour of the proposition. "Architects should concentrate on designing buildings that the majority of people find attractive." While no less than 58 per cent agreed to the simple proposition; "Modern architecture is an eyesore."[3]

Given the unrelenting criticism of modern architecture that has characterised all the Prince's speeches on the subject, it is perhaps just as remarkable that three successive RIBA presidents have gone out of their way to 'welcome' his interventions, and one even sought to place him at the head of a Royal Commission on the state of architecture. In the same way, despite the dissatisfaction with the planning profession implicit in the large public support for the 1988 idea that the Prince should assume responsibility for approving "all major designs", it is perhaps just as noteworthy that the Royal Town Planning Institute should also have given the Prince its "unreserved backing".[4] Over the last five years representatives of English Heritage, the Metropolitan Police, the Royal Fine Art Commission, the Georgian Group, several prominent architects including John Outram, Quinlan Terry, Terry Farrell OBE, the 'urban geographer' Dr Alice Coleman, a clutch of developers and the Archbishop of Liverpool, have also pledged their support.

To command such widespread allegiance in matters of taste it is necessary to touch a deeply felt public prejudice. The extent to which this has been done by the Prince in relation to architecture must therefore be seen as evidence of the thinness of the veneer of authority that the profession possessed before his attacks began. Only a decade ago, architecture, like art, was a creative realm accustomed to being judge and jury in the matter of its own motives and merits, but today this status is lost. As a result of the lack of respect for professional protocol that the Prince of Wales has shown, the mystique of the architectural profession has vanished along with its professional monopoly and its mandatory fee scale. In a few short years, the Royal Institute of British Architects has, in the words of the unregistered, unassociated architect-planner to the Prince, Leon Krier, "lost whatever credibility it once possessed and revealed itself as an ideologically and financially bankrupt organisation".[5]

More obviously. British architecture itself has changed. The plurality of styles that succeeded the hegemony of modernism in the 1970s is already giving way to an official endorsement of the popular taste for the 'traditional' in the form of "Ten Commandments" or, in their most recent form "Ten Principles", set forth by the Prince in the book of his television programme, also called A Vision of Britain. These 'Principles', once codified into planning law, will effectively control the aesthetics of all new buildings. Their implementation will be devolved to the elected and salaried planning representatives of local communities with the implication of an ultimate recourse to the Royal judgement.

Today, in Britain, architects unwilling to operate within this new framework of popular censorship are already being denied new commissions, and those with international reputations are already obliged to find the bulk of their work overseas. Architects whose work has already been criticised by the Prince in his speeches are feeling the consequences in the form of cancelled commissions and increased planning interference. Architects holding unexecuted commissions whose published designs have been attacked by the Prince have been eased out of these commissions altogether in favour of Royally approved substitutes. Completed buildings criticised by the Prince and his followers have had their flat roofs replaced by pitched roofs, been repainted and hidden by earthworks and tree planting, and been scheduled for early demolition and replacement.[6]

Presented in such bald outline, the story of the Prince of Wales' six year intervention into architecture has an obvious precedent, but one which is seldom mentioned. Indeed, on the occasion of last year's *A Vision of Britain* exhibition at the Victoria and Albert Museum, mention of it in a national newspaper was prevented by editorial censorship.[7]

Obviously, comparisons between the growing aesthetic totalitarianism in British architecture today and the suppression of modern architecture that took place as part of the process of cultural *Gleichschaltung* ('harmonisation') of Nazi Germany are not welcome, but they are not hysterical or in bad taste. They are glaringly obvious. Rather than suppress them in the interests of decorum, it is more honest to argue that a wilful complicity with the suppression of creative freedom is involved in the continued failure to bring them into the Royal 'debate'.

Consider the words the Prince himself uses in his popular architectural criticisms. They are so brutal that they have already marginalised the old idea that the design of buildings is a specialist field, like opera or ballet, that is worthy of skilled elucidation by an expert elite. Now any architectural project, large or small, has become public property to be dismissed with such phrases as; "a carbuncle on the face of an elegant friend", "a glass stump", 'a Victorian prison', "a nuclear power station", "a hardened missile silo", "a broken 1930s wireless set", "a grubby launderette" and so on.

The demystifying theory underlying this new demotic perception of the quality of buildings was encapsulated in the Prince's earliest speech on architecture, the famous 'Carbuncle' address delivered on 30 May 1984 in the Royal Palace at Hampton Court on the 150th anniversary of the founding of the RIBA. On that occasion the Prince said: "For far too long architects have consistently ignored the feelings and wishes of the mass of ordinary people in this country... architects and planners do not necessarily have the monopoly of knowing best about taste, style and planning... ordinary people should not be made to feel guilty or ignorant if their natural preference is for more traditional designs."

This accusation is not original.[8] One way or another, it has probably been repeated by every citizen of every civilised country who has ever been brought face to face with the apparently anomalous certainties of an intelligentsia. Typical of such citizens was the young Adolf Hitler who, in the autumn of

1924, was writing a book in his cell in the prison fortress of Landsberg on the River Lech in Bavaria. Of the "Bolshevistic cubistic grimace" of Modern Art, a close cousin to Modern Architecture, Hitler wrote at that time: "Out of pure fear of the clamour of these art apostles who most violently attacked and nailed down as an old fashioned philistine everyone who did not want to recognise in them the crown of creation, one renounced any serious resistance and gave in to what seemed inevitable after all. One was seized with a genuine fear of being denounced for lack of understanding by these half-wits or scoundrels; as though it were a disgrace not to understand the products of intellectual degenerates or cunning deceivers.... In order not to be considered lacking in art understanding, one accepted all their derision of traditional art until in the end one became unsure of what was good and what was bad."[9]

With due allowance for the roughness of Hitler's tongue, the sentiment he is expressing is strikingly similar to that of Prince Charles, and indeed utterances of his on the subject of architecture bear out the comparison. According to Albert Speer Hitler said to him in 1935, apropos a Modern industrial building: "If one of these so-called modern architects comes along and wants to build housing projects or town halls in the factory style, then I say: he doesn't understand a thing. That isn't modern, it's tasteless, and violates the eternal laws of architecture.... Just imagine, Speer, a Christmas tree in front of a wall of glass, Impossible!"[10]

Some 50 years later the Prince of Wales wrote in a similar vein in A Vision of Britain: "If we abandon the traditional principles upon which architecture was based for 2,500 years or more, then our civilisation suffers. Our lives may be dominated by contemporary forms of sophisticated technology, but we are also the heirs of something far greater."[11]

Nor were the Prince and the Dictator at all far apart in their assessment of what this "something far greater" really was. Writing of the City of London and St Paul's in A Vision of Britain, Charles says: "It is not easy nowadays to remember how Wren's City churches used to surround the glorious dome of St Paul's, like so many yachts riding at anchor around a great ship.... The London that slowly evolved after the Great Fire took more than 300 years to build. It took about 15 years to destroy. What was rebuilt after the war has succeeded in wrecking London's skyline and spoiling the view of St Paul's in a jostling scrum of skyscrapers all competing for attention."[12]

Writing more than 60 years earlier and about another country, Hitler inevitably put it slightly differently and appended an anti-semitic element utterly absent from the Prince's speeches, but again his perception was the same: "In the Germanic Middle Ages…. That which in antiquity found its expression in the Acropolis or in the Pantheon, now clad itself in the forms of the Gothic cathedrals, Like giants they stood out over the swarm of small frameworks, wooden or brick buildings of the Medieval town, and thus they became symbols…. But today, if Berlin were to meet the fate of ancient Rome, then the coming generations could one day admire the ruins of some Jewish department stores, and the hotels of some corporations as the most imposing works of our time."[13]

Nor is there any greater dissimilarity between the attacks on "so-called modern architecture" made by Hitler's supporters in the National Socialist Party and the Prince's own mode of architectural criticism already exemplified above. In 1929, Ernst May's housing in the Frankfurt suburb of Romerstadt was described in the Nazi newspaper Völkischer Beobachter as "a collection of stationary sleeping cars" and "cages for apes".[14] In the same year Herman Goering dismissed the houses at the Weissenhof Siedlung as; "Stalls for animals that cause physical and mental illness" and the Völkischer Beobachter noted wisely, "Flat roofs equal flat heads."[15] The sub-human theme recurred in a Nazi description of the house designed by Mies van der Rohe for the 1931 Berlin building exhibition, which was dismissed as "a horse stable", while the Bauhaus buildings by Walter Gropius were described as "Aquariums".[16]

There can be no doubt that the contemporary rebirth of this form of architectural criticism in Britain came with the Prince of Wales' Hampton Court speech. Four days after it, the popular Sunday Express editorialised: "For years architectural trendies have ripped the heart out of our towns and cities, destroying more communities than Hitler's bombers ever could." In the midst of the avalanche of media attention that greeted the 'Carbuncle' speech, this was perhaps the least noticed utterance, but it did touch upon a train of thought that might have led to a connection between His Royal Highness' attacks on modern architecture and those mounted by Nazis.

The *Sunday Express* leader was the first reference to Adolf Hitler to appear in connection with the Prince of Wales' crusade against what he was later to call the "Frankenstein" creations of the architectural profession in England, but it was not the last.[17] In the famous 'Luftwaffe' speech delivered to a professional audience at the Mansion House in the City of London on 1 December 1987, the Prince himself uncannily paraphrased it when he said: "You have to give this much to the Luftwaffe: when it knocked down our buildings it didn't replace them with anything more offensive than rubble... (but) In the space of a mere 15 years, in the 60s and 70s... (the) planners, architects and developers of the City wrecked the London skyline and desecrated the dome of St Paul's."

The sentiment expressed in the newspaper and the speech is very clear. Hitler and his air force may have damaged many English towns and cities during the war, but the damage they did was minor compared to that inflicted by modern architects and planners afterwards by the uncontrolled demolition of old buildings and the erection of what the Prince went on to describe as "voguish innovations and fashionable novelties that appeal to nobody but other architects".

It is this idea of a period of inexplicable licence brought to an end by common sense that is the second clear connection between the Prince's 'crusade' and the treatment of architecture in the National Socialist era. Nazi Germany looked back upon the revolutionary Modern architecture of the Weimar years, and the Great Depression which was its sequel, in much the same way as the Prince and his supporters look back on the years of massive public sector construction in Britain which preceded the energy crisis and the great inflation of the 1970s.

In September 1940, a year after the commencement of the Second World War, the German Library of Information in New York published a very similar book to *A Vision of Britain*. Entitled *A Nation Builds* it illustrated Neo-Classical government buildings, art galleries, museums, airports, VHF radio towers and, most prolifically, housing schemes—all of which later boasted the same pitched-roof, detached houses set in gardens as are today admired by the Prince and his followers in the Community Architecture movement. The book explained the dissimilarity between National Socialist housing schemes and those of the preceding Weimar Republic in the following way:

"Low cost housing projects were the major architectural projects of the Weimar Republic, and although great strides were made in solving the problem of minimum cost dwellings, the tendency was to make a theory of style—materials and function determine form—more important than the needs of the family. Many of these Siedlungen were such stark expositions of the 'house machine' theory that they have proved to be unsuitable for family life. Today the effort is to build modern, efficient low cost housing, using all the technical inventions which have simplified modern building and modern living without, however, losing the home-like quality of the traditional German dwelling."

In all but its national references, this mild reproof might have been written by the Prince of Wales, or by Dr Alice Coleman, who wrote 45 years later of another attempt to solve the housing problem by modern design: "Our vast housing-problems machine has committed one blunder after another in the name of social betterment.... It is the Utopians who should be experiencing the sense of social failure. They have had their day—40 long years of it—and it has become increasingly clear that their social engineering has not worked."[18]

Clearly in pre-Carolingian Britain, as well as National Socialist Germany, the idea that the 'utopian' domestic architecture of the immediate past was responsible for a degeneration of social and family life has a powerful appeal. The conviction that this dehumanisation could be brought to an end by the application of "the eternal laws of architecture", or "the traditional principles upon which architecture was based for 2,500 years" had similarly widespread support. So, too, did the idea of community control in all planning matters, particularly aesthetics.

In this matter particularly the National Socialist planning and building regulation system might serve as a model for what is now emerging in Britain. In Germany, building control officers, or Baupolizei, were employed by 100s of local authorities as small as those that existed in Britain before the local government reorganisation of 1974. Ironically, it was the very unpredictability of their local judgements through 'community control' that led to the passage of a 1936 federal statute that required a local representative of the equivalent to the Royal Fine Art Commission to preview all planning applications to ensure Gleichschaltung another precedent not without its unconscious adherents today.[19]

Thus it can be seen that in both theory and practice there are strong parallels between the system of aesthetic and planning control in architecture that is evolving under Prince Charles' influence, and that which existed in the Third Reich. In Germany, the predecessor, the official war against Modern Art and Architecture can only be considered a minor aspect of the conduct of the Nazi regime, but even so it was not an innocent intellectual game. In the course of Hitler's rise to power and 12 years of dictatorship, the real blood of architects was spilt, the real careers of architects were ruined, real emigrations of architects were forced and real artistic freedoms disappeared.[20]

For this reason, if for no other, instead of being ignored, or jocularly dismissed as rough justice for an unpopular profession, it is time that the growing enthusiasm for designing by 'Ten Principles', planning by 'Community Control', criticising by ridicule and regulating by undemocratic intervention in the planning process was reviewed in its correct historical context.

Launch of the KdF-Wagen, designed by Ferdinand Porsche, Wolfsburg, Germany, 1938

East German Trabants queue to cross the Czechoslovakian border, 1989

The Footmen of Alexandra Road
1990

What a disappointment before Christmas when the East German Trabant was not voted car of the year! There they were, 100s of 'footmen' and 'go betweens' (two meanings of the word), on television every night, any colour you like as long as they were faded blue, a triumph of old-style mass production performing their last kamikaze mission by transporting ungrateful owners to the West. But motoring journalists lack vision. Unemboldened by the occasional forays into controversy of *Time* magazine's man or woman of the year, or even the periodic lapses of the organisers of the Nobel Peace Prize, the guild of motoring writers just went on as usual and crowned some identikit Japanese Rover instead.

Unlike the Skoda, which is the butt of endless jokes—and East German cement, which is not—the Trabant has never been imported into Britain. Too small, too powerless, too old fashioned, too polluting they say. But there was a message in those newspaper photographs of queues of Trabants at the border. Foreshortened by telephoto lenses and monochrome reproduction they were converted into a kind of automotive replica, if not of Royal Crescent, at least of Alexandra Road—as *The Architects' Journal*'s perceptive Astragal pointed out. In fact Trabants and Alexandra Road, are both products of a philosophy of housing, transport, industry, culture and society that is light years away from our present universe of gridlocked hot hatchbacks and unsellable houses, allegedly worth more than £1.5 trillion. They are evidence of Alice Coleman's original utopia, living relics of a way of thinking that is extinct.

Consider what each represents. First the Trabant, commonly mocked by motor-industryless Brits as one of the few vehicles in the world they really can feel superior about, especially last November when transporter loads of them were being collected nightly by the East German government from the streets of Prague and ignominiously shipped back across the border. Clearly not even Erich Honecker's own Trabant would be a 'fast-appreciating investment' like the £500,000 Ferrarris that crowd the classified pages: and certainly no ordinary one would be a match for one of our run-of-the-mill psychopathic twin-turbo, 16-valve, four-wheel-drive hatchbacks with a cockpit like a fighter plane. The Trabant is something from another world altogether: a lost world of innocence where motoring meant simple low-cost unostentatious transportation, as luxuriously upholstered as an underground train and as assertive as a plain pair of jeans and a t-shirt.

Certainly we have no business laughing. We do not have to go far back in time to find cars of our own like that. Even now there are still one or two left amongst the hurtling *bolides* of the motorways. Underneath their lashings of middle-aged make up, the Mini and the 2CV Citroën still are Trabants of a kind and none the worse for it. For the Trabant is the epitome of cheap standardisation, as opposed to frenetic competition. The perfect example of an automobile as ephemeralised as a disposable razor.

The measure of what such wonderful *valuelessness* could mean can be savoured simply by asking the question; "If you were replanning the consumption patterns of the Western world in the light of all we know now, what sort of car would you issue everybody with: an economical Trabant, or near-Trabant? Or 100s of lavish variations on the theme of leather-lined turbo-stereo mobile ego massage parlour that clogs up our cities today?" Before you answer remember that, while the East Germans may have paid a terrible price in boredom, bad food and zero service for it, one thing that everybody who ever went to their part of Berlin remembers is that *there was never a parking problem*.

Now consider Alexandra Road, the last great public housing scheme of the last great public housing London Borough. There we see the architectural equivalent to the Trabant. Massed dwelling units sharing party walls and doubling roofs up with terraces for maximum structural efficiency. The use of a communal heating system for maximum economy. Design for full traffic segregation, and orientation based on the universal requirement for maximum sun and air. Compare this with the typical volume builder's house of the mid-1980s: detached from its neighbours for marketing reasons but condemned to maximum maintenance, maximum heat loss and minimum synergetic use of structure as a result. Like the gas-guzzling turbo, it is extravagantly equipped with separate systems for minimum efficiency: it is oriented for packing onto a site no matter which it faces, and pedestrian/vehicle segregation is positively discouraged so that the family land speed record car can always be parked at the door. Presented in this impartial, unbiased way, the case for "peas in a pod designs"—as Buckminster Fuller's Trabantine Dymaxion house was once described—looks attractive. The only trouble is that it doesn't work.

Some 15 years before the exodus of the Trabants, amid scenes remarkably similar to those that accompanied the destruction of the Berlin wall, Salvador Allende's Chile cast off the shackles of Uncle Sam (as they were then described) and tried to run a planned economy like East Germany's. Predictably one of the first planning decisions was to stop the wholesale importing of foreign luxury cars and permit the domestic production under licence of only the 2CV Citroën and a larger Peugeot. To solve the housing problem the Unidad Popular government did the same thing. Out went decorated American-style two-storey duplexes, and in came Soviet concrete prefabrication machinery from Cuba where, interestingly enough, it had arrived from East Germany a decade before and been used to erect thousands of six-storey walk-ups.

Alas, as everybody who ever drove a Trabant knows, within two years of the start of this enlightened programme Allende was dead and General Pinochet was riding around in a Cadillac and living in a palace.

The best lecture I ever gave
1990

A few weeks ago I gave a lecture at the Interior Design Department of
a large provincial polytechnic. I was due to speak at 2.30 in the afternoon
but the person who invited me insisted that I arrive in time for lunch.
With my carousels squeezed into a T-Group Fresh Foods carrier bag
I travelled first class from London and read car magazines all the way.
When I got there I was met by a professor in dark glasses who drove a
Nissan Sunny. He took me to a restaurant in the city where he was well
known. After we had ordered he explained that, because of "absurd
polytechnic politics" I would have to pay for my own meal but that
I could "claw it back" afterwards.

Over our lunch he enlarged on the absurdities of polytechnic life. Student
morale was at rock bottom, he explained. "They won't do any work and they
give you no respect. As soon as they find out you're not in it for the money
they desert your classes in droves." The department, he explained, had been
"sold down the river". There was no money and the staff were all against
him. He had just been forced out of the headship of the department into
a "promotional" role, arranging external lecturers, handling press briefings,
entertaining and such like. Still, he didn't care. He was going to take early
retirement and pick up a fat cheque. He had given the polytechnic 20 years
of his life and this is what it had got him. No use crying over spilt milk.
The fact was there was no such place as the groves of academe anymore,
now the whole of education was supposed to be a business and its "product"
was supposed to be education. He laughed mirthlessly.

After an agreeable lunch it was time for me to speak. The professor led
me expertly along a tortuous polytechnic route of 100 banging doors to the
lecture theatre. Outside I met the assistant who was going to work the slide
projectors. This was not his job, he explained menacingly, actually he was
a relative of the exiled king of Hungary, but the "technician" who normally
"switched on" the projectors was taking a sickie so he had kindly "stepped
in to help out". Well, only partly stepped in really. Would it be alright if he
left after ensuring that the two projectors were focused?

We entered the auditorium and I looked for the audience. At first I could
see no one. Finally I located a group of about 20 students right at the back.
I remembered this configuration from my own student days. Some of them
were even sleeping on the rows of tip-up seats.

The about-to-retire professor quickly introduced me as the editor of *The Architects' Journal* and sat down at the front. After politely correcting him I made a short speech about the conservation of old buildings being as futile as trying to keep human beings alive for 500 years, and made my pitch for better English Heritage Holograms instead. Why not just keep a picture of everyone and everything you like? That's what soldiers do... I never finished this part of my talk as I could sense these witticisms were not being well received. Instead I signalled to the king in the projection booth and we plunged into merciful darkness.

My slides were, although I say so myself, formidable. I was pretending that I was a visitor from outer space come to investigate the relationship between technology and the natural world on earth so my first slide was a NASA visualisation of a Black Hole in the galaxy of Andromeda. From there I approached the earth in stages by way of all the planets that the Voyager probes had visited. Cunningly I came in past our Moon, taking in some vintage Apollo domestic scenes, and then visited a number of satellites in earth orbit. Finally, I landed at Cape Kennedy—using space shuttle launch shots in reverse—and drove immediately to EPCOT taking in some awesome images of the Grand Canyon on the way. This, I explained, was the idea of the relationship of man-made technology to the natural environment that voyagers from a distant star would pick up if they ever came in to land on spaceship earth. And an admirable one it was too. Not like this stuff. And I showed a collection of pictures of a 1959 Cadillac; the inside of Mad Ludwig's palace at Linderhof; some Memphis furniture; Richmond Riverside; bouncy castles; Japanese work clothes; building FC-2 at Canary Wharf by SOM; Gail Daniels' earrings; Jonathan Glancey in his Jaguar and Rod Hackney's six-wheeled Range Rover.

I paused, then I swung into my real favourites; Gothic cathedrals; stained glass windows; massed VDUs; Dutch land reclamation from the air; early Zeppelins on the ground; black plastic drying tunnels; Congolese pirogues under construction; the new Express Newspapers building by Fitzroy Robinson, the Wolf Rock lighthouse and the East German Trabant before Volkswagen ruined it. This, I said, was the way to go.

It was time to wind up. If architects don't stop humouring the world's mad craving for ornament and permanence soon, I thundered, and get to

grips with simplicity and ephemeralisation instead, we will all fry in
a cancerous greenhouse. Thank you.

The lights came up and there was a long silence. Finally the unlucky
professor did his job and asked a question. How true all that stuff about
ephemeralisation was, he said, but how unfortunate that it had never
been less popular than now! Why was it, did I suppose, that people
had this insatiable craving for Spanish galleons, pieces of eight and
Georgian houses?

I looked sympathetic. The problem was sentimentality I said. Nowadays
everybody was frightened to do anything except set up a poll to find out
what everybody else thought. Most people lacked the nerve even to say,
Spitalfields? No thanks.

The next question came from a student. Didn't I think that all this high-
tech stuff had had its chance and failed. After all there was the Hindenburg,
Ronan Point and the Challenger, there were all those M25 crashes, there was
asbestos in schools, lead poisoning, unburned hydrocarbons, nitrous oxide,
untreated sewage in the Moray Firth and anyway, what would be the effect
of it all on interior design?

I was grateful for the last part. "There will be no effect on interior
design at all", I reassured her. "Today interior designers are in the middle
of golden age of freedom and public respect. There is no bureaucracy to
control them, no rules and regulations to limit their imaginations. Why, if
the world were designed by interior designers, I for one would die happy."
She seemed unconvinced.

"But what about all the pleasure that ancient monuments give to ordinary
people?" Asked another student in a concerned voice. "I suppose you would
want them all knocked down and replaced by more motorways?"

"Well, as a keen motorist", I began, but no one laughed. Mercifully
the professor spoke.

"What Mr Pawley is going to say is that these ancient monuments
are actually being destroyed by tourism. Have any of you visited a
Medieval cathedral recently? It is like the Hillsboro disaster. Buses, cars,
pedestrians, school parties. The very idea that a troubled soul could seek
solace in these ancient Houses of God has been turned into a mockery by
the heritage industry."

How very true that was. I could think of little to add but I tried. "You see it's the problems that are real, not out of date sentimental attitudes. We don't have a choice really. Either we retain the capacity to alter the built environment drastically to suit new needs in the way that it has always been drastically altered in the past by a technological elite, or we will suffocate in a homogenised jungle of fake history. It's as simple as that."

As I returned to London in the train memorising the prices in *Parker's Car Price Guide*, I reflected on a day well spent. I was glad I wasn't taking early retirement.

In pursuit of the ultimate driving machine

1990

There is a therapeutic atmosphere in a green and white BMW showroom. Most people funk going into them but I don't mind. It only costs about £9,000 a go and it's worth it for the free cup of coffee. The cars they put in the showrooms are specially chosen to lure in modest punters, so while there might be an unregistered Five series in dolphin grey right in front for £27,000, somewhere behind it there is sure to be a modest white 320i for £9,995, and alongside that a Polaris 325i on a 'D' plate for £12,995 with only 17,000 miles on the clock. The last one is the one that makes you think. 'D' was August 1986, a long time ago. If the mileage is correct that car has only been driven 3,700 miles a year for the last four years. Is that possible? Look at the body. There are a thousand tiny parking dents in the door and there is something about the paint around the shut lines that a paranoid person might connect with crash repairs after a heavy frontal.... "Can I help you Sir?"

"I'd like to see Jim Brightside please."

"Mr Brightside is out collecting a car. Can anyone else help you?"

"No, Mr Brightside's the man I spoke to on the telephone. It's the car I want to look at that he's collecting."

"And you are, sir?"

"Mr, er... Gomez."

"Would you like a cup of coffee while you wait Mr... Gomez?"

"No thank you."

After a time the receptionist addresses me again from her desk. "Mr Gomez, would you like our valuer to appraise your own car while you are waiting, to save time?"

The valuer in no way resembles my mental image of the genial Brightside. He had a broad Australian accent and sounded as obliging as one of the lads from *Neighbours*. This man is English and looks like Doctor Phibes. The only thing that impresses him about my car is that it is legally parked in a resident's bay. He goes into his antiques roadshow routine. "Lachs silver, hmmm. I haven't seen one of those for a long time. A little out of fashion now but it always comes up better than Polaris." Then suddenly he notices the scratch running from the offside B post to the filler cap. "Oh dear", he exclaims in a concerned voice. "What's this? What a shame...."

"Wait till you see the other side", I joke. "My schizophrenic son kicked the door in."

The valuer looks perplexed. Luckily Jim Brightside turns up in person in the 325 that is the object of my desires. He blips the throttle and his smiling face is revealed as the tinted window slips down. Just as I had expected, he looks like the youthful boss of the Robinson Corporation.

It was Lord St John of Fawsley who first observed that the essence of a BMW lies not so much in its four headlights as its kinked C-posts. Back in the crowded mews behind the showroom you can see how right he was. There must be half a dozen Three Series there. It never ceases to amaze me how different identical cars can look. The 325 Brightside he has driven over is a diamond black two door, a perfect late Big Bang dealers car, still with the original holes where the phone was ripped out when Hazard Brothers sacked 200 staff. Brightside saunters round it running his fingers appreciatively over the colour coded rear spoiler. "Special equipment model", he says. "Esr, e/w, pdm, pas, abs, air, cruise...." I make a joke about the licence number. Its letters spell HLP. Brightside commiserates. English plates are stupid. People here pay a fortune for combinations of letters and numbers that don't mean a thing to anybody. In Australia you can have any initials you like, and in three colours too. It's time for the test drive. "Die Fahnen hoch! Die Reihen dicht geschlossen", I hum to myself as I turn the key. BMWs are very conservative, stealthy almost. They don't care about all that Audi Cd stuff, or flirt with hatchbacks or front wheel drive. Until the new Seven and the new Five came along they just dealt with wind noise by attention to detail, little rubber seals everywhere. More than any of the others the Three series depends for its appeal on the *posture* of the car. Up to 1983 nose in the air. After 1983 a high tail. This particular car is a 1988, almost the last throw of the current Threes. Next spring it will be replaced by something bigger and even more stealthy.

My mind flicks back to a disagreeable experience earlier that morning at Iron Fist BMW across the river. There the sales technique had been entirely different. As I crawl through the traffic towards the beginning of the M40 I relive the whole horrible experience. Unlike tiny London Glades, Iron Fist has a showroom as big as the Ritz, and great sheds of BMWs behind it, stretching back as far as the eye can see.

"Yes?" The receptionist had said sharply when I went in.

"Er, Mr Neil Testyman please."

Testyman had bustled up. Apart from wearing most of a smart pinstriped suit he looked like a harassed schoolmaster.

"Well, what do you want?"

"I telephoned earlier in the week about the 325 auto...."

"When was that, yesterday... the day before? I don't remember. I do wish you people would make an appointment and stick to it."

"Well, I was passing by...."

"I suppose you want to see the car?"

Testyman had led me back through the seven ages of BMW interior decoration, from preternaturally clean white and green, through the purposefully echoing workshop's boom, back into the spacious tomb of cast iron and asbestos where the old cars are. There up against a brick wall and covered in dust was a Zinnobar 325 auto with no distinguishing features at all apart from mud flaps.

"See those mud flaps? Sign of a pretty well looked after car", Testyman had conceded after a few moments.

"Well, it's not my favourite colour", I had ventured.

"Not much I can do about that. Do you want it or don't you?"

"It depends what you will give me for mine."

There was no nonsense about a 'valuer' at Iron Fist. Testyman took a small red book out of his pocket. "What did you say the mileage on your car was?"

"69,000. All motorway, full service history."

"I was assuming a full service history. A 525e with 69,000 on a 'D' plate... It's not even in the book, and I certainly don't need to look at it. It's just an out of date old car. Maybe £3,000—if it's got no dents in it —less if it has."

"But it's no older than this one...."

Testyman had looked at his watch. "Mr Gomez, 99 per cent of our business here is company business. That means new cars. We have about £8 million worth of cars in here and this red one is the only one on a 'D' plate. The only reason it is here at all is because it has only done 11,000 miles in four years, not 69,000 or 100,000. I couldn't retail a car like yours. I wouldn't even try. You ought to be happy that I am even considering taking it off your hands. Now are you interested or not?"

"Er, well, no."

The disagreeable memory fades. Brightside is still chattering away as I practice a few experimental squirts of speed in the black 325 on the elevated section. The engine moans. The tach whirls. "I come from Australia where we drive huge distances", he confides. "69,000 miles is nothing for a big BMW. I just know we can offer you a cracking trade-in against one of our fine warrantied pre-owned cars." But back at the mews half an hour later the valuer is not so sure. The cracking price turns out to be £3,750. Old Testyman at Iron Fist had not been far out after all. Tight lipped I get into my out of date old car and drive away.

Testyman never calls again but the next day Jim Brightside is on the telephone. "Great news Mr Gomez! We did some checking with the wholesalers. I think we can offer you £4,500 for your car against the black 325!" His tone suggests that he has just found buried treasure and is offering to share it with me. Material culture being what it is I almost believe him. That is the power of BMW, the ultimate driving machine.

Exogenous shock
1990

The great energy crisis began on 6 October 1973 when engineering units of the Egyptian army crossed the Suez Canal in an attempt to recover the Sinai Peninsula from Israel, which had seized it six years before. This action began a train of events that was to culminate in a temporary cessation of Middle Eastern oil exports to Europe and the United States and the sudden spectre of fuel starvation. It was what economists came to call an "exogenous shock" to all the economies of the Western world and its consequences can still be detected to this day.

In the United States nothing remotely like it had happened since the spring of 1942 when German U-Boats started systematically sinking tankers on their way from the Gulf ports and Venezuela to the North Eastern seaboard. At that time there were no overland pipelines linking these oil reserves with the most populous regions in the country. These had to be speedily supplied. Between Pearl Harbour and VJ Day 13,400 new oil wells were drilled in the United States; ten billion dollars worth of new refineries were built, and 10,000 miles of new oil pipeline were laid. It was the 1942 energy crisis that led to the discovery of Alaskan oil, a reserve whose exploitation a generation later was to bring problems of its own.

Things were different in 1974, and not just because the crisis was much shorter. For one thing resource exhaustion was not an unpleasant surprise like Pearl Harbour, it was already on the intellectual agenda, along with the population time bomb, the population crisis, the threat of Soviet world domination, and global hunger. And indeed, like all but one of these others, it remains on the agenda today, for the energy crisis was never really overcome, it was merely postponed by economics. Once the actual oil embargo period came to an end, oil supplies from the Middle East were resumed at vastly increased cost. Severe recession coupled with high inflation, a massive increase in international debt, and an ingenious process of 'recycling' Middle Eastern oil earnings back into investment in the West, proved a simpler solution than repeating the drastic government interventions of 1942.

Nonetheless these interventions were considered and mapped out. They ranged from military action in the Middle East to a massive austerity plan for the domestic economy designed to reduce its consumption of imported fossil fuels by 60 per cent. Virtually the only relic of this plan today is the continuing progressive application of fuel consumption restrictions on motor vehicles, originally introduced to save energy, but retained to combat atmospheric pollution. The construction element of the plan, which involved the rationing of process energy for all building materials and components, was never put into operation. United States government researchers very rapidly discovered what was also discovered in Europe: that product life is so long in the world of buildings that saving energy in producing new ones is far less effective than controlling the operating cost of what already exists.

With action at government level soon confined to so-called passive measures, it was left to enterprising individuals to explore the possibilities of an apocalyptic energy architecture. But precisely because construction is a slow process, all that could really happen at first was a change of leadership in the profession. This of course was what had happened at the time of the exogenous shock of the Second World War, after which the Modern manifesto writers of 1914 found themselves honoured academicians. It was their rule of sclerosed modernism that was finally toppled by the energy crisis of 1974. And by then there was a new avant-garde variously called the "Counter Culture" or the "Generation of 1968" waiting in turn for its own promotion.

It was the confrontation of these two generations that was characterised then by Sheldon Wolin when he said prophetically in 1971; "We are all behaving as though our only choice is between Werner von Braun and a bunch of hippies."

What Werner von Braun stood for at the time of the energy crisis was never in very much doubt. The technological elite that he represented believed in science and space travel for the future; system building to solve the housing problem; freeway building to solve the traffic problem; airport building to solve the travel problem; and birth control to solve the population problem. In terms of construction the apogee of their thinking was probably represented by Richard Buckminster Fuller's megastructure projects. Although apparently lionised by the bunch of hippies, Fuller, 1895–1983, had no truck with *Small is Beautiful*, the counter-culture economist Fritz Schumacher's world-parroted book-title slogan in favour of a new peasant autarchy, even though his geodesic domes were to play an inadvertent part in its formation.

While he never opposed the back-to-the-land-movement—"I do not fight forces, I use them"—Fuller never lost faith in macro-architectural creativity. In the 1960s, in partnership with the engineer Shoji Sadao, he had proposed immense structures for the interface between land surface and stratosphere that promised gains in energy efficiency that were appropriate to the scale of the energy crisis. The last and best of them, dating from 1969, was for an intercontinental high-voltage transmission grid capable of delivering electricity across time zones so as to balance out base and peak loads all over the world. Less than a year before the 1973 Middle East War, Fuller had said: "the technical efficiency of our overall economy is of so low an order—five per cent—that 95 out of every 100 barrels of petroleum that we burn are completely wasted".

The thinking of Wolin's bunch of hippies was more inscrutable. Instantly identifiable by their long hair and manner of dress, and politically identifiable by their strong bias to the Left, they had constructed an international revolutionary movement based on a mythology drawn from the Paris 'events' of May 1968; the Cultural Revolution in China; the music festivals that had started with Woodstock in New York State in July 1969; and a dogged opposition to the Vietnam War.

These disparate ingredients did not naturally give rise to an architecture. Indeed within the counter culture not only the whole concept of technology, or "big science", but the idea of ownership and property itself was suspect. "The reality of a common existence of men as a harmonious whole is impossible within the acceptance of property", wrote Draft protester David Harris from a federal prison in 1970, and this opinion was widely accepted.

It was the pride of the counter culture that its most famous images, like the panorama of Woodstock, were devoid of the ideological forms or structures of the earlier mass movement of the twentieth century. There were deliberately no buildings and no serried ranks. The free-forming seas of human bodies were interrupted only by towers for lights, sound systems or cameras. The only real uniform of the counter culture was its recorded music and its televised image of itself. It was the first time in history that architecture had apparently been rendered unnecessary.

But an architecture of the generation of 1968 emerged nonetheless. One of its McLuhanised strands originated beneath the threshold of architectural culture in the streams of images of primitive shelters that the new electronic media of the 1960s beamed in from the *barriadas* of the dispossessed across the world. Another strand was picked up in those remote corners of the United States where the bunch of hippies sought to establish self-governing settlements of their own. What determined the architectural form of these settlements? Not anthropology or politics but chance. According to the pseudonymous Peter Rabbit, author of *Drop City*, the original New Mexico counter-culture builders of 1965 had intended to construct A-frames but, on their way to begin construction, had diverted to attend a lecture by Buckminster Fuller. The result was the famous car-top domes of Drop City destined to be illustrated all over the world. In the end long hair and slightly irregular domes became as synonymous with the movement as feathered head dresses and tepees had been with the North American Indians a century before. Two years into the energy crisis an enterprising counter-culture publisher named Lloyd Kahn had sold 138,000 copies of two broadsheet dome picture books called *Domebook* and *Domebook 2*. His next venture, called *Shelter*, aimed straight for what his readers wanted to see: "Domes, barns, tree houses, houseboats and nomad tents, American Indian wooden structures and Irish farm buildings." Kahn was joined by another entrepreneur named Stewart Brand whose publication, boldly entitled *The Whole Earth Catalog*, consisted of ever larger volumes of news snippets culled from architecture and building magazines, 'how-to' features and propaganda from the self-sufficiency front. Brand's publication soon sold globally and rapidly made him a millionaire.

Somehow, bathed in the uncertain promise of solar radiation, all the disparate dreams of *The Whole Earth Catalog*—from music and revolution to vernacular mud huts and robot settlements—were welded together into an alternative architecture that, by the mid-1970s, was ready to exploit the energy panic that was sweeping through the developed world. The old modern world of larger and larger projects stood revealed as an energy junkie, driven mad by nonsense about 'economies of scale'; paralysed by the weight of its own enormous projects to enlarge its already enormous cities; terrified of its own enormous weapon systems; and addicted to its absurd, enormous cars, aircraft and skyscrapers. And at that instant it became intellectually respectable to contrast it with the virtues of little

people like the street farmers, who sprinkled grass seed all over London
—in an effort to subvert tarmac and concrete by natural means—and in
America with "Folks like Steve and Holly Baer, who heat their home with
the sun (and 90 recycled 55-gallon oil drums). Tom Oates, a North Carolina
craftsman, who still uses DC electricity produced by a water wheel he installed
nearly 40 years ago. John Fry, the South African pig farmer who has completely
powered his house and barns for over six years with methane gas extracted
from his animals' manure. Henry Clews, who now operates two homes and
a business on electricity made with a windplant...." And so on indefinitely
from the pages of the 1975 *Mother Earth News Handbook of Homemade Power.*
Of these 'folks' perhaps the most noteworthy was Steve Baer, who also turned
publisher and contrived to sell more than 100,000 copies of a *Dome Cookbook*
filled with handwritten instructions for making sheet metal icosahedrons.

At this time only the discredited Werner von Braun understood the
reluctance of the corporate 'money making' economy to invest in energy
efficiency of any kind endorsed by folks like 'Johnny Solarseed', a hapless
comic book figure created by architect Dennis Lamoureaux who toured the
United States in a truck in 1976 peddling books on insulation and offering the
simple message: "The solution to the ENERGY PROBLEM is better SHELTER;
and the clever use of SOLAR ENERGY is just MASS UNDER GLASS."

If the scale of Werner von Braun's proposed energy architecture was vast,
so vast that few can grasp it even today, the work of the 'Biological
Architecture' or 'Biotecture' school, the intellectual wing of the self-build
autarchic housing movement, was similarly wish-fulfilling in a different
way. Of the ambitions of the 'Biotecturists' American architect Roy Mason
wrote in the July 1977 issue of a magazine called *The Futurist*; "Neither the
smallest cottage nor the largest metropolis can ever be completely isolated
or cut off from nature. What we should do is build upon this fact instead
of fighting against it. Instead of expending great quantities of energy and
material resources to create and maintain an artificial environment,
biological architects follow two approaches: first they seek to use nature
as a model and design buildings that apply the structural principles found
in nature, and second they try to develop ways in which nature itself can do
the construction work. We shall call the first approach 'biomorphic' and
the second 'biostructural'."

Despite his confident use of the present tense to describe the activities of 'biological architects', Mason's outline programme was doomed to be confined to experiments. Where the technological superhumanism of 1960s groups like Archigram in England and the Metabolists in Japan finally ended up in the art market instead of on the building site, 'biotecture' led to an isolated series of small houses and backyard experiments. There were more of these in the United States than in Europe, but on neither continent did their design establish a genuine low-energy lifestyle, nor did science provide them with the cheap ambient energy sources they confidently claimed were universally available. In England a well-financed experimental energy home project at Cambridge University received a sceptical send-off from the *London Evening Standard* in 1974: "Cambridge researchers are soon to put to the test their claim that there is enough energy in the air to heat and run a home in the damp and chill of an English winter. Mr Alexander Pike, head of the technical research division at the university said; 'We are not eco-freaks. We are trying to establish a firm theoretical framework before we start building hardware.'"

And the scepticism was justified for the Cambridge house, despite a generous research grant, advanced no further than a detailed model and a lot of questions. The German architect Rolf Doernach, whose biotecture projects ranged from a 'farm' near Stuttgart made of living hazel trees bent into arch shapes, to a proposed ocean-going city designed to be housed in a crustacean-structured dome, 'grown' on sunken spherical formwork, made no more progress.

Mason's own career led to the construction of a number of 'organic' sprayed concrete houses billed as 'homes of the future', but these too resolutely refused to unplug themselves from the levels of energy demand common in conventional settlements. In cases where utopian architectural settlements were already under construction, as with Paolo Soleri's Arcosanti in Arizona, the belated addition of solar collectors did little to resolve the same problem.

In the end, the energy crisis proved to be both less acute and more ambiguous than was expected in the winter of 1974. It produced no "massive lifestyle changes" and, in architecture at least, no "design revolution". Under its impact the motor industry and the construction industry turned in opposite directions. Construction clung to its tradition of long life, loose-fit buildings: the car industry developed a new capacity to build short-life, tight-fit cars.

In the end, despite the profusion of designs for solar houses and energy homes that it spawned, the energy crisis did not revolutionise architecture. Its long-term influence upon residential building was marginal. Nor did it much transform the nature of industrial buildings, where process energy consumption so far exceeded the use of energy for heating or cooling that the largest savings were achieved by computerised energy management systems.

The real innovation occurred in the commercial sector. Born out of the synergetic conjunction of modern steel-frame construction, satellite communications links between financial centres, and the recycling into the economies of the West of the fabulous oil wealth generated by the 1974 and 1979 OPEC oil price increases, the financial services building of superbanks, ablaze with light and with their vast computerised dealing rooms generating 500 watts of heat per square foot or more, was ironically the one real and perverse architectural creation of the energy crisis.

Where the big sheds are
1990

If you ever plan to motor west, take the M5 it's the highway that's the best. Round about Avonmouth it gives you a better view of Shedland than any other motorway in Britain. What is Shedland? Well, *ipsa res loquitur* as the lawyers say. When the architectural historians of the late twentieth century finally get round to counting the square footage of planning permissions granted in the 1980s (the way they once counted the number of people at the pop concerts of the 1960s), they will eventually down calculators and look at one another and say; "By the sacred bones of Peter Palumbo, the only real patron of architecture on any scale then was the distribution industry, and Shedland is what they did!"

Because it is a McLuhanised, seamless, decentralised state of being rather than a specific place, Shedland cannot really be localised. Like strips of shredded truck tyre you can find Shedland anywhere there is a motorway. That is the beauty of it. It has no beginning, no middle and no end, only a presence that you are vaguely conscious of as you zoom by listening to phone-ins with one eye peeled for those polite men in the unmarked Volvo 760, and the other worrying about that sluggish bunch of Cavaliers up ahead.

So let us just take one portion of Shedland, so to speak like any large carton of fries at any MacDonalds in the world, and have a look at it. Let's start with my favourite which is called "1916"—the section of the M5 bounded in the south by exit 19 at Gordano, and in the north by exit 16 at Patchway. Running south down the M5 towards this sector of Shedland you can detect the start of 1916 by the appearance of Aztec West on your left. Possibly the world's first science park (or so it seems) this new metropolis was all green fields and villages with names like "Over" and "Catbrain" only a few years ago. Now, with its early Nick Grimshaw buildings already overshadowed by CZWG pomo and carriage trade B1 offices filling up all the gaps, it has become the Hong Kong Island to 1916s Kowloon.

As you cruise the inside lane of the southbound carriageway of the M5, taking in the whole of Aztec's mostly inscrutable western boundary, you feel your pulse quickening. This is a sure sign that you are entering Shedland and leaving Heritage Britain behind. It's like entering a game reserve: from now on you somehow know there won't be another Tudor Rose leisure sign until you rejoin the mainland.

Wow! Only a mile or so after Aztec and already you've seen a gigantic Anchor warehouse grazing right on the hard shoulder. Just after that, over on the right, across the crash barrier and the three lanes of the northbound carriageway, you see more beasts slumbering. There, where the uncut verges have turned to hay and the untended shrubs have already become sizeable trees, you can make out the letters "ZA.USSI .HE .PPLIA..E OF . CIENCE" on the faded silver side of another monster, and then, suddenly, your eyes swock over to the left again and there is the beginning of the Shedland mother lode, Kowloon! Or rather Cribb's Causeway, with its epic quarter-mile long grey profiled steel SAFEWAY warehouse and bright yellow BDP shopping centre. Words flash; "ARGOS", "MAKRO", "Golden Arches", and yes, over there is something immensely bigger. Hovering behind all this on the horizon are the mighty Filton hangars where Concorde was born.

But if you think Cribb's Causeway is the Shangri-la of sheds you are wrong. Over again go your eyes to the right and, just as you sight the great parabola of the Avon Bridge ahead, there it is, Avonmouth! There with its chimneys belching sulphurous yellow smoke, its rows of Cornish Units and BISF houses untouched since the 50s, its big concrete silos and old grey warehouses that were built before they knew how to build 'em cheap and pile 'em high.

A sea of houses, huts, sheds, factories, cranes; ships that look like buildings and buildings that look like ships, all trailing away towards the brown smear of the mouth of the Severn. And all around it are sheds. As you snatch your first nervous glance it seems as though a vast buffalo herd of sheds must run all the way back north to the great bridges over the Severn; all the way south to the great split that lets the climbing, winding motorway through the hills and down onto the Somerset Levels; all the way east to the Clifton ravine, and all the way west to the smudge of Wales on the horizon.

Another mile of this and your heart is really thumping. Right from the apex of the bridge, hanging onto the wheel because you only get one glimpse of it, like a doomed Argentine jet pilot sighting the Canberra in San Carlos Water, over to the right again, day or night, you see the shed of sheds, the glistening white ramp of the Redland plasterboard factory, and around it another whole shed complex called Portbury.

With trembling fingers you indicate left and swoop off the motorway. Round the Gordano roundabout, off due west and there it is right in front of you, so big it looms over the cluster of smaller warehouses that seem to be sucking nutrients from its giant teats. Ughh! Two vast ski-slopes of white painted profiled metal, 50 metres from ground to the ridge. 150 metres long. Its low production shed in the foreground even bigger, another 500 metres long. The nearer you get the more completely it fills your windshield.... Bombs away!

Actually you have to hit the brakes at about this point because the whole Redland complex is protected by chainlink fencing and security guards. This plasterboard factory is the most modern in Europe and the equipment in the production shed is so secret that not even an architectural critic with poor eyesight and no O Level maths would be allowed inside for 1/60th of a second. Instead you have to creep round the perimeter fencing on an unsurfaced track that seems almost as though it was left there for the purpose because it enables you to marvel all the more at the vastness of it all.

Most people who glance at big sheds from the outside think of them as empty, or at least only partly full, perhaps with pallets or boxes or blokes rolling their own. In fact big sheds are always crammed full, fuller than mere humans could ever pack them without the assistance of computers. Real big sheds often have racking from floor to ceiling, with only narrow aisles cutting across from one side to the other down which race automated cranes, rising and falling in flight and stopping only to pick up a pallet, check with Milton Keynes via a bar-code reader, and then swoop on again to the conveyors and carousels and forklift trucks that lead right into the vast trailers of the articulated lorries as big as houses that are the mobile architecture of distribution.

Uniquely the Redland shed is not like that. That is why it looks so different. Not only is its mighty nave steeply pitched, instead of flat-roofed, but it is filled with one vast mountain of Spanish gypsum, shipped across to Portbury in 30,000 tonne bulk carriers and mechanically transferred half a kilometre through the air from the ship's hold to the storage shed by means of a vast, white overhead conveyor. Redland is all surprises but so are most sheds, and you needn't miss them all. Even if you overshoot 1916 altogether you only have to travel another 20 miles before your eyeballs come out on stalks again. This time it's a 300,000 square foot ARGOS treasure house that looks as though it is trying to cross the road.

Notes on the meaning of trivial things
1991

For me it all started the day Hugh Pearman discovered that his Samsonite briefcase was impossible to open the wrong way up. "Look, it has tumblers", he exclaimed delightedly, banging the streamlined grey kryptonite container down none too carefully on the table at Manzis. "They work by gravity.... It just can't be opened upside down. What a brilliant piece of design! If only the human body was designed as well as this briefcase...." I wholeheartedly shared his enthusiasm, and so did everyone else in the restaurant. The scene was like a 1954 *Life* magazine advertisement. We should all treasure such moments. And there I was thinking that good design was getting so hard to find you had to hire a detective.

Great thoughts come unexpectedly, like those vast Zeppelins you occasionally feel cruising around your intestines. The truth that occurred to me that lunchtime was that ideas come out of gadgets, not the reverse. Gadgets do not come out of ideas. The discovery of that briefcase that only opened with its lid uppermost even in pitch darkness or underwater was indeed cause for celebration, but it was not a feat of design. It was one of those things like apposite thumbs that emerged from the vast primeval history of continuous technical development that stretched back to the world of dinosaur bones—or in that case the world's first carpet bag. Like the pocket ioniser or the throwaway camera, if you started out now trying to invent one *ab initio* you would never get there. You would have to have been in the briefcase business or the negative ions business (see driver for details) or the image processing business for generations before the viability of such devices would ever occur to you. Even now there are millions of people walking about with apposite thumbs and failsafe briefcases who do not know how clever they are.

But while what we might call the "spin-on" that leads to such inventions can only be approximated in the kind of closed scientific society you find in an ant hill, a bee hive, or the air conditioned offices in front of a B8 shed in Magna Park, the spin-off from them is literally boundless. Not only are ordinary people all over the world holding their briefcases upside down in wonderment, maybe even winning bets by doing it; but in the title sequences of movies yet unmade aeroplane designers are looking at briefcases and thinking that they could design planes like that, and famous toast designers starring in TV commercials are working on Samsonite toast that cannot ever land on the marmalade side.

In truth the diffusion of ideas from the products of material culture is limitless, and this means that there is no such thing as a trivial step in design innovation. Everything fits into the great evolutionary scheme of things somewhere, even the Dodo and the Cassowary. You may laugh at the "Phantom Pet" that you take for a walk on its rigid lead (you can't see it but you can make it bark or mew when you press a button); the squawking parrot phone; the inflatable swimming pool Cadillac; the half-million candlepower "Nite Tracker" torch; the stunt watch; the digital pedometer; the car security bear (a break-in triggers his incredible 110db Winnie the Pooh siren), or the rollerball 'fat pen' (it fits into your whole hand), but all these incremental mutations have a function in the great evolutionary scheme of things. Behind every one lies the possibility of a chain reaction of the electric ferocity that led from the shape of a cooked lobster claw to the A.C.I.D. three wheeler by Stefan Sielaff that wowed them at the RCA show last summer—all by way of the computer graphic Walt Disney TRON death racer that must have been buried in his subconscious.

But what about the big issues. How can all these trinkets be important at a time when the economy has been handed over to the Bundesbank and all the old ideas are done for? What is there to live for now? Surely not just a multi-lingual talking translator or an electronic ski simulator. Who cares what language they speak or whether they break their legs or not now that the conservation of the past has become as high-tech as science fiction; the great money making nostrum the housing market is dead beyond revival; national sovereignty is out the window; the channel tunnel didn't fail after all, and the future has finally arrived.

And that is exactly the point. From now on, as Thomas Carlyle predicted in 1831; "The whole life of society must be carried on by drugs: doctor after doctor will appear with his nostrum, Cooperative Societies, Universal Suffrage, Cottage-and-Cow systems, repression of population, Vote by Ballot...." And he would have added the innovations catalogue and the leading edge too, if they had been around when he wrote with his skinny quill pen.

Carlyle had his own list of leading edge innovations. He believed that "universal suffrage", "vote by ballot", "cottage and cow" and so on were the nineteenth century equivalents to the twentieth century electrosonic jewellery cleaner. They were the answer to entropic apocalypse: the dreaded arrival of a terminal, unordered economic state that no longer worked on its own (as he believed the Ewok-style subsistence economy of Feudal times once had) but required constant blasts of nitrous oxide suffrage and methanol birth control just to keep it alive. Nor was Carlyle alone in this. All nineteenth century thinkers had their nostrums. William Cobbett predicted the salvation of the workless classes if they stopped drinking tea, and the engineers' PR-man Samuel Smiles thought property ownership was the key to the elimination of drunkenness. But it was Carlyle who got closest to postmodern trinketism. He believed in the necessity of a strong tide of invention, not because he like the idea of it, but because he saw that one half-baked idea after another overcame the inertia of low-energy terminal disorder for just long enough for the beating heart of the whole enterprise to kick into action again. Although we might as well admit here and now that neither Carlyle, Cobbett nor Smiles would have been impressed by Pearman's briefcase, although Jeremy Bentham might have been, these nineteenth century figures, the world's greatest con men almost, came *faut-de-mieux* to the same apparently inadequate solutions to the same apparently insoluble problem of degeneration into meaninglessness in the same trashy innovations catalogue as we look at ourselves.

The advantage of our position, looking back 150 years or so, is that we can see that all their 'inventions' were not worth the paper they were printed on. We the former Imperial English, then briefly the hooligan Brits, and now merely the rebellious right-hand-drive 240-volt tribesmen of the European Community fringe, know that "universal suffrage", "repression of population" and an end to tea drinking are no use at all. After all, the last time we tried laughing at foreigners, when we began congratulating ourselves on the collapse of the misguided socialist economies of Eastern Europe, our own unguided market economy promptly started coming apart at the seams. Now we of all people must see that we are standing at the deathbed of all economic systems.

The nineteenth century political nostrums may be worn out and discredited, creatures of the written word, ideas of a society that existed when Dolphin Square was a gigantic uniform factory for the soldiers of the

Empire. But today we have another set of possibilities that we can see in the Argos catalogue of our culture. The trivial increments of consumer design may each seem annoyingly pointless, but we should never forget that any one of them is capable of becoming the missing link between the disposable nappy and the ozone layer.

The design origins of royal train syndrome
1991

Night has fallen and the brilliantly-lit tube of the standard class carriage hurtles through the darkness, obeying every command of the rails. Forcibly retired from the wheel of my BMW by North Avon Magistrates Court, I stare at a newspaper. "Dead turtle mistaken for human remains", is one of the more promising headlines travelling up to London with me from the country. Another story tells of a planning officer's wife being driven out of a supermarket by locals throwing cereal packets and baked bean cans. The best thing about riding the rails is that stuff like this enables you to keep design in perspective.

Notwithstanding the arrival of the 140 mph InterCity 225 in 1988, with its inboard disc brakes, Maestro-matching acceleration and cruise control, there is still a lot wrong with the design of our trains. It is not just that most of them are old fashioned, although the diesel 125s with an engine at each end have been around for a quarter of a century and their last putative 'High-Tech' successor, the ill-fated APT with its two engines in the middle, was a design disaster of Edsel proportions that was consigned to the Railway Museum at York after less than one week in service. There is more to it than that. In train design it is the sociology, not the technology that counts.

British Rail passenger rolling stock actually reinforces the English class system. You can see that in the way the company, even though it is destined to follow the Water Authorities into dismemberment and privatisation, still maintains the Bourbon waywardness of that other absolute monarchy—the BBC. Enormous practical changes like the disappearance of 'real' breakfast in the dining cars, or the coming of in-train telephones, have no more destabilised it than the advent of the commercial channels did the BBC. Today you may be permitted to telephone from a train to your daughter having coffee in America after her aerobics class, but that doesn't make you important. Under certain conditions, even if you have a ticket, you may not even be allowed to board the train. Certainly you are rarely allowed to eat in the dining car unless you are travelling first class.

At its most extreme the Byzantine fare structure of British Rail means that shattering class contrasts occur. At weekends a kind of feast of fools occurs so that all the people travelling First Class—except a scowling minority right at the front—only pay a tiny surcharge over the standard fare. Midweek there is a savage crackdown and even the First Class passengers can't reach their own First Class lavatories without clambering over vagabonds squatting on the floor of the freezing, high-decibel limbo between the coaches. What sort of tickets do these seatless ones have? You never know. But it is an important part of British Rail's sociological design theory that they should be there. They reinforce the punishing workload of the laptop-and-telephone brigade travelling First Class. Why, if they don't keep their sales up right through the recession they might end up travelling... like them.

Interestingly the postmodern internal arrangements of the new Mark IV coaches have intensified class conflict on the trains. Seeing poverty and squalor of the Lagerlout Division through automatic glass doors gives gravitas to the First Class pleasures of creased plush, chrome, and Westminster City Council-style litterbins. Despite external appearances —the new thin painted lines down the flanks of the locomotives, and the flying swallow above them—train journeys are emphatically not like airline flights. They do not strap people into their social class and bring carefully graded services to them: instead they encourage all classes of passengers to go on sightseeing trips from luxury to the buffet car and then on to the bedlam of Standard Class.

Ironically what kept class on the drawing board at British Rail after nationalisation was the decision in the 1950s to abandon compartment carriages and adopt democratic American-style 'saloons'. This was a well-meaning mistake typical of the utopian years of modern design. The nineteenth century invention of compartments suited the English perfectly, because it encapsulated all the contradictions of the class system.

In those days there were three classes. Third Class compartments accommodated eight people on rock-hard carpet-bag upholstery without armrests, facing each other in fours, secure in the knowledge that life had dealt each of them the same rotten hand. Second Class compartments had the same arrangement but with softer seats, armrests, three pictures of the seaside above each row of seats, and blinds on the corridor side that could be drawn in the forlorn hope that a mid-journey entrant might not have the heart to wake the two stretched out figures occupying eight seats. The final satisfying difference came with the First Class compartment, where only six immense plush seats occupied the same space. First Class passengers only entered an occupied compartment with the greatest reluctance, and certainly only if no unoccupied compartment remained. It was from this genteel respect for privacy of a generation ago that the present raging psychopathology of First Class carriage design stepped off.

Nowadays these compartment trains are mostly gone and spacious saloons have taken their place. But old habits die hard. When a young business person is first promoted to travelling First Class on British Rail he or she thinks it remarkable always to be able to find a seat. But it isn't long before they are not completely comfortable unless they possess the seat directly in front of them too, so they have somewhere to put their feet. Then they start feeling uneasy unless they control all the seats around their table, so they learn to deploy their briefcase, laptop, telephone, coat, newspaper, miniature of Perrier, plastic glass, napkins and bacon sandwich to guard these new frontiers. If things stopped here the process might not be noticed, but after a month or two of long distance runs, even four seats in the First Class saloon begins to feel like Cardboard City. That is the first sign of Royal Train Syndrome, the uncontrollable desire to have an entire railway carriage to yourself.

Nowadays every train has its cases of Royal Train Syndrome. Late at night on any InterCity train there is invariably one raving misanthrope and one alone in each First Class carriage. They relax all over 'their' carriage, put their feet on the seat in front, dump their briefcase up at one end, plonk their copy of Expressions on a table near the middle, toss their ticket on a seat three rows away, and spread out their coat and hat to dry at the other end.

This works fine unless the train draws into a station and 48 Japanese businessmen pour in. When this happens, and occasionally it does, there is a crisis. The Japanese sit down anywhere, as though the entire train were at their disposal. They even sit down around the misanthrope, talking animatedly. One picks up his magazine. Another tries the locks on his brief case. They pass his ticket from hand to hand making remarks in their own language.

When the Royal Train Syndrome sufferer is released by the Railway Police some time later he is made to promise that he will go into therapy. Amazingly most make a full recovery. But then you would hardly expect less from 50 years of British train design and the British class system.

A tenement in Hamburg, Germany, photographed in 1904

Richard Buckminster Fuller, dome over mid-town Manhattan, 1960

High-Tech architecture:
history versus the parasites
1991

Two images can encompass the story of architecture in the twentieth century. Its starting point is represented by a photograph of a Hamburg tenement taken in 1904. Its unachieved, self-ephemeralising end is represented by Richard Buckminster Fuller's famous 1960 project for a dome over 50 blocks of Manhattan. In terms of the contemporary politics of architecture we might say that the Hamburg tenement represents 'history'. What I believe James Joyce had in mind when he called history "the nightmare from which I am trying to awake". The three kilometre dome is what today we would call —with the benefit of the vocabulary of the Prince of Wales—"a vision". Perhaps the canonical vision of the second machine age. A vast post-architectural transparent environmental control envelope intended to be assembled by a fleet of helicopters.

Somewhere trapped between these two images is the present. The process of building—what is now called "building procurement" —no longer an act of creativity so much as a process of immense and unfathomable complexity, involving bureaucracies, statutes, regulations, budgets, policy committees, review boards, special interest groups and others, whose end-product is, in the literal sense of the term, out of control.

Creative or not, the one thing that indisputably results from this process is development. Year after year we see more and more building based on a system of out of date precedents: street widths inherited from a time when there were no cars; houses from a time when 40 per cent of households had live-in servants; densities from a time when the practical limit of load-bearing construction was five storeys; urban identities from a time when it took four day to get from London to York or three months to get from London to New York.

What has 'High-Tech' to do with this? Today it is a term spurned even by those whose work is universally recognised by it. At the recent Future Systems exhibition at the RIBA, consisting of the advanced technology projects of Jan Kaplicky and Amanda Levete, the author was surprised to learn that even the catalogue writers had been abjured by the architects not to use the phrase. Yet it is a very clear and useful descriptor of a much underrated attempt by some architects to teach themselves the methodology of product evolution. Somehow the term High-Tech has come to mean something else. Something most of the architectural profession wants to forget. Something that Lord St John of Fawsley, chairman of the Royal Fine Art Commission, dismisses—as he does so much else—as "Yet another instalment in the iconoclastic destruction of our priceless Heritage"; that John Outram describes as no more than "a form of decoration"; that Robert Venturi has wittily compared to "going to a fancy dress party dressed as Brunel"; that Terry Farrell has disparaged as the "indulgent baroque end-phase of an architectural fashion"; that Sir Andrew Derbyshire has ridiculed as "trying to keep water out with glue"; that even the editor of The Architectural Review writes off as "Redneck" architecture. All of these persons ignore the important distinguishing characteristic of High-Tech architecture which is—notwithstanding the denials by virtually all concerned with it—its indifference to all 'fine art' and 'cultural' values and its adherence to another system of value altogether. That alternative system is the endless process of evolution by which science, technology and design enable us to do more with less: and in the process achieve unique, authentic confrontations between humanity and technology in the built environment.

A photograph of a petrol station in Oregon, taken nearly 20 years ago, shows an architecture that is utterly minimal. "One of the finest remaining examples of a North American corrugated steel fence" plays the part of the street facade. Advertising plays the part of decoration. The whole thing cost practically nothing. It is practically nothing. This is 'ephemeralisation' in architecture, reducing the eternal to a life of one day. Reducing the glory that was Rome to the status of a light show—something that it hardly more trouble to dispose of than it was to make. The seventeenth century clay pipe was an ephemeralised product. So was the nineteenth century cigarette. Today most of the elements of modern life, from cars to sounds and images have been ephemeralised wholesale. Even paper has been ephemeralised—the new Stock Exchange 'Taurus' system will do away with the daily movement of 200 tons of paper in the City of London. Almost everything is ephemeralised except our conception architecture, which adheres to a commitment to eternal values that is wholly inappropriate to our circumstances.

Contrary to popular belief, it is far more ecologically correct to be ephemeralised in the matter of building than to cling to permanence. From 1948 until last year a caravan park containing nearly 200 caravans stood on the seashore in Start Bay in South Devon. Then, virtually overnight, it was removed. The aluminium cladding was sold off the backs of the caravans to be recycled at £250 a ton. The windows were removed and sold as salvage; likewise the sanitary fittings and appliances. The next stage was for the wooden frames to be burned or sold as firewood, and the steel chassis to be cut up with torches and reclaimed for scrap. Now there is nothing left. Like a natural, biodegradable life form this instant town appeared from the resource and energy stream of the economy and, after nearly 50 years of existence, it has disappeared back into it, leaving no waste behind. 'High-technology' could do no better.

High-Tech architecture is contemporary functional design applied to enclosure. Which is to say that it is functional design as the early Moderns understood it, but informed by an awareness of the invisible, ephemeralised, informational, energetic and environmental revolutions that have subsequently created a new post-industrial world—and in the process transformed the real task of architecture. High-Tech finds architectural meaning, not in the fantastic and extravagant exhumation and adaptation of ancient texts and principles of construction, but in the study of how to design buildings that can come and go as the Devon caravan park did: within the fluctuating resource and energy flows of the environment. High-Tech is the acting out of this rational systems enclosure in the cultural world of architecture: where its opponents, particularly architects, constantly seek to deny its legitimacy; and even its most illustrious proponents feel driven to make wholly unconvincing claims that it is somehow descended from the work of Bruneleschi and Bramante. In truth High-Tech is like packaging, it is production engineering for finite buildings. It is the logic of doing the most with the least. Not trivial, but ephemeral, like life itself.

The mobile home is classified as a motor vehicle. The contrast between the relationship of the fixed traditional building to the environment, and the mobile motor vehicle to the environment, is exactly the same as the contrast between High-Tech architecture and Fine Art architecture. One is implicitly transient and of depreciating value: the other is explicitly fixed andtheoretically of appreciating value. In fact 'nomadic' buildings seldom move, and 'fixed' buildings do depreciate. But we prefer not to explore this contradiction.

The activity of design can be found in every field from the extraction and processing of raw materials, through the application of science and engineering to production, to the distribution and consumption of products and their final disposal or reuse. Somewhere in this universe of machine-creation the architect sits. Logically we would expect to find him a key figure holding a command-and-control function, perhaps responsible for the reproductive role of some archetypal giant enterprise like the first Ford production line—reproductive because, viewed objectively, the structure of, say, the automobile is no different from the way in which simple organic life forms like insects are constructed. In effect the man-made version is more or less successfully 'copied' from the natural prototype. And the most important element in this act of 'copying' is the process which leads, by technology transfer, to the emergence of recognisable types of machine, like natural species, that represent plateaux of the familiar.

The 100 year evolution of the car is instructive. It can show a progress from an aeroplane-inspired rear engined, front wheel drive, rear wheel steering mutation—Richard Buckminster Fuller's Dymaxion car of 1933, whose only engineering descendant today is the combine harvester —to the standard front engine, front-wheel steering, rear-wheel drive genotype of 30 years or more stability, represented by the Ford Cortina.

The same endless process is made wonderfully clear by the evolution of the agricultural tractor. The basic elements start off formlessly. On the 1918 Overtime tractor they are almost an abstract composition of the basic elements of the motor vehicle. Then we see the wild, saltatory evolution calm down with fewer mutations, until the elements resolve themselves into a recognisable shape and finally settle down into something like the contemporary Ford that we are all familiar with today.

Beyond these are the strange bye-ways of evolution, to be taken up again or abandoned forever like the dinosaurs. In the case of tractors there was the Austrian Porsche Tatzelwurm of 1915, capable of towing 20 trailers, and its successor of 40 years later the American le Tourneau Superfreighter. And there are the mutations that are produced by miscegenation: The monster Sikorsky sky crane helicopter carrying a house; the upside down train, or monorail; the hovercraft, a cross between a raft and an aeroplane, and the warship with its superstructure resembling a building.

The same kind of evolutionary process can be detected in building, with the prevalence of technologies 'cross-bred' from other fields in a form of 'parasitical' research and development that is well suited to architecture and design where the resources for the systematic study of materials and technology are limited. However, such a logical evolution towards stable plateaux in architecture is more often than not prevented by a non-optimising, non-converging process of design evaluation that declares a plateau at every intermediate stage. It is as though all the agricultural tractors from the 1918 Overtime to the 1980 Ford 6600 were stood side by side and it was claimed, not merely that each was as good as the other but, even more perversely, that the first was better than the last.

Clearly there must be a reason for the continual frustration of the evolutionary process in architecture, and the reason is to do with the nature of the architectural environment. In a Darwinian sense this is so indulgent that the normal processes of natural selection do not apply. For example the much higher cost of restoring buildings instead of replacing them with new ones—in extreme cases involving sums like £5 million for The Queen's House at Greenwich, or £40 million for Lutyens House in the City of London—is nowadays seen as a reason why such restoration should be done, not why it should be abandoned.

The art historical value system of architectural culture lies like a dense fog over the whole field of shelter technology. It is the reason why the architect fails to show up where we would expect to find him, in charge of some building reproduction process on the ladder of product evolution. Instead his activities supplant the functional principle of the survival of the fittest—which serves well enough for the entire natural world—with a degenerate kind of sentimentality. A romanticism that preserves the weak and untypical building species while it ignores or disparages the strong and typical. At its worst it gravely impedes the process of genetic reproduction in construction: the engine of architectural evolution itself. In general we have no expectation that architecture should evolve, such as we possess of the car, the tractor or the helicopter.

A result of this confusion of culture with evolution in architecture is that, despite their different genetic origins, an organically designed modern building—*von innen nach aussen* as the Bauhaus put it—is not held to be innately superior to a decorated facade fronting 1,000s of square feet of serviced floor space. Modern three-dimensional design, in plan and section, produced buildings that really were whole organisms. But the contemporary production of serviced floor space is not organic. It resembles the cancerous reproduction of individual cells rather than the organised genesis of creation. Because today we are suspended in a transitional state between the 'nightmare' of history and the 'visionary' aggregation of individual buildings into larger controlled environments, nobody really knows how the inside of buildings should relate to the outside. A strong spirit would say that this alone was proof that it had already ceased to matter. A profiled steel motorway distribution centre fitted out inside like one of Ludwig II of Bavaria's castles would probably seem alright to most people. Only a few would hold out for the absolute inner and outer consistency attained by Norman Foster in the design of the Hongkong and Shanghai Bank.

While it is true that there is little actual dispute about this matter at present, the grounds for a bitter quarrel do still exist. Peter Pearce, the former Buckminster Fuller associate more recently responsible for the engineering design of Biosphere II, has described the enclosure of serviced floorspace as "minimum inventory: maximum diversity architecture"—the maximum application of the minimum number of components. What the Hongkong and Shanghai Bank called for was "maximum inventory: minimum diversity architecture"—the minimum application of the maximum number of components.

Looking at natural evolution for an answer to this conundrum is surprisingly inconclusive. While there are 'genotypes' in nature where a small number of nearly identical components do make up a large creature—notably plants, snakes, worms and fish—the most highly evolved creatures are actually masterpieces of component specialisation and multi-functional (what Fuller called "synergetic") assembly, which means that specialised components perform more than one function and thus optimise the performance of all other components by reducing their load. This is an interesting question. Far too interesting to be totally neglected in schools of architecture in favour of the study of the Orders, as is presently the case.

Although in theory neither the 'organic' nor the 'cancerous' design approach truly equates with the 'evolutionary' design model that generates progress in mechanical system design, both of them can be related to it. Unfortunately, most architectural design today proceeds from an altogether more primitive level of thinking: that enshrined in the illogical system of prejudices that holds that buildings and machines are utterly different, and what is plainly absurd for one can be entirely acceptable for the other. We have reached a crucial point for the Humpty Dumpty impasse of architectural culture—"a word means what I want it to mean, nothing more and nothing less"—is now bureaucratically dominant. It pervades government departments concerned with design, local authority planning departments, quangos like the RFAC and the Arts Council, the ever-insightful Prince Charles, most if not all academies, and all the media. Its aim today is to contain and define our perception of the built environment, crowding out any non-art historical interpretation of its meaning. It does this literally, through teaching 'environmental perception' to children in schools. Teaching children to find distinctions where there are no differences, and telling them what is architecture and therefore not absurd, and what is not architecture and therefore subject to different rules.

Inevitably this cultural rule by 'perception-control' is doomed to failure because it proceeds from the false assumption that the basic process at work in the built environment is not the evolving interaction between a growing population of fixed and mobile machines: but the struggle to protect a collection of priceless historic objects for posterity. Notwithstanding the depredations of art historical culture upon our power to reason, there have been some evolutionary transformations in branches of architecture, which are protected by their lowly station. Recently, despite their categorical exclusion from architectural culture, larger and more efficient enclosure structures capable of massive replication at minimal energy and material cost have increased and multiplied, progressing towards a new plateau of designed 'ephemeralisation'. These structures owe their existence to the economic power of non-fine art dominated industries such as electronics, distribution and retailing. They are the result of a new, de-culturalised, genetic frequency in building. An optimised rate of replication—say ten years instead of 300 years—that is unconfused by cultural ideas of heritage, conservation, or sentimental camouflage.

It is here that the contribution of High-Tech is most clearly to be seen. What has been identified as the first High-Tech building in England was in fact a potentiometer factory in Swindon called Reliance Controls. It was completed in 1967 to designs by Norman Foster and Richard Rogers, who were destined to become world-famous architects in the years ahead. But Reliance Controls was only incidentally a work of art. Really it was (and still tenuously is at the time of writing) a transitional object, caught midway between fine art 'architectural culture' and true 'Redneck' production engineering. While its 'cultural' antecedents may be clear in the resemblance of its white painted steelwork to Mies van der Rohe's Farnsworth House, the consequence of its transitional status has been to be denied a 'holy place' in the pantheon of architectural culture and to be submitted to a callous industrial fate instead. After 23 years of use as an industrial tool it simply wore out and the company that owned it moved out and sold its site for redevelopment. Reliance Controls is now derelict and vandalised. No conservationist has risen up to defend it. Despite its undisputed importance as a piece of architectural history, no one is putting up a fight to prevent its demolition because it is too compromised by utility to belong to the eternal value system of art history.

Thus, and very properly for disciples of ephemera, the one abiding influence of Reliance Controls will have been the evolutionary effect that its disrespectful treatment as an industrial artefact had upon the subsequent careers of its two architects. Richard Rogers was so dismayed by the insertion of an artless and ill-sited window into the bay next to the main entrance to the building that he resolved henceforth never to design a building of such delicate aesthetic balance that a single minor alteration or addition of this kind could ruin it. The tough, flexible architectural approach that this led to can be clearly seen at the Centre Pompidou in Paris, and at Lloyd's. As for Norman Foster, he went on to develop the deep-plan, single-storey, steel-frame, highly serviced commercial building to levels of technical performance and habitability that are best exemplified at Stansted Airport. In this, as in other buildings, the means employed can still be traced back to Reliance Controls in matters as diverse as the value-engineered fluorescent tubes (recessed into the roof deck corrugations), and the revolutionary single-entrance, single-canteen 'new industrial democracy' according to which the building was planned all those years ago.

Architectural culture may not have helped Richard Rogers and Norman Foster to accept the role of 'evolutionary' architects, destined to dissolve the ancient nightmare of the Hamburg tenement into the ephemeralised megastructure of an enclosed Manhattan, but experience of 'evolutionary' industry undoubtedly enabled them to approach the foothills of a magnificent new transience in their own subsequent work.

The cost of the new culture of cities
1991

We are leaving old Europe behind. Destroying it with sentimentality; telling it that "everything is going to be alright" when it is not. Destroying its identity with all the limitless tonnage of serviced floor space that the market will bear. It is a crime so great that we cannot face it—so we compel our architects to hide it from our eyes.

In Europe, when academics, commentators and politicians talk about architecture and city planning, they only *appear* to belong to one or other of two camps. In fact the dogged fighters for conservation and the enthusiasts for megaprojects for wholesale redevelopment use exactly the same rhetoric. The first group begs for sensitivity, restraint, caution and the need for a tentative, revivalist, regional, site-specific sort of architecture that will disturb the historic appearance of things as little as possible. The second group cries out for exactly the same thing—only they want it stretched around rafts of New World-sized serviced floor space that have no precedent in Europe's Medieval-sized city plans.

What both groups mean by their rhetoric can be seen in the present state of development of all major West European cities. Everywhere there are relics of the old and fragments of the new—as well as plans for more relics of the old and more fragments of the new. What they all have in common is that deep inside them, like the petrol inside a car, there has to be enough high-tech serviced floor space to make them go.

This evasiveness about what 'sensitivity', 'restraint', 'regionalism' and 'context' really mean is the principal obstacle to our coming to terms with the scale of urban regeneration that is really destined to take place in the new Europe. Nobody—except perhaps an American architect in the first few hours after he steps down from the plane that brought him from Manhattan or Chicago—will actually defend the kind of 'insensitive' international commercial architecture and planning epitomised by the high-rise commercial towers that transformed Hong Kong from a horizontal to vertical city in 25 years; or the giant Olympia & York developments in North America and Docklands. But by the same token few German architects will wholeheartedly defend the museum programme of Frankfurt, where a heavy cultural investment in 13 'sensitive' new museums and galleries is expected to counterbalance a vast international airport and a Hong Kong-like forest of 380 merchant banks.

Urban life in the second machine age is strange and disturbing. It has no certainty, and no European city escapes from the state of high anxiety that it creates. There is political panic, but no organised political will to change. No conviction. No one trusts experts or professionals. Everyone suffers from 'information anxiety', the black hole between data and knowledge, the ever widening gap between what we understand and what we think we should understand.

The real source of this anxiety of understanding is the new dissimulation of the urban environment. Today we look at a remote terminal of the electronic information industry and see a Georgian house: we look at a merchant bank and see the church from which its interior has been cunningly converted: we look at a bijou apartment building and see what looks like an eighteenth century waterfront warehouse: we look at a modern electronic office complex with underground parking for 300 cars and see a row of eighteenth century houses. All history has become nonsense. This was not always so. It has happened in the last 30 years. It is worth trying to understand why it happened.

Before the great wars of the twentieth century all cities were the creation of Princes and Republics as seats of power and wealth. Aerial bombardment in the great wars transformed them and introduced a concept of dispersal that outflanked their authority, but they clung to their economic power. Between 1945 and the energy crisis of 1973, capital was captive in cities because major capital movements between countries were successfully controlled by international currency agreements. But in the aftermath of the energy crisis, the recycling of the huge new Middle East oil revenues back into the Western economies became a matter of life or death. At that time the national states abandoned their international agreements and began to act unilaterally. Within five years they lost their capacity to regulate capital flows across their own frontiers.

For the cities of Europe, in particular, this was an important development. Allied to the rapid reduction in transport costs brought about by mass air travel, the encouragement to dispersal offered by autoroute commodity distribution, and the speed of communications ushered in by satellite information technology, it created a new economic order in which the life of cities became a continual negotiation between mobile capital and static opportunity. The term 'static opportunity' is in fact a good economic description of any city in the postmodern world.

Today cities compete like racehorses. We are all familiar with the consequences of this. Among the most trivial is the pattern of advertising that greets business travellers arriving at Heathrow or Frankfurt or Charles de Gaulle with huge signs advertising the delights of Boston, Atlanta and Toronto. The fact that these three cities are all in North America is of no importance. Between and within continents and between and within countries a death struggle between cities is carried on night and day. Even train passengers arriving in London are greeted by signs advertising Bristol, Edinburgh and Liverpool. All our cities display their assets in the shape of special linguistic and labour skills; spectacular centres of consumption activity; impressive command and control functions, and economic inducements in the form of generous grants and loans for incoming businesses.

Just as the museums of Frankfurt were financed by the Bundesrepublik, so was Canary Wharf got off the ground by more than one billion pounds of public money and tax inducements. These funding arrangements in Germany and Britain were typical 'fixed opportunity' inducements, like the architecture of conversation and dissimulation itself. In the new economy of cities architecture, whether megastructural or contextual, it loses its old art historic identity but gains instead the status of a 'fixed opportunity inducement'. If it is successful it will multiply the attractions of a city by the way in which its image is reproduced all over the world. It will attract skilled labour; gain a reputation for spectacular consumption activities, and contribute to smooth-running command and control functions as well. The problem is that, in the process, it loses its intelligibility.

The true success or failure of a city is no longer physical but conceptual in a way that depends upon its global economic propaganda. The reality may be that the whole of Southeastern England, Northeastern France, Belgium, The Netherlands and Luxembourg is destined to become the centre of a continental distribution industry so vast that each country is merely storage space. But that will not be noticed—not so long as the culture of cities can still be focused on the treasures of the royal palaces, the museums, the galleries, the shops and the restaurants of what we will still quaintly call London, Amsterdam, Brussels and The Hague.

Henry Ford and the biospherans
1991

Henry Ford once owned a newspaper called the *Independent* that was written on
an assembly line. One editor wrote the facts, then passed the copy on to another
who added humour, and then to a third who added opinion and so on. This
method did not work very well but Henry Ford could never understand why.
Like Vladimir Ilyich Lenin, he knew that everything was connected to everything
else and a newspaper was a product like any other. His way of producing
a newspaper, like many of the things he did and believed, seem utterly fantastic
to us today, but during his lifetime everything he did seemed reasonable.
In America in the 1920s it seemed reasonable to quite a large proportion of
the population that Henry Ford should be allowed to replan America according
to the principles he had enshrined at the Ford Motor Company. In the end
Henry Ford never did become president of the United States, although he tried
once, but he did create the modern automobile industry in his image. In 1927
his famous Model T was being produced at the rate of one every ten seconds
at a cost of only 1.5 man hours of labour per car. Henry Ford built 15 million
Model T cars between 1909 and 1927. To shift that many units he rewrote the
principles of capitalism. He continually cut the price of the car to increase the
number of people who could afford it, and increased the wages he paid to the
men who produced it. Over the life of the car he halved the profit per car but
quadrupled the Ford Motor Company's sales. At its apogee in the 1920s Henry
Ford's vast production facility at River Rouge was making more than half the
cars in the world.

Now another way of looking at what Henry Ford did is to regard it as the
creation of a new ecosystem that had never existed before; one in which one-
seventh of the working population of the United States was involved by the time
he died in 1947. This new ecosystem was revolutionary enough in reality, but in
his unrealised ambitions Henry Ford's new automobile world extended even
further. It was a dream of a new biosphere almost evolutionary in its scale.
A convinced Darwinian who believed in the survival of the fittest, Ford tried to
create a huge new autarchic community out of the 250,000 workers and their
dependents who worked to produce his cars. In the 1930s he personally
financed research into a kind of 'Ford nation' with its own heritage culture
based on his childhood memories; its own self-sufficient farms and houses;
its own shipping fleet and airline (flying Ford aeroplanes, of course); its own
reserves of raw materials, iron, coal, limestone, timber and silica (for

windscreens and windows); its own soya bean plantations yielding textiles for upholstery; its own experimental soya bean composites for car bodies, and even its own soya bean protein fashioned into a variety of synthetic foods for everyone to eat.

This most fantastic pursuit of industrial autarchy comes to mind in connection with the recent outburst of publicity surrounding Biosphere II, the human experiment that is scheduled to take place near the town of Oracle, Arizona. There, at a cost of between $40,000 and $100,000 (depending on the source of your information), eight volunteer 'Biospherians' will spend two years in another man-made ecosystem: a hermetically sealed container stuffed with plants, insects and small animals. The purpose of this experiment in autarchy is not to produce cars, but to find out whether all or some of the Biospherians will come out alive, and thus whether some sort of accommodation for a commercial enterprise might be built on Mars or the moon.

Like Henry Ford's dream of the self-sufficient car factory, Biosphere II is an attempt to create a completely insulated world within a world. In this case a 3.15 acre glass and metal structure sealed off from the rest of Arizona by 30 miles of neoprene gaskets so perfectly fitted that they will reduce the migration of internal and external atmospheres to below one per cent per year. Within this structure there are microcosmic patches of tropical rain forest, desert (with concrete boulders), 'ocean', savannah scrubland, marshes and arable fields. Some of these climatic zones are almost comically small—the savannah would take under ten seconds to run across—but the object of the whole experiment is not trivial. If it succeeds, and if its oil-rich financier Edward Bass does not run out of money, experiments will be initiated that call for more than one generation of volunteers, human guinea-pigs prepared to embark on a 100 year experiment in autarchy that they hope will not end up like William Golding's *Lord of the Flies*.

Again like Henry Ford's autarchic car factory, which was not truly autarchic because it still required a market of non-Fordians to buy the cars it produced, Biosphere II also has a conceptual flaw in the shape of an unbreakable link to the outside world. Whatever might be true of the proposed future solar-powered version for century-long experiments, the set up that has been tirelessly promoted in newspapers, magazines and TV on both sides of the Atlantic in the last few months will not work without the support of a vast air-breathing five megawatt power plant to keep its pumps and control systems functioning, and operate the heaters and chillers that will hopefully stop its interior temperature dropping below freezing or soaring to a deadly 150 degrees.

While nobody would ever claim that anyone other than Henry Ford was responsible for the research that went into the autarchic car factory community, Biosphere II has an unusually large number of names on its masthead. While Edward Bass may be footing the bill, a metallurgist and Harvard Business School graduate named John Polk Allen, who once founded a commune called the Synergia Ranch, is director of research and development for the project. The planners and designers of the sealed enclosure are variously cited as Carl Hodges, director of Environmental Research Laboratories, the firm that designed the Land Pavilion at EPCOT; and Margret Augustine, a Biospherian nominee who has an architecture degree from something called the Institute of Ecotechnics in London. In all this division of authority the only certainty is that the man who actually designed the crucial space frame structure and its airtight glass cladding was Peter Pearce of Pearce Structures, Los Angeles. Pearce too studied architecture at the Illinois Institute of Technology in the 1960s and admired the work of Charles Eames, Konrad Wachsmann and Buckminster Fuller, all of whom he worked for at one time or another between 1960 and 1982. Like Allen he was an admirer of Buckminster Fuller. He even contributed drawings to the first edition of Buckminster Fuller's monster book *Synergetics*, but his name was not credited in subsequent editions. Now Pearce's opinions of Fuller are said to be mixed. Nonetheless his own creative axiom; minimum inventory: maximum diversity, is a Fullerian concept. It means the achievement of the maximum formal variation with the minimum number of components.

Pearce's space enclosing structure for Biosphere II really does try to fulfil the incredible performance requirement that it should remain airtight for 100 years. But even that may not be enough. As Henry Ford found out with his production line newspaper, technical feasibility is not a guarantee of success. Long before they are in a position to start selling their Mars-based products and scientific information to a starving or superheated world, the Biospherians will probably discover that the weakest link in all dreams of a balanced community of human worker-ants is the dogged irrationality of the human ants themselves.

What London learned from Las Vegas
1991

Robert Venturi is a quiet American who has conducted his career in
architecture with skill and determination ever since he set up in practice
33 years ago. Born in Philadelphia, first generation American son of an
Italian fruit and vegetable merchant who married an English Fabian who
knew George Bernard Shaw, he is one of the phenomena of contemporary
architecture. A transitional but not a trivial figure. A precursor of the rise
of postmodernism, but both a pre-postmodernist and a post-postmodern
himself. In the end, and best of all, a designer at the age of 66 who can still
epater le bourgeois with a new building as he did a quarter of a century ago with
a book called *Complexity and Contradiction in Architecture*. A man simply called
"Bob" in the trade, but punctiliously credited as a partner in Venturi, Scott-
Brown and Associates Inc., in the magazines where his work is illustrated.
Robert Venturi of Venturi, Scott-Brown and Associates, is the man to whom
the National Gallery gave the Trafalgar Square commission that 84 other
architects had struggled for in two competitions over six years: Robert
Venturi, the Yank with a feminist white South African urbanist wife, and
some other Yanks to back him up.

If you ignore *Complexity* and *Contradiction* (a small New York Museum
of Modern Art intellectual earthquake of Bob's own), the Venturis as a couple
(Bob and Denise Scott-Brown, with the aid of associate Steven Izenour) only
really attained widescreen status in 1972 when they mounted an expedition
to the far West and discovered Las Vegas, the mysterious city of gold.

Like nearly all explorers, Bob and Denise were not the first people to go
to a place, only the first people of a certain type. They were the first English
speaking academic architects to stumble upon the brilliant, liquid, seething
krill signs of the mythical Nevada gambling hell. Amazed by these gigantic
structures, as vast and inexplicable as Easter Island statues, they raised their
doctorates and took possession of the territory in the name of architecture.
Las Vegas, the psychedelic and semiological drug overdose of a desert city
(they announced on their Lewis and Clark-like return to the East Coast) could
be used by architecture as an elixir of youth. If it were taken in very small
doses, a tiny drop of this kaleidoscopic hologram of illuminations could be
used by any architect without dependency. It wouldn't be the end of the art,
like prefabrication. Rather, like marijuana, the fantastic illuminated signs
were 'almost alright'. The Venturis called their book *Learning from Las Vegas*.

What they had seen in Las Vegas was another language more powerful by far than architecture. Like the town in *Invasion of the Bodysnatchers*, Las Vegas in the late 1960s was a place where signs had already taken over from buildings. The buildings were nothing, just el cheapo boxes, the signs were everything, another civilisation, an anti-thetical semiological language poised to take over the world. There was only one more champion left for it to fight—architecture—the gaunt geometrical old timer who had held on to his title for 2,000 years. Bob was for the gaunt geometrical old timer.

He looked at the weird new challenger up from polycarbonate out of electrification by computer, and thought he could take him on. In a way his career ever since has been trying to make information take a dive for architecture. Long before anybody else Bob Venturi realised that all buildings are as alike as T-shirts. The only interesting thing about them is the message on the front.

"We know of no spectacle so ridiculous as the British public in one of its periodic fits of morality", observed Lord Macaulay in an aside that has become famous. And he might have had the saga of the National Gallery extension in mind. "Shapeless", "hapless", "a bad joke", "despicable", "wretched".... And that was just the quality press. The queen of the professional journals came up with "picturesque mediocre slime". When the Venturis' scheme for the National Gallery extension was first published the roof came in on them. Word quickly got around that it was OK to go all out on this one, just like Canary Wharf. And when the critics and the 84 disappointed architects had finally yelled themselves hoarse, a firm called Capricorn, allegedly London's only remaining firm of blacksmiths, had a go. Outraged by the specification it received from the Venturis for laser-cut steel railings, balustrades and gates for the building, the firm replied with an instinct for runway denial that was pure vindictive England. Capricorn's MD wrote, not to the architects, but to gallery chairman Jacob Rothschild and the press; "This design is an appalling insult to the craft of blacksmithing, to the National Gallery, to the art world and to this country."

Somehow the Venturis survived this. Later on Denise survived the showing of a 50 minute film about the National Gallery that had originally been transmitted in the United States under the title *Robert Venturi and Denise Scott-Brown: a partnership in architecture*—but was economically screened by the

BBC as *Robert Venturi: back to the future*. Over this one Bob was characteristically philosophical; "I don't know", he told me when I met him last year, "Denise seems to belong to an unlucky generation of women architects. The older ones like Eileen Gray and Charlotte Perriand didn't seem to have a problem of recognition; and the younger ones like Elizabeth Plater-Zyberk are very successful. It's a transitional period I guess." Denise is not so sure. Her contribution is coming in a book called *Architecture, a place for Women?* It is called "Sexism and the star system in architecture".

About the ups and downs of the National Gallery project, Bob has been philosophical too. Apart from regretting the lack of trust between architect, contractor and subcontractors in England, the furthest he will go is to say that he is not keen to work here again. He says he has taken a vow not to discuss the job at all until the building opens; "Talk to me then", he urges. "Then I will tell all, I promise." Denise is only slightly more forthcoming on the phone; "I will say this. It has been very hard. The quality of the contractors was very poor and we had to have stand up fights to get the quality we wanted. But we kept everything that mattered. In the end I think we taught them quality."

Lambasted as it was early in its career, the building has been picking up friends recently. Even now, if you look at it properly across Trafalgar Square (and do not perversely concentrate on the plant room vents at the back as certain critics do), it is difficult not to be impressed. Bob himself says it is a very simple building, banal almost, but then he stops. "No. I've learned never to explain anything to the British. It puts them off. They prefer to believe things are tremendously complicated."

"How could you call little me an invasion?" Venturi once said when he was accused of spearheading the mass arrival of American architectural firms in London; and it is true that his contribution has been of a different character to the commercial presence of Skidmore Owings and Merrill, Tribble Harris Li, Hellmuth Obata & Kassabaum, Kohn Pedersen Fox and Johnson Burgee.

Venturi is a shy, slightly stooping figure who looks more at home in a lounge suit than in a hard hat on a building site. But the deception is in character, for even his Philadelphia office is less grand than it sounds; visitors soon finding that its imposing address, 4236 Main Street, is actually a converted warehouse in a run down suburb called Manayunk.

Despite his bruising experience with the National Gallery, Bob remains not only a confirmed Anglophile ("I don't take it to extremes, like wearing tweeds"), but a thinker of genuine influence. Even though few English architects have actually seen such modest but seminal buildings as the Guild House in Philadelphia or Dixwell Firehouse, New Haven, all of them will have heard of his books, and a surprising number remember hearing him lecture here in the 1970s. Some might even have seen the very first article he ever published on architecture—in *The Architectural Review* in 1953, long before he was known in America.

"I only wrote those books because we had no work and I had nothing else to do", he says now. But taken together his widely circulated books and (mostly) little buildings were tremendously influential in the difficult years between 1965 and 1975 that marked the sea change from modern to postmodern architecture all over the world. Venturi was never flippant or what-the-hell, like SITE or Gehry. He always worked out what things really meant and why he was doing what he did. The very fact that he is so well endowed with work in the United States today is the reason it is impossible to write him off as a transitional figure like so many others, someone who made his career in that historic gap between the new-old and the old-new. In the end his conditional dismissal of modern architecture was farsighted and authoritative. "It is a simple fact that nobody any longer wanted all the buildings all over the world to be the same", he says. But he still reserves his admiration for Aalto, Le Corbusier, and Frank Lloyd Wright, combining them with a litany of earlier figures, a surprising number of them English.

"English architecture", he says, "has a special capacity for taking the rules and breaking them." It is a characteristic that appeals to the Anglophile in him and it encouraged him to include one particular feature in his National Gallery design: a frieze of Renaissance painters' names just like the frieze of architects' names that the Venturis have around the dining room walls of their Philadelphia home. There is no precedent for it in the original National Gallery building, but if you look very closely you will see the same chiselled lettering, enormously large, on the walls of the Seattle Art Museum on the other side of the world.

What's in a name?
1991

What, or who, are The Million Dollar Man and Virgil, Sergeant Slaughter, The Heart Foundation, The Ultimate Warrior, The Orient Express, Demolition, The Legion of Doom and The Mountie? They are the names of American wrestlers on satellite television. Names taken from words and phrases in fact, fiction and history, business, rock music and language. What about 33, 75, TZ, SZ, Guilia and Giulietta? They are the numbers and names of cars, of course, but they too have been used more than once. Motor manufacturers are inveterate collectors of names and numbers; they buy them and copyright them extravagantly. There is a good reason for this. Executives in the motor industry who 'name' successful cars get promoted, while executives who 'name' unsuccessful cars get fired. Nothing stands in the way of the use of a successful name. When the Ford Sierra was launched in 1983 there was already a Sierra on the market, a kit car made by a firm called Dutton. Ford simply bought out the name and left Dutton a pale shadow.

Names seem to have a life of their own and many leap from the animal world to the world of machines before stepping from one type of machine to another. Panther, Jaguar, Tiger, Pinto and Wasp did that. Spitfire was the name of a ship, then of an aeroplane, then a car. Typhoon was the name of a fighter plane, then the name of car, then the name of a trimaran. Mustang was the name of a horse, then the name of a fighter plane, then the name of a car. The Adler was a car and a typewriter. A Daihatsu was a Japanese landing craft, now it is the name of a motor vehicle manufacturer. The Bisiluro was an Italian torpedo bomber, then it became the name of a racing car. XR-2, XR-3 and XR-4 were all names of post-war experimental rocket aircraft, then they were the names of American cars, then the names of English cars.

The Ford Fairlane was named after Henry Ford's Fairline estate near Dearborn. The Ford Model A of 1927 was named after the Ford model A of 1900. The names of all four cars in the unsuccessful Edsel range of 1957—Corsair, Citation, Ranger and Pacer—became successful later when they were attached to different vehicles, only two of them Fords.

There have been six ships in the British Navy named *Ark Royal*, eight named *Invincible*. Jonah Barrington used to be the pen name of a popular columnist at the *Daily Express*. 50 years later he was a squash champion. There have been 20 published writers called Shakespeare, 50 called Hardy, 200 called Smith. What is the significance of these names when they hop from snake to car to aeroplane, or metamorphose from generation to generation like caterpillars into butterflies? We think nothing of calling a huge ship powered by gas turbines and armed with nuclear missiles after a tiny ship that four centuries ago put to sea with stone cannon balls, pikes and boarding nets. It must be something to do with the incantatory power of names that they can smooth the way for such total transformations and make them instantly acceptable.

Despite this obvious power, names are not universally used in this way in architecture. There may be some subliminal professional advantage in the possession of an ancient architect's name, but if so it remains unproven. In architecture there was an eighteenth century Robert Adam and now there is a late-twentieth century Robert Adam. But, according to the ARCUK register, there are several Fosters, several Rogers, several Wrens, Grimshaws, Stirlings, Butterfields, Hawksmoors, Taylors, Wyatts and Pratts. Even in the nineteenth century there was more than one Gilbert Scott, Shaw, Street and Waterhouse. Then there are the phonetic resemblances: Goff and Gough; Ellis and Elles, and the misdirected letters....

In Milton Keynes the road layout of the new city was accomplished without reference to old names—V8 and G6 and such-like served well enough for boulevards—but the old villages in the designated area kept their names and became the titles of kilometre squares. In at least one case a name was kept for a time and then abandoned. The rustic sounding Bean Hill, with its revolutionary corrugated aluminium houses, became The Gables after pitched roofs were put on them. In a way this decision too, like the hasty removal of street names after the overthrow of a dictator, or the subtle conversion of a place with a bad name like Windscale into a place with a good name like Sellafield, also reflects the power of names.

Unlike the new Erewhon of Milton Keynes, the London Docklands Development Corporation has made fanatical attempts to keep old names everywhere, even though the old landscape of wharves, basins and warehouses over which it presides has been almost totally wiped out by redevelopment. Perhaps the survival of so unlikely a project as Canary Wharf owes more than we think to the retention of a quaint-sounding old name in place of something like Cashtown, UK. And in the same way the lingering death of high-rise council estates all over the country owes more to the practice of naming them after here today and gone tomorrow politicians instead of the ancient districts in which they were built. A hypothetical New Stonehenge for example, might not have been demolished as readily as Ronan Point.

Stansted and the triumph of big sheds
1991

Although it was ten years in the making, Foster Associates new £200 million Stansted Airport Terminal building and its satellites sprang suddenly into the public consciousness. This was because throughout the 1980s, while it made its way through outline and detailed design, official and unofficial approvals, and finally construction and fitting out, the architectural issue that obsessed England was not the potential of advanced technology construction, but the challenge posed by the architecture of the past.

It was the issue of the relationship of modern architecture to historic architecture that gave force to the interventions of Prince Charles. Interventions that set the agenda for the media reporting of architecture during the decade. During this time the whole concept of architecture as an independent creative discipline fell into disfavour. Such was the power of the historic conservation lobby that nearly 500,000 old buildings were granted immunity from alteration or demolition. The emphasis on historical architecture in an urban context was reinforced by the most popular new building of the 80s, which was a London office complex disguised as a row of large Georgian houses designed by the Classical Revival architect Quinlan Terry, and by the unsuccessful outcome of the greatest architectural adventure of the decade, the bid to erect a posthumous Mies van der Rohe building in the centre of London.

In England there has always been a tendency to emphasise historic urban issues because the intelligentsia lives and works in historic towns and cities, often in the oldest and most picturesque quarters. Furthermore today's architectural critics and commentators tend to be unfamiliar with the issues of economic policy and construction management that underly most commercial construction. A surprising number cannot drive and thus never travel the motorways. Most have never visited a factory or a distribution centre: never travelled to an offshore oil platform: never seen a container port or a cargo ship. Their ignorance of all these matters contributes powerfully to their vision of the world. It explains why they concentrated on historic towns and cities while the economic infrastructure of the nation was being assembled elsewhere.

During the 1980s a new architecture was being built in non-historic England. While forests were being cut down to provide paper to debate the merits of the various proposals for an extension to the National Gallery in

London's Trafalgar Square—in the end no more than a small building on a site that had been a car park for 40 years—all over the country millions of square metres of business park and distribution centre floor space was being constructed at breakneck speed. Outside the towns and cities, at 1,000 motorway access points, whole new commercial complexes were springing up with no reference to the supremacy of history at all. This new 'abstract urbanism' was ignored by critics of architecture: yet in economic terms it outweighed in importance all the fine art architecture of the preceding quarter century. Today, after a decade of frenzied construction, these office, manufacturing and distribution parks boast over 30 million square metres of new serviced floor space. They are the new operational centres of the British economy. Their architecture is the architecture of 'big sheds'.

Big shed architecture is not small, vertical and ornate like the historic architecture upon which most English critics concentrate. It is vast, horizontal and plain, as befits the unobstructed rural sites upon which it is built. In such areas steel-framed, flat-roofed, laser-levelled floor plates of 25,000 square metres are not unusual, and 50,000 square metres is not unknown. In some parts of the country these great boxes of big sheds line the horizon like stationary sleeping cars. Cheap offices or expensive distribution centres, they are inscrutable from outside but conceal secret inner worlds. Some contain extraordinarily expensive mechanical handling equipment. Often they are air conditioned or refrigerated, their operations are controlled by computer from 100s of miles away.

These enigmatic big sheds are not national but international in their design. They are the unacknowledged 'International Style' architecture of the world consumer economy. They are also the first steps towards the realisation of the supra-architectural megastructures dreamed of by Richard Buckminster Fuller in the 1950s. They are the buildings of the "flatscape with containers" that Reyner Banham first wrote of in 1966. The "non-plan" cities of the future that Cedric Price visualised in 1969. The 50,000 square metre Stansted Airport Terminal by Foster Associates, 30 miles north of the centre of London and 14 miles from the M25 orbital motorway, is a big shed. In fact it is one of the largest and most beautiful big sheds ever built.

Although possessed of a world reputation for fine art architecture of the highest aesthetic importance, Norman Foster has also had a long association with big sheds. In some ways he can claim to have invented the genre. Beginning in 1967 with the electronics factory at Reliance Controls, designed in association with Richard Rogers, he went on to design a succession of commercial and industrial buildings and projects in the years that followed. As early as 1972 he was working on a major expansion of the conventional limits of the big shed. Working for an international leisure consultancy, Foster Associates designed two large motorway-access single-storey structures intended to enclose shopping malls and leisure parks. Each one was to have provided 40,000 square metres of serviced floor space beneath a space frame roof—by comparison with the modest 3,200 square metres enclosed at Reliance Controls. In 1974 another client commissioned what might have become the largest big shed in Britain if it had been built, a mammoth 160,000 square metre distribution centre for German cars at Milton Keynes.

In these unbuilt projects, as well as more modest completed industrial units like the 2,200 square metre SAPA extrusion factory at Tibshelf, and the much smaller 850 square metre showroom and warehouse for Modern Art Glass at Thamesmead, the origins of the vast Stansted Terminal building can be seen. Like Stansted, all these projects were large, horizontal 'umbrella' enclosures that hugged the landscape and were plugged into an existing transport infrastructure. The proposed German Car Centre at Milton Keynes, in particular, with its almost military landscaping of long earth berms, massive 24 metre structural bays, 800 metre frontage and full length open bay along one side used as a giant *port-cochere*, prefigures many aspects of the 50,000 square metre Stansted Terminal.

All the Foster Associates big shed buildings of the 1970s were prophetic in their emphasis upon ground-hugging horizontality and existing transport infrastructure. Seen in retrospect the work of nearly 20 years confirms that the idea of huge, flat rectangles of serviced floorspace, cruising half-buried through the landscape like submarines running on the surface, yet connected by the umbilical cords of access to road and rail networks, must have taken root in Norman Foster's mind at the end of the 1960s and worked through one commission after another to achieve its most developed realisation.

Nor did this idea effect only commercial projects. The Sainsbury Centre for the Visual Arts of 1978 is an art gallery, but it is also a big shed, a five-times larger version of the Modern Art Glass factory of five years before, connected by the same ribbon of road to the rest of the country. In this sense it is linked to the 24,000 square metre Renault Distribution Centre of 1983. There Norman Foster raised the size of the floor plate by six times again and even returned to the giant mode of the German Car Centre with the same 24 metre bay width, but the same matrix of existing transport infrastructure remains.

In 1981, when the Renault building was still in the process of design, the outline commission for Stansted Airport Terminal arrived. Despite having only one runway, Stansted Airport is destined to become the third great London airport after Heathrow and Gatwick. Today it accommodates up to eight million passenger movements a year: fully expanded with four satellites it will be able to handle 22 million. True to big shed genealogy, the accommodation of these passenger movements revolves around transport infrastructure. At Stansted the heart of the operation is a covered intersection of three transport systems. The most important of these is the existing 227,000 square metre former United States Air Force runway, one of the longest in England, built in the mid-1950s to receive military transport aircraft en route for Germany and under-used ever since. The others are the M11 motorway, giving access to the M25 and the entire national motorway system; and the new twin-track rail spur off the main London to Cambridge route that permits express shuttle trains to run direct from beneath the Stansted Terminal to Liverpool Street Station in the heart of London in 40 minutes.

Foster Associates' task at Stansted was to enclose the passenger and baggage facilities and movement systems that would make this tri-modal transport interchange operate smoothly and, as far as possible, on one level. This resulted in the conception of a single large umbrella roof covering an immense public concourse with submerged servicing and a new railway station. There were from the beginning three overriding architectural requirements: minimal structure: maximum use of daylight, and maximum concealment of services.

Foster Associates started with the umbrella roof that would enclose all functions. They took an abandoned centrally supported roof module system, originally sketched out for the Renault building, and began to develop it further. Using tension members within splayed struts, and setting a square shell of roof deck between each central support, they were able to push the column spacing out to 36 metres. Suspended glass cladding for the walls and more roof daylighting than had ever been incorporated into any previous big shed building—with a promised saving of 500,000 kilowatts of lighting electricity a year as a benefit—enabled this umbrella to become almost the sole visible part of the building. The roof in particular possesses an extraordinary visual lightness. Before the cladding was installed it resembled an enormous formation parachute landing, photographed at the point of touchdown. Today it still floats 15 metres above the grey granite paved concourse, barely apparent to the airport users below. There is no lighting, heating or service function of any description attached to the underside of this cluster of metal shells, not even a sprinkler system. And above it, where the Renault PVC roof membrane was penetrated by no less than 90 steel columns and 360 tension rods, Stansted's PVC roof membrane is continuous, with no penetrations, no expansion joints, not even a single rainwater pipe. It is the most breathtaking roof since the Middle Ages.

At concourse level all that is visible of the mechanism that sustains this epic roof are the rows of squat quadruple tubular column structures that contain the square risers for a dense mass of servicing technology. Above are the splayed struts of the parasol roof: below is what is in effect an eight metre raised floor. This is the deep 'undercroft' that contains the railway station, the mechanical handling equipment, heating and cooling machinery, servicing and communications technology, all hidden underground in the same way as the engine room of a ship is hidden below the waterline. Right down at the bottom of this 'engine room' are the shallow pad foundations for the roof. Using the topography of the site, the architect was able to plant a forest of 36 quadruple tubular steel trees at centres of 36 metres. The trunks of these trees rise to a height of 17 metres but, at half their height, they are connected by the in-situ coffered concrete slab of the concourse. At 17 metres the branches of the trees spread out to support the roof shells 23 metres above the undercroft floor.

Like all truly large horizontal buildings Stansted Terminal is difficult to view adequately except from the air. The topography of the site makes it difficult to see from a distance on the ground and its ingenious changes of level—ground level becomes basement, first floor becomes ground —mean that it is only from the large car park to the south, or from one point on the access roundabout, that the way in which it plunges into the landscape like a huge ship into a giant wave can be understood.

Once inside, the Terminal itself is spectacular in a surprisingly understated way that is better experienced than described. Apart from a modest use of stained glass in the region given over to a complex of concession cabins on the concourse, it is the austere and unnerving quality of space and light that strikes a visitor, rather than any design feature, rather like the experience of the Sainsbury Centre but on a vaster scale. The grandeur of the grey Sicilian granite floor in what is after all a public service building is not obvious but subliminal. The structural steelwork is simply painted. Only the fire-hose reels in the 'trees' glisten in stainless steel, echoing the shape of the analogue clocks above them.

At the time of writing only one arrival and departure satellite is in use (the second is still under construction and a further two can be added), and this is reached by rail shuttle transit system. The satellites, each one nearly one-third as long again as the Terminal, have braved an inadequacy of resources that stems from their relatively late inclusion in the design. Ingenuity and discipline alone, coupled with vast areas of glazing and a cheap form of metal cladding on plywood, are not really adequate to overcome the narrowness and spartan perpective offered by their almost penal interiors.

In the earliest design configuration, the aircraft at Stansted were to have docked on the northwest side of the Terminal and the passengers were to have walked straight through it to their surface transport in the simple manner of air travel in the 1930s. This was Sir Norman Foster's ideal. In the end operating requirements, security and cost made this ideal unrealisable. Thus what has survived is horizontal, but not without considerable changes in level. The huge, squat big shed of the Terminal itself is landscaped with a muscular grandeur appropriate to the openness of the site and the vastness of the great runway and its associated transport infrastructure. It is an envelope as economical as that of the Hongkong and Shanghai Bank was expensive: a structure as light as that of the Sainsbury Centre was heavy —and an authentic milestone on Foster Associates' road to the eclipse of history and tradition in architecture.

Martin Pawley, Garbage House, 1974

Martin Pawley, 'Car Collector', Florida, 1977

And you thought your car
was good for nothing
1992

Since this is my last column before a General Election that seems certain to plunge us into a hung parliament, proportional representation, Scottish independence.... In short the biggest changes in our nation's history since the Norman conquest, I think I will defer my comments on that subject for the time being and tell a story instead.

Years ago when I was a visiting professor in America, I carried out a research project. At that time, which was just after the 1973 energy crisis, all environmentally concerned Americans had just forsworn big cars and taken to driving Volvos with five mph bumpers and bicycle racks. The academic community had gone even further and convinced itself that all cars were bad. As a result, the professors in the department where I taught spent interminable lunchtime seminars agreeing that the age of air conditioning and skyscrapers was at an end, and a new era of log cabins, wood-burning stoves, polystyrene bead insulation, windmills and underground houses had begun. Now as the only foreigner present, I remained sceptical of this. I knew from personal experience that you could run a three tonne Cadillac Coupe de Ville with fins and a seven litre V8 engine in New York for the same amount of money as it cost to run a miserable Volkswagen Beetle in London. Inevitably it was not long before my scepticism came to the surface. One 'brown-bagging' day I announced; "You Americans talk a lot of nonsense about energy. Why don't you forget about all this 'alternative technology'? There is so much slack in your economic system that you only have to improve its energy efficiency by five per cent and you will hardly notice the difference."

This outburst was greeted with a thunderstruck silence. Then somebody said something distinctly uncomplimentary about a visiting professor who drove around in a 'pimpmobile' during a fuel shortage and then had the nerve to criticise decent bike-riding Volvo drivers. At this the seminar hotted up. "You don't need log cabins", I said. "Why not just use tractors to tow airliners to the end of the runway and save millions of gallons of jet fuel?" But this too fell on stony ground. After all we were an architecture school, and our answer to the energy crunch had to be a building answer—hence the new interest in thatch, adobe and timber. One student summed up the faculty view when he said; "Neither cars nor aeroplanes have any future. It is only a matter of time before buses and trains replace them completely."

"That's nonsense", I said. "You can make more energy out of a car than you can ever save by using buses or trains."

Next year I found myself teaching in North Florida instead of upstate New York. That was where I carried out my research project, with five graduate students and a budget of $20,000. Our task was to develop low cost techniques for improving the energy performance of rural housing. Now, as anybody who travelled through the Southern states of America in the 1970s will attest, rural poverty was widespread and oppressive. Survey data showed that more than one quarter of the rural households in North Florida not only had no sanitation, but no water supply either. Instead, people drove their cars with the boot full of empty plastic milk containers to collect water from someone who did have a well. Bizarre and tragic contrasts such as these: electricity and cars but no water: colour TV but no furniture, formed the real-life background to our drop-in-the-ocean research project at the school of architecture.

The first thing we tried was to solve the water problem by rainwater collection, using pits dug in the ground and lined with polythene sheets. Then we made 'cheap' wood-burning stoves from oil drums. Then we explored different ways to insulate the rotting timber shacks with newspapers and rags; then we attempted a kind of primitive 'air conditioning' by blowing air through underground ducts made of old tyres laid in trenches. To be honest none of this stuff worked, but even so we transported a genuine abandoned rural poverty house to the campus to experiment on.

It was then that we started work on the car-collector. The idea for this device stemmed from the discovery that almost all the run-down former tobacco-workers' shacks that we were dealing with had a junk car outside. The more I thought about it, the more I came to believe that if only we could find a way to turn the car body into a solar collector—without even having to move it from where it had stood for years, picturesquely overgrown with kudzu grass and nettles—we might snatch something of value from the jaws of Marie-Antoinette academic irrelevance after all.

We started with an engineless Plymouth Arrow that was given to us by a junk yard. We stood it in the sun, stripped out its interior and replaced it with a 120 metre coil of 13 mm black polythene pipe. Water pumped through this pipe came out hot. Then we started to pull air through the car using the fan from a broken air conditioner and a drier hose, trying to turn it into a space heater as well. But despite painting the car black and leaning it up against the side of the house at a convincing solar angle, this didn't work. It was not until we hit upon the idea of drawing more air through, instead of trying to make the car hotter that we had any success. With the aid of the huge 'air conditioning' tyre duct we finally drew out 25,000 BTU/hr one afternoon. Of course, any fool could do this in Florida in August, but it was an inspiring moment. Assuming we could collect rainwater, and factoring our torrid summer temperatures down to winter levels, we convinced ourselves that it was possible to service and heat run-down shacks with old car bodies.

Within a year I had moved again, this time to UCLA to study waste reclamation projects in Los Angeles. But to this day I still wonder if the upstate New York people ever heard about my solar car collector, and, if they did, what they thought about it.

Nigel Coates: from Nihilist to planner
1992

Step through the Dickensian archway from Old Street past the overflowing dustbins and you are in a time warp. It is the Soviet Union circa 1929. That Constructivist tower of metal windows in front of you must be the fire escape of a workers' club by Melnikov. Wrong. Look at the powerful Suzuki 750 parked by the armoured door and the strange Bulgarian lettering reading "Branson Coates Architects". No, this is London 1992 alright, a place where things are as they really are.

The door lock buzzes. Up the timber staircase you go, landings caulked like the decks of a clipper ship, into a brightly lit space like a small Soho loft. The Branson Coates office is a polished wood-block floored ex-rag trade warehouse where carefully unchosen music plays, untrimmed flush doors laid across trestles support at least 20 drawing boards, and computers trail wires in gay abandon.

"Our clients like it here", beams Nigel Coates, emerging like Count Dracula. "The last thing they want to see is a slick grey carpeted 80s-style office with huge debts to go with it."

Doug Branson materialises too and smiles in agreement. "When you ask them what they think of it, they always say 'It's different.' Their other parameters are clean/dirty, fresh/dowdy. We come on the clean/fresh side."

Then Branson drifts away and Coates and I sit down like schoolboys at a simple wooden table. Two headless chromed manikins stare down at us. There are dogs wandering underfoot. No one pays any attention. It certainly is different.

When I come to I realise that Coates is a dazzling sight. Apart from myself he is the only person in the office wearing a suit—but his suit glints with the subtle effects of man-made fibres known only to a few. Nigel Coates IS the *avant-garde*. His blue shirt with no tie, bullet haircut and wire-framed glasses enhance his resemblance to an encyclopaedia of mythological figures of the twentieth century. He seems amazingly confident. Perhaps because the pages of history are written in his face: glasses by Leon Trotsky; eyes by Reggie Kray; haircut by Erich von Stroheim, energy by Andrew Lloyd Webber; menace by... Mishima?

Whoever the visitor, Nigel Coates has ways of making himself talk. Almost shyly he produces a Sir Norman Foster-style notebook. It has within its pages the most extraordinary sketches in 2B pencil. "I have a moviemakers' way of drawing", he explains, leafing through. He stops at a spread dominated by a number of wobbly ellipses labelled with words like "iconade", "bodyfeeld", "ecolone", "swervex" and "pumplanning". They are so odd that I write some of them down.

"I like playing with words. They are not real words, just play words, but that's the way that ideas move", he says.

The way these particular ideas moved was towards a project for the Vogue 75th anniversary issue last year, showing Coates's vision of London in the year 2066. Decoded, the wobbly ellipses are elements of the city. The field in which they float is the Thames. Most of them are projects for new buildings, riverfront gardens and floating islands. Somehow they come together into a mass of sinuous blimpish Finsterlinian shapes squeezed straight from the tube. Quatermass jelly (as we used to call it) is everywhere. It bubbles over the north circular road and invades King's Cross. Bits squeeze across the river. A giant arch of bone rises over North Woolwich. I marvel at the bizarre mixture of the mundane and the exotic. The possible and the impossible. I have said it before and I will say it again. All architects who succeed, do so by not looking too far ahead. It is an art. The art of the architect.

Nigel Coates started as a joke. Then in 1980 his bare, half-paint-stripped flat was written up by Peter York for *Harpers' and Queen*, copied for *Cosmo* and featured again in *Brutus*. Soon he was teaching at the AA and editing a magazine called NATO. Serious AA futurists like Jan Kaplicky, found it difficult to take him seriously. Elsewhere, the embunkered crowd at the Bride of Denmark, surrounded by the signatures of celebrities gone by, decided that he and all his works were cynical, chaotic, and more or less the end of civilisation as they knew it. It was at this time that RIBA external examiners Jim Stirling and Ed Jones went so far as to refuse to pass the work of his students. But then someone said the word 'Japan' and all bets were off. In 1985 Coates and Branson formed their practice and remodelled the Metropole restaurant in Tokyo. Then the Caffe Bongo. Those who came to laugh stayed to cheer.

A conversation with Coates reveals immediately that he has an extraordinarily clear mind. He is able to see what is there, not just what might be put there. Any fool, as they say, can work out what ought to be done: what takes intelligence is to work out what is actually happening, and that is what Coates can do. In the middle of the 1980s boom Coates understood that the City of London was a vast building site, a city renewing itself, not the priceless heirloom at risk that existed in the mind of the Prince of Wales. What he saw in Tokyo intensified this insight. There the metamorphism was raised to the power of ten: a city replacing one quarter of itself every year. As a result, where other architects might construct immaculate white models of whole areas of the city cleared of scaffolding, great flapping sheets of polythene, premix concrete trucks, roadworks, cones, grime, noise, traffic jams, advertising hoardings, drunks, dossers, wastelands, ruins and clamped cars; Branson and Coates produced even larger models redolent of dereliction and desperate expedients. Made out of bits of junk with paint thrown over them, and the same sorts of funny words as we see in the black Coates notebooks, the image of the city they conveyed was nonetheless more real than any conventional development model—from the synthetically tidy images of the Intelligent Buildings Group to the three-cornered-hat Norman Rockwell visions of Carl Laubin. What Coates portrayed was the reality of old crumbling, new overlaid London. Whatever you thought of it, it was the truth. It was real, not an illusion. And for that reason it was there for the taking. A dynamic desperate wasteland to be cruised by a gang led by Nigel Coates on his powerful Suzuki.

Coates was into planning early. When the GLC was expunged, he and his AA students did a plan for colonising County Hall with layers of real chaos and called it Ark Albion. Then they did a King's Cross plan for the ICA Metropolis exhibition. The community groups opposed to the blister/park/carpet Foster Associates master plan took a fitful interest in this, but they were not really ready for him. The Branson Coates master plan did not look at all like Sir Norman Foster's tidy arrangement. In fact Coates thinks Foster's plan, like Canary Wharf and Broadgate, is obsolete. It all comes under the heading of 'grey carpet'. Architecture robbed of all the dynamic, ephemeral features of real urban life. He himself is more into giant cones, permanent scaffolding, eternal roadworks, more flapping plastic, more litter. More, not less, of everything.

It seems strange to talk of an architect best known for Kienholz/Dufy restaurant refurbs, weird heavy metal shops, hotels, bars, department stores and more shops ("Retail? We can't seem to shake it off.") about planning —but a planner he is. He has that calm in the face of chaos that got Milton Keynes onto the ground; got Lord Holford his audience with the Queen, and got the New Towns started 40 years ago. Visions of London are two a penny. They have been all the rage of late. But all of them need a borrowed £50 billion to get started, 20 years of guaranteed economic stability and the planners' equivalent to martial law to get them finished on time. Coates' view is that, what with public inquiries, local interest groups, financial crashes, loony local authorities, fogeys, contextualists, inclusivists and the random interventions of the *Baupolizei*, none of these conditions can be met. In London—if not Paris—the completion date for that sort of utopia is always safely immersed in doubt.

His own approach to planning is different. It is softer, faster, more flexible and infiltrating. One per cent for art? Pfui! Even on small budgets he will spend 30 per cent or more. Big jobs or small he always starts from what is there, not from what he wants. The existing built, half-built and unbuilt infrastructure is what counts. He works on top of that. As a planner he conceives the kind of transformation to London as a whole that was achieved by Ron Herron at Imagination, but on a cosmic scale. "Don't forget, everything can be converted", he says of London's 20 million square feet of unlet grey carpet. "Everything can have a programme brought to it. I know a lot of people think an apocalypse is coming, but I don't. All we have to do is forget about utopia and make the best use of what there is. If we do that, in 20 or 30 years London can crawl out from under the mess of obsolete architecture and planning and express what it really wants to be again."

A full and Frank talk
1992

Frank Gehry was born in Toronto in 1928. He trained at the University of Southern California and Harvard, then he worked for Victor Gruen, Hideo Sasaki and William Pereira. He set up in practice in Los Angeles in 1962 and built many small houses. In 1977 he remodelled his own Santa Monica house with profiled aluminium and chainlink netting and got taken up by the theorising classes. Dubbed "the first deconstructionist" by Charles Jencks, his feet hardly touched the ground when he was sent round the world with Peter Eisenman as one half of a national double act. "He's the thinker, I'm the t'inker", he said. By then his Santa Monica house was being compared with "the spatial stratifications of Guarino Guarini".

The first mention of Guarino Guarini in connection with the work of an architect is a solemn moment. Guarini was a seventeenth century architectural spin doctor who gets called in when all other methods of classification have failed. In the happy-go-lucky days of the California Aerospace Museum, Gehry had possibly never heard of Guarini, but his apologists had. In 1988, when the time came for the former bricoleur to meet the widow of Walt Disney to talk about designing a $150 million 2,400 seat Los Angeles Walt Disney Concert Hall, it was "Get me Guarini!" And fast.

Last June Frank Gehry confronted a packed audience of 500 in the Chemistry Auditorium at London University. In that company he seemed small and pale, a bookish-looking man in a well-cut blue business suit and striped shirt. Completely out of place in a mob of students auditioning for a repainting of *The Raft of the Medusa*. You might have thought he was an evangelist because of the patient way he smiled and waited until it was quiet enough for him to talk. Then he began.

"I looked at the name tags, but he didn't come." The audience looked baffled and he smiled at their bafflement. Then came the punchline; "The Prince I mean."

At this a burst of laughter defused the uncertain temper that always lies in wait for the famous and successful when they address an audience of wannabees. Soon Frank was on his way, talking about building fish-shaped buildings; about the Los Angeles riots; about the shame of the metal detectors at the gates of Santa Monica schools; about his "anger against postmodernism"; about chainlink fencing and corrugated metal and the "it's alright" quality of buildings that look like binoculars or jugs, and about how cities "have gotta be built by more people than just one".

Next morning I report to the lobby of the Russell Hotel. I am staring at the multi-coloured marble balusters and the Annigoni portrait of the Queen when he appears.

"Did you choose this hotel?" "Nope."

"Do you like it?"

"Nope."

"Do you know who designed it?"

"Do you?"

"Nope."

When this is over we find the bar and sit on two highly polished Chesterfields. Frank Gehry orders water.

"I guess you will be wanting to talk about Prince Charles", he opines. "No. Americans are always far too polite about him."

"Oh really?"

"Yes, Cesar Pelli said he agreed with every word the Prince said, but it did him no good. Charles attacked him anyway."

"Is that so? Well, I don't feel polite about your Prince Charles. I don't agree with what he says. I think he's an anachronism. He's a kind of protected species. Royalty has nothing to do with what is really going on in the world today. He's not doing any good, he's doing harm. He's trying to roll back the present and you can't do that. Besides all his ideas are based on a version of the nineteenth century that never existed, its been all cleaned up. Sure, he has a forum, but he's wasting it."

"Mr Gehry, you're a Pritzker prizewinner aren't you?"

Pause and wary look. "Yes, I am."

"Well, the Pritzker Prize is awarded for 'significant contributions to humanity'. If Prince Charles' attempts are so poor, what have you done?"

Gehry looks like a man struck by a low-yield nuclear device at five o'clock in the morning, but he recovers quickly.

"I'm just a liberal do-gooder I guess", he says evenly. "The worst kind."

There is a long silence while he ruminates uncomfortably in his Chesterfield.

"Contributions to humanity.... Well, maybe a good businessman could sort it out, but I doubt it."

Another long pause.

"Do you know anything about the riot people in Los Angeles?" He asks suddenly, not waiting for an answer. "We live in Los Angeles and we can't leave. We tried to help them. We called the agency up and went to visit them. You hope they are going to need architecture but they don't. They are culturally very rich. They don't need architecture. They need self-respect."

"What exactly is self respect?"

"I don't know. But I know what you need to get it. You need to be able to send your kids to the store to buy ice cream and not have them get arrested. You know, that's what happens. They go to buy an ice cream and they get arrested."

"If self-respect has nothing to do with architecture, how can architecture help humanity?"

There is another ruminative silence.

"Do you know what the Los Angeles riots really were?" He asks, and again answers. "They were an arms raid. They raided the gun stores. Now they've got more firepower than the police."

Another long silence. But still he won't leave the subject of humanity, and still he won't *tu quoque* his way out of it.

"What have I done for humanity? What *can* you do for humanity? You're stuck in your own juice. I told them we would take two youngsters from the riot district who wanted to be architects into the office and put them through training. We'll do that."

There is a strong strain of what might be called riot appeasement running through Gehry's thinking at the moment. He may not be a pacifist in the sense of being opposed to war, but he is passionately concerned about the breakdown of civil order. For a man whose projects appear to have laughably little to do with anything social or even political, or even related to the economic system in a Fosterian, Rogersonian or Grimshavian sort of way, he seems obsessed by the idea of the destruction of the city. He returns to the issue of the Los Angeles riots repeatedly and keeps predicting more riots and worse ones.

In a conversation that tries to hop about the world of architecture and buildings he seems always to be trying to connect the *good* idea of many different architects collaborating over the design of cities, with the *bad* idea of the bloody riots. If style wars need not involve personal animosity, he seems to be saying to himself, why should racial differences involve personal animosity? But he knows the parallel is not very convincing. Just because he and Eisenman can get along together—even though Gehry rolls his eyes expressively when I read out some Eisenman stuff about "exponential torque" and "asymptotic tilts"—that doesn't mean there will be no more war in the ghetto. Just because he and Claes Oldenburg can get along together —even though that one pair of binoculars has crowded Gehry's whole building off several magazine covers—it doesn't really add up to a crusade for urban peace. Anyway, wasn't it the Modern Movement that had the architectural answer to all these problems?

"Yeah, they knew what they had to do. Some of them still do. Ken Frampton still thinks he knows what to do."

His tone suggests that he is not a modernist of that sort himself, yet he still talks about his "anger at postmodernism". What does he mean by that?

"I mean that when all that postmodern stuff started up I didn't think modernism was washed up. It still had a long way to go. It was full of possibilities. All the electronics. Distance working. Electronic shopping. Flying to the Moon.... I know what modernism is. I still believe in it. modernism is having the nerve to live in the present. That's why I think I am still Modern. I'm not burrowing in the past. My work is not irrational. I don't just throw all the blocks up in the air and draw them where they land. I live in the present." Then he thinks for a while.

"But the French don't think so. They are disappointed in me. They hate my American Cultural Center, they thought I was going to bring them all kinds of hotshot technology from the States and I didn't."

"You mean like a Starfighter stuck on the side?"

"I guess, but you know I never did want an F-104 on the California Aerospace Museum anyway. I wanted a Messerschmitt 109F, the most beautiful fighter plane ever made. You can junk your Spitfire and your Mustang and your Zen, no, what was it? Your Zero. The 109F was perfection. But the client wouldn't have it because it was a Nazi plane. I told them you could buy one from Romania. Have a Romanian plane, with Romanian markings. I wanted to make two important points with that plane. One, that elements of war could be beautiful. Two, that aerospace development could lead to destruction. But it was no good. We ended up with the F-104, about the worst American warplane ever made, and painted in United Nations markings."

Is it surprising that Gehry should be so obsessively knowledgeable about the different models of Me109? The Me109E had ugly tailplane struts and the 109G had big bulging gun tubs under the wings. The 109K? Well, that wooden rudder. He is absolutely right about the 109F of course. What exquisite taste. But how can you be into all that stuff and just go on calling yourself a "middle class slob" and a "do-gooder" and worrying about the riots?

"I don't know. Times have changed. I guess we Americans don't take ourselves so seriously as you Europeans do."

The case for an un-creative architecture
1992

One day in 1935 there was a great scandal. The celebrated violinist Fritz
Kreisler admitted to a journalist that for 30 years he had been inserting
pieces of his own composition into recitals of the works of seventeenth and
eighteenth century composers. Kreisler came under virulent attack, but he
was unrepentant. If his listeners could not distinguish between the pieces
he played and genuine baroque music, he argued, why should it matter
whether they were forged or not?

The Kreisler episode has its analogues in architecture today. A modern
building may be no more than a piece of industrial design, "like an
enormous typewriter", as Robert Venturi once put it, but its unique
combination of industrial components is still considered to be intellectual
property, like the alleged compositions of Couperin, Stamitz and Albinoni
that were actually Kreisler fakes. In this way architecture, like music, is
inextricably bound up with an erroneous idea of individual creativity.

Why this should be is not clear. Architects know that getting a building
built is not like writing a book or painting a picture. It is more like winning
an election, after undergoing a process of immense and unfathomable
complexity involving many personalities, products, consultancies, schedules,
contractors, bureaucracies, statutes, regulations, budgets, policy committees,
review boards, protest groups, etcetera. Even a small building can involve a
cast of thousands, amongst whom only one—the architect—is trying to
create something original. In such circumstances creative architecture is a
myth, as Kreisler proved.

Is there then a case for un-creative architecture? In my book *Theory and
Design in the Second Machine Age*, 1990, I argued that the real, as opposed to
the mythological, profession of architecture should shift its ground from
meretricious claims of creativity based on art history and 'meaning'
—a realm where, as the Prince of Wales has demonstrated, expertise is
already completely consumerised—to the more challenging field of
technology transfer.

Technology transfer is what happens when the methods or processes
developed in one industry are applied to a completely different one.
Its history is immense and uncharted, often bizarre. In the fifth century
AD, the dome of the church of San Vitale in Ravenna was made from
earthenware pots, still with their carrying handles, in a tour de force of

technology transfer executed in pursuit of lightness. 1,500 years later pots of a similar design were being fashioned out of worn-out auto tires. The Middle Ages saw a long series of largely undocumented transfers from wooden ship construction to timber roof construction. Later scissors were adapted into spectacle frames and the machinery devised to make bone china was used to make chocolate. In the nineteenth century the first rolled iron beams, made to support the decks of ships, migrated ashore to become not only structural beams in buildings but railroad tracks. In modern times the cavity magnetron tube has made its equally unlikely way from aircraft radar to the domestic microwave oven.

Technology transfer has all the unpredictable wonderment of genetic mutation and yet in construction its importance has been direct and seminal. 40 years after a small reinforced concrete boat was exhibited in Paris, reinforced concrete building became common. In the same way all-steel ships preceded steel buildings, and the steel masts of steel ships led the way for radio transmission antennae and power transmission pylons.

Like shipbuilding, the auto industry has been a great source of technology transfers. Its cold-rolled steel chassis beams led to the family of round tubes, square tubes, angles, channels and space frame members that are used in construction today. At the behest of pioneer technology transfer architect Eero Saarinen the auto industry developed neoprene gasket glazing for curtain wall systems. Aerospace too has proved a fruitful source of transfers. Complex alloy castings and large panel raised floor systems for commercial buildings have been developed from those used in large passenger aircraft. In the same way the vast array of composites and adhesives developed for aerospace applications by the chemical industry has filtered into innumerable applications in construction.

Stochastic and unplanned as it is, the adaptation of the technology of one field to advance another is a tremendously efficient process. In architecture its capacity to exploit the product of research and development of any field without actually paying for it, adds up to a parasitic form of R&D well suited to the needs of an impoverished and fragmented profession with no profits to plough back into research on its own account.

Technology transfer is a process far better attuned to the needs of a globally organised construction industry than fine art architecture can ever be. And yet even those architects who most dramatically use technology transfers today, temporise over its importance. Norman Foster is well known for his ingenious use of components and materials that have their origin in industries far removed from construction: solvent welded PVC roofing derived from swimming pool liners; gaskets of neoprene developed originally for cable-jacketing; structural glazing and enamel glass 'fritting' from the auto industry; superplastic aluminium and metallised fabrics from aerospace; roof-eaves tensioning devices from trailer sidescreens; raised floor systems from jetliners.... All these, along with techniques of presentation culled from aviation magazines, are to be found in his buildings and projects: yet he does not believe that this "interesting but uncreative process" can supplant the fine art tradition upon which the architectural profession depends.

Leading European architects like Richard Rogers, Jean Nouvel, Terry Farrell, Benthem Crouwel, Nicholas Grimshaw, Weber Brand and Richard Horden—the last of whom designed the 1984 Yacht House, a sophisticated technology transfer building with an alloy mast structural frame and many nautical components—also acknowledge the presence of technology transfer in their designs and cite it as evidence of modernity in their buildings, but they too shrink from espousing it as a theory of architecture in itself.

To conceive of architecture as founded upon the pursuit of technology transfers, each based upon Buckminster Fuller's technological law of doing more with less, means to accept that it is no longer a 'creative' activity in the fine art sense, but a process of multi-sourced element combination. Technology transfer can open up this process of combination to the whole genetic pool of scientific and industrial activity everywhere. It is an activity literally waiting for a profession to take it over.

Lunch with Leon Krier
1991

It's not easy having lunch with Leon Krier. He'll arrange to have his passport and money stolen that morning so he has to go to the police station, and then he'll have to deal with builders in his house. He won't remember to phone the upstairs room at Manzis to tell you about this until he is already 30 minutes late, and he won't actually arrive until he is 90 minutes late. Then he will confess that he has already eaten and he'll only drink coffee while you have to talk through your whitebait and seafood salad and drink a bottle of mineral water and a bottle of Corvo on your own. Still it's worth it. This man is as close an advisor to Prince Charles as Rod Hackney ever was. Better yet, he is the man entrusted with bringing our future monarch's vision of the urban regeneration of Britain to life at Poundbury, the unsuspecting 600 acres of Duchy of Cornwall land at the foot of ancient Maiden Castle that was looped into the little town of Dorchester by the construction of a bypass some seven years ago.

Like his equally famous brother Rob, Leon Krier is an impressive figure. Obeying Noel Coward's advice to the ambitious he always dresses like a stockbroker, albeit with a white scarf, and nowadays even his wild old Abbie Hoffman hairdo has shrunk to Bart Simpson dimensions. Somehow his most notorious utterances; "Auschwitz, Birkenau and Milton Keynes are children of the same parents", or "Most architects consider the erection of a column more dangerous than a nuclear power station", seem entirely reasonable when he sits down and fixes you with his affable but penetrating gaze. My boy, he seems to say, the attention of the world has to be gained by one means or another. Once it has, we successful men can always leave such things behind us.

In Leon Krier's case it was not so much death camp Milton Keynes as praise for Hitler's architect Albert Speer that made his name a household word. In the 1970s he befriended Speer and wrote two books about his architecture and a notorious article saying it was not Speer but Hitler's rocket man Werner von Braun who should have been sent to prison for 20 years: Speer should have been flown to the United States to redesign Washington. The same article deplored the callous demolition of Nazi classical buildings in Germany after the Second World War. It was published in the conservative *Die Welt* and sent a thrill of horror through Germany. Today Krier still shakes his head over Germany. He shakes it twice over two Germanies united. Born the son of an ecclesiastical tailor in Luxembourg, by the age of 45 he has enough achievements to his credit, and enough demonstrations of courage and integrity to look back on, to be able to give his opinions boldly, without fear or favour, or even too much concern for the accuracy of details. "There is a total revival of modernism in Germany", he sighs urgently, as though it were something like AIDS. "A stupid, uninformed modernism. They are completely blocked. When you ask them why they must be modern, they just have these stock phrases; 'You can't put the clock back', things like that."

Can this be true, I wonder? Even the German government exhibition at last year's Venice Biennale was devoted to the work of the Classicist Heinrich Tessenow, the mentor of Leon's own special subject, Albert Speer?

"Was it? I do not know. I did not see it."

"But you were in Venice?"

"Yes, I was there but I did not have time to see it. I can tell you that this year I was invited to Germany to take part in a symposium in Dresden about whether to rebuild the Frauenkirche, the huge circular church that was destroyed in the 1945 bombing of the city. I took up at least one part in nine of the symposium arguing that not only should the Frauenkirche be rebuilt, but the whole of the old city plan should be restored in place of the modernist scheme built under the DDR. Everybody else was opposed to the rebuilding of the church. There were TEN REPORTS in the German newspapers of this symposium, NOT ONE mentioned my suggestion about the plan. That is why I say there is a complete domination of modernism."

Unsurprisingly, in view of their age, both the Kriers were schooled under modernism, but their experiences differed. Rob, the elder, says his brother, boldly introduced the work of Le Corbusier, Gropius, Mies and Frei Otto into the Technical University of Munich in the 1950s, when the sleepy provincial school was in the grip of "a boring conservatism". So successful was he with Frei Otto in particular that he went on to design a house for him in steel and glass.

Leon's experience was different. Ten years later he spent a year at the Technical University of Stuttgart. It was the annus mirabilis of 1968 when the whole world's universities were in turmoil, but not Stuttgart. There Leon quietly produced classical designs for his studio projects and equally quietly received no grades. At the time when students were storming the administrative offices of the University of Strasbourg, Krier was on a visit to that latter-day Bauhaus, the Hochschule fur Gestaltung at Ulm, attending a seminar on colonies in outer space. At the end of his first year he felt out of it. He wrote to James Stirling in England, sending him some of his drawings and asking for a job. Why on earth did he choose the then modernist Stirling, and why England?

"I always admired his Leicester Engineering building. It has a remarkable discipline and symmetry...."

"Discipline? Symmetry? But it is not classical. It is not even functionally modern. It is wilful, self-indulgent...."

Krier shakes his head pityingly. "Not well put together, I admit, but a masterpiece."

"Where was Stirling's office at that time?"

"75 Gloucester Place. Sarah Miles lived upstairs."

"Sarah Miles?"

"Sometimes she opened the door. I saw her in a film recently."

"Did you enjoy living in London?"

"I hated it. I hated all England. I swore I would never return. It was so provincial. Luxembourg City with a population of 60,000 was more urban than London."

20 years later Leon Krier is an expert on England and he can smile at such memories, That one year at Stuttgart was the only architectural training he ever did. And now he is a master planner on two continents. Master planner! The one postmodern title that everyone covets and nobody really understands.

I decide to try to summarise Krier's position on modernism from his writings. His broad strategy, I suggest, is to use his powers as a planner and polemicist to fight the evil force of industrialisation, that dehumanising state of slavery that modernism merely serves. All industrial states, he believes, are engaged in promoting the fragmentation and destruction of cities by zoning that separates out life and work instead of bringing them together. But although it is powerful, this industrialisation is not invincible. In fact he once wrote that it was "only an episode between craft cultures". If this is true, then our present is no more than a transitional state between industrialism and the coming new age 'craft culture' that will use computers, electronics and technology in life enhancing ways. It is into this latter context that his Poundbury development for the Prince of Wales will fit.

Krier nods through most of this but he cannot remember having written the bit about industrialism being only an "episode". I quote him a reference and he shrugs. When I stop he seems to think I have been too hard on modernism, the architecture of industrialism.

"The evils of modernism were not in what it did, but in what it denied", he says sagely. I am surprised. Can this really be the same modernism that was responsible for Auschwitz and Milton Keynes?

"No, modernism is not responsible for industrialisation", he goes on. "It simply has an abstract, negative relationship with it. It does so many unnecessary things and prevents things that really need doing from being done.'

For example?

"Housing. The whole idea of mass housing was unnecessary. All today's suburbs are a multiplication of cells without a nucleus, they have no public buildings so they are not towns. Besides, there was no need to re-invent the house. Its evolution was complete 200 years ago. It had already been invented, like the wheel. Modernism's 'housing' is like the use of styles by the nineteenth century historicists: it is inappropriate, the use of an inappropriate language."

If that is so, how is it 'appropriate' to build 244 fake 'Georgian' houses in Dorchester?

"They will not be fake. They will not be 'Georgian'. They will be vernacular houses, the dominant Dorset vernacular. That is what most houses are like there."

What about the high density of the development and the use of a greenfield site at the foot of the ancient hill fort of Maiden Castle?

"I would build on Maiden Castle itself if I was allowed to. It would make an excellent hill town."

I have more than a suspicion that he is joking but I continue. What about his own building at Poundbury, the great tower, and what about the covered market, the church and the little shops.... Are they 'appropriate' in the age of video and satellite TV?

"You know as well as I do that if public buildings are built they will be used. Shops and markets don't have to be 'started'. You only have to stop 'stopping' them from happening."

But what will the TOWER be used for?

"It can be used for any public purpose. Meetings, things like that. Oh, and the top will be used for microwave aerials."

I look at Krier closely. We have been talking for an hour and a half and he is on his tenth cup of coffee. This time he definitely is kidding. It must be time to go.

Zaha escapes the pull of gravity
1993

Zaha Hadid has a good story about what happened once when she applied for an entry visa into the United States. Because she was a woman from an Arab country the man at the embassy did not believe her when she said she was an architect. "If you are an architect", he said shrewdly, "tell me who Antonio Gaudi was." Zaha told him that Gaudi was a Catalan architect, a master of structural plasticity who was born in 1852, designed some of the most famous buildings in Barcelona, and died in 1926 under the wheels of a tram. "OK Zaha", said the man, "I guess you are an architect."

If only the rest of the world were so easily convinced! In a way Zaha Hadid's career over the last 15 years has been like one long encounter with that immigration officer: she has existed to prove that she is an architect. And sitting at a table in the converted schoolroom that is her office in Bowling Green Lane, it it clear that the final, incontrovertible proof has only just arrived. Zaha Hadid is recovering from flu. She is swathed in a black cloak and unwisely smoking Marlboro Lites 400 at a time. "People did not think I was a stayer", she says of her long apprenticeship in the avant-garde. "They all thought I would give up and go away."

Well, they were wrong. Before her on the table is a black folder containing black and white Helene Binet photographs of her first real building. Flip, flip, flip go the vinyl pages, each one showing a detail construction shot, a mass of reinforcing bars here, a spectacular concrete cantilever there, a panelled section of concrete wall bearing shuttering marks, a knifedge concrete finish, then finally the whole structure, 90 metres long and looking like an experimental rocket plane wheeled out of its hangar for a world air speed record bid. This freestanding concrete form is astounding in its acute angularity, its solidity, its matter-of-fact, junk-on-the-ground-all-around genuine construction site factitiousness. In a way it is all the proof and none of the proof for, from the photographs, the function of this structure can be no more than a wild guess. One thing it is not is conceptual architecture. It is dynamic solid, physical and big. In fact it is Zaha's one million pound fire station for the Vitra factory at Weil in Switzerland, nearly completed already and opening next spring.

Zaha Hadid was born in Baghdad in 1950, the daughter of an economist who studied at the LSE. She grew up, read mathematics at the American University of Beirut, and came to England in 1972. She graduated from the

AA in 1977 and, encouraged by Rem Koolhaas and Alvin Boyarsky, went straight into teaching there, exploiting her creative wilfulness, her superb draughtsmanship and her penchant for strange geometrical projections. In 1979 she amazed that part of the architectural world that was paying attention to such things with a radical entry for the House for the Irish Prime Minister competition. She amazed the rest of the architectural world three years later when she won the $100,000 Hong Kong Peak competition outright, with a feast of spiky cantilevers never before seen. Although the Hong Kong Peak was never built, the prize money enabled Zaha to open her London office. More importantly it rehabilitated an entire generation of 'conceptual architects', most of them out of the AA, who had been written off by the critics as mere artists unlikely ever to build a real building.

Zaha Hadid had grown up within the protective environment of the AA school, Prince Charles' "Frankenstein Academy", and she broke out of it by winning the Peak. Until then, despite being hailed in 1977 by her tutor and mentor Rem Koolhaas as, "a planet in her own inimitable orbit", by 1982 she had done no more than remodel her brother's flat in Eaton Place in the style of an explosion—an event that did not bring her planet to the attention of the astronomers of the real world. It was only when her drawings were retrieved from the Peak competition reject pile by Japanese architect and Royal Gold Medallist Arata Isozaki that great things began to happen. Like Eero Saarinen at the Sydney Opera House competition a quarter of a century before, Isozaki somehow convinced all his fellow assessors of what he called "the uniqueness of expression and the strength of logic" of Zaha's entry. "It must win because it gives itself up to the forces inherent in style itself", he said.

The Peak was a shot heard round the world. Zaha subsequently obtained commissions in Holland, Japan and Germany on the strength of the fame it brought her. Of its shockingly radical design she later said; "The architecture was like a knife cutting through butter, devastating traditional principles. When I did it I almost believed there was such a thing as zero gravity. I can actually now believe that buildings can float. I know they don't but I almost believe it." Today her recollections of that great event are more pragmatic. "It was a breakthrough because people were not prepared for it. It was important to a lot of architects because it showed that there was another way to do things after all."

After the Peak came the Moonsoon restaurant in Sapporo and another competition win for a £40 million Düsseldorf Media Centre which is still under way but has yet to advance to building regulations approval. Perversely the Vitra Fire Station arrived by another route. Rolf Fehlbaum, already the enigmatic patron of Grimshaw, Eva Jiricna and Frank Gehry, had approached her to design a chair in 1988. At the time she was designing her celebrated —and alas uncompleted—three metre-wide six-storey restaurant in Tokyo. Seeing this bizarre structure Fehlbaum enquired one day; "Would you like to design a fire station?" "Of course", said Zaha, as though it were the most natural thing in the world. And so perhaps it was, for Frank Gehry, so rumour has it, who was originally invited to design a Vitra chair store that ended up as a chair museum.

Somehow in the conventional surroundings of the old school house in Bowling Green Lane, with Zaha swathed in a black cloak contrasting with the jaggedly patterned orange carpet, it seems justifiable to probe her own personal sensitivity to radical forms. After all the Vitra Fire Station is not like Bob Venturi's Dixwell Firehouse, or even the fire station that she insists was once designed by Peter Eisenman. Aside from looking like a military secret made out of concrete, it also looks as though you *could* park fire engines under it if you wanted to, but you might rather put sculptures there or nothing at all. In other words... IS IT A REAL FIRE STATION?

The ghost of the immigration officer hovers over our conversation but he does not speak. Curiously enough, although they are highly technical-looking, the drawings don't help much. Some could be taken for measured drawings of traces left in the Andes by extra-terrestrial visitors, while others have reassuringly pedestrian words lettered onto them, like 'gymnasium', 'training facility', 'washdown area', things like that, allied to bizarre plan shapes.

Zaha affects to be unimpressed by my question about how REAL it all is. "It has four walls and a roof. Well, five...." She begins again. "Because the walls are not at right angles.... The walls control where you stand in the rooms." Then finally; "Space is a strange phenomenon. Everything is important, proportion, height, colour, temperature.... It is not the same as virtual reality." But do these strange shapes really have effect on people? Apparently at Harvard they did.

"When I showed some slides of the Vitra Fire Station a strange silence and chill fell over the whole lecture hall. You couldn't hear anybody breathing. Nobody said anything, but afterwards several people commented on it. They all felt it. The same thing happened when I showed the slides at Columbia."

Had she ever felt such a sensation?

"It is catching a moment of space, like catching a moment of time", she reflects. "I suppose I can say I felt it once myself when I was in the Mies van der Rohe National Gallery in Berlin. Not a space I particularly like, but it is how you feel in a space at a particular time. Buildings are always a surprise."

What does it feel like to have completed a real building at last?

"Three things. First, the experience was good, I had a fantastic client. Second, the stigma is lifted—the stigma of never really having built anything. Third, confidence. Confidence that there is a simple way to do such a building, and that, for not very much more money, a client really can get a much better building."

She said buildings are always a surprise. Did Vitra get what it expected?

"Vitra didn't know what to expect. I think that, because it was a fire station, Fehlbaum thought it might be red. It's not. So it was a surprise to him too."

Tales of the obsolescent
1993

On the 24 November 1983 I bought a state of the art typewriter for £1,100. It was an Olympia Supertype, a business machine the size of an aircraft carrier, the latest in a long line of German typewriters built like guns and intended to last forever. Of course, I knew about word processors in 1983 —according to *Time* magazine Raquel Welch used one—but I believed that a serious journalist needed a serious typewriter. Besides, the Supertype was not old technology. It was an interesting transitional machine. It had a small cinemascope-shaped screen above its keyboard across which scrolled words made of little green dots in the shape of the last 24 characters you had typed. This was called a buffer. It enabled you to correct your errors before they reached the paper. Progress indeed. And there was more. The Supertype had an 8k memory. It could remember and summon up 16 different business letters, or one document 1,000 words long.

Once I learned to use it, I was very satisfied with this machine. Right through 1984 I thought it was great. By 1985 there was even a Supertype II, with a 48 character buffer and a 16k memory. But I knew that was no good either. The truth was that these Jurassic machines, Olympias, Olivettis, Remingtons and IBMs, were not only the culmination of 100 years of typewriter technology—they were the swan song of the typewriter itself. Just before Christmas 1985 I bought a word processor for another £1,100. An Atari 520ST with a monochrome monitor and an Epsom printer. For the same price as the Supertype it could create and manipulate documents on a TV-size screen, recall and print them automatically, and store 32 times as much information. By 1988 the Atari had improved so much that it had 1,024 times as much memory as the Olympia Supertype and cost a quarter of the price. In that year I traded in my Supertype for £100 against a 1 megabyte Atari. No matter how committed you felt to typewriters, the paperless way was best. Ten years after I bought the Supertype, I could word process ten times as fast on a PC with access to 20,000 times as much memory for not much more than £500. The truth is that something terrible happened to typewriters in the 1980s. They changed from serious office equipment to catastrophe theory at work. Today they are virtually extinct. There is no use for them. Not even accessing old data, which remains the principal, indeed the only use for old computers.

Obsolescence is an interesting subject, and not just where office machinery is concerned. Another major casualty of the 1980s was the public telephone box. Another product that did not go down without a fight. The celebrated red K2 telephone box of 1924, designed by Sir Giles Gilbert Scott—coincidentally also the designer of another piece of 1980s obsolescence, Battersea Power Station—soon attracted the conservation barflies. Before long this cast iron museum piece was routinely described as "one of the finest pieces of industrial design every produced" and a book by Gavin Stamp was published, extolling its virtues. But whilst comparisons with the Parthenon and the Baths of Caracalla filled the air at the Royal Fine Art Commission, the industry for whom this piece of industrial design had been intended began to undergo a revolution of its own. One that rapidly passed a death sentence on the whole idea of telephone boxes as little buildings.

Radio telephones, once confined to the cars of tycoons, had suddenly become terminals in a new national cellular network. As the 80s progressed, tales proliferated of stranded motorists summoning aid, press reporters filing stories from the street, and stockbrokers stemming losses from the pavement. Even as the conservationists were triumphantly listing individual cast iron telephone boxes, more and more ephemeral designs came into use. Designs whose only purpose was to mark the end of the telephone enclosure, and herald the birth of the pocket telephone in its place.

By 1988, when Mercury, British Telecom's private enterprise competitor, introduced three lightweight telephone shelter designs of its own, to widespread critical derision, Stamp, by then the doyen of telephone box historians, was moved to complain; "In the chaotic state of modern British architecture, no designer is capable of producing a telephone kiosk as assured and sophisticated as Scott's." This, of course, was true. But the reason was to be found, not in 'the chaotic state of British architecture', but in the rapid advance of miniaturised electronic communications.

If the typewriter is already in the dustbin of history, and the telephone box dying of a cancerous proliferation of telephones, what of the clock? Here is a victim of 80s obsolescence that has been devoured by the machine environment in a process more like cannibalism. 500 years ago the clock enjoyed the status of a tracking satellite dish today. When Giuliano da Sangallo remodelled the great Lorenzo de Medici's villa, he equipped it with a huge clock and sundial that dominated its garden facade. As late as 1900 the clocktower was still regarded as a major technological device. Of course by mid-century the wristwatch had superseded the public timepiece, but that was just the beginning. By 1980 the digital clock had exploded over the entire spectrum of consumer goods from cookers to jewellery. It was impossible to buy a car without a clock. Wallets incorporated digital clocks, so did handbags, diaries, rulers, calculators, radios, computers, briefcases, television sets, stereos, videos, rings, portable tape players and telephones. By the end of the decade the clock had ceased to be a unitary object at all. It had become an accessory. A part of everything else.

The 1980s was a decade of slaughter in the world of machines. Hot metal printing went the way of typewriting, its huge ancient installations torn out and sold for scrap. Monochrome photography took a terrible pounding from colour, then computer-generated images began to threaten the whole future of film. In the media, video tape replaced film overnight. In business hot desks replaced dedicated workstations, fax machines came back from the dead to eclipse computer modems, and fax modems counter-attacked and drove them out again. On the road, engine management systems replaced carburettors, and sundry accessories including laptops, telephones, tyre-inflators and hot-drink makers, clustered around cigar lighter sockets no longer used to light cigars. In entertainment, CDs wiped the floor with cassettes and LPs disappeared. In recreation, sales of sailing dinghies were eclipsed by sales of sailboards, and sales of speedboats by sales of jet skis. Calculators attached themselves to wristwatches like parasites, and then fell away again.

What can we learn from all this? As technology evolves new species, leaving no recess in the market unfilled, its wonderful seething mass of invention, like a shoal of arctic krill at the mercy of the great whale of consumption, leaves behind it a trail of corpses. These are old machines and obsolete devices in their millions. Most of them find their way into landfill, but a few fall into the hands of interior decorators, curators of museums, private collectors, conservationists and such-like individuals. These scavengers upon industrial production perform the task of transforming technology into culture. For what obsolescence teaches us is that culture is no more than the consumption of the obsolete.

Invasion of the body snatchers
1995

Art History is today's fastest growing discipline. Apart from its incredible rate of expansion, the oddest thing about it (motto: "Keep up to date with the past"), is that it is so young. Believe it or not, Art History is no older than the motor car.

Art History grew out of 'connoisseurship', which is a posh word for making lists of collections of valuable things. By this time last century, Art History's leading lights had turned collections of these lists into books that were a cross between public opinion polls and music charts. The spoils of colonialism meant that they had a lot of lists to work with. Even the Great War, with its popular revulsion against Monarchs of the Glen, rattan chairs and umbrella stands made out of elephant's feet, failed to shake Art History. The Modern Movement, a rebellion against it, did no good.

By the time we reach the present, after another World War and dose of Socialism, Art History has the whole person-made environment in its grip through valuation, insurance, taxation, tourism and Heritage law. Minimalist bits of Modern architecture, built as a rebellion against academic classification, are now high-flying performers in the Art Historical value system. Even 25 years ago it would have been inconceivable that an Ernö Goldfinger house would one day be "saved for the nation".

Now everything has become a priceless example of something or other, and nothing is too young, too big, too small or too different to show up on the Art Historical charts. Before long Richard Rogers' designed-to-be-altered Lloyd's building will be 'protected' from change in the same way as open fields that still bear traces of Saxon villages are protected from agriculture.

Somewhere there is a central directorate of Art Historians where they digitise all their data. Today they police the environment, missing nothing. They record every chink of light falling upon a 'priceless' painting; every unauthorised act of metal detection in the countryside; every fanlight front door and upvc replacement window; every waterlogged brain that tumbles out of a Medieval skull when it is dug up (I swear that last one is true), and every attempt to replace a working 1923 factory diesel engine with a new one.

Art Historians are at the leading edge of technology. They X-ray buildings, use electron microscopes, cellular telephones and laptops, recording everything they see. They analyse 1950s plastic tableware, matchbox tops, old Beatles albums, cinema posters, air raid shelters and paint on walls. Everything belongs to them. It's like *Invasion of the Body Snatchers*. Thousands of new ones are being trained every year.

Invasion of the vibrators
1996

"The mind becomes a glutinous slab that takes impressions and Oxford Street rolls off upon it a perpetual ribbon of changing sights, sounds and movement. Parcels slap and hit; motor omnibuses graze the curb; the blare of a whole brass band in full tongue dwindles to a thin reed of sound. Buses, vans, cars, barrows stream past like the fragments of a picture puzzle; a white arm rises; the puzzle runs thick, coagulates, stops; the white arm sinks, and away it streams again, streaked, twisted, higgledy-piggledy, in perpetual race and disorder. The puzzle never fits itself together, however long we look."

A long quote, but worth it for its evocation of real urbanism, as opposed to the Arcadian substitute being peddled by the Vibrators; the growing number of people in London who have given up having 'visions' and started saying that they want to make the city more 'vibrant' instead.

This group has been having things all its own way recently, with its mass meetings in Westminster Hall and its trails of celebrities from the arts and parliament. No one ever seems to mock its Hiroshima and Nagasaki plans for universal pedestrianisation and formation cycle-riding; no one ever queries its crackpot schemes for floating cafes and pedallos on the Thames. How one longs to subject the Vibrators to a dose of real urban life! Like a week in Shanghai, where everybody really does ride a bike and the authorities are at their wits end trying to stop them. Either that or a quick voyage down the Thames estuary to find out what tide lifts and choppy water are all about.

When you think about it, it is extraordinary how removed from reality the Vibrators have become. They take heart when they move into lofts in Clerkenwell, believing that this is proof of a resurgence of city life. It never occurs to them to wonder why so much property in Clerkenwell became vacant, or why it was so cheap. They see no connection between their own presence there and figures that prove London has lost nearly one and a half million jobs since 1961—including half of those in manufacturing—and labour demand is still falling. When confronted with this paradox they deny it, saying the tide has turned. When did it turn? Last weekend probably. Why was that? Quick as a flash; "Because of tourism." Tourists have taken the place of all the lost workers so we don't notice their absence. When you think about it, that means, in a spooky X-Files kind of way, that the city is growing a new phantom population, never indigenous, always changing.

Such thoughts flood into the mind whenever a genuine bit of urban vibration surfaces through the hype. The quotation from Virginia Woolf at the head of this column for instance. Not renowned as an urbanist; not generally listed with Mumford, Abercrombie or Sharp; but in 1932 she wrote the essay on Oxford Street from which the quote comes, and it puts any of the pioneer town planners to shame. So perfectly does it evoke the lost hustle and bustle of real, working urbanism that someone should read it aloud at the next Vibrators meeting.

Frank Lloyd Wright fights for his life
1996

Tradition, as Frank Lloyd Wright once acidly observed, is not as old as people think. But being right and enjoying it are not necessarily the same thing. A return visit to his winter studio at Taliesin West in Arizona—once *near*, now in Scottsdale, once *near*, now *part of* Phoenix—would show Wright's ghost where resistance to change can lead. Today, standing on the prow of his desert ship, once 26 miles from the nearest human habitation, Wright would be only a hop, skip and a jump from red, pitched-roof suburban houses and skeins of electricity pylons that block out his once spectacular view across the desert to Camel-Back Mountain.

So much for the chances of tradition when pitched against progress. But it is also a tradition, as Eddie Murphy wisely observed in *Coming to America*, that times do, and must change. And so they have at Taliesin West, and not just outside. A visitor today sees evidence of time and change everywhere. In the studios (where once purists objected to the replacement of draped canvas with fibreglass roof panels), today they would have to object to the opaquing of all side and roof lights with painted out glass and makeshift blinds. Admitted to the holy of holies, the drafting room, one does not have to look far for the culprits. Down the row of tables you see serried ranks of monitors, virtually unknown in Wright's time. Although a cheery tour-guide Taliesin assistant insists that Wright would have been the first to welcome CAD if it had existed 50 years ago, one looks at this one-thousandth example of the incompatibility of monitors and modern architecture with deep misgivings. Trite and stupid as it is, it is a tradition as good as any of Eddie Murphy's that monitors do, and must, have near-darkness to be usable. So out the window has gone the transparency, the airiness, the open-fireplace exposure of the original Taliesin architecture. Today the symbols of Wright's *Truth against the World* go with the flow. You can see it in the neat base model Jeep Cherokee, de-badged and painted desert red, with Wright's square spiral logo and "Taliesin Architects" in loose-pack Wrightian lettering on the doors. You can see it inside the visitor centre where there are piles of black Taliesin sweat shirts, stained-glass, T-shirts and baseball caps.

All this adaptation may be inevitable but it must have been forced upon Wright's rag-tag and bobtail heirs. And indeed it has. For it turns out that this very month Wright's descendants apprentices are threatened with the loss of the title School of Architecture, unless they can gain recognition from the United States National Architecture Accreditation Board.

When it comes to *The Future of Architecture*, CAD monitors, jeeps, T-shirts and tour guides are clearly not enough. Anyone asking about the building is directed to the library, where there used only to be books by and about Wright. Apparently now it is different. But the signs don't look good for organic architecture. Besides, it is 4.00 pm. No more tours today. The cash desk is closed.

The rise of the engineer
1996

"I like engineers", the American humorist Will Rogers once said. "They look like people who are minding their own business." You can see what he meant, but that was more than 60 years ago and nowadays things are a little different. Were he alive today Rogers would almost certainly have rounded his observation off with something like; "By the way, what is their business?" And you can see what that means too. Engineering has become a profession that is expanding deep into a lot of territory that used to be other people's business, all the way from project management to undersea archaeology and economic forecasting. While architects increasingly get in each other's way because of their constantly growing numbers (there are a million in practice across the world today, and half as many again undergoing training), engineers (whose university places go unfilled) infiltrate on all fronts with the skill of Ninjas on a dark night. How they do this without ever emerging as prominent personalities is part of the secret of their capacity to look as though they are minding their own business. In Britain, where a century ago the names Brunel, Telford, and Stephenson were household words, scarcely one person in a thousand knows the name of a living engineer. Being celebrities hardly enters into it. The fact is that in the world of construction their powers increase daily.

This can be seen in different ways in different parts of the world. In the Orient the Asean countries mechanise and put the finishing touches to their first wave of infrastructural building since colonial times. In the United States a massive programme of energy, waste and pollution reduction is transforming the role and scope of engineering in building construction. In Eastern Europe the former Comecon countries have undertaken massive indebtedness in order to modernise their obsolete industrial, transport and communications systems. In Western Europe, after a long period of what can only be called structural correctness, the heroic structural engineering vision of the nineteenth century is returning with a vengeance. Already Britain and France have been joined by an undersea tunnel that was first proposed two centuries ago. Now Denmark and Sweden are to be joined by a system of bridges, and there is even talk of a tunnel beneath the Straits of Gibraltar that will link the continents of Europe and Africa for the first time in 100,000 years. All of this is engineering on the grand scale, even when it appears to be merely building, as with the giant 40, 50 and 70-storey towers under construction in Asia. Increasingly the architectural element shrinks in significance compared to the daring of the structure, and in the end the structure is the work of the inscrutable engineer. By comparison, architects, having spent the last 30 years striving to remove risk from the practice of their art, now find that risk is not only interesting, but lies at the very heart of all constructional enterprise, without which there can be no growth and no development at all.

Into the twenty-first century architectural treatment—as a proportion of total construction cost—seems destined to shrink below the infrastructure yardstick of five per cent, to something more like one or two per cent. It is not for nothing that we approach the millennium with our largest engineering firms ten times the size of our largest firms of architects. And if despite everything our architects do still seem to be clinging to the top of the pyramid of construction, it is surely through popular inertia in the public perception of what they do, rather than an informed admiration for their contribution to the solution of the problems and challenges of the built environment. In the United States design and build construction has advanced from virtual non-existence in the early 1970s to nearly 20 per cent of the construction market. In the European Community the figure is double, with more than 40 per cent of all building construction carried out by contracting organisations that employ architects, not by architects overseeing the work of construction companies as they are supposed to in the pages of popular fiction.

In such circumstances, engineers increasingly become the crucial figures as far as legal responsibilities and the underwriting of risk are concerned. Because of their intuitive affinity for the increasingly complex construction of buildings that are more and more combinations of finished assemblies rather than organic structures grown from sites and contexts rooted in history, they are free from the dead weight of tradition that dogs the architectural profession. So much so that they must already represent the greatest threat to the charismatic status of the architect to have emerged in centuries. They have not only made crucial contributions to the realisation of most of the architectural landmarks of the present century—the Sydney Opera House, the Centre Pompidou, and the Hongkong and Shanghai Bank to name but three—but their special talents have drawn architects in swarms to their coat-tails. The second stage of a typical international architectural competition today will boast a short-list of architects up to half of whom are in association with the same firm of engineers.

Brought up in a world of certainties, engineers may lack sophistication in client relationships, but as construction projects consolidate and ring-fence their teams, it is increasingly engineers who are appointed first and act as conduits for later architectural commissions. It is because architects know that engineers are a source of jobs that they do not protest more vehemently when, as in the United States today, engineers start claiming authorship of projects that architects would once have considered their own as of right. In the long run the only hope for the primacy of architecture may lie in the evolution of building technology itself. As Antoine de Saint-Exupéry once wrote, "Perfection is achieved not when nothing is to be added, but when nothing can be taken away. At the end of its evolution, engineering seems to vanish."

Perhaps it will.

After postmodernism, terrorism
1996

Writing 30 years ago the late Charles Moore, father of Postmodernism in America, said that in future, "If architects are to continue to do useful work on this planet, then their proper concern must be the creation of place... to make a place is to make a domain that helps people know where they are and, by extension, who they are."

In broad terms Moore's plea—that architecture should deliberately aim for uniqueness by taking its cues from history and context rather than picking up on such novelties as airports, factories, skyscrapers and autoroutes—stopped modernism dead in its tracks. Within 20 years postmodern architecture had given birth to a whole new category of 'Stealth' buildings that combined a regional 'heritage' appearance with space age interiors the International Style would never have dreamed of.

The combination of old and new and the separation of interior and exterior were the crowning achievements of postmodernism. It must have been a bitter blow to Moore himself, who died in 1993, to see how directly they led to another kind of 'International Style', the unmistakable style of the giant mixed-use commercial developments that are now under construction everywhere from Berlin to Bangkok. These schemes, with their architecture of new versus old, interior versus exterior and plan versus elevation, are united only in their dedication to a serviced floor space as universal and general as the International Style ever was, but they look like places. They are what has enabled the followers of Charles Moore to say that they really have "helped people know where they are and, by extension, who they are".

It is in this sense that postmodernism has carried out Moore's mission to the letter. A little disappointing to see a Chinese temple on top of an American skyscraper perhaps, but you can't dispute that it tells you where you are and who you are. Unfortunately what it can't tell you is that the triumph of postmodernism was by no means the Armageddon of style wars that it was cracked up to be. No sooner did the struggle between internationalism and uniqueness settle down to an uneasy compromise, than another villain lumbered onto the stage. A villain more deadly to architecture than any killjoy arrogance of modernism or decorative historicism of postmodernism had ever been. The new is another 'ism', of course, but it is not a style. Instead it is the enemy of all styles. Its name is Terrorism, and it bids fair to put an end to architecture as we know it, once and for all.

The architecture of terror begins with the universally acknowledged need to protect the highly serviced and vulnerable technologies of the modern world. Faced with a terrorist threat, governments, banks and developers seek to safeguard these structures by seeking the advice of military experts. As time passes and the terrorist threat, far from evaporating, becomes a continuous, low-intensity war, the influence of these security experts spreads from advising on retrofit technology—designed to make existing buildings and installations more resistant to attack—back up the line to planning decisions about where facilities should go so as to make attack difficult and escape after it impossible. In Northern Ireland this kind of planning began a quarter of a century ago and continues to this day.

After planning decisions come directives to architects. When the level of terrorist attack rises sharply, or the damage it causes begins to run into billions of currency units, calls to "design it out" become impossible to resist. This happened after the 1993 and 1994 bombs in the City of London. It also happened after the 1993 World Trade Center and 1995 Oklahoma bombs in the United States. It happens after ETA attacks in Spain, after Tamil attacks in Sri Lanka, Palestinian attacks in Israel and the Lebanon, cult attacks on urban systems in Japan. It happens everywhere. And one of its most obvious but least talked about effects is upon the appearance of buildings.

In their day, the International Style and postmodernism both dealt with changes in historic architectural elements: shape, shadow and line, fenestration, proportion, prospect and function. Where the security adviser becomes the lead consultant, these elements do not change so much as disappear. Since the first rule of security is to make the target inconspicuous, any architectural tour de force is out of the question. Urban sites in general are discouraged. Landscaping, including trees and shrubbery, must be kept away from buildings. Glass cladding for external walls is banned and transparency everywhere is suppressed by floor to ceiling splinter screens. Windows in external walls are discouraged. Decorative features that might obstruct surveillance cameras are deleted. Recesses, reveals and returns, undercrofts and external access stairs are not allowed (they provide hiding places for bombs). Public access to atriums is denied, all entry and exit points are minimised in number and monitored at all times, cars are not allowed near buildings and car parks are sited far away.

The results of these and a hundred other measures will be to create a styleless architecture, its buildings nondescript fortresses of serviced floor space that will only breathe freely inside their own armoured carapace. In contemplating such structures our thoughts return to Charles Moore. Like prisons such places will certainly help people know where they are and, by extension, who they are.

Meeting the future everywhere
1997

One of the most quietly impressive buildings I have ever visited is the Boeing Customer Service Training Center at Tukwila, near Seattle. A $100 million complex overlooking its own ornamental lake, this training centre for air crew and ground staff who work with Boeing aircraft was completed to designs by Callison Architecture, the Seattle firm that also built most of Bill Gates's Microsoft campus at nearby Redmond.

From outside the Boeing building is not particularly dramatic. At most it might be described as slick in the American commercial manner, with a pleasantly landscaped site, button-down aluminium cladding and flush-fitting Darth Vader glass. But the exterior of the building is a lot less important than what goes on inside it. There, people are taught how to fly and maintain Boeing commercial aircraft, a task that is performed, not only without the aid of expressionistic architectural metaphors, but without real aircraft either. Instead the centre's 800 students and 1,100 Boeing instructors follow a heavy on-screen curriculum of computerised task simulation and multiple choice testing.

The point at which I realised that the Boeing training centre was not so much boring as astounding, came when I was about half way through the cavernous hall of flight simulators, a long rectangular triple-height space populated by what look like oversized lunar excursion modules feeding from great bunches of cables and hydraulic pipes. Each of these modules is in Boeing colours with a type number, like 747–400, painted on its side. Inside, each has a fully furnished, fully instrumented flight deck with high definition video screens in place of the windows.

Walking through the hall of simulators it comes as a shock to realise that all of them are in use, fully crewed by individuals who believe they are somewhere 1,000s of miles away—on the polar route to Japan perhaps, or making a final approach to Bangkok International Airport. It is a realisation made all the more shattering by the modest factitiousness of the architecture. Everything here might seem normal, but it is not. The crews locked away in their gently swaying slices of aeroplane are like brains severed from their bodies and dispatched to different parts of the world, all of them somewhere, but none of them here. In this sense the hall of simulators is a vast illusion, a working model of virtual reality. Today its occupants think they are flying. Tomorrow they might be chairing a teleconference, studying the

Japanese economy, practicing surgery, or strategy. Because it can be everywhere at once, yet still in one place the great hall of simulators has infinite possibilities.

At the moment, for example, it would be a priceless gift to place in the hands of the Messianic wing of the intelligent building movement, a group of fundamentalists whose dream of buildings as "value-free responsive and supportive environments for the achievement of business objectives" has been greeted with something less than glee by the Millennium community. Were these fellows able to fly the openly sceptical out to Seattle for a quick simulator trip back to England, they would have much less trouble explaining the difference between efficiency and effectiveness at conferences.

From here to modernity
1997

If you thought the 'Modern Age' ended when the word modern gave place to the word modernism, you were right. Only now the word modernism has in turn been supplanted by the word modernity. There is a considerable difference. Ten years ago even the wishy-washy word modernism still suggested a bit of backbone, the suggestion of an underlying ideology that might be related to socialism, communism or even fascism. Today's modernity is quite different. It is a prim, politically correct sort of word, but deeply fascinating to the cultural commentators of *Kaleidoscope*, who love its powerful subliminal associations.... Nudity, maternity, insanity?

Of course, the supplanting of old words is a continuous process. Day after day neologisms muck out the Augean stable of the dictionary. If they didn't, new values and interpretations would never get a roof over their heads. The only problem with this sort of churning is that it goes backwards as fast as it goes forwards.

I only realised this when I noticed the uncanny similarity between the language used to promote information technology today, and the language used by the heroic pioneers of civil aviation 60 years ago to describe the potential of flying. Antoine de Saint-Exupéry who, as a pilot of the Modern Age was one of the pioneers of hazardous airline routes that are now carelessly flown by 1,000s, eulogised in his books the boundless liberty and adventure of flight in exactly the same way as today's IT enthusiasts extol the freedom and daring of GSM mobile connectivity and PC card data/fax modems.

He also understood the role of old language in limiting innovation and change. "To grasp the meaning of the world of today", he wrote in 1932, "we use a language created to express the world of yesterday. This is because the life of the past seems familiar to us. But the past is not really familiar, only its language is familiar." To a Modern thinker like Saint-Exupéry, the liberating power of aviation was actually being reduced by the use of the language of ships and the sea to describe it. If he were in our place he would be complaining that the potential of virtual reality is being wasted because we talk about it in the obsolete language of aeroplanes and flight.

The declension modern, modernism, modernity is a small matter by comparison. Modern is assertive—you either are or you aren't. Modernism is already weaker—it at once concedes the possibility of many other isms.

Weakest of all is modernity, whose modern element is entirely pathological, no more than a kind of BSE in the semantic food chain.

The most remarkable thing about this semantic betrayal of the Modern is that it happened in a lifetime. Sir Denys Lasdun, for example, has lived from the age of aviation to the age of IT; he has lived from Modern, through modernism, on into modernity. In his early years he fought to put buildings up, now he fights to stop other people pulling them down. I wonder if anyone has asked him which of the three words he prefers?

Seat pocket aliens
1997

Ever wondered how important graphics really is? Take planes. Although you are routinely urged to familiarise yourself with the contents of the safety card in the pocket of the seat in front of you, very few people do. That is because it is considered bad luck to be seen reading it intently. God knows what would happen to anybody who read the safety card roaring with laughter at the comic adventures of the folk depicted on it. There may even be an airline regulation against this. Nevertheless, as graphic illustrations of what to do to save your life, aircraft safety cards are in the same brain category as crash test dummies. Their behaviour is so different from that of real people that they might as well be creatures from another planet.

In one way the safety card people do come from another planet, or at least their airlines do. Unlike ours, theirs have no pilots or cabin attendants. They don't need them. However often their planes take off, they never manage to land again. Instead they crash on billiard table-smooth green fields or mill pond oceans. None of this deters their passengers, the safety card people. They learn at their mothers' knee not to wear spectacles or high heeled shoes whilst flying, and always to remove their false teeth while extinguishing all smoking materials. Prudently they speak three languages, never eat or drink on flights, nor carry any cabin baggage, lest one of their frequent crash landings leave them with a tray of hot food and three double whiskies on their lap, and a rucksack on their head. Even more amazingly, all this preparation does not make them dull and boring people. Not at all. They have developed their own ways of passing the time before the inevitable crash, mostly doing things we would not do. For example they snort oxygen frequently and force their children to inhale it too. They also spend a fair amount of time in prayer, either bowing low, their arms locked under their knees, or hugging the back of the seat in front of them. Other times they crawl down the aisles on their hands and knees and practice opening the cabin doors.

When the inevitable happens and the safety card people's plane loses the will to fly, they take the news philosophically. If their plane is over a billiard table, they do not bother with any nonsense about runways, aprons or motorised gates. Instead they snort some oxygen and crash straight away on the green. Then they open the cabin doors and throw them away, pull the cords to inflate the bouncy castles, slide to the ground and run off in all directions. They are just as carefree when they come down in one of the smooth, swimming pool-coloured seas they are so accustomed to. Unlike ordinary passengers they always have plenty of headroom inside the cabin to put on their life vests, flash their lights and blow their whistles. That done, quick as a flash they throw out the doors, turn the inflatable slides into boats, and the last you see of them they are floating away in a big bouncy castle singing songs.

The myth of monumentality
1997

As every student knows, the second of Sir Henry Wotton's three conditions of architecture is 'firmness', which follows commodity and precedes delight. Dating from the seventeenth century, all these conditions remain unquestioned, or at least firmness does, when it is properly modernised into structural strength, permanence and monumentality. The absence of dissent is understandable. If we enjoy a lively public concern about the design of buildings—as opposed to the deadly public indifference that greets the design of ships or airliners—it is because people naturally assume that they will be around forever.

However, widely accepted though this view may be, there are exceptions to it. Temporary buildings are, of course, not meant to be permanent, but these days there are other buildings, built in anticipation of a long life, that turn out not to have one—for example city centre office buildings of the grandest type. The reason for this downturn is not hard to find. In recent years many of these flagships of commerce have taken a hammering at the hands of information technology, not only because they have difficulty in keeping up with its space demands, but because management telepresence, which is one of the principal achievements of information technology, has made many buildings seem superfluous, ill-sited, or no longer well-adapted to the needs of the people who work in them.

What this means in plain language is that when buildings that have been designed for one purpose turn out to be in urgent need of costly reconstruction to suit another purpose—which one might say is the case with the many office buildings now being converted into apartment blocks across Europe —it does not require immense mental powers to see that some discounting of their value at the investment stage cannot be far behind.

Despite this logic, when confronted with the question of the impact of telepresence upon the prospects for architecture, few architects see great dangers in it. One distinguished Asian architect, who has worked in the Philippines and mainland China as well as his own country, is particularly insistent that the threat is illusory. "Cyberspace will always be temporary, like being in an aeroplane", he says. "Sooner or later you have to land somewhere or you crash. It is like thinking you can drink champagne all your life then finding out that you need water. Water is reality. Architecture is reality. Architecture is permanent."

Nearly all established architects take this view. East and West they believe that buildings are monuments, not instruments. The enormous cost of the construction process, the length of time it takes, the cultural importance attached to it, all of these are persuasive arguments in favour of the idea that architecture will always be regarded as a weighty matter by clients, planners, financiers and the public. Cyberspace or no cyberspace, buildings will remain the epitome of permanence, as they have been since ancient times. The idea that electronic simulations of distant places might one day seriously threaten their status seems implausible, not least at a time when preparations to celebrate the Millennium involve grand building projects whose very object is to act as historic markers for centuries to come.

Impregnable as this traditional view might seem, there can be no doubt that the arrival of telepresence in business has had an impact on property values. At the most elementary level it has, for many practical business purposes, conquered distance, and in doing so established new criteria for the specification, performance and location of new buildings. We know this is true because many major design firms, simply through the installation of teleconferencing facilities (which they have been quick to adopt), have demonstrated that remote control can supplant direct control, and distance working supplant working in the same building. By purchasing advanced communications equipment, these building users are demonstrating that ideas of space and distance that used to determine the size and location of buildings 20 years ago, have already been altered. Indeed, part of the alteration has been the massive enlargement of the scale of operations open to architects, an enlargement that has made global practice a reality.

Enthusiasts for virtual worlds in architecture may be reluctant to lock horns with traditionalists in the matter of permanence versus the temporariness 'that has to land somewhere or you crash', but they cannot do so indefinitely. The moment they admit that cyberspace has implications for architecture and urban design they beg the question of what these implications are. Will telepresence bring about revolutionary changes in planning, transportation, energy consumption, infrastructure, population distribution and employment, or will it not? If the answer is that it will, then how can these changes fail to impinge on the idea of permanence that lies at the heart of architecture?

Sooner or later the value of permanence to architecture is going to be questioned. To a degree it already has been, as we can deduce from the reduction in real construction cost and the increase in construction speed that has taken place over the last ten years; notwithstanding an improvement in thermal performance, an improvement in environmental control, and a massively increased quantity of information technology in first class office buildings all over the world that should have cost more. In the United States major design firms now accept that facilities management, alterations to existing buildings and the mapping of client 'exit strategies' now accounts for a significant proportion of their workload—in effect they are being paid to undo the downside of old-style monumentality in preparation for a more flexible future.

Follow this line of reasoning further and you rapidly reach the conclusion that, contrary to popular belief, telepresence might not even be an information or an entertainment issue. It might principally be an architecture and planning issue. The kind of issue in fact that architects will only be able to confront by coming to terms with impermanence in ways Sir Henry Wotton never dreamed of.

Soft drinks cans stacked in a New York supermarket, 1976

Martin Pawley, detail of the Dora Crouch House, Troy, New York, 1976

So long recycling, here comes secondary use

1997

For years recycling has been everybody's answer to resource exhaustion, litter, the environmental crisis and everything else. I know. Back in the 1970s, when I tried to persuade the American Can Corporation to supply millions of worthless off-grade cans to the construction industry for voids in concrete work, I was told that recycling was a better answer. In Salvador Allende's Chile, where I worked with the Ministry of Planning to produce a metal emergency housing system out of car body parts, politicians argued that recycling the steel would be better. When I demonstrated to officers of the United States Environmental Protection Agency that non-return glass bottles were so strong you could build a multi-storey building out of them, I was told no, it was still better to smash them up and recycle the bits. Even when I turned to experimenting with tension nets made from car tyres—which are impossible to recycle—I was told to think about burning them in huge incinerators to generate electricity instead.

The trouble with fashionable ideas is that they have a life of their own that makes them impervious to reason. For the last 30 years sorting household trash, collecting cans, smashing bottles in so-called bottle banks, saving milk bottle tops and carting huge quantities of newsprint to recycling centres to save the rain forest (even though newsprint has never been made from hardwood), has been the epitome of responsible citizenship. But now all that has changed. The truth has burst through like one of those methane fires that plague old landfill sites. It's official. Recycling was all hype. It has been an economic disaster. Even wheelie bins don't work.

Ironically enough, considering the pabulum that has emanated from there on the subject of waste management for the last 20 years, the first place to have officially discontinued recycling is Washington DC. There, it was announced last April, an audit had revealed that recycling consumer-sorted garbage was costing the city $200 a tonne, while collecting it wholesale would only cost $25 a tonne. By switching back to indiscriminate waste collection the city will save $2.5 million a year. To those who object to the waste of resources the city says; "Residential recycling is of zero social value if it loses so much money. The savings from incineration and landfill disposal could be put to better use." True enough. But what about the waste?

Perhaps it is at last time for secondary use to take over from recycling. Pioneered in its modern form in the 1960s by John Habraken, who designed 'a brick that holds beer' for the Heineken Brewery, secondary use involves designing in a post-consumer function or disposal route for every retail container or piece of packaging produced. Construction applications are particularly attractive for this because consumer distribution systems ensure that concentrations of reusable waste are always found where building is taking place. A legal requirement for design for secondary use could give waste containers and packaging a market value that would make collection and storage an economic proposition. Better yet it would give architects and designers something more important than arts and lottery nonsense to think about.

A night to remember
1998

This is the time of year for resolutions but I have nothing to resolve. In fact
my powers of resolution, instead of straining forward into 1998 and beyond
(as they so often do), insist on dwelling on painful episodes from the past.
In particular that dinner at the Mansion House ten years ago when Prince
Charles praised the Luftwaffe for doing less harm to London during the blitz
than the post-war planners had done after it.

Although this was Prince Charles' last big push at architecture, he did
not dominate the evening in my eyes. The cynosure of my eyes was the great
Satan Robert Maxwell, then owner of Architectural Press, sitting in splendid
isolation at the far end of the high table. Throughout the proceedings no
one spoke to him and he spoke to nobody. He sat there impassive, next to
an empty chair twiddling his fork, a shambling monster of a man, made
even more monstrous by the height of the podium upon which the high
table stood.

As a journalist, I was seated at the lowly press table, almost underneath
him. But as the dinner wore on and speeches were made, I became more and
more obsessed with the idea of speaking to him. This was a golden
opportunity, perhaps the best I would ever have. The owner of the *Daily
Mirror* and the founder of the *European* was sitting barely five feet away.

I had good reason to approach a press baron. A new regime at *The
Guardian* threatened my position as critic. The powers wanted a 'consumer
of architecture' to write about the subject. Preferably someone who would
appreciate Rod Hackney's timber guttering and applaud the Prince's plucky
attacks on architects. They did not want an enemy agent steeped in
architectural lore. They wanted someone who would fearlessly denounce
architects by name; someone who could run off a long list of anti-social
tower blocks at the drop of an 'eyesore'. Someone who would get indignant
about satellite dishes and out of town supermarkets, someone who would
traipse around old buildings and tirelessly launch campaigns to save them
for the nation.

I couldn't believe that Robert Maxwell would be like that. Cap'n Bob
was made of sterner stuff. He had come up the hard way. He knew that you
couldn't make an omelette without breaking heads. So I decided to sieze my
chance and slip away from my seat under cover of the gluttonous hubbub of
800 diners and their attendant waiters. Quickly I stepped to the high table

which was almost level with my head and looked up. Maxwell loomed above me like a gigantic Michelin Man.

"Excuse me Mr Maxwell", I said. He looked at me dully, stopped playing with his fork, and nodded for me to go on.

"I just thought", I said, "It must be time the *Mirror* had an architectural writer. I'd like to offer myself for the job."

He focused his eyes on me for the first time.

"Do what?" he grated in a deep voice.

I repeated myself.

He looked at me for a second or two.

"Piss off", he growled, and turned his attention back to his fork.

Terminal architecture
1998

At the turn of the nineteenth century Guglielmo Marconi, 1874–1937,
the inventor of wireless telegraphy, performed transmission and reception
experiments that required huge amounts of electrical energy. Before the
advent of the directional aerial, to send a spark-gap signal across the Atlantic
from Ireland to Nova Scotia required 300Kw of electricity at 20,000 volts.
In order to supply this amount of power Marconi's experimental radio
station in County Galway, Ireland, with its eight transmission masts over
60 metres high, had a staff of 150 and a turf-burning power station to which
fuel was delivered day and night by a special narrow-gauge railway.

Transatlantic transmissions in Morse code were not all that Marconi
achieved. In the summer of 1899 he used the same sort of equipment to
describe reality in a much more marketable way. With a 23 metre aerial
rigged from the mast of the steamer *Flying Huntress* he reported the results
of the Kingstown yacht races. His Morse signals were transmitted several
miles to a 60 metre aerial on shore and then telephoned to the offices of the
Dublin Daily Express, where they were published in the newspaper's evening
edition on the same day—before the yachts themselves had even returned
to harbour. The edition was a sell-out, and rightly. With this primitive
equipment Marconi had not only sketched out the possibility of the sort of
instantaneous electronic awareness that is now marketed in a much more
developed form by radio and TV, he had glimpsed the massive market that
was waiting for it.

Knowing the result of a distant yacht race before the boats had returned
to harbour might seem a trivial matter to us today, but it was a milestone:
a fragment of the huge mosaic of reality that is nowadays put together at
enormous expense by the media 24 hours a day to substantiate every
eyewitness account of every interesting event within its reach, from
childbirth to the outbreak of a war. This giant mosaic of reality obeys all
the rules of perception that have governed human and technological records
since mechanised memory first became possible. Like one of those vast,
inaccurate maps of the known world pored over in the Vatican during the
age of exploration and discovery—but with the added dimension of
instantaneous time—the media mosaic has room for every fragment of
wireless, cinema, radio and video history that was ever broadcast. Like
headlands, bays and great rivers plotted on the fringes of unexplored

continents, we find there such landmarks as the 1912 film footage of the Suffragette Emily Davison being ridden down by the King's racehorse; the 1937 radio commentary on the burning of the Zeppelin *Hindenburg*, and the Zapruder film of the assassination of John F Kennedy. In the construction of this gigantic mosaic, technology, in the shape of the camera, the cinema projector, radio, TV, video and multi-media, has turned possession of the map of reality from an exclusive resource of the ruling class into a mass consumption item, like electricity, gasoline or food.

A century after Marconi's yacht races, electronic awareness, the field that he and other nineteenth century pioneers like Hertz, Maxwell and Popoff created, has become the world's largest industry, responsible for ten per cent of the Gross National Product of the world. Yet despite its acknowledged economic importance, the electronics industry still possesses no unified field theory to explain what it does. Specifically, of course, we know that the electronics industry manufactures devices based on the application of electro-magnetic phenomena. These devices range from silicon wafer chips to wide area network computer systems; recording and replaying devices for sound and image; video machines, security cameras, transmitters and receiving equipment, clocks, watches, monitors, scanners and many, many more things.

But generic terms like "communications equipment", "electronic goods" or "control mechanisms" barely convey an appropriate sense of an industry absorbed in the creation of a cosmic image of reality, devised and marketed in the shape of a machine version of consciousness. Nearer the truth would be an assertion that the generic product of the electronic age is technological immortality, for the production of reality cannot be far short of immortality itself. We can see this in the endless soap opera of celebrities and royals kept alive in ghostly form by magazines and newspapers. We can see it in the posthumous media careers of prominent figures from the past—pre-eminently Adolf Hitler, who appears on a TV channel somewhere in the world every night, frequently in post-synchronised colour, more than 50 years after his death—or Clint Eastwood or Sean Connery, who never appear to age or, even more eerily, the expanding afterlife of the actor John Wayne, who died in 1979 but, through digital magic still walks and talks in TV commercials and in 1997 topped a Harris poll that asked Americans; "Who is your favourite movie star?"

The complex of networks and mechanisms that holds such celebrities in suspended animation is constantly evolving towards higher and higher fidelity and more and more continuous coverage, but already it constitutes a multi-faceted robotic mirror that mimics more and more of the natural processes of all human perception. Because of the professionally recorded lives of celebrities it is now the manufacturer and vendor of electronic appliances who is the ultimate arbiter of the fidelity of our own senses of seeing and hearing, touching and understanding. And the electronics store will not close its doors until its ultimate product, a device that can simulate life itself, is to be found everywhere. By means of that product, programmed to understand and replicate everything it sees, the electronics industry will eventually gain access to the whole genetic pool of human consciousness.

Today the map of reality that is being drawn by the spectrum of products of the electronics industry already approximates to a kind of immortality. A synthetic universe that we have mistakenly taken to calling "virtual reality", when it would be more accurate to call it "secondary reality"—the product of all the sensory-simulating devices that we buy to blot out our own 'primary reality'. It works in somewhat the same way as the blindness of glaucoma works when it painlessly blots out sector after sector of the visual acuity of the human eye. The difference in the case of the spectrum of electronic recording devices, from video cameras to foetal heart monitors, is that their processes do not so much blind us, as change the nature of what we think we have seen. In the century since Marconi this electronic glaucoma has turned the old primary reality that our organic senses confront us with into an incoherent and fragmentary pattern that we no longer believe. We no longer trust our own, or each other's, remembrance of events. Instead we attach more credence to secondary reality, the image captured by the video, or better yet the robot security camera.

Today the market in secondary reality works like the property market. If we think of the big electronics manufacturers and media groups as counterparts to nineteenth century landlords controlling vast estates, then we can see the parallel. These electronic space owners lease or sell 'secondary realities', through wholesale distributors and retailers, to consumers, who are the end users. Long before the death of Diana Princess of Wales, a columnist for the London *Times* described the ceaseless reporting of the activities of the British Royal Family by the media in almost exactly these terms.

"The Royal saga is a market phenomenon that defies regulation. It is the industry's seam of gold, a product guaranteed to sell worldwide and for astonishing sums of money. Few British readers will realise the voracity of the global appetite for Royal Family stories. Magazines in a dozen languages are devoted to it. A Royal Family headline will boost street sales from Los Angeles to Lusaka, from Nice to Nagasaki. Two paragraphs will syndicate for 1,000 pounds. A good picture will go for tens of thousands. The Sun increased its sale by 100,000 copies merely by printing a story about the Duchess of York."

Thus the operations of TV network, newspaper, magazine and radio are all part of the same vast marketing operation that is selling leases and granting mortgages in secondary reality. Mortgaging up to 100 per cent —enough reality to approximate to immortality, which is the point where time begins to stand still and reality decisively shifts from the primary mode to the secondary mode: the point where each one of us becomes for a time a media member of the Royal Family or John Wayne himself.

This transference of realities is a huge business and it operates at all levels. In addition to the not inconsiderable number of professional and amateur persons who earn money from their knowledge of celebrities and TV and media events, there are persons whose possession of a physical characteristic similar to that of a celebrity offers them a remunerative, though often temporary career. According to the executive producer of a TV talent show where such individuals often appear; "It's essential to sound like a chosen star, singer, band, politician or member of the Royal Family. To look like them is the icing on the cake." Apparently make up artists are on hand to transform sound-alikes into look-alikes within 45 minutes.

Through the labyrinthine workings of the reality marketing mechanism, each one of us is progressively ceasing to be a *producer* of primary reality, and becoming instead a *consumer* of secondary reality. This process is gradual and barely recognised at present, but the transformation, when it has been accomplished, will be complete. To illustrate how far the change has already progressed, it is interesting to contrast two forms of investment in reality:

the old-style primary reality construction of buildings, which is denominated in space (18,000 square metres of floorspace and so on), and the new-style secondary reality production of television drama which is denominated in time (hours of programming, minutes per episode, and so on).

To build a new mid-range office building in London today (1998) costs about £680 per square metre. That is the datum cost of creating 'real estate'. The corresponding cost of 'virtual estate' is difficult to compare exactly, but television drama is an established genre that makes a good starting point. We might therefore compare the cost of putting up an office building in a conservation area with the cost of producing a TV costume drama based on a historical novel, say Jane Austen's *Pride and Prejudice*. Unlike putting up an office building on an urban site of fixed dimensions, which is a factual task, making a TV series is a fictitious activity measured in minutes of recorded reality captured on film or tape. Every hour of usable costume drama costs somewhere in the region of £1 million, or £16,000 a minute to produce. Thus one square metre of primary reality building costs as much as two and half seconds of secondary reality TV drama. In other words, were it possible to trade shares between space and time, between primary and secondary realities, a modern 1 million square metre office complex could be built for the same cost as 700 hours of TV costume drama.

Fanciful though these calculations may seem, such figures do possess a supporting logic. *Pride and Prejudice* has been serialised repeatedly, most recently over only six episodes with a total of four hours of viewing time, which is equivalent to the construction of only 5,700 square metres of office floorspace. But then the production cost of the adaptation in no way represents its full earning potential. If we include repeat showings, video sales, airlines, music spin-offs and international marketing, 700 hours is a very modest figure indeed. Nor are the limits of the original novel necessarily fixed, as the site boundaries of the building are. Like the Korean War hospital drama M*A*S*H, a classic example of secondary reality TV, *Pride and Prejudice* too can look forward to offspring with a considerable life ahead of them.

M*A*S*H was originally a feature film about an army hospital in the Korean War which was extrapolated into a TV sitcom which was in turn stretched into an endless series of sitcoms loosely based on the same idea.

But whereas the original event, the primary reality Korean War, only lasted three years, from 1950 to 1953, the secondary reality TV version enjoyed a life of 14 years. Given intelligent marketing *Pride and Prejudice* might well match this record, ascending to the same level of electronic immortality by means of successive series. The same long life awaits the succession of actresses who will play Jane Austen's heroines. Elizabeth Bennett for example, the leading character in *Pride and Prejudice*, theoretically died 200 years ago. In practice she has risen from the slab several times, ready to star in sequels yet unborn.

Before leaving *Pride and Prejudice* and its derivatives we can develop our original comparison between building design and TV production to its logical conclusion by applying a multiplier based on the number of employees in the office building, and comparing the resultant figure with the size of the audience attracted to the TV series. This way we shall be able, even more directly, to compare the relative economic value of primary reality and secondary reality today, and produce some surprising results.

Assuming that our million square metre office complex ends up employing 10,000 *workers*, we can set that figure against the 11 million TV viewers, watching for 40 minutes every week, who were the consumers of the first run of the most recent TV version of *Pride and Prejudice*. This comparison shows us that not only is a one million square metre office development equal in cost to only 700 hours of TV, but it may already be a much poorer investment. This is not because it takes more or fewer persons to build a building than to make a TV series, but because the working behaviour of the *workers* in the office complex is increasingly coming to resemble the behaviour of the *viewers* 'consuming' the 700 hours of TV.

While a one million square metre office complex might provide an occupation for 20,000 persons for a 1,920 hour working year (a total of 38.4 million hours) at a construction cost of £677 million; the same expenditure on drama production for TV would result in 700 hours of viewing, which could occupy 11 million people for 7.7 billion hours at first showing alone. In other words an equivalent period of *occupation* to 200 years of work by 10,000 people in the office complex.

The difference here is between a construction process designed to provide for occupation by a relatively small number of people for a long period of time, and a production process designed to *occupy* a very large number of people for a much shorter period of time. In economic terms this is a highly significant change. All existing secondary reality industries, such as radio, television and the cinema and their peripheral merchandising are based on it. The point often missed is that these are pioneering financial entities based upon secondary reality. They point the way towards massive changes in demand for, and requirements of, buildings in the future.

The rules of secondary reality business—which are still being written—will one day make it unremarkable for a corporation in any field to occupy 11 million persons for 40 minutes one day a week, while remaining dormant for the rest of the time. In economic terms such an enterprise would be no different to today's primary reality corporation that keeps office hours and employs a staff of 50 for ten years. Furthermore TV costume drama, whilst popular, is by no means the most prolific generator of secondary reality business opportunities. Major sporting and music events far exceed its yield, as do unpredictable, one-off, current events of a dramatic nature. A television phenomenon contemporaneous with the first serialisation of *Pride and Prejudice* in Britain, for example, was the first OJ Simpson trial, which attracted audiences so vast that, at peak viewing hours it could be said to have *occupied* two million persons every ten minutes worldwide. Even more remarkably, on Saturday 6 September 1997, the funeral of Diana Princess of Wales attracted a larger audience still. The service was held in a cathedral with a seating capacity of 1,900, but according to estimates, more than a billion people watched the event on TV. It was broadcast live to 187 countries with commentaries in 45 languages. In Britain itself 31.5 million viewers —three quarters of the adult population—watched the ceremony on TV. In Japan, three of the five national television networks broadcast the event live. If ever proof were needed of the 'reality' of celebrity or the existence of the 'global village', or the economic potential of both, the death and funeral of Diana Princess of Wales provided it.

Film, TV and recording companies already operate according to irregular bursts of activity, unconventional balances of timing, and audiences rather than clientele—all of which makes the presentation, or even the necessity for, a permanent architectural identity for them difficult if not impossible to imagine. And they are not alone. Right across the spectrum of electronic, reality altering enterprises—from national (soon to be global) lotteries that offer "new reality lifestyle" jackpot prizes, to the humble designing of web sites on the Internet—there are unconventional business entities coming into existence that reflect the infinite number of ways in which the sale and leasing of reality is destined to become the biggest post-industrial business of all.

While it may seem no more than a piece of sophistry to match the words "employment" with "occupation", and "worker" with "consumer", the sweeping redundancy of traditional patterns of employment, and the technological annihilation of traditional careers, suggests that some such cost-efficient transformation is already far advanced. Changing balances of power threaten the status of the factory worker, the office worker, the professional and the service industry employee alike. At the same time increasing self-employment, personal mobility, distance working and home working—and the steady convergence of all so-called 'jobs' into clicking keyboards and watching monitors, which is nowadays as much an activity of the unemployed as it is of those who make their living enterprising everything from currency speculation to sailing round the world against the wind—is steadily closing the gap between having an 'occupation' and being 'occupied', literally, in another world.

The reunion of the world of work and the private world, is indeed a massive social event, marking the reversal of more than two centuries of separation, but it is an index of how far from the ball our eyes have wandered that so far we barely understand that it is happening. Of the shape and size, the wealth and ambition of the new economic entities that electronic realities are bringing into existence, we know little, except that they should be carefully watched and their growth measured, for they are the clients of the twenty-first century, and theirs will be the authentic architecture of the information age.

The strange death of
architectural criticism
1998

Original wording: "Who is the man responsible for this historic series of achievements? He is a slight, bespectacled 51 year old with a reputation for unconventional thinking...."

Revised version after subject has checked copy for factual errors. "Who is the man responsible for this historic series of achievements? He is a slim, energetic figure in his early 50s with an infectious smile and an undiminished curiosity about the world...."

Some people might say there is no more wrong with this than a photographer doctoring up prints in the darkroom; "Just lighten up the sky a bit love, and get rid of the graffiti."

The trouble is that not everybody agrees with the cosy arrangement whereby more and more architectural magazines and vanity-published monographs clog letterboxes and bookshops with digitally cleansed images and wall-to-wall testimonials of praise. Where, they say, is the withering criticism that you get in TV reviews?

I can still remember the last piece of take-no-prisoners criticism I saw in an architectural magazine. It was Gavin Stamp reviewing Quinlan Terry's building at Downing College. By the time I had finished reading it—as is sometimes the case with a TV review by Victor Lewis Smith—I feared for the life of the writer. This was no ignorant or silly review, nor one aimed at a licensed punchbag like the East European cars that used to be road tested for laughs by *Autocar*. Instead it was an utterly dispassionate demolition job. I am quite sure Quinlan Terry read it. I am quite sure that it did him good, and I am quite sure that he remembers every word of it today. But if he had supplied the photographs and drawings and "checked the copy for factual errors", would it ever have seen the light of day?

According to the *Concise Oxford Dictionary*, criticism means "the work of a critic", and the word critic means "one who pronounces judgement". The root of the word lies in the Greek *kritikos*, from *krites* meaning judge. What then is the role of the contemporary critic who—in order to protect his or her sources of information, transparencies, invitations, freebies, job, et al —writes that everybody who is well known is a genius, and everybody who is not is on their way to being one? Surely it is that of the *krites* who finds every accused person innocent. There are such judges, and there are such critics, and there is a word for the kind of moribund culture they create.

Compared to building, criticism may be as futile as trying to make a car go faster with a whip, but it has the force of tradition behind it. Unlike the reality of practice, the unreality of criticism teaches us that buildings should be something more than mere images erected around serviced floor space. Architects know the falsity of this proposition. They know that all buildings are bits of other people's ideas, the flotsam of plagiarism, the work of unsung assistants, the result of prejudice, bureaucracy, money, time and wayward subcontractors. But when they embark upon criticism they forget it all and take to literary licence like a warm bath.

Where air conditioning
meets its match
1999

"Only connect!" Once a much-quoted exhortation to join prose and passion from the novelist EM Forster, then the motto of a mobile phone company. Now a plaintive cry across the divide that separates art history (what things look like), from air conditioning, safe-water plans and heat recovery systems (how things work out).

Only connect! Five years ago there was a demonstration of electric cars in Florence. With a scrunch of gravel an eager little solar powered Kevet L-Jet leapt away. Round the carriageway of the Palazzo dei Congressi it sped, until it passed under the shadow of a tree. Then it slowed to a painful crawl. One by one all the other electric cars revealed similar limitations. They had room for only a single occupant. None had headlights, windscreen wipers or heaters. This did not deter the director of the event. "I live only for the day when all can drive cars such as these, and we shall have no more pollution and noise", he announced, presenting the conference grand prize to the driver of a car hardly any wider than its own number plate that had allegedly been driven over the Alps from Munich powered by the sun.

Only connect! A far cry from sun-drenched Italy is the superheated oven of Riyadh. There, far from experimenting with alternative energy, the natives invest recklessly in air conditioning, which at peak times accounts for 70 per cent of Saudi Arabia's electricity consumption. Sitting as they do on top of a quarter of the world's known oil reserves, the Saudis are generally unconcerned about this. Their electricity bills are heavily subsidised and more than a few households leave the air conditioning running in their homes when they go abroad for the summer, to prevent the intense desert heat from damaging the interior decorations. In such circumstances it might seem impossible to make headway with threats of an energy crisis, but it is not entirely. Just as in Europe a politician or an administrator can always be found to announce with a straight face that the future of the motor car lies with derivatives of the Kevet L-jet and not the Audi TT coupe, so in Saudi Arabia it is possible to find a deputy minister for electricity who has to hand enough flip charts, facts and figures to prove that the sweltering desert kingdom is on the brink of an energy crisis. Like the saintly Jimmy Carter in 1970s America, Abdul Rahman Tuwaijri is on a diversionary energy trip. He says that either the Saudis have got to learn to live in temperatures of 110 degrees fahrenheit like their desert forebears, or they will have to stump up

£75 billion to triple their country's generating capacity. At this, of course, most Saudis merely reach for their cheque books, but Mr Tuwaijri pretends not to notice. Like drunken driving in the West, energy consumption in the Middle East is always good for a scary government advertising campaign.

Only connect! A subcontinent away from Riyadh is Bangladesh, where something much worse is happening. Before 1970 millions of Bangladeshis drank from shallow wells or natural ponds frequented by cows and water buffalo, so cholera and dysentery flourished. To conquer these diseases 1,000s of deep tube wells for drinking water were dug in the 1970s and 1980s, using materials and technical assistance supplied by UNICEF. Only years later did it become apparent that the tube wells also transmitted carcinogenic doses of naturally occurring arsenic to those who drank the water. Today the digging of tube wells continues because a return to surface water would mean many more deaths from dysentery, even though the World Bank estimates that 18 million people in Bangladesh are poisoning themselves as a result. Only connect!

A brace of fins du siècles
1999

For people of a certain age it is impossible to relate the term fin du siècle to the dying months of this year. Difficult to relate it to any period except the turn of the last century, when the age of Napoleon, Jane Austin and Queen Victoria gave place to the age of Adolf Hitler, Ernest Hemingway and Fergie. That was a turning point in history indeed: one minute the tremendous pageantry of kings, emperors and Empires putting the finishing touches to the environment: the next a catalogue of disasters culminating in the shock of an environment preparing to finish off mankind instead.

According to Marshall McLuhan, artists can prefigure this sort of thing. They can transmit messages in their work that predict the downfall of regimes. But no such warnings were received in 1914, only jubilation. Like stock market crashes and earthquakes, collapses of Empires are not predicted as a matter of policy. To be sure, until the mid-twentieth century, revisionist historians strove to fudge a provenance for the plain surfaces and empty spaces of Modernism out of the mess of Victoriana, but their efforts now seem specious. Nothing in Europe before 1914 was really Modern. Anomalous perhaps, like the Crystal Palace, but not Modern. Modernity came from America by way of the cinema—like most of twentieth century life.

On the eve of the twentieth century the rooms of quite ordinary houses were so full of coal and coke and accumulated bric a brac that it required a servant industry to keep them clean. The great contribution of Modernism was to redirect the destructive finality of the Great War into sweeping all that junk away. But by mid-century, when science had made such monstrous wars impossible, the empty rooms of modernity were becoming impossible in their turn. The servant class was becoming extinct, mechanical and electronic appliances of all kinds had multiplied, and the stop-go flow of images from America had become continuous, wired for sound and delivered by television. As a result empty rooms began to fill up again and the definitive image of domestic space shifted to the dimly lit war room, the control centre and the flight deck. Exteriors no longer mattered, they became disguises. Glass cladding no longer meant transparency. Transparency no longer meant access. Like birds flying into glass doors humans could no longer enter where they could see, but only where the could be seen.

Toss in a hundred thousand CCTV cameras and that will guarantee that 1999 will not presage the kind of global disturbances that began in 1914. For beyond our millennium lies, not another great clear out and another empty room, but a multiplication of uninhabited rather than empty spaces. Robotised spaces that already exist, containers of such vastness that the miniaturised electronics required to deal with their daily business will be lost within them.

The idea that we are living through a fin du siècle whose outcome can be compared to the great changes that took place at the end of the Victorian age is a fantasy. The past has never been more securely modernised than it is today. The future never more tightly programmed. Only the present remains at liberty like a criminal, armed and dangerous. For while the Modern pioneers of the twentieth century, artists and architects, dealt fiercely with the issues of their time, the architects of the twenty-first century have difficulty in keeping pace with the here and now. For them it is as though design had decided to seek refuge in science fiction in order to escape from science fact.

For the beginning of such a portentous century, the biggest Ferris wheel in the world, rotating but going nowhere, is an appropriate symbol.

The new life of Albert Speer
2000

Popular images of architects change over time. 150 years ago, Gustave
Flaubert, author of *Madame Bovary*, included the image of the architect as
"a dreamer who always forgets the stairs" in his dictionary of received ideas.
And so he remained for a century or more until Ayn Rand's Howard Roark
turned him into a women's magazine hero, young, handsome and hoping
for nothing more than a crack at the new town hall.

By the 1960s Howard Roark had aged considerably and was treading
the boards in Joan Littlewood's *The Projector* as the servile tool of ruthless
developers. Then he became identified with the tragedy of the tower blocks,
and began to be hunted down in his elegant Georgian house by journalists,
dragged out and charged with responsibility for Ronan Point, Broadwater
Farm, comprehensive redevelopment, overspill estates and windswept plazas
everywhere. Before long Princes of the Realm and TV pundits were cheered
to the echo when they denounced him as an arrogant brute.

Abruptly, with the coming of the Lottery and millennium bonanza, this
terrible baiting ceased. As a result, where 20 years ago media and public alike
would have been baying for blood, now they greet falling glass, wobbling
bridges and untoward skyscrapers with an indulgent smile. So far so good.
But just as the profession has begun to emerge from its bunker mentality
in anticipation of a spell of universal approbation, the shadow of a truly
terrifying role model has fallen across its path. It is the ghost of Albert Speer,
architect, war criminal, and one of the most successful autobiographers
of modern times.

The real Albert Speer, Hitler's architect and minister of armaments,
died in London in 1981, 15 years after his release from prison. Now, against
all probability, he has risen again as a theatrical character of Hamlet
proportions. He first appeared on the stage playing a supporting role in
Richard Norton-Taylor's *Nuremberg*. Then, last year at the Almeida he
received top billing in Esther Vilar's *Speer*, a fiction in which, in old age, he
is lured to East Germany to use his tremendous organising skills to save the
bankrupt socialist economy, but ends up debating the morality of his life and
work over a model of Hitler's Germania, with its enormous dome.

This year Speer has graduated yet again. Given an incredible four hours
instead of Vilar's 90 minutes, and his full name as the title he appears,
alongside the famous model of Germania again, in David Edgar's *Albert*

Speer at the National Theatre. A play drawn from the encyclopaedic biography by Gitta Sereny. This time the stark, dramatic sets enhance the prominence of the model (the actor playing Hitler uses the dome as a recliner whilst holding forth to his acolytes), while the diverting parody of a classical master class by Tessenow ("Whatever is successful is bound to be simple"), and the telling depiction of the impossibility of rejecting opportunity when it presents itself—even at a railway station—conspire to give Speer's Faustian tale a timeless currency.

Where Hitler and his courtiers are trapped beyond redemption in their period uniforms and barbaric rituals, Speer, seldom in uniform, makes the leap from 1941 to 1981 in modern dress. Here is a man who shows that it still is possible to be 'purely technical'. A man who (one thinks), could leave the theatre at any time to be reunited with one of his V2 rockets at the Science Museum, or teach a class a lot about the management of new technology. An architect moreover whose works are all destroyed but whose model of an unbuilt city has entered the image cascade of the twenty-first century. An architect who saw into the future of all architects everywhere.

Traffic congestion and confusion
2000

The great American developer Trammell Crow, who created modern Dallas, once said; "I like congestion. It's better than recession." It sounds like a flip remark but Crow was right. Congestion isn't a problem, it's the political opportunity of the twenty-first century.

Crow wasn't the author of another adage—that it is always easier to tell people what to do than to find out what they are really doing—but he might as well have been because it bears powerfully on the future of congestion. An example of *what is really going on* is the way buildings have to go on taking the rap for the energy squandered by transportation.

For years architects have accepted the specious argument that half of global energy is guzzled by buildings. Filled with guilt they go home and stuff more mineral wool into the roof space, invite more radon indoors, mortgage the house for a heat pump and learn to talk baloney about wind towers and low-e glass. What they should really do is square up to the so-called energy experts with a smart rejoinder like; "OK. What shall we do about the other half?"

They are entitled to do this because construction is essential. It was there before the Industrial Revolution and certainly before transport. Go back just 200 years and transport—in the sense of an industry employing one in every six persons in the European Community—doesn't exist. How on earth did the world survive without it? By growing up autarchically. In those days they knew that dragging huge stones from Wales to Salisbury Plain was not a sustainable activity so they only did it once. Now we have thousands of articulated trucks doing the equivalent trip every day.

The key to ending irresponsible transportation is not to raise its cost punitively, as the government has been doing. That will only prolong its life. Much more effective to allow congestion to overwhelm it and thus bring on the new age of immobility—the answer to the energy crisis, the pollution crisis, the Concorde crisis, the road rage crisis, the asylum seeker crisis and 99 per cent of all other known crises.

Can congestion really do this? According to the American Highway User's Alliance, a body representing 215 driving and road organisations, it cannot fail. Short of a massive recession or the sort of drastic restriction of civilian motoring that was enforced in the Second World War, road traffic congestion will continue to increase faster than population, driver numbers and car registrations. The average American already spends 434 hours (18 full days a year), in a car. Soon the figure will become unsustainable as a vicious circle of population growth, more car registrations, fewer occupants per vehicle, increasing adoption of car travel over other modes of transport, and more car journeys takes over. In Indianapolis it already has. The city's population increased by only 17 per cent (150,000 persons), between 1982 and 1997, but the number of vehicle miles driven there went up by 103 per cent—creating as much congestion as if the population had increased by a million.

Multiplied by the 32 per cent increase in the United States population between 1970 and 1997, the doubling of car registrations and the 65 per cent increase in licenced drivers, all this amounts to a predictable deadline for gridlock. Yet it is the best kept secret in the world: it is the reason for globalisation, Internet banking, e-wholesaling and retailing, supermarket deliveries, soaring urban land values, car company mergers, £50 billion bids for mobile phone licences, media groups, video phones and telefactor gloves.

The end of transport won't be a disaster, it will be a new frontier. Trammell Crow was right, congestion is the answer.

America: it's 24–7 at Mission Critical
2001

The best thing about a trip to America is the boost it gives to one's vocabulary. There are always new words, expressions and axioms, and all of them, it seems, born since you were last there. This time it's not only words but numbers too. For example it isn't long before you start to believe that every job in America, from delivering the mail to building houses, is done 24–7— twenty-four hours a day, seven days a week. As for new expressions, the demise of the 'Quick burn' dot coms has had a silver lining for architects at least. Every motivated design firm above minimum size is now working 24–7 on 'BOOT projects' (Build, Operate and Transfer), or else monstrous 'Mission Critical' data storage buildings, the new electronic fortresses designed to keep businesses operating through typhoon, tornado or terrorist attack and possibly even nuclear war.

This is where the expressions come in. "The KISS principle" may be old hat, and 'If it ain't broke don't fix it" can practically be attributed to Chaucer, but how about "The fastest growing business is always the smallest"? or "It's like drinking from a fire hose"—the last being a frequent description of the rate of increase in client demand for extremely secure data storage.

Mission Critical buildings are in some ways the US equivalent to the 'hot sites' that were set up in London during the IRA bombing campaign, and particularly in the aftermath of the Canary Wharf bomb which, it has always been rumoured, did destroy a number of not-so-secure data stores and put the wind up a lot of corporations. But where the UK hot sites were merely nondescript addresses from which business could continue in the event of computer crashes, fire or terrorist damage at head office, the American 'Mission Criticals' are up-front pieces of architecture. They may not go to the extreme of allowing 'naming rights' as colleges and hospitals do—"The Jerry Lewis Mission Critical Building" in big letters across the front, for example—but they are so large, so expensive, and so 'hidden in plain sight' that they invite curiosity in a land where information is free.

Not surprisingly most American architects see Mission Criticals in a dramatic light. Like the hideouts of James Bond villains they are deliberately sited far from fault lines, flood plains, railways, highways and airports, recognisable only by their subtly concealed 'satellite farms'. Depending on the level of staffing and duplicated equipment needed to protect the 24–7 operational availability of their racks of servers, they can cost eight to ten times as much as ordinary office floorspace to build. This is partly reflected in their heavy duty construction. They are proofed against 200 miles per hour winds, and some even have 'sacrificial roofs' designed to blow off if they suffer too much damage—exposing a second roof underneath. They have to be able to generate their own power, not only because they need to be isolated from grid failures but because, in operation, they consume as much electricity as 2,000 homes. All of this equipment gives them a net to gross that is the reverse of any conventional office building. A typical Mission Critical might have a footprint of 10,000 m² but only 1,000 m² available for servers and employees.

The place of these buildings in the cosmology of building types is a matter of hot debate. Some maintain that they are the last redoubts of the corporations of the 'old economy', defending the accumulated information of years of monopolistic power as though it were buried treasure. Others point to clients among the surviving 'new economy' dot coms, still trying to attain credibility by fitting themselves into the big picture at last.

Ordering buildings like hamburgers
2001

It is a truth universally acknowledged that anyone in search of a justification for dabbling in architecture other than a mad desire to take a drink from the firehose of art history, must be in search of a seriously commercial firm. By seriously commercial is meant a firm with offices in the City—not in Hoxton, or on the river—a firm where the senior staff wear identical suits; where the sliding glass doors open and close by themselves; where the only reading material in the reception area is the in-house magazine—and where the in-house magazine contains such blood-curdling, totalitarian, non-art historical mission statements as the following: "A building is a means to a business objective. Integration of the construction process helps achieve this objective by complete dedication to the client's needs from the entire design and construction team."

Clearly compared to 'cultural architecture', commercial architecture is strong stuff. A place where the blood on the carpet is real blood, the desks cleared by midday are real desks, the drastic decisions taken really are drastic. Why? Because, as our militant in-house magazine explains; "There is nothing more frustrating than watching a project slide further and further away from its intended date of completion while its cost rises higher and higher. In some way everyone on every team can help prevent this happening. It is their duty to do so whenever they can." It may be OK to be three and a half years late with the Jubilee Line Extension. But in the world of commerce, directors fall on their swords, whole teams get fired, people go out of business and subcontractors don't get paid.

It is because of this difference that there are two worlds of architecture. One is populated by celebrities who are ceaselessly praised, the other is populated by unknown or reviled people who carry visiting cards with titles like President, Principal, Design Director, Vice President and Director of Communications. The people in the former group have an unreal job to do —who needs another art gallery? But the people in the latter group have an impossible job to do. Their job is to try to make architecture and building work at the speed of a fast food restaurant.

This has always been impossible—think of the way Canary Wharf cruised sedately into bankruptcy ten years ago—the buildings were going up and the market was going down, but no power on earth could synchronise the two movements. Now, with the fall of the dot coms—a fall, incidentally, that could just as well be blamed on the poor supporting performance of the construction industry (the most fragmented industry in the modern world), as on the greed, the herd instinct or the madness of investors—the demand for speed in construction is going to become even more insistent. Having once seen 2,000 m² offices remodelled in eight weeks from the first phone call, tomorrow's clients are going to be trying for six weeks max. And if these clients also realise the pointlessness of the obstacles being put in the way of fast building by the planning bureaucracy, the conservation agencies and the friends of the views of St Paul's....

Ever since IT introduced business at the speed of thought, business has dreamed of being able to order up buildings like hamburgers—"A whopper office floor with full retail wrap please, and could I have extra parking with that?" What it doesn't want to order up is a lecture series on cornice lines, or months of archaeology. And if it doesn't get what it wants? Well, there are other firms, other parts of the country, even other countries. Commercial architecture already knows that.

Rocket science at the AA

2001

Two students dressed in black stand in front of a packed house. They are presenting their project. One is wearing what looks like a straitjacket festooned with Velcro and zips. The other one does the talking. He advises us that we all want to transform our bodies into objects and a black zippered body suit like that worn by his colleague will make it possible. He demonstrates that his colleague's arms are zipped tight to his sides and his legs zipped together. Then, by inviting him to adopt a crouching position and judiciously zipping other zips, he converts him into a frighteningly boulder-shaped bundle small enough to travel hand baggage.

Shocked by this display, this particular invited juror is struck by the thought that anyone passing the AA building, with its two blue plaques and its button down Georgian facade, would never in a million years guess what was going on inside.

Next up is a man whose exhibit A is a sheet made up of 100s of cigarette papers. This he has photographed as it wafts to the ground, studied the structural implications of, and otherwise pumped dry of all significance. Less imaginatively another aspirant has designed a 400 foot table with a restaurant to fit, and made a huge model of Deptford. Another has tried to cross an animation of Jackson Pollock painting with the plan of the Schroder House, and another the Greenwich Village meat packing district with Prada—the result being data-generated shapes worthy of Claes Oldenburg or Paul Rudolph.

I begin to get it now. It's the people outside who are crazy. The presenters are basically setting up processes that will generate mutations, then giving names to the mutations and assigning meanings to them. The trouble is that the resulting data fascination can be as deadly to a designer as instrument fascination is to a pilot. Take the group that takes a slice of landscape near Lisbon, cuts it up into rectangles and then plays a randomising game of pass the parcel with it. Is this rocket science?

Another one just might be. It starts out illustrating the automatic balance achieved by the processes of crop rotation, fallow fielding, contour cropping and inter cropping in agriculture, and then promises to apply the same harmonising principles to urban planning, permitting for example seasonal development.

But wait, there's more. There are 16 wooden pieces each representing a dream. There is a student who has followed people using mobile phones in the street and made a map of their movements. He has taken six hours to get from Acton to Bedford Square on foot by following the directions of everyone he asks, and who has finally cast himself in plaster to see what immobility feels like because he wants a house that will reconfigure itself around him at will.

Next comes branding and some high quality image making. Several Guinness commercials are shown. For some reason a fragment of the Panopticon finds itself inside a Portakabin. Curtains herald the conversion of the podium level of Centrepoint into a cult cinema, and Rolex diversifies from watches into self-defence with a jewel-like stun gun.

And finally comes the capsule hotel. This one starts off made of shipping containers and ends up as a nest of demountable, transportable foam-cored plywood capsules, enough "to sleep 46 students". The bed, "a capsule in itself", is to be built in prototype form over Easter. And thus ends an all-day jury at the AA. The hall is packed with spectators from beginning to end. If it were not for that, I would urge everyone to attend the next one. It is, as Tony Blair once said of the dome, "a monument to our creativity and a fantastic day out".

Shooting at statues

2001

Somebody once said that history is something you make, not something
you keep, a thought to bear in mind when considering the recent outburst
of iconoclasm that had Afghanistan's ruling Taleban unleashing anti-tank
missiles, artillery shells and dynamite upon religious artefacts including the
famous Buddhist statues at Bamiyan that had survived for 1,500 years.
The destruction followed swiftly upon a new law calling for the destruction
of all pre-Islamic 'false idols'.

Predictably global public opinion was outraged by this event, which was
almost universally seen as an act of intolerant vandalism, but aside from the
practical impossibility of preventing it, lay the question of its status as living
history. Iconoclasm never gets a good press, but it does have a long record,
starting with the destruction of Troy and Carthage in the Ancient world, and
moving on to modern times via the fall of Constantinople; the smashed
Medieval stained glass of the English Civil War; the excesses of the French
Revolution and the Paris Commune; the Russian Revolution; the bombing
campaigns of the Second World War; the cultural revolution in China;
the anti-urbanism of Pol Pot and the widespread demolition of Communist
statuary in the former satellite states of the Soviet Union at the end of the
Cold War.

The truth is that history so boils over with instances of wanton destruction
that it might even be said to consist of them, especially in the realm of
architecture where destruction by demolition is seldom unmourned but seen as
the ultimate gesture of disapprobation nonetheless. This being so, how can we
manage to draw distinctions between the religious and the political, and the
political and the sociological, in an area where one person's vandalism can be
claimed as the enactment of another's ideological gesture? For instance how
does the terrorist demolition of the public services building in Oklahoma City in
1995, compare with the spate of high-rise housing projects dynamited by city
authorities in Britain and America in the 1970s and the 80s.

Given what we know of the motives of the perpetrators, Oklahoma might
be described as an ideological event, whereas the dynamiting of high-rise
housing in general could be considered to be a series of sociological events.
The ethical difference between them being that one was a heinous crime
punishable by execution, while the other was considered (at the time at least),
to be an enlightened response to changing standards in public housing.

In many ways we operate a double standard in all our dealings with the destruction of sacred or historic artefacts, whether they be giant statues, historic buildings or the bones of Saints. We profess to see no connection between the sack of Carthage and such miscellaneous merriments of modern times as the carpet bombing of the great cities of Europe and the obliteration of Hiroshima and Nagasaki in Japan during the Second World War, the 'precision' bombing of Iraq, or the attempted demolition of Serbia by NATO aircraft from an airbase near you.

Where the religious crusade of the Taleban is concerned we put a different spin upon it. In our secular, inclusivist, commercialised way we respond to the destruction of statues half as old as the civilised world, not really spiritually, but with eyes firmly focused on the long term marketing possibilities. Thus within 48 hours of the cannonade in the Bamiyan Valley came the announcement that an Anglo-Irish 'Task Force' had been formed to protect all such cultural treasures from extremists, wars and natural disasters. By the time you read this it will already be at work lobbying governments and funding bodies and sending experts to emergencies all over the world to persuade institutions and authorities to invest in their treasures and promote access to them instead.

Hong Kong's space shuffle

2001

Circling above the islands of the Pearl River delta, waiting to land at a crowded Kai Tak Airport, used to give visitors to Hong Kong a grandstand view of an urban civilisation without parallel on earth. Hong Kong Island, as densely packed with skyscrapers as cigarettes in a packet, and its hinterland dotted with massive evidence of earth movement and landfill. Today, in the twenty-first century era of Hong Kong International Airport, the heavily built-up coastal strip either side of Hong Kong harbour is no longer the city's most obvious feature. That honour falls to the ubiquitous evidence of excavation in the landscape. Everywhere on the Kowloon peninsula and in the New Territories there are great cuts and scars, as though giant carving knives had been taken to the sides of hills and mountains. Slope control, as this cutting and stabilising is called, like the work of tunnelling, bridging, road building and the reclamation of more and more land from the sea, is part of Hong Kong's ceaseless search for building land. A search satisfied only by tremendous feats of engineering.

All cities are museums of architectural history—even Brasilia, even Milton Keynes—and each is chained by geographical location to its own special set of circumstances. Apart from this location there is only the unpredictable course of human events to shape their destinies. But this is no small matter. So great is the sway of chance that different circumstances at different times can convert a city into a radically different place. Hong Kong for example, is one of the most extreme and remarkable of all the world's cities.

Seized from China by the British in 1841, the colony has only recently been restored to its former owners, an event that makes the city's geopolitical importance unpredictable for years to come. Today Hong Kong may be a giant but, as a city it is new, only the last 50 of its 156 colonial years having seen any great development. The massive high-rise powerhouse of the last years of colonial rule is a creation of the Pacific War of 1941–1945. Then Japan seized the colony by force as part of an attempt to create an East Asian economic region not totally dissimilar to the arrangement that exists today. The attempt was a failure, but the goal remained within reach. Ten years later, after 1949, when the defeated Kuomintang had fled to Taiwan and mainland China had fallen under Communist rule and become embroiled in the Korean War, Hong Kong became the Eastern equivalent of West Berlin—an island refuge from collectivised tyranny.

In the 1950s it was the pressure of immigration and the press of booming population upon the tiny enclave that forced Hong Kong's growth into the forest of skyscrapers that exists today. First houses covered the shoreline; then the houses were replaced by apartment towers, and yet more land was recovered from the sea. Finally even the balconies of the apartments in the apartment towers were turned into apartments themselves. What the long term effect of the removal of the land frontier with China will be upon this crazy pattern of building and rebuilding remains to be seen.

In terms of architecture what could be termed the aesthetics of density has barely come to terms with the historical infrastructure. Much of its sparse modern history is confined to short essays, among them those by the German novelist Tilman Spengler, who writes about old Kowloon, black market gold dealing and, most interestingly, the sociological significance of the city's retail display windows. Hong Kong's windows, he believes, with their elaborate displays arranged in depth, act as a kind of virtual space that relieves the pressure of the immense population upon the city's crowded pavements and elevated walkways.

Tall buildings: the end of a civilisation
2001

Every opinion has a function, and it did not take long for the shock and
horror of last week's suicide attacks on New York skyscrapers to convert
itself into an outpouring of opinion reminiscent not so much of Pearl
Harbour, as is claimed, but of the sinking of the *Titanic*, as the historian
Andrew Roberts has said. The strength of his parallel—as opposed to
the various other parallels advanced in the wake of the event—is that it
acknowledges, in addition to the tragic loss of human life, that this was not
only a technological disaster but a disaster for technology. The drama may
have shared some elements with earlier historical events—the blowing up
of the battleship *Maine* that triggered the Spanish American war of 1898,
or the Paris Concorde crash of 2000—but it was no more the first war of the
twenty-first century as president George W Bush declared than was Chernobyl
the last war of the twentieth century.

What we can see of Chernobyl, with the perspective of 15 years, is that
it did lasting harm to the development of nuclear power, setting it back to
an extent that may soon cause power shortages that a hastily resuscitated
nuclear industry will be agonisingly slow to make good. In the same way,
setting aside (although this is all but impossible), the appalling human cost
of the destruction of the two towers of the World Trade Center, that event
will do lasting harm to the development of high-rise construction which
in turn will threaten the whole concept of high-density urbanisation.

It is this effect that is of particular interest to architects. Literally
before the dust had settled in New York, commentators had already saddled
this new steed—the vulnerability of any prominent tower building to
a fuelled-up airliner flown into it at hundreds of miles an hour by a crew
of suicidal hijackers—and galloped into print with demands for an end
to all high-rise building.

As is well known, the 110 storey World Trade Center towers were
designed long after the 1945 crash of a twin engined aircraft into the Empire
State building. Contemporary claims that Minoru Yamasaki's towers would
withstand the impact of a Boeing 747 were prompted by memories of this
event. But this time it was different. The eventuality of the napalm-like
combination of 300 tonnes of airliner impacting one of the towers at high
speed with a full load of jet fuel on board was never taken into account.
As a result, while both towers remained standing even after the full impact

of the aircraft, neither could withstand the tremendous heat generated by the combustion of thousands of gallons of jet fuel that softened their steel structure and led to progressive collapse.

The argument that such a collapse could or should have been 'designed out' of the buildings by fire engineering is spurious. No fire engineer foresaw that huge quantities of jet fuel might explode on contiguous upper floors, nor did the security review that followed the abortive 1993 terrorist bombing consider such an eventuality. Terrorists had turned cars and lorries into bombs before, but no one considered that men with pocket knives could turn passenger-laden airliners into huge incendiary bombs and occupied office towers into death traps until it actually happened.

Only in retrospect does the fact that each World Trade Center tower had 250 lifts but only three escape stairs for 25,000 people seem inadequate, or the four hours it took to evacuate the building in 1993 seem alarming. Like the cathedrals of the Middle Ages, buildings like these were beyond criticism. They represented the highest achievement of a civilisation.

How to get famous by not building anything

2002

In America you compete by building; in Britain you compete to build. That used to be the big difference between the two countries in the old days when British architects and planners used to be invited to lecture the Americans on public housing and new towns. Now it is even worse, what with CABE and Health and Safety too on the UK side and the lecturing trend going into reverse. If you are pretending to be designing an airport for the next ten years the best thing you can do is to get yourself swamped by a big American name, like Bechtel did the JLE, only sooner.

But let's look on the dark side for a moment. If this doesn't work, can you make a career out of not building anything at all? Surprisingly you can. Play your cards right and you could even find yourself at the sharpest cutting edge since Prince Charles upstaged Charles Correa at Hampton Court. Who knows, you might even end up lecturing stateside.

There are three stages to a career in disarchitecturalisation (as we call it). The first is objecting. This is as simple as it sounds. All you do is let it be known that you think that a proposed major development is 'questionable'. Questionable is a very useful word because, oddly enough, people never question it, yet it strikes the victim like a dagger to the heart. You can for instance look at the computer-generated image of a major pedestrianisation scheme and privately consider that it looks like the Alexanderplatz at the height of the DDR, but you mustn't say that. Just murmur that it looks 'questionable' and others will supply the comparisons while you garner the gravitas.

After a few months of questionablising you will be able to appear on You and Yours without passing a sleepless night wondering what to say, and you will be invited to uproarious drinks parties at English Heritage where people will start to let you into all kinds of secrets.

The second stage involves making use of all the data you have accumulated during your 'questionable' campaign. You do this by speaking at a prominent public inquiry in your own recognisance and reading out a long deposition consisting of lavish praise for every person or organisation that has ever supported your own one word analysis. This excruciating personal praise element will shield you from possible counterattacks that might otherwise hint that perhaps you are a bit 'questionable' yourself. But don't worry, you are almost home and dry.

The creative stage comes last, but it is worth waiting for. This is when you throw off your cloak of negativism and subtly advance your own vision of a revolutionary disarchitecturalised built environment consisting exclusively of Grade 1 historic buildings deployed in a vast sculpture park lined with processional ways. There will be no 'questionable' elements in this city of the future. There will be no houses, no office blocks, no conspicuously modern buildings of any kind, and no motorised traffic either. Citizens will wander from palace to cathedral to mausoleum on foot, or else on battered three-speed bicycles with wickerwork baskets on their handlebars.

Obviously at this point you may have to stump up a few bob for digital images of your own, but yours will be cheaper than anyone else's because all that has to be done is to delete the 'questionable' buildings and traffic from well-known views of St Paul's. Now it will be your turn to be praised! Your proposed phase one demolition of 148,795 objectionable buildings will be described as "dramatic", "thought provoking", "radical", "farsighted" and best of all "essential". With any luck you will never need to use the word 'questionable' again.

Stern view of a Dutch East Indiaman, 1720

Stern view of a Royal Navy Battle Cruiser, 1936

Battleships hold the key to the future of tall buildings

2002

Frank Lloyd Wright once said that inferior minds work by comparison while superior minds work by analogy. As an aphorism this matches Buckminster Fuller's better known one about the task of design being to do more with less, so that even if resources dwindle there can still be more for everyone, but in either case the use of analogy to tease out technology is a gift from the Gods because it really works. Take clocks for example. They started out as sundials rooted to the spot, then they got their solar mechanism so they could be mounted anywhere they could be seen; then their mechanism shrank down to the size of a pocket watch; then a wrist watch, then something so small that its flashing digits can be fixed to anything from a credit card to a car.

Tales of miniaturisation like this chase each other down the centuries; the development and extinction of the camera; the weight of coinage; the output of an engine; the mass of a bridge structure; the cost of a photo-voltaic cell, the size of a mobile phone and so on, until after a time it all becomes too easy. That is when the analogists task becomes to find out the exact change points in this process of evolution, not just glossing over them or, better yet, to actually predict these major shifts on the basis of data taken from completely different fields. In short that's when you use the methods of meteorology and market research to predict the future of structures and machines.

To show how analogue aphorisms can produce answers where nothing else can, let's have the past predict the future by means of an analogy so arcane that it may never have been explored before—the decline and extinction of the battleship as a model for the fate of tall buildings. We can start with a passage from David Howarth's *Sovereign of the Seas*, a history of British sea power, published in 1974. "The affairs of nations are often guided by sentiment rather than logic, and battleships in every age were wonderful creations. They had a fierce feline beauty like a tiger, 'a fearful symmetry'; and even when they proved impractical, their beauty may have had some martial value in itself, to give confidence to a nation that possessed them, and give pause to a nation that did not."

Now consider the same passage with the word battleships replaced by tall buildings: "The affairs of nations are often guided by sentiment rather than logic, and tall buildings in every age were wonderful creations.

They had a fierce feline beauty like a tiger, 'a fearful symmetry'; and even when they proved impractical, their beauty may have had some political value in itself, to give confidence to a nation that possessed them, and give pause to a nation that did not."

Clearly the sense of the passage is not destroyed by the substitution, so let us assume that the analogy is not either. Here is another passage; "So the great battleships survived, and the people took comfort from their existence, as they always had. But more and more of the strength of each battleship was being diverted to its own protection."

Making the same substitution in this passage we have the following; "So the tall buildings survived, and the people took comfort from their existence, as they always had. But more and more of the strength of each tall building was being diverted to its own protection." Once again the sense of the passage has not been destroyed by the substitution, but its message has become predictive. Now it is a harbinger of 11 September 2001.

Saved by the intelligent toilet
2002

Every day in every way Japan is becoming more and more important. The world's second biggest economy may be stuck on the rocks of deflation but even the newspaper articles that try to convince us that we are not heading in the same direction make riveting reading. With the Nikkei index at a 20 year low, trading at less than a quarter of its 1990 volume, the Japanese economy has been stagnant or shrinking for a decade. Its corporate sector is choked with heavily indebted property, retail, and construction companies that are trapped in an undeclared insolvency, with too many bad debts and too few customers to borrow from banks that have their own £250 billion bad debt problem. No wonder business commentators here and in the United States have started to talk about a second Great Depression. The whole Japan thing holds a gloomy fascination everywhere.

Everywhere, that is, except in Japan. There, above the cloudbase of the stultified macro economy, a feverish culture of Designer Keynesianism called Chindogu has developed, its growing number of exponents cheerfully working long hours in cramped innovation centres producing potentially marketable novelty items such as the portable zebra crossing, the golf hoe (weed your garden whilst practising your swing), and the 360 degree panorama camera. The line between ingenuity and farce lies at the heart of Chindogu but it is a mistake to dismiss its potential on the strength of the ideas of its lunatic fringe. For every solar powered cigarette lighter there is a driver operated taxi door, and for every driver operated door there is a Walkman and a global market opening up for it.

It is in this spirit of suspended disbelief that we should consider the recent focus of Japanese ingenuity on the development of the flushing toilet and its seat. The small ideas here have all been focused on the automation of the person/machine interface encountered when going to the loo. At first the gadgets were simple—the flushing action has operated the warm water tap on the wash hand basin on upmarket Japanese toilets for years—but lately the proliferation of support functions has begun to leap from the quaintly exotic to the seriously medical. One recent invention is a toilet that glows in the dark and lifts its lid when an infrared sensor detects the presence of a human being, while a competitor has announced a lavatory that does all that too, but also deodorises the bathroom and resets its temperature for every user by means of warm or cool air jets. Yet another at the pre-launch stage of development opens its lid in response to a verbal command and uses a voice synthesizer to greet users by name and offer them personalised advice.

But these seem frivolous by comparison with the line of inquiry being followed by Matsushita Electric, one of the biggest innovators in the toilet field. Matsushita has taken up the idea of the 'throne' as a diagnostic device capable of giving a BMI (Body Mass Index) reading for every user by passing a small electric current through their buttocks. But the company plans to go farther, turning the whole bathroom into a home diagnostic centre and the toilet into a means of measuring weight, fat, blood pressure, heart rate, urine sugar, blood and albumen. These readouts will be sent to the users' doctor as text messages by a cellular phone built into the toilet providing a means for remote health monitoring.

It might seem impossible that a humble device like a toilet could bust the Japanese economy loose from its pack ice of deflation, but it isn't entirely impossible. Like nearly all Chindogu ideas it is already 49 per cent brilliant.

Why prefabrication fails
2002

The history of attempts to industrialise house production is a big subject, principally because in a free market the 'less' of innovation can never compete with the 'more' of the existing housing stock. This is why prefabricated, modular or temporary homes always end up being confined to captive populations—soldiers, refugees, prisoners, students, the homeless, and now key workers. But contrary to the apparent belief of the chairman of the government's Housing Forum, this does not mean they were chained to a tiny sector of the housing market in the past. As long ago as the Second World War, under conditions of appalling scarcity, 2.7 million allied troops were accommodated in hutted camps in England and Wales for the best part of two years in the run up to the Normandy landings. Then, after the war was over, the government's Emergency Factory Made programme was committed to producing 500,000 new technology prefabricated houses between 1945 and 1947, and actually achieved 170,000 before an economic crisis led to the programme being discontinued. During the war in America a similar housing programme had relocated eight million war workers over four years by mass-producing prefabricated dwellings. Clearly the problem was not insuperable, even where a mobile home industry hardly existed, which was the case in England in the 1940s.

Nearly 60 years later the factory production of houses remains a matter of priorities and lateral thinking: the first a requiring sustained resolution on the part of government: the second a willingness to depart from the traditional demarcations between industries. Thus the 1945 AIROH house was an aluminium dwelling designed and produced by the aircraft industry, while the PORTAL house was developed by a consortium of motor industry engineers and the ARCON was developed by the steel industry. Today's broad search for key worker housing production capacity should be similarly drastic. It should start with the capacity of the building industry, move on to seize derelict or unoccupied property, then move on to the three alternative industries, aircraft, motor vehicles (with special emphasis on the potential contribution of producers of commercial trucks and vans), followed by an investigation of the potential of caravan makers and boat-builders, pool house, green house and conservatory manufacturers, tent makers, rolling stock manufacturers and so on. Every possible enterprise with space-enclosing capability. Ignorance of the importance of this 'broadband' approach is a cause of the failure of previous attempts to bring about a salutatory evolution in construction that could defeat the idea of the individual building as a priceless object by showering it with replicas —as happened to portraiture under the impact of photography.

I had some small experience of this phenomenon some 30 years ago when I was in Chile during the Allende years. The country was in a state of near bankruptcy, importing second hand concrete panel building systems from the Soviet Union and East Germany but unable to import engines, transmissions and spare parts for the Western motor vehicles running on its roads. My contribution was to propose that the closed down production line for small and large Citroën vans (whose flat panel bodies were manufactured under licence), be reopened so that the corrugated body panels, doors, windows and other useful parts could then be assembled as metal panel housing units. The Chilean ministry of planning had already shown interest in this idea and at one time it appeared that the Citroën Chilena plant would be partly reopened to run up a prototype. Unhappily, despite calculations showing that at least 5,000 units could be completed in a year, this never happened. Although seductive drawings were made, the local socialist housing committees strongly opposed the idea. With the overthrow of the Allende regime, like so many housing dreams it never flew.

Technological jewels in the crown
2003

"Sonic geriatric." So editorialised *The Times* in a leader last week commenting on the decision to take the surviving handful of Concordes out of service after 27 years of crisscrossing the Atlantic at twice the speed of sound. Nor was the newspaper alone in not being able to think of anything more profound to say on the subject. As the flood of last minute ticket sales has shown, Concorde is, unusually, going to be allowed a dignified retirement —as opposed to being banned from the airways for damaging the ozone layer or playing the villain in a second ghastly fireball. If asked to predict the aircraft's final fate, most people—even after the space shuttle *Columbia* catastrophe—would settle for "put it in a museum", "make it the prime exhibit in a supersonic theme park", or prop it up at a dashing angle outside an RAF base. "Fiery coffin" would have come nowhere. Too much like tempting providence even to mention. Nonetheless, taken as a whole, the Paris Concorde fire and the Columbia shuttle tragedy must have had some effect upon the decision to take the aircraft out of service.

Tragedies like the sinking of the *Titanic*, the burning of the Hindenburg and the explosion of the Comet airliners are the creative milestones of technological evolution. Just as the famous journeys of the great discoverers illuminate the study of geography, so do the tragedies of air and space, and the immense appetite for minutely detailed information about them that is always shown by the public, confirm that a technological society is not necessarily a post-historic society and indeed may never be one.

While there are civil and structural engineering disasters to match those of sea and sky it is hard to call to mind buildings of the modern age that have been both celebrated and incinerated in the same inspiring way. The best-known example of this genre must be the Crystal Palace, built, dismantled, rebuilt and then burned to the ground inside the space of 80 years. But a less well known and much smaller project is important nonetheless. The late Reliance Controls potentiometer factory in Swindon is an almost exact contemporary of Concorde. This building, the last collaboration of the two great architects, Norman Foster and Richard Rogers, both of who now have seats in the House of Lords, was completed in 1965 and demolished only 13 years ago. As a building Reliance Controls was brilliantly simple and brilliantly cheap. Its structure consisted of a welded steel frame composed of only four elements—combined columns and crossheads, main beams, purlins, and external diagonal bracing—and its cladding was the same profiled steel sheet on roof as well as walls. Instead of windows it had a floor to ceiling glass wall and apart from its ground slab no wet trades were involved in its construction.

Like Concorde, Reliance was tremendously popular as an idea. It received considerable publicity when it won the first ever *Financial Times* Industrial Architecture at Work Award and from then until its demolition it was a place of pilgrimage for architects and students. The trouble was that, like Concorde, the people who admired it were enthusiasts—the people who worked in it day after day hated it as much as the people who endure the noise of Concorde's engines thundering overhead. When asked in a BBC documentary for his opinion of the building, the firm's managing director, who had worked at Reliance from the beginning, described it as "a biscuit tin" that heated up intolerably in the summer. He volunteered to push the button to demolish it himself.

Clearly every work of genius leaves space in its wake for improvements.

The defining moment of Modernism
2003

Everything has its defining moment these days. Every week there is a defining moment in fashion; every month a literary prize; every year a car of the year. The whole process, including awards for new buildings, already exceeds the number of recipients available. Like Saddam Hussein's parliament, it ends up with more seats than candidates and every candidate sure of a seat. At one level all this may simply be the invisible hand of capitalism at work, creating employment for public relations firms, but one thing it certainly isn't is history.

History is something you make, not something you save. If it does have defining moments they are not the product placements that our awards and commemorative plaques have become. The Industrial Revolution is a good example. Historians agree that there was such a thing and that it utterly transformed Britain between the eighteenth and twentieth centuries, but by no stretch of the imagination can 200 years be described as a "defining moment". At most it is a cautious generalisation. Not that it can be entirely dismissed for this reason—as we can easily see if we try to sharpen our focus on its component events and begin listing precise dates for the building of canals and railways, the launching of ocean liners and the completion of fireproof warehouses as well as the erection of the Crystal Palace. In this sense the more precise we get, the further from the truth we stray, until in the end we have to fall back on something like a non-momentous generalisation in order to be able to discuss the matter at all.

Does the problem of the defining moment disappear if we substitute a looser phrase like "Modern Age" for "Industrial Revolution"? To some extent it does, but mainly because it opens the floodgates to art history. As a result the defining moment of Modernism has come to be hailed not only as the prefabrication of the Crystal Palace in 1851, but in the rear view of a house built in Vienna in 1912 and the arrival of non-representational art in the galleries of Paris. It has also, of course, been identified with the 1903 flight of the Wright brothers' biplane; with the success of the first Benz automobile in 1886; with the appearance of the 32 knot *Turbinia* at the 1897 *Spithead Review*; with the deaths of Captain Scott and his companions in Antarctica in 1912; with the first successful flight across the North Atlantic by Alcock and Brown (which ended in a crash landing in Ireland); with the first solo, non-stop flight across the Atlantic from airport to airport by

Charles Lindbergh in 1927; with the explosion of the first atomic bomb over Hiroshima in 1945 and most recently with the destruction of the towers of the World Trade Center in New York in September 2001.

Setting aside the last two, which raise questions of another kind and should perhaps be excluded for being more postmodern than modern, it now behoves me to produce my own contender for the defining moment of the Modern Age. It comprises a single photograph of a man in a parachute descending from an airship over Roosevelt Field at the New York City end of Long Island. The airship in question is the R34, a British copy of a German Zeppelin, and the date is 6 July 1919. The parachutist is Major Pritchard, the first man to arrive in America by air, having boarded the airship four days earlier in Scotland.

To cross the Atlantic by airship and arrive in America by parachute! Surely nothing could be more futuristic, more functional, more poignant, more MODERN than that.

Porsche 911: the genetically modified machine
2003

"Artefacts evolve using themselves as the point of departure: they contain the conditions for their own development. The structure of the object moves to match the future conditions in which it will be employed."

Gilbert Simondon, *Du mode d'existence des objets techniques*, Paris 1958, 1989.

Tony Hatter is one of five ex-Royal College of Art graduate students working in the 35 strong Porsche Design Department in Stuttgart. He studied transportation at Coventry Polytechnic and then did two years post graduate automotive design at the RCA from 1979 to 1981. As Hatter remembers, it was his ambition even in his school days to design for Porsche, but the process of getting there was difficult. "As soon as I graduated from the RCA I applied to the company but there were no vacancies at that time", he recalls, "so I tried elsewhere and worked for Opel for five years before approaching Porsche again in 1986. This time the company accepted me and I have worked in the design department ever since."

From 1995 to 1998 Hatter worked in the racing division. He designed the bodywork and paint splash graphics of the three GT1 cars, including the winner of the Le Mans 24 hour race in 1997. He was also responsible for the 'optical appearance' and livery of the racing division at that time. Today he looks back on the Le Mans effort as "The ultimate experience of my life."

Hatter has worked for years on 911 series cars. Of the current road-going version he says simply; "It's not a car to drive at 300 kilometres an hour down an autobahn. It is a car for piloting swiftly along country roads. It enables you to enjoy a tremendous sense of achievement doing that." He is deeply respectful of those responsible for the car's careful evolution. "It is evolution, not revolution", he insists. "The car has always been the sum of incremental changes. You might say it lost its way slightly with the 964 model, but the 993 got it back on track. Now there's the water-cooled 996. The evolution of the 911 will never stop. It is based on a philosophy, not a style."

The difference between a philosophy and a style is a pattern of change. It was adherence to a philosophy that enabled a tiny engineering company in post-war Austria, a country under military occupation after the Axis defeat in the Second World War, to produce a prototype sports car so much more advanced than those of other countries. It was a pattern of change that enabled it to become the most famous in the world within a generation.

The first Porsche car I ever saw was a 356. It was during a school trip to France which included the Palace of Versailles. The most memorable thing about the day was that silver shape moving slowly past the visitors in the gardens. I ran to see what it was and it drove right past me, its vestigial bumpers seeming only millimetres above the ground, its wheels with their huge chrome hub caps almost completely hidden from view, its exhaust note oddly clattering.

That was in 1953, so it must have been a very early car. Coming from England I had never seen anything like it. Nothing so small, so extreme or somehow so private. A ground-hugging exoskeletal creature of aluminium beaten into uncompromising curves.

It was many years before I properly understood how the Porsche philosophy of engineering and design had enabled that car to emerge from the wreckage of war-torn Germany, or what it was that made it so superior to its competitors. The elucidation came to me in part from a passage in Antoine de Saint-Exupéry's *Wind Sand and Stars* in which the famous aviator is marvelling at the clean appearance of the closed-cockpit, low-wing, retractable undercarriage metal monoplanes that had evolved out of the old strut and wire braced wooden biplanes of the early years of flight; "It is a shock to realise that all visible evidence of invention has been refined out of these machines so that they look like products of nature", wrote Saint-Exupéry. "They are objects so natural that they might be pebbles polished by the waves."

The Porsche 356, too, was a machine that looked like a product of nature, and so was its successor the Porsche 911. Like Gilbert Simondon's artefacts that draw their future from within themselves, the 911 grew out of its predecessors and thereafter not so much evolved as metamorphosed over a lifespan in excess of 35 years. During that time it has flaunted its inherited capacity to dissolve invention within itself so effectively that in its present manifestation, despite a very significant redesign, it retains enough of its historic purity of form to enable one to say, not that it has been changed, but that it has been repeatedly reborn.

There is no doubt that the Porsche 911 was the offspring of the Porsche 356, but in the taxonomy of machines, as in the taxonomy of natural species, there is no simple starting point. The entwined engineer/designer/driver

DNA that was in the bloodstream of the 356 went through three changes in 17 years of production before it metamorphosed into the 911. Going further back the prototype 356, the first ever Porsche, the 'weekend sports car' of 1948 with all but its body taken from the pre-war Volkswagen Beetle, contained even older genes. At the level of fundamental engineering the rear-mounted air cooled 'boxer' engine and the torsion bar suspension reached back to the 1934 Auto Union grand prix car and the NSU project 12 (an earlier design by Ferdinand Porsche for a people's car). From here the trail back is harder to follow but still exists. There must ultimately be some reference to the Austrian Paul Jaray's streamlining patents and the Porsche 'boxer' aero engine of 1912.

Unlike the insight of Saint-Exupéry, the essence of Gilbert Simondon's insight is that not only inherited genes but predictive genes as well are present in the inanimate organism. Thus the Porsche 911 would not merely be descended from a cast of glorious ancestors: from its 1964 production version onwards it incubated its own future together with the means to modify it.

In the world of plant and animal species such genetic modification is achieved by inserting a construct that has three parts: a desired gene, a marker gene and a promoter or catalyst. The marker gene enables the construct to select the correct cells for the modification, while the promoter inserts the desired gene. The incremental process of automobile design is a close analogue to this process. The desired outcome plays the part of the desired gene; the parts of the car affected by the achievement of this outcome play the part of the marker, and the promoter is not only the designer but the market maker and the driver. Because of this similarity it is possible to compare the genetic modification that produces a pest-resistant strain of wheat, with the design modification that significantly enhances any aspect of the performance, safety or comfort of a car.

When dealing with a car with the long and illustrious pedigree of the Porsche 911 there are numerous instances of such designed modifications. They extend back from the present to the date of the car's introduction, and back before then to the design regime and the reigning technical ideas of the time when it acceded to the status of a project. This can be seen in the way that the new model 996 incarnation of the 911 possesses what could be called pre-foetal, foetal, infant, young, mature and senile elements side by side, all genetically blended into an indivisible whole. In the car's bodywork, electronics and mechanical engineering there are not only buried assumptions that date back to before the introduction of the first version of the 911 in 1964, but also design features that have emerged much more recently—for example as a result of new environmental legislation, changes in the customer base, or conditions of severe traffic congestion that in 1964 did not exist. Were one to spread out all the images and documents necessary to take a synoptic view of the whole 35 year history of the Porsche 911 one would see this clearly. Put simply, it would become evident that the first half of the car's life was spent getting bigger and heavier, gaining power and reputation, while the second half has been spent subtly divesting itself of the appearance of all these Darwinian attributes whilst retaining their substance in a concealed form. Thus the outrageously exhibitionist 1975 three litre turbo—which must represent the fulcrum of road-going 911 hubris versus late model discretion—can be contrasted with both the modest original car and its wolf in sheep's clothing present incarnation, the plain-looking model 996. The 1975 car may boldly carry its American five mph bumpers and whale tail like a bulldozer and backhoe, but the defiance does not last. From then on disarming emphases began to proliferate on all the road cars. The brakes, for example, (which are philosophically as well as practically the antithesis of the accelerator), were once considered of so little visual importance that they were hidden by steel wheels and chrome hub caps. Now they have become such powerful symbols of motoring survival that they are on ostentatious display, prowling like wild animals behind the spindly bars of their see-through alloy wheels. In the same way the car's headlamps, once boldly raised to command the road and establish the aggressive lunge of the wings, now recline invisibly, dissolved into a rounder, flatter curve and deconstructed into busy multipurpose lamp clusters beneath a smoothly moulded transparent cover.

There are other examples of this metamorphosing of imagery. Austere painted steel, once proof of circuit mettle on even the most luxurious dashboard, is now banished in favour of leather, wood or (non-structural) carbon fibre. Air conditioning, once a power-sapping obstacle to sports car performance, is now standard even on open-top cars. Thin-rimmed steering wheels of huge diameter, made of that now extinct post-war German cream-coloured plastic, are now replaced by thick-rimmed airbag-fat steering wheels of tiny diameter. Even the magnificent horizontally opposed six cylinder air cooled engines, once gloriously exposed simply by raising a metal cover, are now totally concealed under a cloak of accessories, electronics and water jackets. Most drastic of all, the puissant flare of the front and rear wheel arches, introduced to accommodate wider tyres and subsequently seen at its most extreme in the various turbo versions up to and including the statuesque 959, is now dissolved into the deceptive blandness of a longer, wider car with gentle side modelling, more predictable curves, less aggression, more discretion, less promise, more concealment. So much is this the case that only the fastback coupe roof and side windows, a styling cue held over from the model 993 (now regarded as the last of the 'old style' 911 cars), and the new racing shark's mouth air intake below the integral front bumper, enable the 996 to be seen as a reformed character rather than simply an anonymous one.

It is no accident that the science of genetics has assumed a burning importance in so many fields. Students, who shy away from traditional university subjects, queue up to study this important new discipline that promises massive change from microscopic interventions. We are told that by genetic means desirable characteristics can be enhanced and undesirable characteristics diminished, with the result that species survival is ensured. Crops, livestock, fish and poultry, all line up for performance optimisation by this means. Why not cars too?

DNA is unique to an individual, and to any individual line. But for 100s of years human beings have refined thoroughbred plants and animals in order to maximise beauty, performance and intelligence without understanding its mechanism at all. Ships, aircraft, buildings and other industrial products have been developed and steadily improved over time. Today, at the end of a century that has seen industry evolve from the limits of steam and muscle power to the micrometric precision of the robot assembly line, we have products that are continually rendered more perfect in their relationship with their environment by design.

In the last half century the harmful exhaust emissions of Porsche cars have been reduced by 95 per cent. The proportion of the car that is recyclable has risen to 87 per cent. The use of solvents, CFCs, heavy metals, non-reusable packaging and water in the production process as well as the product has been drastically reduced. And yet, at the same time performance, fuel consumption, road holding and comfort have been improved beyond measure.

In a conscious emulation of nature, design has created innumerable machine species, of which among the most prolific are cars—and perhaps the most successfully perfected of all cars is the Porsche 911.

Nonsuch Metropolitan University summer school

2003

Hi, there! Well, it's great to be back. The name is *Garth G Prendergast Jr* director of Nonsuch University's third annual design summer school, and I want to persuade you to come along. Yes it's May, the time of year when all the marketing pedagogues want you to come to their colleges and meet the best design teachers in a boiling creative ferment that has raw energy zap, zap, zapping across the synapses all the way to the end of summer and beyond!

So why come to Nonsuch? Because this year we have an even longer list of teachers and lecturers with funny names, and lots more lecture slots called "tba". The line up is so good that if I had my younger days all over again I'd sign up myself. If it weren't for my consultancy cataloguing the ruins of Baghdad—before they get ruined all over again by insensitive, inappropriate and worse still unsustainable redevelopment—I would be there with you at Nonsuch every step of the way! But that's enough from me, let me hand you over to Nonsuch U's emeritus professor of summer school admissions *Sigi Moleslinger.*

Well thank you *Doc Prendergast*, we'll sure miss you on the podium, but hey! We really do have the greatest ever line-up of summer school teaching fellows. There will be the MOBILE studio run by adjunct professor *Gigli Montaniero. Gigli* is a partner at *Duck Zany Trubshaw*, New York, and this year at the summer school he will be assisted by *Begnamino Quartz* (sole trader, Strange Furniture Designs Inc, Madrid, Texas). Next up will be the STATIC studio, this searching brainfest will be moderated by *Jemima Puddleduck* of Noseblast with help from *Putney Swope* on tea-chest bass straight from those notorious Sustainex trials in Siberia. This will lead on to a revisit to Nonsuch's best known work in progress, RUN RUN by Prof *Nurmi Bannister* and his team of dancing academix.

WARP follows in the culpable hands of *Lars Burp* and the team from Pocohontas was innocent, (top Boom club in Okinawa). Next up is HOUSING, an evergreen subject given a new twist by *Patsy O'Pottle* and *Stephanie Bonhomie* from Cidervat, both professors at Ye Olde Butterscotche Universitye, Chipping Norton.

Next up is a new one for Nonsuch, MORPHING, with *Jane Gomez* and the *Lightfoot* trio, three professors of landscape planning with a catchy thing about rhythm in the bunker.

CITY is another newcomer with vibrant break dancing administrators only too ready to show there really was a worse place to be than the Bastille.

And now for the main festbilt exercise in subcutaneous fat. It is the preliminary list of names for the MOREGAMES travelling symposium which will link up with the summer school for the last two action-packed weeks of the summer school. By popular request we have a definite maybe for *Carlos Winterbottom*, co-founder of TSK TSK together with *Jeff Arnold*, *Sitting Bull* and *Asimo*, *Johnny Appleseed*, *Old Man River* and *Mike Mendoza*.

But the best is always last and it has to be Rotterdam that is bringing it over. Kite designer *Mike Trekbike* of GOSH will give a design studio on SPIES and he defies anyone to finish his course without having learned how to assemble their own courtyard cctv system.

Early Bird registrations win a ten per cent discount. Call MAYBUG on the 24 hour hotline at the Global Research Centre for sustainability. With thanks to the organisation group at Battleaxe, aka *Jerome Kitchen*, Tabletop Enterprises, Littleknown U, Klondike Street, Anchorage, Alaska.

PS. If this is one summer school email list too many for you, simply reply "enough already" in the subject line, and we'll desist from sending you further dispatches.

Return of the phone box
2003

It goes without saying that the first law of technological development
—that synergy makes all products evolve towards their own extinction
—is indisputable. Which is to say that as products get better they also
get more vulnerable to a takeover by other products.

The takeover concept explains why structural systems appear to evolve
towards lightness and simplicity, while motor cars evolve towards weight
and complexity. For example a square metre of cold rolled steel cladding
weighs about one tenth as much as a square metre of old-style hot rolled
steel framing; but the Mark IV Volkswagen Golf weighs nearly twice as
much as its Mark I ancestor. The former does less for less, while the latter
does more for more, yet both are more efficient than their predecessors.
The cladding, having been value-engineered within a millimetre of its life,
has become the most economical space encloser known to man, while the
current Volkswagen Golf packs air conditioning, ABS and electric everything,
not to mention drinks holders and leather upholstery. Odd though they
might seem, these are examples that are worth pursuing to their possible
ultimate fate. For example the cladding might finally be overtaken by climate
control—or more accurately some sort of outdoor air heating system derived
from giant patio heaters—while the car is already itching to become the
nucleus of a high-tech motor home with add-on inflatable rooms.

But enough of these idle speculations. What we need is a news item to put
them to a better test. Luckily last week one turned up in the shape of the rebirth
of the telephone box, a bare five years after the death sentence was passed on it
by the upstart mobile phone. Now mobile phones are the best ever examples of
the first law of technological evolution. From hefting battery packs the size of
suitcases in the 80s to apparently talking into thin air by the end of the 90s,
phone users have never let students of miniaturisation down. Their evolution
has been meteoric and almost all one way because opposition to their
supporting forest of transmission masts, coupled with fears of brain damage
from electromagnetic radiation, though widely publicised, have never caused
them to break stride. While the masts are paradoxical accretions (the smaller
the phone the more numerous and prominent the antennae), the real
casualties have been the network of terrestrial telephone boxes, some very
old indeed. During the 1990s a war broke out between the defenders of
'traditional' Giles Gilbert Scott telephone boxes and the rather more edgy

promoters of so called 'contemporary' designs like those produced by Mercury and Orange, companies that later went so far as to launch a competition to redesign mobile phone masts so as to make them seem less conspicuous, with the aid of Prince Charles as one assessor and the daughter of John Betjeman as another.

In the event the development of new designs for telephone call boxes turned out to be largely irrelevant to their removal, which came about as a result of increasing complaints about their use as advertising space by prostitutes. If only they had hung on for a few more years! For today the 'wireless' technology that enables mobile phones to call one another is capable of radio signal performance or Wi-Fi. As a result Verizon Communications Inc, the biggest American local phone company, has fitted out 150 New York phone booths into 'hot spots' with chairs and counters so that customers with laptops can connect wirelessly to the Internet from up to 100 metres away. By the end of the year there should be 1,000 of them covering all Manhattan.

Not-so-smart intelligent buildings
2003

One sure sign of a recession in the property business is the way the term 'intelligent buildings' drops out of use. As a handful of historians will remember, it first came into vogue in the early 1980s when magazines like this one started publishing technical drawings of buildings that looked like circuit diagrams. Buildings with brains seemed unstoppable after that. Their high point was 'Big Bang' when the City let it all hang out in pursuit of economic growth. In those heady days information technology was like Ecstasy. You could hardly open a newspaper without seeing hard-faced businessmen laying down the law on the 24 hour business environment, the new stock exchange Taurus system, or the role of new technology at Broadgate and Canary Wharf.

But then, only a year after 'Big Bang', there was 'Black Monday'. The FTSE fell to 1565—which makes today's 4,000-odd look comfortable —the world's stock markets crashed and the property market began to slide. What was the use of raised floors like platform shoes and storey heights rivalling St Paul's when the Taurus dealing system had to be abandoned with the City shedding jobs like a punctured fuel tank? In the boom years of the 1980s, 180,000 new jobs had been created by expanding financial services in London. Three years after the crash more than 50,000 of those jobs had been wiped out.

The last man off the sinking ship was Paul Reichmann, the developer of Canary Wharf. He started building his supertanker of an intelligent building in 1988, when the pack ice was already advancing over the horizon. Reichmann thought he knew what he was doing. His 800 foot tower was going to be built so fast that it would outrun any recession. Only two years after work on it began, the first tenants moved in.

Number One Canada Square was a phenomenon. It had as much floorspace in one building as in the whole of the original Broadgate. It had dealing rooms nearly six metres from floor to floor—although they were fitted out as normal office floors in the end. But it was no good. "If you were so intelligent", Reichmann must have cried of his great building when Canary Wharf went into receivership in 1992, "why didn't you keep me rich?"

Charles Darwin understood the limits of intelligence. He knew that it was no use any species trying to bulldoze its own environment into submission. The environment lays down the rules. If the species prospers, fine. If not, no appeals tribunal and no compensation. Viewed as a gigantic piece of industrial design, like a rack stereo system writ large, Canary Wharf was a triumph. As an instrument of wealth it was a disaster that bankrupted its creator. Its 'intelligence' gave it no defence against ice age economics. After the collapse of Olympia & York, most of the development team fled from Docklands to China to build 'intelligent buildings' there.

The only way Reichmann could have ridden out the crash at Canary Wharf would have required a conceptual revolution, one that is nowadays foreshadowed by 'hot-desking' and in 'in-car working'. All he needed to do to set up his alternative financial centre was to spend a few bob on hard standing and provide sandwich bars for 20,000 IT-equipped BMW drivers. That way his 'intelligent building' would have been able to disperse overnight when the crash came. The cars might have ended up banger racing or being recycled into profiled cladding or knives and forks.

So remember the next time you hear the siren song of the intelligent building. If they are so stupid that they can't even save their owner from bankruptcy, how intelligent can they really be?

Assembly line of the Beech Aircraft Corporation, Wichita, USA, 1945

A section of a prefabricated AIROH house, London, 1945

Henry Ford and the limits
of prefabrication
2003

Whenever talk turns to the housing crisis someone is bound to proclaim that millions of new prefabricated houses are the answer. "Just like car production old boy." And of course you can compare car, or better still van production with house building. Four Ford Transits joined together would make a decent starter home, and there could be no argument about its feasibility. 50 years ago the Bristol Aeroplane Company was turning out modular aluminium dwellings at a rate of one every ten minutes. If they could do it then, we can do it now. And if we still can't do it now then the reason can only be because we have erected barriers to prevent ourselves doing it. Barriers like the artificial scarcity of land created by the planning system; the untaxed owner-speculation that diverts resources, and most of all the absence of a charismatic figure like Henry Ford, founder and first president of the Ford Motor Company.

Henry Ford was a man who could have solved the housing problem. He had already solved the transport problem. At the beginning of the last century motor cars were as scarce and expensive as houses are today, or at least they were until Henry Ford created the world's first modern mass-produced motor car, the Model T Ford. From the outset he intended to keep this vehicle in production until he had motorised the whole world, but in the event production of the Model T Ford ceased after only 14 years. During those years 15 million Model Ts were made in factories on production lines altogether capable of turning out a car every ten seconds. This performance enabled the Ford Motor Company to take over 57 per cent of the entire United States car market in ten years and then to venture into overseas markets, but even that was not enough. Ford's marketing method was simple and universal: a completely standardised product—"Any colour you like as long as its black"—and a no-nonsense slogan—"It Gets You There and It Brings You Back." There were to be no face-lifts or performance models, but there were regular price reductions designed to increase Model T ownership among first-time car buyers.

This bargain basement strategy worked brilliantly in the early years, when demand for motor cars was still indiscriminate, but it failed dismally when General Motors' low cost Chevrolet division opened a styling studio (eventually destined to employ 1,400 designers), and fitted its cars with such luxuries as electric starters and hydraulic brakes. By 1927, the last year of

Model T production, sales of the car had fallen so far that Henry Ford was compelled to close down the factory while a new car, the Ford Model A, was designed from the ground up according to less Spartan principles.

The lesson of the Model T can be summed up in two words—market saturation—of which the Ford Model T was an early casualty. This condition arises when demand for any particular good or service is satisfied but production continues unabated. When this happens alternative marketing strategies are required—price cuts, technical improvement of the product or service, increased advertising, or other inducements. It was here that Henry Ford failed. He had the means to hand to build a car for everyman, but he had no idea how to sell a car to any man who already had one already. That was the new task that, for the first time in history, devolved upon the technicians, designers, stylists and even architects of the late 1920s, and that was where the production of cars parted company with the production of houses. Instead of housing the world, we taught it to drive.

The end of an interface
2003

I grew up in the information age. Not necessarily the knowledge age I agree, but certainly the age of data. I can distinctly remember the smouldering argument over how the word 'data' should be pronounced, and whether it was singular or plural. To say DAHTA in those days was to be determinedly patriotic, whereas to say DAYTA was to be currying favour with the Yanks. As we all know, the Yanks won in the end, which was only fair as they invented the typewriter, the first word processor.

Today most people don't know how important typewriters once were, and scarcely one in a million would know that when the United States entered the Second World War, all the typewriter factories in the country except one were converted to the manufacture of small arms, fuses, shells and other munitions. The exception, the Woodstock Typewriter Company, was authorised to produce up to 18,000 typewriters a year for military use. At first sight this measure might seem to indicate that typewriters were not of great strategic value, but they were. Within a year further US legislation called for the surrender to the military of all surplus typewriters, and 650,000 more were acquired for the armed forces by this means.

In Britain even more drastic measures were passed into law. From 7 May 1943 all typewriters were rationed and no typewriter was allowed to be bought or sold, even privately, without a licence. This did not prevent a ship laden with typewriters striking a mine during the Normandy landings with the loss of 20,000 machines.

My own first data processing instrument (after pen and inkwell at school), was an ancient Erika portable typewriter with a QWERTZ keyboard instead of a QWERTY. I kept this machine for many years on the basis that, in conjunction with half a dozen sheets of foolscap paper and a bottle of Tipp-Ex, it might come in useful during a power cut or a nuclear attack but it never did. Instead it gave place to an Olympia electric and then an enormous Olympia Supertype Electronic, a typewriter that actually had an 8k memory. From then I moved on into bona fide computer word processing and found out that data was no longer the issue. Information had taken over and increased floor heights, air conditioning, false ceilings, raised floors, enormous risers and so on were everywhere. But now the problem was not communication so much as too much communication.

Nowadays electronic office equipment makes it so easy to send a message that everyone, from rocket scientists to checkout persons, has to be taught to restrain their urge to communicate. Even then the emerging scale of the problem suggests that such education may be useless. According to a study carried out five years ago by American office equipment manufacturer Pitney Bowes, the average office worker now deals with 190 messages a day in the form of 52 telephone calls, 48 emails, 22 voice mails, 21 letters, 15 faxes, 11 post-it stickers, 10 telephone messages, four written notes, four overnight delivery packages and three cellular telephone calls.

Pitney Bowes describes this avalanche of distraction as "highly disruptive", but that is surely too circumspect. University of Chicago researcher Carstairs McKillop, in the throes of his own study of information overload, has no hesitation in going further; "We have all got used to thinking that the biggest threat to employment comes from automation", he says. "But the big threat to jobs now comes from non-task related information, and that is mushrooming. Hiring more people doesn't help because it simply generates more disruptive information. Unless something is done, nine to five as we know it will become untenable."

It's an ill wind...
2004

Last December an auspicious gathering took place at Kill Devil Hills, a large sandbank off the coast of North Carolina that is the hallowed spot where Orville and Wilbur Wright, two bicycle builders from Dayton, Ohio, made the first powered flight 100 years before, on 17 December 1903. Unfortunately, unlike this earlier occasion, all did not go well with the re-enactment that had been planned. A crowd of 1,000s, including President George W Bush, assorted astronauts and 'Right Stuff' jet pilots, had braved heavy rain to witness the centenary flight. This required the replica 1903 Wright 'Flyer' to stay in the air under the control of its pilot for 12 seconds and land not less than 120 feet away from its starting point, to match the original feat.

But alas this performance proved beyond it. The attempted flight was even postponed from the historically correct 10.45 am in hopes of better weather, but to no avail. When the 'Flyer' was finally released to run down its wooden rail and take to the air, its nose reared up and it fell back with one wing in a pool of water.

To say that this outcome disappointed everyone present would be an understatement, but perhaps least so for members of the small but Hydra-headed gang of naysaying protesters who have always claimed that the Wright Brothers were not the first to achieve controlled and sustained flight, or, if they were, they did not do it in 1903 but years later, by which time there were considerably more contenders whose claims would have to be considered in the light of the events of 1908 when the brothers had shipped a much improved version of the 'Flyer' to France to demonstrate its greater capabilities.

But if the naysayers were heartened by reports of the worrying limitations of the replica 1903 'Flyer'—apparently in pre-Centenary 'flight tests' it would only leave its launching plank against headwinds of 16 to 22 kilometres per hour. Less wind and it wouldn't unstick. More wind and it became impossible to control—they didn't say so loudly enough to shake the confidence of the most important ayesayer of all, President George W Bush. Clearly aware of the controversy, his speech, which he delivered before the abortive take off, was already in counterattack mode. He began by quoting from a 1903 leader in The New York Times as follows: "All attempts at flight are doomed to failure because to build a flying machine would require the combined and continuous efforts of mathematicians and mechanics from one million to 10 million years." After a pause he delivered the punch line —"As it turned out, the feat was performed only eight weeks after the editorial was written"—to prolonged laughter and applause as he made his way to his helicopter and left.

And left behind him the whole question of the ayes and the nays in more of a flux than ever. For 100 years before the episode of the non-flying replica 'Flyer', a professor at the Smithsonian Institution named Samuel Pierpont Langley, who was receiving funds from the United States War Department to develop his own experimental flying machine the 'Aerodrome', which he had catapulted 50 metres from a houseboat into a lake in October 1903, shortly before the Wright Brothers made their first flight. A contest of claims had ensued which ran on for nearly 20 years but was terminated abruptly when it was discovered that the 'Aerodrome' rebuilt by Langley's supporters in 1914 had been extensively altered from its 1903 iteration. At this Langley's funding was cut off and the Wright Brothers were vindicated.... Until 17 December 2003 perhaps?

The nine ages of transport

2004

Transport is such an amorphous term that we are often tempted to regard it as a fact of life, like death or taxes. This is a big mistake. Transport is a living mutating thing. It lives and breathes as we do and often, even when it appears to be stone dead, turns out to have metamorphosed into something else, even after hundreds of years of factitious service.

The first age of transport is exploration, because it is in the discovery of the otherness of other places that the idea of travelling from A to B is born.

The second age in the life of transport begins when the surveying or formalisation of the route from A to B and B back to A again has been accomplished. This applies whether the journey is made on foot, by car, by boat, by air, or any other way.

The third age of transport has arrived when infrastructure is drawn to the route to facilitate its operation and exploit its location. Typically distribution centres, tunnels, bridges, harbours, runways or pipelines come into this category, any structure that facilitates the carriage of passengers, goods and services between A and B.

The fourth age of transport comes with the multiplication of complementary feeder routes so that A to B and back again becomes enmeshed in the omni-directional network of other routes, existing or proposed.

The fifth age of transport comes with the beginning of saturation, when the passenger and cargo use of the route and the network it now serves has become so heavy that it threatens to become an obstacle to traffic, rather than a destination.

The sixth age of transport comes when this sheer 'M6ism' of A to B brings about a massive search for a solution and tolls are imposed. This so-called "Option C" solution soon leads to the additional imposition of an all-day congestion charge, which is raised until use of the A to B route has dropped to an acceptable level.

The seventh age of transport marks the beginning of its metamorphosis. Travellers now actively avoid the A to B route rather than seeking it out. Instead of being cited in tourist literature as a work of genius that inspires national pride, the route has become the butt of jokes. With the passage of time the state of maintenance of the route becomes a by-word for neglect.

This is the stage that approximates to the present level of road traffic management in the South East of the United Kingdom today.

The eighth age of transport continues the metamorphic process begun by the seventh. Avoidance of the route has now become a national pastime. There is increasing emphasis on microwave and satellite communication systems and telephone lines as means of conducting business in A to B land without actually going to either place. Finally, after an accident in which many people die, a Royal Commission is appointed to look into the whole matter. Sure enough in due course the principal recommendation of this body is that the A to B route be permanently closed and its function taken over by "new communications technology in place of movement". Asked to explain what this means, a government spokesman says; "It's like how letters became weightless when they were replaced by emails."

Thus the ninth age in the life of transport begins precisely when the medium loses its physical form and ephemeralises itself into an IMAX-quality image of B seen from A, and A seen from B.

This sort of remote command capability has been sought by the military ever since the Second World War—since when the technology has improved immeasurably. Use it and route A to B will actually work better 'closed' than it ever did open.

The myth of the urban future
2004

"In the country were neither means of being clothed nor fed. Mechanical appliances in agriculture had made one engineer the equivalent of thirty labourers, there were no efficient doctors for an emergency, there was no company for loneliness and no pursuits.... Instead there was a vision of city beyond city. Cities on Great Plains, cities beside great rivers, vast cities along the sea margin, cities girdled by snowy mountains.... Everywhere now through the city-set earth the same cosmopolitan social organisation prevailed and everywhere, from Pole to Equator, the whole world was civilized. The whole world dwelt in cities."

This extract is taken from the celebrated science fiction novel by HG Wells *The Sleeper Awakes*, a volume still admired for its insights into the causes and consequences of the future. First published in 1898 its action takes place 150 years later in 2048. Wells' concept of the British Empire in his distant future was of a civilisation of cities, advanced, globalised megastructures, ruled by a corrupt elite. The most striking element in this picture is the total urbanisation of the population, and the evacuation of the countryside that is its corollary. Wells' vision of 2048 is compelling, and remains so as is evidenced by its influence on science fiction films ranging from Fritz Lang's *Metropolis* to Ridley Scott's *Blade Runner*, that continues to this day. Its terrifying idea of the triumph of the megacity now has the status of a Holy Writ. No one can gainsay it, not even to say that it is not true, that Wells was wrong about cities. The myth of an inevitable triumph of the city has hoodwinked politicians, historians, and social commentators for more than a century.

Given the durability of the urban myth it is surprising how little attention has been paid to an almost synchronous anti-urban prediction. Only five years after the publication of *The Sleeper Awakes*, a very different and completely contradictory book was published in London. *Tube, Train, Tram and Car*, by Arthur Beavan, argued convincingly that the combined effect of these, then new, means of transport—coupled with the increasing distribution of electricity—would be to open up vast areas of previously inaccessible countryside for development by dramatically shrinking time and distance along all-weather corridors into and out of cities, thus giving birth to the commuter lifestyle that survives to this day.

Beavan sees the principal benefit of this coalition of new technologies as making slum clearance possible but he concedes that the creation of cheap rural building land further out is also a factor. He also foresees suburban railway stations becoming transport interchanges with large car parks for motorcar commuters.

But 100 years later, Beavan is forgotten while Wells' world of cities uncannily anticipates, not our present, but the urban future so extolled in *Towards an Urban Renaissance*, the 1999 report of the Urban Task Force chaired by Lord Rogers of Riverside. This report also fails to acknowledge the rise of private transport in the shape of the motorcar and thus misses out the greatest agent of land use change of the twentieth century, the motorcar and the disurbanising recolonisation of the countryside that it has brought about. Because it presents an essentially nineteenth century image of the city of the future, *Towards an Urban Renaissance* shares this blind spot with Wells. It shows us that despite more than 100 years of motoring and 50 years of motorway construction—all of which has encouraged dispersal and decentralisation in living and working patterns all over the world—our official vision of the future remains stubbornly urbanised and historicised, compact and densely populated.

Flying antiques
2004

Rebuilding old aircraft, I suppose, is no more reprehensible than restoring old buildings, and is certainly an activity just as susceptible to compromise, dilution and the laws of entropy as they might be applied to the authenticity of historical objects. Because these are profoundly interesting matters in many fields, from time to time I like to purchase a copy of *The Aeroplane* (motto "History in the Air"), to see how the eternal struggle between the fundamentalists, who insist on keeping their authentic vintage aircraft flying at air shows, and their opponents who favour a high-value, low-risk replica approach.

Apologists for the former group claim that in terms of spectator numbers air shows are the second biggest outdoor sport in the world. Apologists for the latter group can point to the worrying frequency of accidents involving vintage aircraft and the sheer scarcity of replacement wrecks to be restored. Nor is this all. Beyond these rather obvious weaknesses lies the prospect of absolute extinction because of a growing 'technology gap' between what are now considered vintage aircraft and what the 'cottage industry' level of aircraft restorer can be expected to undertake. A Soviet MIG 15 jet fighter of Korean War vintage, for example, would represent the limit of technical feasibility which is why there are V bomber static displays but no flying V bombers. Replacing the obsolete engines alone would present insuperable difficulties. Any former military aircraft classified as complex, which in effect means jet powered or post-Second World War, is unlikely to be airworthy and still flying in private hands for very much longer unless it has been extensively modified or fitted out with a new identity—a process that depends on the use of a 'works number'.

There is no equivalent to this gold standard proof of identification in the schedule of 'buildings at risk' simply because none is necessary. There are as many projects as there are architects, always were, and always will be, but when you are talking about aircraft, especially military aircraft, it is a poor machine indeed that cannot muster 100 examples manufactured, and many run to 2,000 or 3,000. And paradoxically these can be the rarest of all. So what does the aerial conservationist do? He or she gives up the search for a lost Messerschmitt in the Carpathian Mountains and heads for an air show in Texas, then to an air museum, and then to somewhere else where pilots and air groupies gather.

This time the object sought is a more manageable size. No more fruitless negotiating with Russian peasants over rumoured crash sites 60 years before, this time the handover is in an air conditioned bar in Rio de Janiero.
The prize is the original manufacturers 'Works Number' which is the be found on a small plate riveted somewhere appropriate. Having secured this prize the purchaser, either by the above method or by buying one at a high maintenance car boot sale, you so to speak 'own' the identity of the aircraft in question, whether it physically exists or not. Once you have a works number you can attach it to any aircraft of the same generic type and, more importantly, you can paint it in any authentic colour scheme that ensures you a fly-on part in the next big budget Second World War movie. When it comes to Messerschmitts an authentic works number opens the door to 5,000 aircraft of which 4,999 were no doubt destroyed years ago but with an identity plate the rest can even be cottage-industrialised back into life as a static display or a replica. Either way all is not what it seems in the world of aerial husbandry. It is a bit like switching the tax disc on a car.

Heavy bottles for a picnic

2004

Last term at my son's school his year did a project on Victorians. The net was broadcast like that in order to admit almost anything that could be described as Victorian dress, or sung to the words of a Victorian song, or wielded like a Victorian scythe. Beyond that there was little I could contribute to the project except to calm an ashen faced victim when he returned from a museum visit with a grim tale of how children had been sent down the mines in the century before he was born.

I was thinking about that side of Victorian life when something struck me. Perhaps child labour was not really explained by anything to do with the exploitation of children but was simply an early example of value engineering; a way of obtaining the minimum sized labour unit for the task, as in the case of boy chimney sweeps and cabin boys. Clearly this line of thought could not be presented to the rest of Year Three in the cheerful tones of their form teacher, but it could be used to reveal some of the similarities and differences between ancient and modern that would otherwise be lost in the tide of Morris dancing with balloons that was already taking the lead. Take for instance the evolution of the sailing ship which started the nineteenth century as a 100 tonne vessel with a crew of 50 and ended it as a ship with a displacement of 2,000 tonnes and a crew of ten. Was this not value engineering at work, and ephemeralisation—doing more with less —for that matter? The Victorian age was the age of ephemeralisation to an extent and with a speed that seems entirely beyond our powers today when our imitation of the Victorian consists of little more than the production of common goods with luxury trappings.

And yet there is a similarity. Glaring down on my desk for the last 20 years has been a Codd bottle, a glass container for drinks like lemonade and ginger beer that date from the Victorian age. Patented in England in 1886 by Hiram J Codd, this all-glass bottle was resealing and reusable and remained in popular use well into the 1920s. The Codd bottle could be charged with a carbonated drink protected from leakage by a captive glass marble running in a groove to affect a seal except when held back by gas pressure.

Looked at through contemporary eyes the Victorian Codd bottle still has much to recommend it. It is made of only one material, recyclable glass, which is made from sand, and is thus cheap and limitlessly available. It is also reusable and manufactured in standard sizes, one of which, either by chance or by international standardisation, is 330 ml—almost exactly equal to the present day 333 ml all-aluminium Coca-Cola multi-pack can. Here for sure is a comparison that will show an example of Victorian superiority.

But does it? The glass bottle is easily smashed (and each bottle contains its own motive for this in the shape of the glass marble inside it). But far more important than breakage is the simple question of weight. Empty, a Victorian Codd bottle tips the scales at 594 grams; filled, its weight rises to 910 grams but 316 grams of that difference is the weight of solid glass. In the case of the contemporary multi-pack aluminium can, the difference is shattering. The empty can weighs less than 0.5 grams, the full can 316 grams. The benefits of ephemeralisation are drastic when applied to the Codd. As a teacher remarked after translating grams into tonnes: "No wonder they needed a coach and four just to go on a picnic."

The strange world of luxury watches
2004

As I have observed on this page in years past, a sure sign of the approach of Christmas is a massive increase in advertising for luxury goods. Jewellery, expensive clothes and country houses vie with exotic cars and watches. As if by magic, Porsche becomes the most profitable motor manufacturer in the world, and Ferrari the only non-ailing branch of the Fiat Empire. But fabulously expensive timepieces are the real technological snowdrops, and they live in a world of their own. Posh cars may still have to be taxed and insured like ordinary cars, and expensive houses may still leak water when it rains, but costly watches lead a charmed life. Even the freakish ones that are certified capable of enduring desert heat, arctic cold and the pressure of the ocean floor seldom take a journey longer than the one from the wall safe to the box at the opera and back again. Yet despite this exclusivity their economic performance exceeds that of any other techno-bauble by a huge margin. Why this should be I do not know. But I do know that it is not because of a global scarcity of watches. You can find perfectly usable Chinese watches in the goody-bags your children bring home from birthday parties that cost practically nothing, but these are not luxury goods. They don't have magic powers.

Not like the Seiko "Sportura kinetic chronograph" for example, which is described in advertisements as being "powered by the movement of your own body, no batteries to change". This wristwatch comes with its own propaganda message which, it must be admitted, loses something in the translation from the original Japanese. "It's not your clothes. It's not your handwriting. It's not your TV shows. It's your *watch* that tells most about who you are."

Or it used to be. Now, as a result of the inscrutability of popular attitudes to the charismatic power of costly watches—which are, after all the nearest to a piece of genuine nanotechnology that most of us will ever come to —luxury watchmakers today are living lives of quiet desperation when it comes to promoting their product.

For years there was only one kind of luxury watch advertisement. You would find it in the solus spot in the bottom right hand corner of the front page of every broadsheet newspaper in the country. But now that broadsheets are fast disappearing something different is needed and the watchmasters are all looking for it. The universal picture of a watch except for Patek

Philippe ads, which also showed a picture of the small child who would inherit your watch when you die, all the other watchmakers were torn between boasting about their space age chronometric technology, and trying to glue it to their earlier boastings about ancient traditions of craftsmanship. They are doing this either by larding their advertisements with background images of jet fighters and pilots (Breitling), or by depicting a watch with four dials or six dials. Others less imaginatively lay as much emphasis on the leather strap as the watch itself (A Lange & Sohne), or throw technology to the winds and come up with an antique face and a barefaced claim of extraordinary longevity. Well placed at the time of writing were Omega (in business for 150 years) and Ulysse Nardin (156 years), but both topped by the unsinkable Breguet, which claims to have been in the luxury watch making game since 1775—before the Declaration of Independence let alone the French Revolution.

Meanwhile, alone in their palatial underground workshops the luxury watchmakers of Switzerland churn out the same seductive images of chunky manacle-type watches programmed to tell the time with split-second accuracy until the year 2200, when their batteries finally run out.

The young dig in their heels
2005

The worst thing about the future, said a young friend of mine, is that it's so boring. It's always on television and if you miss that it's in the Sunday newspapers. What's really interesting is the past. The guys just can't get enough of it. Everyone I know is obsessed with shooting radar into the ground to find old tombs, digging up plague pits, reconstructing Roman cities, X-raying skulls, counting teeth....

A typical young person's view, I thought. When you get a bit older, I replied, you'll find yourself much more interested in the future. That's when you'll find out that the future is entirely created by old people. They didn't send teenagers into space first you know. The astronauts were middle aged and even the monkeys were old.

Where did that idea come from?

Well, whatever happens, happens first in America. In architecture everything worth a light from Frank Lloyd Wright to Frank Gehry has come from America. The best Archigram ideas like computer city, the cushicle and the suitaloon came from America via NASA and the space race.

So. What's that got to do with old people?

In America today an entirely new kind of society is creating itself with its own system of housing, its own system of communications and its own corporate backing. And everybody in it is over 60 and single.

Sounds like a cult to me.

Well, maybe. But on the other hand maybe not. Have you ever heard of Slab City?

No.

It's an abandoned military base in California right on top of the San Andreas Fault. A place where people who live on the road take a break. Not just a few drifters but 1,000s of senior citizens who cruise the American West from the deserts in the South in the winter, to the forests of the Pacific Northwest in the summer. They just follow the seasons.

That doesn't sound very futuristic to me. Americans have been doing that for years, in the 60s they called them snowbirds.

A few have been doing it for years, but now the numbers are doubling every decade. There's reckoned to be well over a million now. The increase in early retirement, advances in geriatric medicine, new motor home technologies, all of that is making it easier and easier to have no fixed abode.

American motor homes are not like our poky caravans you know, they can be more like mobile condominiums. The whole phenomenon is like a real life Archigram, all of it, except that everyone's old. They are the pioneers. 'Listen to the old' was the slogan of Dr David Suzuki, the Canadian doyen of West Coast anthropologists. "Listen to the old", he used to say, "They know what's going to happen to you." Before moving pictures and recorded sound the memories of the old were immense reservoirs of collective wisdom.

Just a minute. What was that you said about corporate backing, where's the corporate backing for these aged pioneers?

It's been in all the papers. I'm surprised you missed it. Last year the Sony Corporation decided that its future lay in linking consumers to services through television, computers and mobile phones. Sony isn't a manufacturer of consumer electronics any more, it's a provider of digital network services to what it calls a "network-centric world".

Which means?

Which means that nobody will need to be in one place any more. Everybody will be given a telephone number at birth. Nobody will actually have to live anywhere. Worldwide, they will be able to live everywhere.

And old people think that's a good idea do they?

Listen to the old my boy! Remember, they are the ones who know what's going to happen next.

How total urbanism will come to grief
2005

There is a pattern to all totalitarianism, whether of the Left or the Right, and you can recognise it immediately. It starts when the same goal is endorsed by everyone. To be topical let's say it's something called "Total Urbanism". What about total overcrowding, you object. Nonsense you are told, for that we'll double all densities and forthwith! Short shrift at the hands of these zealots then and the planners are even quicker off the mark, opening the floodgates on every infill site in town. Suddenly Opera Houses, Art Galleries, Hotels and Museums become fabulously important. The words "Culture", "Vibrant", "Regeneration", and "Sustainability" will ricochet around the academies like bullets in a shootout and pretty soon every project will be deemed worthy of a prize.

Stage two in the development of totalitarianism occurs when the 'proof' kicks in. That's when it turns out that 'urban researchers' have discovered that free people in a democratic society always gravitate towards urban life. From Ur of the Chaldees to Milton Keynes, rural man has always yearned for a life below decks packed like a sardine into a terrifying municipality as notorious as the *Titanic*.

Up to this point, opposition to the pro-city band wagon has been encouraged—for target practice naturally—but also to help the urban crusaders get yet more money for yet another bureaucratic layer, yet more consultants and advisors to ensure that everything is of course "of good quality", or at worst "of world class". For now a lack of money is becoming a burden. Despite the apparently unstoppable tide of world urbanisation found by earlier researchers, time is beginning to take its toll ("What? Five years already and nothing done!"). The gang of urban promoters gets together again and decides the city needs encouragement of a different kind. From now on it's no more mister nice guy. If mankind's great urban dream doesn't net them another three billion pounds, well then... well.... There won't be any urban revolution after all, only unspeakable suburbanisation everywhere.

Which, of course, is correct, because what is trying to happen in the city today is a counter revolution, not a revolution. If it were otherwise we should not see flats and houses priced far above what salaried workers can afford, nor find standing room only on unreliable commuter trains with runs of more than one hour or more. Such indicators do have an effect, it is true, but it is not to increase the appeal of the sidewalk cafes, remorselessly increasing traffic, and copious pedestrian areas. Instead these and other pressures join the great push for decentralisation that began with Victorian public health measures, enlisted the aid of the railway boom, gained irresistible strength from the fear of bombing in two world wars, and attained its greatest success in the decades of planning for dispersed development that followed them.

No matter how much money is thrown away in pursuit of the mythological metropolis of the future, it can never overcome the centrifugal force of the evolution of technology nor the will of individuals to live where they wish and at a reasonable distance from one another. Examples from many fields prove this. The animal sciences show us that, in our version of intra-species aggression, territorial dispersal is the only way to avoid conflict. In the same way, the information technology revolution of the twentieth century legitimises the resultant dispersal by rendering most face to face encounters unnecessary. These truly are powerful forces whose resultant changes will not be easily reversed.

The answer to a historical conundrum
2005

As a student of history I have always been fascinated by my own period
—by which I, of course, I do not mean my own place in history, but the
events that took place around the year of my birth, which for the purposes
of this reminiscence will remain at an authentic 1938. This year, more than
any other prior to the bombing of Hiroshima seven years later, must have
gone straight to the top of the class for Saturday afternoon quarterbacking.
Besides, who would ever want to dissociate themselves from such a dramatic
year whose political matrix remains the subject of heated debate among
academic historians to this day? In Europe it takes in the implementation
of the reunification of Germany and Austria, and Neville Chamberlain's
"Peace in our Time" deal with Hitler over the break-up of Czechoslovakia.
All these consequences of the Treaty of Versailles either came to a head
in 1938 or, like the Winter War between the Russians and the Finns, or the
start of the Second World War itself in 1939, were clearly foreshadowed
by the general European mobilisation in the previous year.

This is the sort of response you would expect to a query about the year
1938, but there is another way of looking at the contribution of one year to
a longer historical progress. Thus against the oft-repeated tale of the Munich
agreement, wrought by hapless and corrupt politicians as well as obsolete
and deluded military men, there is a ready substitute to replace the
lamentable democratic tendency to fight the last war over again instead
of searching for the key to winning the next one.

How was it that as early as 1938 a defeated country like Germany,
completely lacking in petroleum, with its iron ore reserves confiscated
by the Treaty of Versailles, with no nickel, no tungsten, zinc, lead or copper,
and perhaps most surprising of all, no government planning framework
to undertake the huge task of remedying this state of unpreparedness.

The answer was of course not solely an economic one: it lay in part with
the militaristic nature of the Nazi regime and its paymasters. But even more
fundamentally it depended upon the scientific and technological
infrastructure bequeathed to the Nazis by the world famous Imperial regime
they had ousted in 1933. Led by its peerless chemical industry from the latter
part of the nineteenth century German science and scientific research led the
world. First the Chemist Karl von Linde succeeded in liquefying air and
turning it into a raw material. Then came Fritz Haber's synthesising

ammonia from nitrogen, a discovery that solved the shortage of nitrates for fertilizer and explosives to such an extent that by 1938 German factories were synthesising six times as much fertilizer from the air as had been imported from the cliffs of Chile in 1914. Air liquefaction was later developed as a source of rare gases, which like argon, neon and xenon, revolutionised the lighting industry. Alchemical achievements like these were readily translated into their military equivalents and then fed into the industries most directly concerned. But while her science and technology alone made Germany the most technologically advanced country in the world by 1938, they played a no less important role in converting the country into the most energy efficient as well. This process of radically mobilising the entire population that took place under the aegis of an organisation called—*Verwertung des Wertlosen* —"Finding uses for the Useless". This outfit rode on the back of a handbook of the same title with an introduction by Reichskomissar Herman Goering and a translation into English was published in London in 1944 under the title *Science and Salvage*. This book thus becomes, in all probability, the first serious attempt in modern times to codify and organise the available data on recycling and waste processing.

With the passage of time it has become increasingly obvious that much can be learned from a study of the performance of the losing side in the Second World War if we wish to understand one pattern of breakdown —where an energy-starved but technologically sophisticated nation went down with its blast furnaces glowing and its production lines moving to the very end. Short of that point there are also organisational, if no longer technical, lessons in the extent to which the Germans did achieve great economies and material substitutions, bizarre contrasts between the futuristic and the ancient, as when cart horses towed jet fighters to runways and autobahn filling stations sold wooden logs instead of petrol.

The biggest house sale in history
2005

In 1940 when this dear offshore island of ours was in even greater danger from continental Europe than some think it still is today, with German tanks already lining the cliff tops of Northern France, and the French government in flight from Paris and drafting surrender documents, the British prime minister devised a mammoth gesture intended to keep France in the war at all cost. In the event, the measure Winston Churchill proposed was dramatic but also impossible, for it offered the French people equal citizenship with Britain, which is something like France giving Germany to Argentina. Actually such propositions are not quite as rare as one might suppose. Unusual but not unprecedented, might be a better descriptor.

Such measures became part and parcel of the unsatisfactory settlement of the treaties of Versailles and Saint-Germain that brought an end to the great war of 1914–1918, for as part of the Peace Settlement of 1919–1920 most of the states of Central and Eastern Europe were required to sign treaties or make declarations ensuring that their racial minorities would receive equal treatment under the law. These rights were guaranteed by the League of Nations, which conspicuously failed to uphold them 20 years later.

About 100 years before that reorganisation of a continent came the Louisiana Purchase, the biggest land sale in history wherein the United States of America purchased from Napoleon Bonaparte's France the whole of the Mississippi Valley up to the Rocky Mountains, an area of 830,000 square miles acquired at a cost of only 15 million US Dollars in 1803. Another 60 years passed before another historical anomaly came along. On this occasion the government of Imperial Russia was eager to sell and the United States government was eager to buy. By 1867 a deal had been worked out and Alaska had changed hands for four million US dollars. Then the most recent standoff, the United States versus Canada in the matter of another border dispute, which was resolved in 1903 by means of neutral adjudication, the Canadian government opened its cheque book and finally settled a long standing border dispute over Alaska at a Territorial level.

Now I am sure we all understand that this is merely speculation, all the figures are round numbers, surnames only and so on, but the point is that wherever huge numbers of anything are concerned money will come tumbling after. Thus if it was possible to buy 8,300 square miles of prime virgin plantation in the deep south of the United States in 1803, then it would be reasonable to expect to have to pay at least double the same sum to make the same transaction 100 years later, and probably three times as much after 300 years. The difficulty would be, of course, to find a responsible client body, eager to make such a transaction, human mortality being what it is, on such uncertain terms. Meanwhile, we have to make do with leaseholds of 999 years (already challengeable at law), freeholds that are borrowings in all but name; five pound meals in a million restaurants; an improbable estimate of 67 million credit cards in circulation, the grand total adding up to a much quoted one trillion pounds, the bulk of it consisting of mortgage and credit card transactions.

So what can be done? Nothing could be simpler, but first we must divest ourselves of any reliance upon the remedies (chiefly do nothing), offered by all the Parties and rely on history instead. For example: the history of mass population movements in the twentieth century. Or why not spread our net a little wider.... Why not see what the going price is for equal citizenship with France is on the Bourse.

Ludwig Mies van der Rohe, Farnsworth House, Plano, USA, 1948

Granada service station at Heston on the M4, England, 1988

Notes

The Time House

[1] This parallel was developed by Robert Boguslaw into a book entitled *The New Utopians. A study of system design and social change*, New Jersey: Prentice-Hall, 1965.

[2] Rosenberg, Harold, *The Tradition of the New*, New York: McGraw-Hill, 1965, Chapter 19, "The Orgamerican Phantasy".

[3] This does not seem too unfair a description of the concept Banham originated in his "A Home is not a House", *Art in America*, April 1965.

[4] Banham, Reyner, *Folkestone Conference of Experimental Architecture*, June 1966.

[5] The celebrated experiments with Planarian worms carried out between 1958 and 1961 by JB Best and I Rubinstein in Washington. Quoted in Ardrey, Robert, *The Territorial Imperative*, London: Collins, 1967.

[6] Goffman, Erving, *Asylums: Essays on the social situation of mental patients and other inmates*, New York: Doubleday Anchor, 1961.

[7] Searles, Harold F, *The Nonhuman Environment*, New York: International Universities Press, 1960.

[8] Kelly, Burnham, *The Prefabrication of Houses*, London: Chapman & Hall, 1951.

[9] Habraken, NJ, *De Dragers en de Mensen (Frameworks for Living)*, Amsterdam: Scheltema & Holkema Ltd, 1961.

[10] Kubler, George, *The Shape of Time*, New York: Yale University Press, 1962.

[11] Kubler, George, *The Shape of Time*, New York: Yale University Press, 1962.

[12] Kubler, George, *The Shape of Time*, New York: Yale University Press, 1962.

A new kind of message in a bottle

[1] Fitzgerald, Frances, *The Fire in the Lake: Vietnamese and the Americans in Vietnam*, London: Macmillan, 1973.

My lovely student life

[1] University Grants Committee, "Enquiry into students' progress", *RIBA Journal*, 1968.

Two triumphs of twisted wire

[1] The name 'Jacintosh' was compounded from Jack Tramiel (the president of Atari computers) and the Apple name 'Macintosh'.

[2] The author was told by a partner at Palmer & Turner that the escape refuges which Foster used to articulate his building were "advisory" rather than "mandatory" elements in the Hong Kong fire codes applicable to the bank.

Technology transfer

[1] Barbara Miller Lane (*Architecture and Politics in Germany: 1918 to 1945*, Cambridge, MA: Harvard University Press, 1968) quotes Walter Gropius in 1919: "The old forms are in ruins, the benumbed world is shaken up, the old human spirit is invalidated and in a flux towards a new form." Conrads and Sperlich (*Fantastic Architecture*, London: Architectural Press, 1963) quote Bruno Taut in the first issue of the magazine *Dawn* in 1920: "Space. Homeland. Style. To hell with them, odious concepts! Destroy them, break them up! Nothing shall remain! Break up your academies, spew out the old fogeys.... Let our North wind blow through this musty, threadbare tattered world."
Anatole Kopp (*Constructivist Architecture in the USSR*, London: Academy Editions, 1985) provides similar quotations from the Russian Constructivists.

[2] Fry, E Maxwell, *Fine Building*, London: Faber and Faber, 1944.

[3] "Industrialisation of the process of construction is a question of new materials.... Our technologists must and will succeed in inventing materials that can be industrially manufactured and processed and that will be weatherproof, soundproof and insulating. I am convinced that traditional methods of building will disappear." Mies van der Rohe, G, No. 3, 1924. Or in a later version: "It will soon be possible to break altogether with the tradition of putting stone on stone or brick on brick and move in the direction of rational fabrication." Bernal, JD, *The Social Function of Science*, London: George Routledge & Sons Ltd, 1939 (quoted in Saint, Andrew, *Towards a Social Architecture*, New Haven: Yale University Press, 1987). As late as 1962, Herbert Ohl, the German expert on industrialised building, wrote: "The artistic and formal interests of the last hundred years have taken the task of the architect away from productivity, in spite of all attempts to rescue him.... The architect must realise that the machines, processes and appropriate materials of

industry are the effective means for the production of buildings."
Architectural Design, April 1962, p. 162.

4 I have twice witnessed this process at work when Berthold Lubetkin
addressed groups of younger architects in 1985 and 1986. Many of the
questions put to him take the form: "But surely if you were in practice
now, you would behave as we do and not be as intransigent as you were
then?" To his credit, Lubetkin never concedes this point.

5 "The outside of a house should be dictated by the inside, as the form of the
animal body is dictated by the skeleton, the disposition of the organs and
the functioning of the various systems—blood circulation, nervous and
muscular systems and so on... communications, drainage, services and
so on." (Bertram, Anthony, *The House: a machine for living in*, London:
A&C Black, 1935.) There are more famous examples of such clarity of
thought in the oeuvre of Le Corbusier, and earlier ones in Loos, but
Bertram is particularly robust, mocking the occupants of 'Tudorbethan'
dwellings by demanding to know why they do not wear doublet and
hose etc..

6 I am indebted to Richard Horden for this example.

7 Banham, Reyner, *Theory and Design in the First Machine Age*, London:
Architectural Press, 1961.

8 Quoted in *Theory and Design*, pp. 325 & 326. A similar thought can be
discerned in a quote from Edwin Lutyens dating from seven years earlier
still: "The modern architecture of so-called functionalism does not seem
to me to... show yet a genuine sense of style—a style rooted in feeling
for the right use of materials." (*Country Life*, 20 June 1931.)

9 Quoted in *The Buckminster Fuller Reader*, ed. Meller, James, London:
Jonathan Cape, 1970.

10 Schon, Donald, *The Reflective Practitioner: how professionals think in action*,
London: Temple Smith, 1983.

11 Rand, Ayn, *The Fountainhead*, New York: Bobbs-Merrill, 1943. An exhaustive
study of the relationship between Rand's hero and stylistic rationality is to
be found in Andrew Saint's *The Image of the Architect*, New Haven:
Yale University Press, 1983.

12 The repeated appearance of the Farman 'Goliath' in *Vers une Architecture*
is a case in point. Le Corbusier made no effort to employ the materials

and methods of contemporary aircraft construction, but he did emulate the appearance of wing struts seen obliquely—using them as columns —and the visual relationship of planes to solids—as with wings and fuselage. The ability to see complex structures in this formal, analytical way may be uniquely architectural. The engineer Peter Rice has described it as "A fine visual appreciation of the way the engineer's design is perceived. (The architect) refines the form in relation to an image so that ultimately it is explainable at a simpler level." One of the very few direct technical influences of the aircraft industry on construction in Britain during the Modern period came from the Great War airship programme, when the task of solving the large number of simultaneous equations generated by segmented circular space frames led to the development of new methods of calculation for lattice girders. Southwell, Richard, *Methods of Calculating Tension Coefficients*, London, 1920. The direct copying of American industrial building by the European pioneers is discussed in detail by Reyner Banham in *A Concrete Atlantis*, Cambridge, MA: MIT Press, 1986.

[13] For a discussion of the obsolescence of the Lloyd's building see Martin Pawley, "Into the Unknown", *The Architectural Review*, October 1986, p. 88.

[14] The Peter Rice quote is from a profile of the engineer published in *The Architects' Journal*, 21 & 28 December 1983. The Michael Hopkins quote from *Building*, 8 November 1985. The concept of technology transfer as a limited, non-intellectual, non-creative approach to design emerged in conversation with Norman Foster during 1985. The term 'redneck' to describe it was contributed by *The Architectural Review* editor Peter Davey.

[15] The 1985 'Grand Buildings' competition brief called for a minimum gross floor area of 18,000 m^2 within the framework of plot ratio, daylight angles and fire regulations governing the site. Future Systems' design provided 23,000 m^2 gross with a remarkable 89 per cent, 20,500 m^2 net lettable. In addition, the repositioning of the suspended floors within the envelope offered unprecedented flexibility—of a type crucially relevant to designs like Lloyd's.

[16] Bowley, Marian, *Innovations in Building Materials*, London: Duckworth, 1960.

[17] The exhibition of a rowing boat made of concrete reinforced with a rectangular mesh of iron rods at the Paris Exposition Universelle

of 1855 is recorded by SB Hamilton (*A Note on the History of Reinforced Concrete in Buildings*, London: HMSO, 1956) as antedating the first reinforced-concrete building by ten years, and the first large-scale use of reinforced concrete for building by 40 years.

A precedent for the Prince

1 A partial list compiled by the author in 1988 included: trade with Australia, homeopathic medicine, inner city aid, marine archaeology, dyslexia, AIDS, the German Officer Corps and the Luftwaffe, adventure training, business efficiency and sex and violence on television.

2 *The Sunday Express*, 30 October 1988. These were among the results of a poll carried out by Telephone Surveys Limited among 1,000 adults throughout the country following the showing of Prince Charles' television film *A Vision of Britain*.

3 *The Sunday Times*, 24 September 1989. These were among the results of a poll carried out by Market Opinion and Research International among 2,009 adults in 147 constituency sampling points in Great Britain. Data were weighted to match the population profile.

4 A number of these 'pledges of allegiance' occurred at an Urban Design Group meeting held in May 1988. The event was reported under the headline "HRH No Charlie, Architects Assert" in *The Architects' Journal*, 18 May 1988.

5 Leon Krier in conversation with the author, 12 August 1989.

6 Peter Ahrends, of Ahrends Burton Koralek spoke of a collapse of commissions in the aftermath of the 'Carbuncle' speech and the abandonment of the National Gallery extension project. Richard Rogers and Norman Foster both have more work overseas than in this country and have both been denied major London commissions since 1984. Arup Associates' Paternoster project has been attacked by the Prince —"like putting St Paul's in a prison camp"—and is, at the time of writing, likely to be aborted as a result of the resale of the development site. There is a strong possibility that any new consortium will employ Leon Krier as planner and John Simpson—designer of a surprisingly well-financed 'alternative' scheme that has been under development for nearly two years—as architect for the project instead. Large numbers of 'topless'

Modern houses and maisonettes all over the country have been retrofitted with pitched roofs since 1975, notably Norman Foster's 'Bean Hill' estate at Milton Keynes. The Arup Associates Plessey superconductor factory at Roborough near Plymouth, described by the Prince in 1987 as "looking like a high-tech version of a Victorian prison", has since been repainted grey and surrounded with earthworks planted with trees to conceal it from view. The Skipton Building Society headquarters at Skipton, criticised by Prince Charles as "obtrusive", is to be demolished and rebuilt even though it is less than 20 years old.

[7] 'Fifth Columnist', Astragal, The Architects' Journal, 20 September 1989.

[8] This outburst embodies the one perception that the Prince has brought to all the fields that have engaged his attention. On 15 September 1988, for example, he rounded on an audience of TV and film dignitaries at the opening of the Museum of the Moving Image in London with, "It is palpable nonsense to say that violence on TV has no effect on people's behaviour. The people who say this are so-called experts who attempt to confuse ordinary people so they feel they do not know what they are talking about!" The same sentiment was expressed by George Bernard Shaw in his play A Doctor's Dilemma in which the line "All professions are conspiracies against the laity" appears. The Soviet dictator Josef Stalin, too, had his own version, according to Berthold Lubetkin's RIBA President's First Invitation Lecture delivered on 11 June 1985. Stalin said in 1935, "The assumption that the specialist knows better drags theory and practice into the bog of reactionary cosmopolitan opinion."

[9] Hitler, Adolf, Mein Kampf, unabridged translation by the New York New School for Social Research, Boston: Houghton Mifflin, 1939, p. 360.

[10] Quoted in Elaine Hochman, Architects of Fortune, New York: Weidenfeld & Nicolson, 1989, p. 236. The idea is of course not "impossible" at all in architecture. 20 years before Hitler made his remark, Paul Scheerbart wrote: "If we want our culture to rise to a higher level, we are obliged, for better or for worse, to change our architecture. And this only becomes possible if we take away the closed character from the rooms in which we live. We can only do that by introducing glass architecture, which lets in the light of the sun, the moon, and the stars, not merely through a few windows, but through every possible wall, which will be made entirely of

glass." Scheerbart, Paul, *Glass Architecture*, ed. Dennis Sharp, London: November Books, 1972.

[11] HRH The Prince of Wales, *A Vision of Britain*, London: Doubleday, 1989, p. 9.

[12] HRH The Prince of Wales, *A Vision of Britain*, London: Doubleday, 1989. pp. 55–58.

[13] Hitler, Adolf, *Mein Kampf*, unabridged translation by the New York New School for Social Research, Boston: Houghton Mifflin, 1939, p. 363.

[14] Miller Lane, Barbara, *Architecture and Politics in Germany 1918–1945*, Cambridge, MA: Harvard University Press, 1969, p. 247, n. 31.

[15] Miller Lane, Barbara, *Architecture and Politics in Germany 1918–1945*, Cambridge, MA: Harvard University Press, 1969, p. 254, n. 81.

[16] Hochman, Elaine, *Architects of Fortune*, New York: Weidenfeld & Nicolson, 1989, p. 75.

[17] HRH The Prince of Wales, *A Vision of Britain*, London: Doubleday, 1989, p. 10.

[18] Coleman, Alice, *Utopia on Trial*, London: Hilary Shipman, 1985, p. 184.

[19] Quoted in Hochman, Elaine, *Architects of Fortune*, New York: Weidenfeld & Nicolson, 1989, p. 265.

[20] Elaine Hochman (*Architects of Fortune*, New York: Weidenfeld & Nicolson, 1989) notes that of 37 German nationals associated with the Bauhaus before 1933, 12 emigrated, two were jailed and 23 remained in Germany.

Sources

001 "The Time House"
     Architectural Design, September 1968
002 "Looking for a sound"
     Architectural Design, May 1969
003 "Meeting Buckminster Fuller"
     Building Design, 6 March 1970
004 "A new kind of message in a bottle"
     Extract from *Garbage Housing*, 1975
005 "My lovely student life"
     *A Continuing Experiment: learning and teaching at the
     Architectural Association*, 1975
006 "We shall not bulldoze Westminster Abbey:
     Archigram and the retreat from technology"
     Oppositions, Winter 1976
007 "Thoughts on the design of houses and banknotes"
     Skyline, March 1978
008 "This England—coming home"
     RIBA Journal, November 1980
009 "What does vernacular really mean?"
     RIBA Journal, August 1981
010 "The defence of modern architecture"
     RIBA Journal, May 1983
011 "Sex, violence and design"
     Blueprint, November 1983
012 "Self-build workstations: a partial history"
     The Architectural Review, November 1983
013 "Norman Foster 6.0, 6.0, 6.0"
     Blueprint, May 1984
014 "Building revisits: Coventry Cathedral"
     The Architects' Journal, 9 May 1984
015 "Building rcvisits: Hunstanton School"
     The Architects' Journal, 23 May 1984
016 "The most important building of the twentieth century"
     The Guardian, 3 December 1984

017 "Heavy stuff this symbolism"
     The Guardian, 17 December 1984
018 "Beyond messing about in boats"
     The Architects' Journal, 19 & 26 December 1984
019 "Office design in Eternia"
     RIBA Journal, May 1985
020 "Quinlan Terry: beyond the tantrums of Modernism
     The Guardian, 1 May 1985
021 "Plucky Jim"
     Blueprint, July/August 1985
022 "Doubts about Lloyd's"
     The Guardian, 30 June 1986
023 "Two triumphs of twisted wire"
     The Architects' Journal, 22 October 1986
024 "Dan Dare: an extremely small step for mankind"
     Blueprint, December/January 1986
025 "Welcome to the house of fun"
     Blueprint, October 1986
026 "A winter school"s tale"
     RIBA Journal, March 1987
027 "Objects of our time: the Piccadilly Line train"
     The Architects' Journal, 15 April 1987
028 "Tower blocks and tourist castles"
     The Architect, July 1987
029 "Technology transfer"
     The Architectural Review, September 1987
030 "The secret life of the engineers"
     Blueprint, March 1989
031 "Life in the urban war zone", (extract from *Theory and Design in the
     Second Machine Age*), *Blueprint*, October 1989
032 "Lost arks of the air"
     Blueprint, April 1989
033 "Dymaxion: the car that never flew"
     Blueprint, September 1989

034 "Is ecology all hot air?"
     Building, 17 August 1990
035 "A precedent for the Prince"
     The Architectural Review, January 1990
036 "The footmen of Alexandra Road"
     RIBA Journal, January 1990
037 "The best lecture I ever gave"
     Blueprint, June 1990
038 "In pursuit of the ultimate driving machine"
     Blueprint, August 1990
039 "Exogenous shock"
     The Architectural Review, September 1990
040 "Where the Big Sheds are"
     Blueprint, November 1990
041 "Notes on the meaning of trivial things"
     Blueprint, Dec 1990/Jan 1991
042 "The design origins of royal train syndrome"
     Blueprint, February 1991
043 "High-Tech architecture: history versus the parasites"
     AA Files No. 21, Spring 1991
044 "The cost of the new culture of cities"
     Blueprint, March 1991
045 "Henry Ford and the biospherans"
     Blueprint, April 1991
046 "What London learned from Las Vegas"
     Blueprint, May 1991
047 What's in a name?
     RIBA Journal, July 1991
048 "Stansted and the triumph of Big Sheds"
     A+U, October 1991
049 "And you thought your car was good for nothing"
     Building, 27 March 1992
050 "Nigel Coates: from nihilist to planner"
     Blueprint, May 1992

051 "Frank Gehry: a full and frank talk"
Blueprint, July/August 1992

052 "The case for uncreative architecture"
Architectural Record, December 1992

053 "Lunch with Leon Krier"
Blueprint, December/January 1992

054 "Zaha escapes the pull of gravity"
Blueprint, February 1993

055 "Tales of the obsolescent"
Blueprint, September 1993

056 "Invasion of the body snatchers"
The Architects' Journal, 2 March 1995

057 "Invasion of the vibrators"
The Architects' Journal, 29 February 1996

058 "Frank Lloyd Wright fights for his life"
The Architects' Journal, 14 March 1996

059 "The rise of the engineer"
World Architecture 45, April 1996

060 "After postmodernism, terrorism"
World Architecture 47, June 1996

061 "Meeting the future everywhere"
The Architects' Journal, 13 March 1997

062 "From here to modernity"
The Architects' Journal, 20 March 1997

063 "Seat pocket aliens"
The Architects' Journal, 29 May 1997

064 "The myth of monumentality"
World Architecture 54, 1997

065 "So long recycling, here comes secondary use"
The Architects' Journal, 31 July/7 August 1997

066 "A night to remember"
The Architects' Journal, 8 January 1998

067 "Terminal architecture"
Architectural Design, February 1998

068 "The strange death of architectural criticism"
The Architects' Journal, 2 July 1998

069 "When air conditioning meets its match"
The Architects' Journal, 22 July 1999

070 "A brace of fins du siècles"
The Architects' Journal, 21 October 1999

071 "The new life of Albert Speer"
The Architects' Journal, 13 July 2000

072 "Here comes the age of immobility"
The Architects' Journal, 31 August 2000

073 "America: it's 24–7 at mission critical"
The Architects' Journal, 8 February 2001

074 "Ordering buildings like hamburgers"
The Architects' Journal, 15 February 2001

075 "Rocket science at the AA"
The Architects' Journal, 15 March 2001

076 "Shooting at statues"
World Architecture, May 2001

077 "Hong Kong's space shuffle"
World Architecture 98, July/August 2001

078 "Tall buildings: the end of a civilisation"
The Architects' Journal, 20 September 2001

079 "How to get famous by not building anything"
The Architects' Journal, 11 April 2002

080 "Battleships hold the key to the future of tall buildings"
The Architects' Journal, 19 September 2002

081 "Saved by the intelligent toilet"
The Architects' Journal, 17 October 2002

082 "Why prefabrication fails"
The Architects' Journal, 5/12 December 2002

083 "Technological jewels in the crown"
The Architects' Journal, 17 April 2003

084 "The defining moment of Modernism"
The Architects' Journal, 1 May 2003

085 "The Porsche 911, a genetically modified machine"
RCA Exhibition Catalogue, 2003

086 "Nonsuch Metropolitan University summer school 2003"
The Architects' Journal, 15 May 2003

087 "Return of the phone box"
The Architects' Journal, 22 May 2003

088 "Not-so-smart intelligent buildings"
The Architects' Journal, 24 July 2003

089 "Henry Ford and the limits of prefabrication"
The Architects' Journal, 9 October 2003

090 "The end of an interface"
The Architects' Journal, 6 November 2003

091 "It's an ill wind…"
The Architects' Journal, 26 February 2004

092 "The nine ages of transport"
The Architects' Journal, 18 March 2004

093 "The myth of the urban future"
The Architects' Journal, 25 March 2004

094 "Flying antiques"
The Architects' Journal, 30 September 2004

095 "Heavy bottles for a picnic"
The Architects' Journal, 4 November 2004

096 "The strange world of luxury watches"
The Architects' Journal, 25 November 2004

097 "The young dig in their heels"
The Architects' Journal, 3 March 2005

098 "How total urbanism will come to grief"
The Architects' Journal, 10 March 2005

099 "The answer to an historical conundrum"
The Architects' Journal, 17 March 2005

100 "The biggest house sale in history"
(MP's last published essay)
The Architects' Journal, 14 April 2005

Bibliography

Books

Masters of Modern Architecture—monographs on the life and work of Le Corbusier, Frank Lloyd Wright, Mies van der Rohe, Richard Neutra, Oscar Niemeyer, Paul Rudolph, Philip Johnson and Eero Saarinen, London, 1970–1973

Architecture versus Housing, London, 1971

The Private Future, London and New York, 1973

Garbage Housing, London and New York 1975

Home Ownership, London, 1978

Building for Tomorrow, San Francisco, 1982

Theory and Design in the Second Machine Age, Oxford, 1990

Buckminster Fuller: a biography, London, 1991, and Tokyo, 1994

Design in Exile: the architecture of Eva Jiricna, London, 1991

Future Systems: the story of tomorrow, London and Basel, 1993

The Hauer-King House: Future Systems, Architecture in Detail Series, London, 1997

Terminal Architecture, London, 1998

Norman Foster: a global architecture, New York and London, 1999

Twentieth Century Architecture: a readers' guide, Oxford, 1999

Hellmuth Obata and Kassabaum, introduction to monograph, Sydney, 1999

Anthologies

"The Time House" is included in the anthology *Meaning in Architecture*, London and New York, 1971

"My lovely student life" and "Demilitarisation of the university" are included in the anthology *A Continuing Experiment: learning and teaching at the Architectural Association*, edited by James Gowan, London, 1975

"Doubts about Lloyd's" is included in the anthology *The Bedside Guardian*, London, 1986

"Plucky Jim" and "Making the Future Work" are included in the anthology *From Matt Black to Memphis and back again*, London, 1989

"A prefab future" is included in the anthology *Built to Last*, London, 1992

"The electronic cottage" is included in the anthology *The Name of the Room*, London, 1992

"The Redundancy of Urban Space" is included in the anthology *Die Zukunft des Raums (The Future of Space)* edited by Bernd Meurer, Frankfurt, 1994

"Decline of the urban centre" is included in the anthology *Last Exit Downtown*, edited by Michael Monninger, Basel, 1994

"Vom Verschwinden der Städte: Architektur im Informationszeitalter" is included in the anthology *Schöne neue Welten?*, Munich, 1995

"Architecture versus the new media" is included in the anthology *Intelligent Environments*, edited by Peter Droege, Amsterdam, 1997

"Auf dem Weg zur digitalen Desurbanisierung" is included in the anthology *Virtual Cities*, edited by Christa Maar and Florian Rotzer, Basel, 1997

"Stadtwelten—Wirkliche Illusionen, illusionare Wirklichkeiten" is included in the anthology *Der Sinn der Sinne*, Munich, 1998

"The arena" is included in the anthology *Winning: the Design of Sports*, London, 1999

"Chek Lap Kok: the airport as saviour of the city" is included in the anthology *Vertigo: the strange new world of the contemporary city*, London, 1999

Martin Pawley contributed to all four published volumes in the series *Norman Foster: buildings and projects*, London, 1989 to 1996, and wrote the introductory essay to Volume 2, 1989

Additionally, he contributed entries on Richard Buckminster Fuller to the encyclopedia *L'art de l'ingenieur*, published for the Centre Georges Pompidou, Paris, 1997

"The Porsche 911, a genetically modified machine", *RCA Exhibition Catalogue*, 2003

Magazines and Newspapers
The following list includes all major magazine and newspaper articles from the period 1968 to 2005. However, space forbids the inclusion of the many hundreds of column pieces that Martin Pawley contributed regularly to the The Architects' Journal, Blueprint, Building, RIBA Journal and World Architecture during this period. Only those columns that are included in this anthology are referred to below.

AA Files
"High-Tech architecture: history versus the parasites", No. 21, Spring 1991

de Architect
"Luchthaventerminals: integratie luchthaven en stad" (The design of the new passenger terminal at Hong Kong International Airport), Dossier 7, November 1998

The Architect
"Tower blocks and tourist castles", July 1987

Archis
"After Armageddon: the decline of a profession" (The 1994 BBC2 documentary revisited), May 1998 (Amsterdam)

Architectural Design
"The Time House" (First publication of Martin Pawley's AA Diploma thesis in short form), September 1968
"The Time House" (Second publication of Martin Pawley's AA Diploma thesis at full length), March 1969
"Looking for a sound", May 1969
"The Agora at Dronten" (A critique of multifunctional space), July 1969
"Habraken's frameworks for Living" (Critique of housing design system using supports and detatchable units), January 1970
"Businessman expendable, hippie irreplaceable", January 1970
"The shape of trade" (Discussion of new world trade centres), February 1970
"Architecture versus the movies" (Special Issue on Expo '70, Osaka), June 1970

"Finland: where have all the followers gone?" (Survey of the state of the
    modern architecture in Finland after 1968), August 1970
"The Other Shelter Problem" (Discussion of air raid shelter production
    during the Second World War), September 1970
"Caroline go to canvas city, your friend Linda has been busted" (Report on
    the Third Isle of Wight music festival), November 1970
"Garbage Housing" (Argument for the integration of consumer wastes into
    the construction process), February 1971
"The Beaux-Arts since '68" (Special issue by Martin Pawley and Bernard
    Tschumi dealing with the reorganisation of the Ecole Nationale
    Supérieure des Beaux-Arts in Paris), September 1971
"Housing: the need for a revolutionary myth" (Learning from radical housing
    policies in developing countries), February 1972
"Garbage Housing" (An account of early experiments in building with
    consumer wastes), December 1973
"The Cost of not treating Housing as a Consumer Product" (Comparison of
    production of housing and consumer goods), August 1976
"Terminal Architecture" (Early draft of introduction to book used as an
    article), February 1998

L'Architecture d'Aujourd'hui
"The Kingdom of Inflation" (Effects of high inflation on the public housing
    programmes), December 1974
"Richard Rogers et Norman Foster, du succes a la victoire" (Richard Rogers
    and Norman Foster, from success to victory), May 1986
"Richard Rogers, Norman Foster, du succes a la victoire" (Comparison of
    personalities of Britain's two greatest architects), October 1986
"Michael Hopkins: stade de cricket a Marylebone, Londres" (Critique of
    Hopkins' Mound Stand at Lords cricket ground), December 1987

The Architects' Journal
"Information Systems" (Special issue written by Martin Pawley and
    Tony Cole), 1 January 1969
"The DOE Housing Awards" (Survey of history of DOE Awards showing
    changing pattern), 30 April 1975

"Housing at St Michael's Hill, Bristol" (AJ building study), 7 May 1975

"A thousand million components" (An argument for technology transfer as a means of accelerating the production of low cost housing worldwide), 13 October 1976

"Building at £6 per Square Metre" (Feature on the construction of the Dora Crouch house), 27 October 1976

"Attic Archives" (Astragal note on similarity between designs by Biltin Toker from 1960 and Zaha Hadid 1983), 21 September 1983

"Building revisits, Modern Critical Successes" (Includes Leicester Engineering building, Coventry Cathedral, Hunstanton School and Walter Segal's low cost house), 9 May, 23 May, 6 June, 20 June, 25 July 1984

"Escape to Sea" (Account of the author's sailing experiences), 19–26 December 1984

"Vorsprung durch Technik" (Review of Peter Cook's exhibition 21 years—21 ideas), 1 May 1985

"New York giant" (The proposed 135-storey SOM Coliseum project), 19 June 1985

"Monopoly in reverse" (The rise of the home owners' equity economy), 24 July 1985

"Building revisits, Glass architecture: the English descendants of Farnsworth" (Includes Farnsworth house, house by John Winter, house by Peter Aldington and house by Michael Hopkins), 4 September, 18 September, 2 October, 16 October 1985

"Near East tower" (Proposed 60-storey tower in Whitechapel), 19 March 1986

"Rehousing Jordan's Palestinians" (Report on a fact-finding visit to Amman), 26 March 1986

"Stirling's Mansion House" (Report on Peter Palumbo's second project for Mansion House Square), 21 May 1986

"The rise and fall of the public sector" (A survey of the origins and fate of council housing), 20 & 27 August 1986

"Objects of our time: the racing trimaran" (The design and performance of Adrian Thompson's racing trimaran Paragon), 17 September 1986

"Two Triumphs of twisted wire" (Information technology at Lloyd's and the Hongkong and Shanghai Bank), 22 October 1986

"The man who loved metal" (The life of Jean Prouve), 25 February 1987
"Objects of our time: the Piccadilly Line train" (The design and performance
    of a classic underground train), 15 April 1987
"Biting the hand" (Astragal reports on a tour of Germany), 17 June 1987
"Low energy High-Tech" (Richard Horden's Stag Place office project),
    2 September 1987
"Pioneer and prophet" (Maxwell Fry Obituary), 16 September 1987
"Modern movements" (Story of Nic Bailey's racing trimaran),
    2 November 1988
"Scrap value" (In praise of ephemeral buildings), 21 March 1990
"Lubetkin's last project" (Phillip Island penguin observatory),
    5 December 1990
"Invasion of the body snatchers" (MP column), 2 March 1995
"Invasion of the vibrators" (MP column), 29 February 1996
"Frank Lloyd Wright fights for his life" (MP column), 14 March 1996
"Meeting the future everywhere" (MP column), 13 March 1997
"From here to modernity" (MP column), 20 March 1997
"Seat pocket aliens" (MP column), 29 May 1997
"So long recycling, here comes secondary use" (MP column),
    31 July/7 August 1997
"A night to remember" (MP column), 8 January 1998
"The strange death of architectural criticism" (MP column), 2 July 1998
"When air-conditioning meets its match" (MP column), 22 July 1999
"A brace of fins du siècles" (MP column), 21 October 1999
"The new life of Albert Speer" (MP column), 13 July 2000
"Here comes the age of immobility" (MP column), 31 August 2000
"America: it's 24-7 at mission critical" (MP column), 8 February 2001
"Ordering buildings like hamburgers" (MP column), 15 February 2001
"Rocket science at the AA" (MP column), 15 March 2001
"Tall buildings: the end of a civilisation" (MP column), 20 September 2001
"How to get famous by not building anything" (MP column), 11 April 2002
"Battleships hold the key to the future of tall buildings" (MP column),
    19 September 2002
"Saved by the intelligent toilet" (MP column), 17 October 2002
"Why prefabrication fails" (MP column), 5/12 December 2002

"Technological jewels in the crown" (MP column), 17 April 2003
"The defining moment of Modernism" (MP column), 1 May 2003
"Nonsuch Metropolitan University summer school 2003" (MP column),
    15 May 2003
"Return of the phone box" (MP column), 22 May 2003
"Not-so-smart intelligent buildings" (MP column), 24 July 2003
"Henry Ford and the limits of prefabrication" (MP column), 9 October 2003
"The end of an interface" (MP column), 6 November 2003
"It's an ill wind..." (MP column), 26 February 2004
"The nine ages of transport" (MP column), 18 March 2004
"The myth of the urban future" (MP column), 25 March 2004
"Flying antiques" (MP column), 30 September 2004
"Heavy bottles for a picnic" (MP column), 4 November 2004
"The strange world of luxury watches" (MP column), 25 November 2004
"The young dig in their heels" (MP column), 3 March 2005
"How total urbanism will come to grief" (MP column), 10 March 2005
"The answer to an historical conundrum" (MP column), 17 March 2005
"The biggest house sale in history" (MP final column), 14 April 2005

The Architectural Review
"Self-build workstations: a partial history" (Account of design and
    performance of the author's seven self-build workstations),
    November 1983
"The designer of the Hongkong and Shanghai Bank" (An interview with
    Norman Foster), April 1986
"Lloyd's: into the unknown" (A critique of the Lloyd's building),
    October 1986
"Technology Transfer" (The uncharted history of technology transfer),
    September 1987
"A precedent for the Prince" (A comparison between Nazi and Carolingian
    approaches to architecture), January 1990
"Exogenous Shock" (Lessons of the 1970s energy crisis), September 1990

Architecture Today
"Industry: economic imperatives and constructive solutions" October 1990
"Bernard Tschumi's folly" (The new media school at Le Fresnoy),
    March 1998

Architectural Record
"To the mannerism born" (The Sainsbury Wing of the National Gallery),
    October 1991
"The case for uncreative architecture" (An argument for more emphasis
    on technology transfer in architecture), December 1992

A+U
"The Four Paradoxes of British Architecture" (A survey of current tendencies
    in British architecture), February 1974
"Richard Rogers and how the future could really work", May 1990
"Foster Associates' third London airport at Stansted", October 1991

Arquitectura y Vivienda
"La tradicion de las grandes naves: el nuovo aeropuerto de Stansted"
    (Stansted and the tradition of Big Sheds), 38, 1992

Bauwelt
"Die 'Stadtkrone' und ein Solitar" (The commercial heart of the City of
    London has failed to attain critical mass), No. 46, 8 December 1995
"Delirious Dome" (Critique of Millennium preparations in England),
    No. 40/41 30 October 1998

Berliner Zeitung
"Eine Stadt sieht rot" (An account of the impact of IRA terrorism on the
    planning and administration of the city of London since 1969),
    10 August 1997
"Ein Königreich für einen Bürgermeister" (The prospect of a new mayor
    and assembly for London), 27/28 December 1997
"Obelisken un Raketen" (The work of Taiwanese architect CY Lee),
    14/15 August 1999

Blueprint

"Sex, violence and design" (A celebration of the design of military hardware), November 1983

"Norman Foster 6.0, 6.0, 6.0" (A profile of Norman Foster), May 1984

"Is there life after the Zanzibar?" (An interview with Julian Wickham), July/August 1984

"Home sweet homestyle" (An investigation into booming DIY), October 1984

"Plucky Jim" (An interview with James Stirling), July/August 1985

"The second cleverest man in all England" (A profile of Stephen Bayley), September 1985

"Dan Dare: an extremely small step for mankind" (Survey of resurgence of Dan Dare literature), December 1985

"Learning to live with the Rector" (A profile of Jocelyn Stevens at the RCA), February 1986

"Come back austerity, all is forgiven" (A critique of the relationship of design with the national economy), May 1986

"The English School" (Review of the Royal Academy exhibition Foster, Rogers, Stirling), October 1986

"Shoot out at culture gulch" (Competition among new museum impresarios), June 1987

"The science man" (An interview with Neil Cossons of the South Kensington Science Museum), October 1987

"History is bunk" (A review of recent design histories), December 1987

"Who's in charge?" (Critique of the Thatcher era's rebuilding of London), June 1988

"Architecture's all our yesterdays man" (Review of career of Charles Jencks), February 1989

"The secret life of the engineers" (Interviews with Frank Newby, Tony Hunt and Peter Rice), March 1989

"Lost arks of the air" (An exhibition of airship hangars), April 1989

"The car that never flew" (The story of Buckminster Fuller's rear engine, front drive car), September 1989

"Life in the urban war zone" (Prediction of the ultimate collapse of cities), October 1989

"The Greatest Landlord in the World" (Interview with Jennifer Jenkins of the
    National Trust), February 1990
"In pursuit of the ultimate driving machine" (What happens when you try to
    buy a BMW), August 1990
"Where the Big Sheds are", November 1990
"Notes on the meaning of trivial things" (Ideas come from gadgets, not the
    other way around), December 1990
"Design in exile" (The work of Eva Jiricna), December/January 1991
"Royal train syndrome" (The class-ridden psychology of railway carriage
    design), February 1991
"Zero gravity" (A profile of Ian Ritchie), March 1991
"A new departure" (Critique of Stansted air terminal), April 1991
"Henry Ford and the biospherans", April 1991
"What London learned from Las Vegas" (An interview with Robert Venturi
    and Denise Scott Brown), May 1991
"Post coffee table" (An interview with Charles Jencks), November 1991
"A singular view" (An interview with Leon Krier), December/January 1992
"The man with a plan for London" (An interview with Peter Hall),
    February 1992
"Chairman Balfour" (An interview with the new chairman of the AA),
    March 1992
"The engineer unchained" (An interview with Santiago Calatrava),
    March 1992
"Face to face with the new president" (An interview with Richard
    MacCormac), April 1992
"In search of the spirit of Ecstacity" (An interview with Nigel Coates),
    May 1992
"Making paper architecture concrete" (An interview with Peter Cook),
    June 1992
"A full and Frank talk" (Interview with Frank Gehry), July/August 1992
"The man with Olympian ambitions" (Interview with RIBA Director General
    Bill Rodgers), October 1992
"Library on the runway" (Critique of Foster Associates' Cranfield library),
    November 1992
"Zaha escapes the pull of gravity" (Interview with Zaha Hadid), February 1993

"The discreet charm of the redundant object" (Lessons of the rapid
    obsolescence of products in the 1980s), September 1993
"Those fabulous Krier brothers" (Review article), October 1993
"Bigness and Bellini" (An interview with Mario Bellini), March 1996
"Bridging the Gap" (Why there is a bridge building renaissance in England),
    October 1996
"Invasion of the Millennarians" (Four highly unlikely Millennium projects),
    January 1997
"Who Killed Archigram?" (An account of the turning point in the career of
    the famous five), January 1998

Building
"Is ecology all hot air?", 17 August 1990
"And you thought your car was good for nothing", 27 March 1992

Building Design
"Meeting Buckminster Fuller" (Interview with Richard Buckminster Fuller),
    6 March 1970

Casabella
"Il trionfo dell' anatra" (The Sainsbury Wing at the National Gallery),
    No. 536 June 1987
"Torquay: conservazione o commercio?" (Commerce becomes conservation
    in Torquay), No. 538 September 1987
"Libera iniziativa o totalitarismo" (Docklands and the abolition of the GLC),
    No. 539 October 1987
"Prigioni: una crisi progettuale progettata" (Differing views over the design
    of prisons), No. 544 March 1988
"Gli antefatti di King's Cross" (The Foster masterplan for King's Cross and its
    problems), No. 545 April 1988
"Attenzione, arrivano gli 'Skeuomorphs'" (New computer building by Robert
    Adam deliberately designed to look old), No. 546 May 1988
"Il Design Museum, ovvero il Museo delle Cose Materiali" (The opening of
    the design museum), No. 548 July/August 1988
"Un vestito per Goldfinger" (Controversial plans to overclad a building by

Ernö Goldfinger), No. 551 November 1988

"La democrazia di male in peggio", No. 557 May 1989

"Terry e i pattinatori" (The Terry Farrell plan for the South Bank),
No. 559 July/August 1989

"King's Cross: crisi, ma quale crisi?" (Problems begin to overwhelm the
King's Cross redevelopment project), No. 565 February 1990

"La complessita del globulo", No. 567 April 1990

"Stairs for Stars" (The work of Eva Jiricna), No. 574 December 1990

"Dallas nel cuore del paese di Shakespeare" (Critique of the new
Birmingham concert hall), No. 579, May 1991

"L'aeroporto di Stansted a Londra di Foster Associates" (Critique of Stansted
air terminal), No. 580, June 1991

"Il Principe colpisce ancora" (Prince Charles intervenes again), No. 589,
April 1992

"Verso un funzionalismo storico?" (Michael Hopkins' project for a new
parliament building), No. 592, July/August 1992

"Future Systems: finalmente si construisce" (At last a job for Future Systems),
No. 594, October 1992

"Un gioiello nella polvere" (Critique of Foster Associates' Cranfield Library),
No. 596, December 1992

"La Nuova tragedia del Reichstag" (Dangers of the inconclusive result of the
Reichstag competition), No. 605, October 1993

"La fabrica della biblioteca" (The saga of the British Library), No. 607,
December 1993

"Ovest, est & ritorno" (The exporting of Western design styles to the Orient),
No. 630-631, January/February 1996

Crafts

"Notes on the ideological bankruptcy of post-Modern furniture" (Polemical
attack on post-Modernism), March/April 1985

Design

"Building for Business at Oxford" (Critique of the new Oxford School of
Management by Ahrends Burton and Koralek), August 1969

Designer
"Editors laid bare" (Editors of design journals describe their lives), May 1983

Design Book Review
"Design for the real world?", Winter 1987
"Prince Charles and the Architects" (A survey of the Prince's recent
    interventions), Summer 1989

Designers' Journal
"Carpeting the columns", December 1987
"Boots time capsule" (The SOM designed headquarters for Boots revisited,)
    April 1988

Deutsches Architektenblatt
"Gesucht: die Wirklichkeit. Architektur im Informationszeitalter"
    (The convergence of manufactured an real realities in architecture),
    April 1998

Deutsche Bauzeitung
"Glashaus Clifton Nurseries" (Advanced technology in postmodern dress),
    February 1986
"Digitale Entstadterung" (Shortened version of Digital Urbanism),
    September 1997

Direction
"Gift of the Gorb" (An interview with Peter Gorb design guru of London
    Business School), November 1988

Elle Decoration
"Who killed country style?" (Motorway service area styling moves into the
    provinces), Autumn 1989

The European Magazine
"The Accountants are Coming" (Why French architects no longer lead a
    charmed life), 17–23 October 1996

Foundation

"Port Side" (Norman Foster's early work for the Fred Olsen shipping line),
Issue 1, Spring 1991

"Natural Cool" (Experimental buildings using natural ventilation),
Issue 2, Autumn 1991

Frankfurter Allgemeine Zeitung

"Architektonische Stealth-Bomber in der Altstadt" (Architectural stealth
bombers in the City), 9th March 1992

"Die visionare Dorfgemeinschaft" (Prince Charles's dream of Poundbury),
May 1992

The Guardian

"Of Mies and men's inspiration" (Peter Palumbo's bid for a Mies van der Rohe
tower at Mansion House Square), 13 August 1984

"Out on a limb in Bedford Square" (Alvin Boyarsky and the AA school),
27 August 1984

"The future is a classic cover-up" (Critique of Robert Adam's Amdahl
computer building), 10 September 1984

"How to put modern architecture into a towering rage" (End of the National
Gallery competition fiasco), 21 September 1984

"The art of good intentions" (Review of RIBA exhibition of architectural
drawings), 5 November 1984

"The art of Colonel Richard Seifert", 19 November 1984

"The planning row over Salisbury cathedral car park", 8 December 1984

"The Prince and the planners" (Prince Charles and record of the Royals in
architecture), 25 February 1985

"Building becomes a racing craft" (Critique of Richard Horden's yacht
house), 25 March 1985

"A joy for the maker and user" (First part of three part series on the future of
architecture: an interview with Ted Cullinan), 29 April 1985

"The line running from Palladio to Palumbo" (Second part: an interview with
Richard Rogers), 30 April 1985

"A good slate roof against disaster" (Third part: an interview with Quinlan
Terry), 1 May 1985

"An end to the tower of babble" (Defeat for Palumbo over Mansion House
    Square), 22 May 1985
"Building the sum total of their fears" (Why do competitions always produce
    the wrong result), 27 August 1985
"What's wrong with DIY?" (Response to Rod Hackney"s defence of
    community architecture), 9 September 1985
"Yankee bet on the Isle of Dogs" (The beginning of Canary Wharf),
    4 October 1985
"Planet of the IRPS" (The Divis Street flats in Belfast), 26 November 1985
"How Lloyd's gambled on the past" (Critique of the new Lloyd's building),
    11 December 1985
"Friends of the hearth" (Self-build housing in Lewisham), 15 January 1986
"Final fling in the Imperial twilight" (Eyewitness account of the opening of
    the Hongkong and Shanghai Bank), 8 April 1986
"The architecture of Lloyd's is like modern poetry—it doesn't rhyme like a
    limerick, but the beat is there", (With Richard Rogers on a tour of the new
    Lloyd's building), 30 June 1986
"A man with designs on the destruction of apartheid" (An interview with
    Hans Schirmacher, South African architect against apartheid),
    18 July 1986
"Lots of energy but no luck" (A casualty of Milton Keynes energy world),
    8 September 1986
"Unarrested development" (Survey of the building revolution after Big Bang
    in the City), 23 September 1986
"The Prince and the paupers" (Report on the first conference of community
    architects), 29 November 1986
"All the history that fits" (Contribution to a survey of postmodernism in the
    arts), 3 December 1986
"Today Hackney, tomorrow the world" (An interview with the new RIBA
    president, Rod Hackney), 12 December 1986
"City of lost dreams" (Berthold Lubetkin's work at Peterlee),
    29 December 1986
"Land of the rising rhizome" (The architecture of Kisho Kurokawa),
    8 January 1990
"Out of the Hothouse" (The demolition of Reliance Controls), 19 March 1990

"Living on the edge of time" (The rebirthing of Alexandra Road), 2 April 1990

"First simulate, then stimulate" (Survey of computer simulation techniques in
architecture), 4 June 1990

"The Invisible Architects" (Architects working in backlands sites), 9 July 1990

"Who puts the kit into architecture?" (The new BBC headquarters at White
City), 3 December 1990

"High-Tech heritage for Mr. Pickwick" (The arrival of Esperanto architecture),
31 December 1990

"Crumbling pillars of strength" (Review article on the failure of property
developers), 3 September 1992

"Architect who preferred penguins to princes" (Review article on Berthold
Lubetkin), 10 September 1992

"Leon Krier: architecture and urban design" (Review article), 1 June 1993

"Heteropolis Los Angeles" (Review article), 26 October 1993

"The high-rise hopes that fell to earth" (Review article on the history of tower
blocks), 9 April 1994

The Independent

"Why Mr. Venturi has played to the gallery" (Critique of the Sainsbury Wing at
the National Gallery), 26 June 1991

"Red brick cannot disguise a monster" (Camouflaging a giant distribution
centre in Warwickshire), 14 August 1991

"How the Big Bang created a City of Dinosaurs" (Consequences of
overbuilding in the City during the 1980s boom), 30 December 1992

"The toughest nut in Oxfordshire" (Speculations on the future of the giant
Upper Heyford airbase), 27 August 1996

InterCity

"Brave new world postponed" (Failings of modern architecture over 21 years),
May/June 1987

"Mr. Venturi comes to town", November/December 1987

"Leonardo: man of the millennium", February 1989

Lichtbericht

"Die Architektur nach Foster, Rogers und Stirling" (Comparison of three
   great English architects), March 1987

The Listener

"Getting off the ground" (New building in liberated Czechoslovakia),
   7 June 1990

Marxism Today

"Building Blocks" (Reasons for the failure of system-built housing),
   March 1988
"Motor showdown" (Car design is out of step, as usual), September 1990

Modern Painters

"John Summerson, defender of modernism" (Review essay), Volume 4
   Number 1, Spring 1991

New Society

"Electric city of our dreams" (Hong Kong is the model for the redevelopment
   of London's docklands), 13 June 1986
"The incredible shrinking home" (Survey of the volume housing industry
   during a boom), 25 July 1986
"Charlie's Angels: Prince Charles' architectural fad" (Decline and fall of
   community architecture), 3 April 1987

New Statesman & Society

"Power stations: museum buildings have stolen the limelight" (A survey of
   new museums and art galleries), 12 April 1991
"Hamlet without the Prince" (V&A motor show with no cars), 26 June 1992

The Observer

"Norman conquers the establishment" (Profile of Sir Norman Foster),
   31 July 1994

The Observer Life Magazine
"Zaha Hadid" (A profile of Zaha Hadid), 19 February 1995

The Observer Review
"On the horizon with Mark and Mo" (Labour Party policy for architecture),
    27 March 1994
"The City stirs and reaches for the sky" (Rebuilding the NatWest tower),
    10 April 1994
"The good, the bad and the ugly" (The Royal Fine Art Commission's
    guidelines for good buildings), 24 April 1994
"And they all look just the same..." (Shell redesigns 40,000 petrol stations
    worldwide), 8 May 1994
"Through the round window" (Critique of Richard Rogers' Channel 4
    building), 12 June 1994
"The draughtsman's contract" (New home of the National Monuments
    Record Centre), 26 June 1994
"Constructing a collage of time" (Interview with Karl Sabbagh), 17 July 1994
"Artists of the floating world" (Critique of Future Systems Hauer/King
    house), 21 August 1994
"Measuring the impact" (The engineers who design networker trains),
    11 September 1994
"... and a cast of thousands" (Investigation into the authorship of buildings),
    23 October 1994
"Seattle goes soft" (A visit to the Microsoft campus), 13 November 1994
"Airborne with the flying buttress" (Critique of Michael Manser's Eastleigh
    Airport), 4 December 1994
"Form, function and fame" (A profile of Sir Richard Rogers), 5 February 1995
"Peas in a pod" (Results of a student housing design competition),
    12 March 1995
"A matter of principal" (The AA chooses a new head of school)
    26 March 1995
"Save us from the savers" (Against conservation), 23 April 1995
"Transparent but not clear" (Critique of the new European Court of Human
    Rights), 25 June 1995

"Tunnelling under sacred turf" (What the Royal Court theatre will do with its lottery money), 24 September 1995

"Splendour in the glass" (Critique of the new NCM insurance building at Cardiff Bay), 1 October 1995

Open House International

"A strategy for the resolution of the conflict between mass housing and consumer aspirations" (reprint of paper delivered to the International Housing Conference, Santiago, Chile, in September 1972), Vol. 13 No. 1 1988

Oppositions

"We shall not bulldoze Westminster Abbey: Archigram and the Retreat from Technology" (An explanation of the failure of Archigram to find clients for advanced technology buildings), Winter 1976/77

Parliamentary Review

"Stimulation to the Heart" (Why the Foster/Trafalgar House skyscraper proposed for the City should be built), January 1997

Progressive Architecture

"Singular Houses" (Feature includes the Dora Crouch house, Troy, New York, designed by Martin Pawley and built from consumer waste), August 1976

"Peterborough Court and Siblings" (The Goldman Sachs building in London), March 1992

Punch

"Jaguar's chequered flag history" (The decline and fall of a British car manufacturer), 19 January 1990

"Into the time machine" (Report on the Ideal Period Home Show), 2 February 1990

RIBA Journal

"This England—coming home" (Martin Pawley returns to England after many years in the United States), November 1980

"What does vernacular really mean?", August 1981
"The defence of modern architecture", May 1983
"Office design in Eternia", May 1985
"A winter school's tale", March 1987
"The footmen of Alexandra Road", January 1990
"What's in a name?", July 1991

Royal Academy Magazine
"The New Reichstag" (Account of award of commission to rebuild the Berlin
	Reichstag to a non-German architect), No. 54 Spring 1997
"Journey to the Interior" (The rise of minimalist Tadao Ando),
	No. 60 Autumn 1998

Skyline
"Thoughts on the design of houses and banknotes", March 1978

Stadt Bauwelt
"Theorie und Gestaltung im Zweiten Maschinenzeitalter", (Review publication
	of a chapter from the German translation of *Theory and design in the
	Second Machine Age*), No. 36 September 1998

Tatler
"Shirley Porter, Brand Leader" (Profile of the leader of Westminster City
	Council), September 1985
"Cruickshank's Georgian Buildings" (Report on 'New Georgian' movement
	in Spitalfields), October 1985
"The power brokers of architecture" (Three dealers in deals), March 1987
"Maggie's Man's Man" (Profile of Conservative Central Office spin doctor
	Michael Dobbs), June 1987
"Architects of our time" (The building of Broadgate), May 1989

10+1
"Why rebuild a phantom City?" (Critique of the rebuilding of Berlin),
	No. 23 May 1998, Tokyo

Topos

"Altes Land und neue Medien" (The impact of the new electronic media on
rural land use), June 1994

Tribune

"Put not your trust in Princes" (A view of the consequences of the Prince of
Wales' interventions in architecture), February 1990

Vogue

"The AA: hothouse or madhouse?" (A history of the AA and its distinguished
alumni), August 1992

World Architecture

"Pierre Vago: a testament of 60 years" (Profile of a veteran French architect),
No. 20 November 1992

"Decline and fall of Carl Zeiss Jena" (A history of the famous optical firm and
its revolutionary buildings), No. 20 November 1992

"Callison the big number eight" (Profile of Callison Architecture a large
American practice in Seattle), No. 33 January 1995

"Born in the USA" (Profile of Kohn Pedersen Fox international),
No. 34 February 1995

"Region and Identity in America" (A profile of NBBJ, Seattle),
No. 35 April 1995

"Two plus two equals five" (A profile of Gensler, a large American practice),
No. 39 September 1995

"HOK is a work in progress" (Profile of the largest American practice),
No. 40 October 1995

"Success story of an English architect" (A profile of Chris Wilkinson
Architects), No. 45 April 1996

"The rise of the engineer" (MP column), No. 45 April 1996

"Constant values: changing strategies" (A profile of the Minneapolis practice
Ellerbe Becket), No. 46 May 1996

"After postmodernism, terrorism" (MP column), No. 47 June 1996

"Learning from experience" (A profile of the German practice Bremmer
Lorenz Frielinghaus), No. 49 September 1996

"The myth of monumentality" (MP column), No. 54 March 1997

"A New Architect for China" (A profile of Taiwanese architect CY Lee),
    No. 55 April 1997

"Over the top is what it takes" (A profile of John McAslan and Associates),
    No. 63 February 1998

"Building in the past and for the future" (A profile of Rhode Kellermann
    Wawrowsky + Partner), No. 65 April 1998

"XX marks the spot" (A profile of XX Architecten, Delft), No. 69
    September 1998.

"Shooting at statues" (MP column), No. 96 May 2001

"Hong Kong's space shuffle" (MP column), No. 98 July/August 2001

World Link

"Architectural Haute Couture's dying days" (Corporate America no longer
commissioning great architecture), September/October 1992

Picture Credits

Arcaid/© Richard Bryant: 132

Architectural Press Archive/RIBA Library Photographs Collection: 104, 105, 156

Archive of the Luftschiffbau Zeppelin GmbH Friedrichshafen: 185

John Donat: 184

Richard Buckminster Fuller Papers, M1090, Dept. of Special Collections,
Stanford University Libraries, Stanford, California: 38, 237

Louis Hellman: 4, 12

Ian Lambot: 133

Martin Pawley collection: 22, 23, 39, 157, 196, 197, 206, 207, 266, 267, 316,
317, 354, 355, 378, 379, 404, 405

Sherin Aminossehe/RIBA Library Photographs Collection: 236

Index

Aalto, Alvar 256
A Vision of Britain 198–199,
   200–201, 203
Ackerman, James 126
Acropolis, the 202
Adamski, George 141
Addams, Charles 123
Adler, Cy 194
Admiral Grosvenor 140–142
"Aerodrome" flying machine 385
After the Planners? 78
AIDS 284, 410
AIROH prefab houses 107, 360,
   379
Airship Industries 186
Albinoni, Tomaso 280
Alcock, Captain John 364
Alexanderplatz, Berlin 352
Alexandra Road 208–209,
Allen, John Polk 252
Allen, William 55, 58
Allende, President Salvador 17,
   210, 318, 361
Allinson, Ken 60
Ambasz, Emilio 126
Amdahl Computers 118,
American Embassy, New Delhi 50
American University of Beirut 288
Americas Cup 189
Amsterdam 68, 249
Anthony Hunt Associates 173
Apollo Programme 166
Apple Macintosh 138
Appleyard, Bryan 76
Archigram 59, 60–67, 166–167,
   169, 224, 396–397, 413, 429, 437
Archigram 1 59
Archigram 3 60, 69
Archigram 4 61
Archigram Opera 59
Architects' Journal, The 13–15, 18,
   20–21, 58, 212
Architectural Association, The 13,
   48, 59
Architectural Design 13–14, 20, 58,
Architectural Press, The 14, 66, 123,
   320
Architectural Review, The 13, 20, 97,
   126, 239, 256
Architecture versus Housing 17
ARCON 360
Arcosanti 224
Arendt, Hannah 94, 110

Arnheim, Rudolph 55
Arnstein, Karl 187
ART NET 66
Arup, Ove 64, 174–175
Ashmolean Museum, Oxford 53, 60
Aspersion Tensegrity (Fuller) 61
Asplund, Gunnar 76
Atelier Faugeron 49–50
Augustine, Margret 252
Auschwitz 283, 286
Auto Union 368
Automatic Train Operation (ATO)
   153
Automobile magazine 192
Axis Defeat, World War Two 366

Baghdad, Iraq 288, 372
Baird, John Logie 140
Bamiyan Valley 346–347
Banham, Reyner 15–16, 26–27, 60,
   123, 144, 162–163, 170, 261
Bar-Hillel, Mira 77
Barnhart, Clarence 74
Bass, Edward 251–252
Battersea Power Station, London 293
Battery Houses 145
Battle of Britain 142
Bauhaus 85, 162, 202, 242, 285
Baupolizei 204, 274
BBC Building, Portland Place 91
BBC Radio Centre 168
BBC World Service 88
BBC2 15, 57
Beatles, The 143, 296
Beavan, Arthur 388–389
Beech Aircraft Corporation,
   Wichita, Kansas 106, 378
Beefeater II 114
Bentham, Jeremy 231
Berchtesgaten 110
Berkeley, (University of) California
   53, 55
Berlin 154–155, 202, 209, 210, 291,
   304, 348
Berlin Wall 210
Best-Rubinstein Experiment 29
Betjeman, John 375
Big Bang 20, 110, 216, 110, 376
Binet, Hélène 288
Binney, Marcus 94
Biospherans 251–252
Biosphere II 243, 251–252
Birkenau 283

Blake, Peter 107
Blenheim Palace 129
Blueprint magazine 15, 18, 20, 64,
   107, 143
BMW 18, 20, 125, 154, 215–218,
   233, 377
Boeing 747 136, 186, 350
Bonaparte, Napoleon 86, 159,
   334, 402
Booker, Christopher 76
Borromini, Francesco 126
Bowley, Marian 170
Boyarsky, Alvin 14, 289
Bracken House 176
Bramante, Donato 240
Brand, Stewart 222
Brand, Weber 282
Branson Coates Architects 271
Branson, Doug 271–273
Brasilia 50, 54, 348
Breguet 395
Breitling 395
Bride of Denmark 123, 272
Bristol Aeroplane Company 380
British Broadcasting Corporation
   (BBC) 15, 57, 61, 88, 91, 168, 233,
   255, 363
British Rail 233–235
British Telecom 293
Broadacre City 179
Broadgate, London 180, 273, 376
Brunel, Izambard Kingdom 239,
   301
Brunelleschi, Filippo 158–159
Brutalism 99–100, 102, 175
Brutus magazine 272
Buckingham Palace 145
Building Construction (Mitchell) 72
Building magazine 15
Building News 79
Bullitt 35
Burgess, Sterling 189–191
Burke, Edmund 159
Burroughs, William 36
Bush, George W 350, 384
Bushnell's Turtle 86

Cadillac 16, 66, 210, 212, 230, 268
Cadillac Coupe de Ville 18, 268
Caffe Bongo 272
California 60, 99, 186, 275, 396
California Aerospace Museum 275,
   278

Cambridge 119, 175, 224, 263
Cambridge University 224
Camus, Albert 52
Canary Wharf, London 135, 179
Cape Kennedy 212
Capricorn Blacksmiths 212
Captain Hunter 141
Car Collector, 1977 267
Caracalla, Baths of 293
Cardington 186
Carlyle, Thomas 230–231
Carrington, Blake 117
Carthage, Battle of 346–347
Casabella magazine 15
Centre Georges Pompidou 173,
    175–176, 245, 302
Chalk, Warren 59
Challenger 213
Chalmers, Richard 147
Chamberlain, Neville 400
Channel 4 110
Charles de Gaulle Airport 249
Checkpoint Charlie 155
Chernobyl 129, 350
Chevrolet 380
Chiattone 166
Chile 17, 210, 318, 361, 401
Chindogu 358–359
Christiani & Nielsen 174
Church of San Vitale, Ravenna 280
Churchill, Winston 96, 402
Citroën 108, 209, 210, 361
Citroën 2CV 108, 210
City Wise Conference 146
Classical Revival 107, 108, 119, 121,
    171, 260
Clifton Nurseries building, London
    171
Coates, Nigel 271–274
Cobbet, William 231
Coca Cola 393, 47
Codd bottle 392–393
Code of Conduct (RIBA) 79
Coin Street 93
Coleman, Dr Alice 146, 198, 204, 208
Collectivisation Programme 182
Columbia space shuttle catastrophe
    362
Columbia University, New York 291
Comet airliner 362
Commercial Union Plaza 129, 131
Commission for Architecture and
    Built Environment (CABE) 352

Community Architecture
    movement 203
Complexity and Contradiction in
    Architecture 253
Conceptual Architecture 66
Concorde 136, 227, 338, 350,
    362–363
Constructivists 60
Cook, Peter 58, 59, 60, 61, 65–68
Cornwall, Duchy of 283
Correa, Charles 352
Cosmopolitan magazine 272
counter-culture 220, 222
County Hall, London 273
Cousteau, Jacques Yves 77
Coventry Cathedral 95–98
Coventry Polytechnic 366
Coward, Noel 283
Crompton, Alastair 141
Crompton, Dennis 59, 60, 64
Crouwel, Benthem 282
Crystal Palace 334, 362, 364
CSS HL Hunley 86
Cultural Revolution, China 221, 346
Czechoslovakia 207, 400
CZWG 226

D magazine 13, 52–53
da Sangallo, Giuliano 293
Dan Dare 140–142
Dance with a Stranger 119
Dangermouse 76
Daniels, Gail 212
Darwin, Charles 376
Davies, Colin 174
DDR 284, 352
de Medici, Lorenzo 293
de Stijl 60
Derbyshire, Sir Andrew 239
Die Welt 283
Disney World 142, 154
Disney, Walt 154, 230, 275
Dissolving City 64
Dixwell Firehouse, New Haven 256,
    290
Docklands, London 247, 258, 377
Doernach, Rolf 224
Dome Cookbook 223
Dome over mid-town Manhattan
    237
Domebook 222
Domebook 2 222
Dora Crouch House 17, 317

Downing College, Cambridge 119,
    330
Dr Finlay's Casebook 119
Driver, Stanley 150
Driving Motor (DM) car 159
Drop City 222
Duck Zany Trubshaw 372
Duke of Edinburgh 76
Dunleavy, Patrick 80
Düsseldorf Media Centre 290
Dymaxion Car 39, 190–191, 241
Dymaxion House 42, 88, 162–163,
    209
Dynasty 117

Eagle 140, 142
Eames, Charles 82, 252
East Germany 210, 336, 361
Eckener, Hugo 185
École Nationale Supérieure des
    Beaux-Arts, Paris 13, 49
Ecological Fantasies 194
Ecstasy 376
Eichmann, Adolf 77
Eiffel Tower 51
Eisenman, Peter 275, 278, 290
Elliot Paul 51
Emergency Factory Made
    programme 360
Empire State Building, New York 350
Engels, Friedrich 77
English Civil War 346
English Heritage 180, 198, 212, 352
Enterprise Culture 182
Enthoven and Mock 56
Environmental Research
    Laboratories 252
EPCOT 142, 252
Epstein, Jacob 98
Erhard, Werner 109
Erith, Raymond 120
Esher Report 147
Eternia 117–178
EXPO '70, Osaka 64

"Farewell PKO376W" 18
Farnsworth House 148, 245, 404
Farrell, Terry 92–93, 198, 239, 282
FC-2, Canary Wharf 212
Features-Monte Carlo 65
Fehlbaum, Rolf 290–291
Ferrari 394
FIAT 177

Fiat Empire 394
Fiat Tipo 177
Financial Times Industrial
    Architecture at Work Award 363
First Machine Age 182
First World War 41
Fitzgerald, Frances 41
Florida A&M University,
    Tallahassee 17
Flynn, Errol 115
Folkestone International Dialogue
    of Experimental Architecture 68
Ford 6600 242
Ford Capri 157
Ford Cortina 241
Ford Escort 1.3 194–195
Ford Model 'A' 257, 381
Ford Model 'T' 380–381
Ford Motor Company 194, 250,
    380
Ford Mustang 257, 278
Ford Sierra 2.0GL 147, 257
Ford Transit 380
Ford V-8 190
Ford, Edsel 233, 257
Ford, Gerald 71
Ford, Henry 250–252, 257,
    380–381
Foster Associates 90, 94, 133, 184,
    260–263, 265, 273
Foster, Norman, 10–11, 21, 82, 90,
    94, 134, 136, 139, 167–170, 174,
    176, 243, 245–246, 258, 261–
    263, 265, 271, 271, 282, 362
Fournier, Colin 60
Frampton, Kenneth 127, 278
Frauenkirche, Dresden 284
French Revolution, The 346, 395
Freud, Sigmund 29, 125
Frost, Robert 159
Fry, Max 82, 158, 163–164
Fuller, Richard Buckminster 10
    (foreword), 16, 19, 38–44, 60, 61,
    62, 91, 106–108, 145, 162–164,
    167, 189, 190–192, 209, 220,
    221–222, 228, 237, 238, 241,
    243, 252, 261, 282, 356
Fun Palace 144
Future Systems 169, 238
Futurism 85, 119
FV 453 190, 191

Gage, René 155

Gale, Adrian 147
Gallot, Jacques 50
Garbage House 266
Garbage Housing 17, 47
Gaudi, Antonio 288
Gehry, Frank 256, 275–279,
    290, 396
General Pinochet 210
George, David Lloyd 151
Georgian Group 198
German Car Centre,
    Milton Keynes 262
German Library of Information,
    New York 203
German U-Boats 219
Glancey, Jonathan 212
Goering, Herman 85, 202, 401
Goldfinger, Ernö 295
Golding, William 251
Goodman, Robert 78
Goodyear Corporation 187
Governor's Palace, Brasilia 50
Graf Zeppelin 90, 185, 187
Graf Zeppelin II 187
Graff-Baker, William 150
Granville Brothers 189
Graves, Michael 91, 93, 112, 126
Gray, Eileen 255
Great Depression 186, 203, 358
Great Fire of London, the 201
Great Northern, Piccadilly and
    Brompton Railway 151
Greater London Council (GLC)
    145, 273
Greene, David 60
Grimshaw, Nicholas 176, 226,
    258, 290
Gropius, Walter 127, 163, 202, 284
Gruen, Victor 275
Guarini, Guarino 176, 275
Guest, Hubert Gascoigne 140
Guild House, Philadelphia 256
Guimard, Hector 175

Habbakuk 86
Haber, Fritz 400
Habraken, John 147, 318
Hackney, Rod 212, 283, 320
Hadid, Zaha 21, 288–289
Hall, Peter 144
Hamilton, Richard 96
Hampson, Frank 141–142
Hampton Court 19, 200, 202, 352

Happold, Ted 173
Harpers' and Queen magazine 272
Harris, David 221
Harris, Vicki 95
Harvard Business School 252
Harvard University, Boston 29, 275
Hatter, Tony 366
Hayward Gallery 86
Heathrow Airport 149–152, 249, 263
Hellmuth Obata & Kassabaum 255
Hemingway, Ernest 51, 123, 334
Herrenchiemsee Castle 154
Herron, Ron 59, 60, 274
High-Tech 74, 82, 86, 90, 100, 108,
    115, 119, 120, 129, 136, 139, 167,
    168, 171, 173–178, 213, 230, 233,
    238–240, 245, 247, 374
Highpoint Flats 174
Hillsboro Disaster 213
Hindenburg Disaster 62, 186, 213,
    362
Hindenburg Zeppelin 187, 323
Hitler, Adolf 78, 110, 200–203,
    205, 283
Hochschule für Gestaltung, Ulm 285
Hodges, Carl 252
Hodgson, Geoffrey 193–195
Hoffman, Abbie 283
Hogan, Pilot Captain Henry
    Brennan 140
Hongkong and Shanghai Bank
    133–139, 142, 169, 243, 265, 302
Hong Kong Island, China 226,
    348–349
Honk Kong Peak competition 289
Honecker, Erich 208
Hopkins, Michael 168, 176
Horden, Richard 90–91, 93, 168–
    170, 282
Howarth, David 356
Hughes, Robert 76
Hunstanton School 99–103, 105, 174
Hunt, Tony 173–176
Hussein, Saddam 364
Hutchinson, Max 173

IBM 62, 93
IBM typewriter 87, 292
Illinois Institute of Technology 99,
    252
Imagination 274
IMAX 387
Imperial War Museum 98

Industrial Revolution 27, 170, 338, 364
Inmos 175
Instant City 62, 64
Institute of Contemporary Arts, London 60, 273
Institute of Ecotechnics, London 352
Intelligent Buildings Group 273
Intercity 225, 223
International Building Exhibition (IBA) 155
International Style, the 162, 261, 304–305
Invasion of the Bodysnatchers 254
Isozaki, Arata 289

Jackley, Nat 95
Jaguar 212, 257
Jameson, Conrad 76
Jaray, Paul 368
Jaspers, Karl 52
Jefferson, Thomas 110
Jencks, Charles 14, 58, 76, 109–112, 159, 275
Jenkins, David (preface) 13–21
Jennings, Helen Huntington 95
Jiricna, Eva 290
Johnson Burgee 255
Johnson, Philip 82, 121–122
Jones, Ed 272
Jones, Inigo 143
Jordan, Robert Furneaux 97
Joyce, James 238

K2 telephone box 293
Kahn, Lloyd 222
Kai Tak Airport, Hong Kong 348
Kaplicky, Jan 169–170, 177, 238, 272
KdF-Wagen 206
Kelly, Burnham 30
Kenchington Little 176
Kevlar 163, 171
Kill Devil Hills 384
King's Cross 179, 272, 273
Kohn Pedersen Fox 255
Koolhaas, Rem 289
Korean War 326–327, 348, 390
Korsakov, Rimsky 94
Kowloon Peninsula, China 348
Kreisler, Fritz 280
Krier, Leon 21, 127, 199, 283–287
Krier, Rob 155
Kubler, George 32, 34

Kuomintang, the 348

La Santé, Paris 48
La Villette 173
Labour Party 125, 145, 186
Lamoureaux, Dennis 223
Land Pavilion, EPCOT 142, 212, 252
Langley, Samuel Pierpont 385
Laubin, Carl 273
Le Corbusier 54, 78, 103, 163, 171, 173, 256, 284, 408, 409
Le Mans 366
le Tourneau Superfreighter 241
Leicester Engineering Building 127, 285
Levete, Amanda 238
Levin, Bernard 76, 84
Lewis and Clark 253
Lewis, Jerry 119
Life magazine 229
Lincoln College, Oxford 53
Lindbergh, Charles 365
Linderhof Castle 154
Lipton, Stuart 93
Little, Douglas 100–103
Littlewood, Joan 144, 336
Liverpool Street Station 263
Lloyd's Building 129–130, 134, 134–138, 167, 295
Lockhart, JG 113–114
London Bridge 179–180
London, City of 129, 201, 203, 239, 242, 273, 305
London Evening Standard 224
London Residuary Body 145
London School of Economics, LSE 288
London School of Pop 57
London, Swinging 57
London Underground 149–151
London University 179, 275
London Wall 179–180
Loos, Adolf 171
Lord Carrington 76
Lord Holford 274
Lord Macaulay 254
Lord of the Flies 251
Lord Snowdon 175
Lord St John of Fawsley 216, 239
Los Angeles riots 275, 277
Los Angeles, California 18, 72, 88, 169, 252, 270, 275, 277, 325
Louis XIV 41

Louisiana Purchase 402
Lubetkin, Berthold 79–80, 174, 182
Luder, Owen 77
Ludwig II of Bavaria 107, 154–155, 203, 212, 243
Luftwaffe 320
Lutyens House, London 242
Lutyens, Sir Edwin 81, 123
Lynn, Vera 95

MacQuedy, James 14
Maiden Castle, Dorchester 283, 286
Maisonrouge, Jacques 62, 65–66, 68
Mansell, Nigel 173
Manser, Alan 'Joe' 150
Mansion House, London 203, 320
Mansion House Square 124, 129, 160
Manson, Charles 62
Manzis, London 229, 283
Mappin & Webb Triangle 135
Märkisches Viertel 155
Marquis de Sade 61
Mars Landing Programme 161
Martin, Ian 18–19
Martner, Gonzalo 17
Marx, Karl 77
Mason, Roy 223–224
Massachusetts Institute of Technology (MIT) 66
Matsushita Electric 359
Mavrolean, Basil 125
May, Ernst 202
McKillop, Carstairs 383
McLuhan, Marshall 81, 96, 154, 221, 226, 334
Me109 E-K 279
Menil Gallery 173
Mercedes Benz 154, 364
Messerschmitt 278, 390–391
Metabolists 224
Metropole Restaurant 272
Metropolis exhibition, ICA 273
Middle East 193, 219, 248, 333
Middle East War 221
Middleton, Robin 58
MIG 15 390
Miles, Sarah 285
Miller, Herman 117
Milne, Teddy 95
Milton Keynes 142, 228, 258, 262, 274, 283, 286, 348, 398
Mississippi Valley 402
Modern Art Glass showroom and

warehouse, Thamesmead
262–263
Modern Movement 60, 81, 97, 120,
134, 163, 166, 170, 278, 295
Moleslinger, Sigi 372
Montaniero, Gigli 372
MoonSoon Restaurant, Sapporo 290
More, Thomas 25
Morris, Marcus 140
Morrison, Elting 83
Mosley, Sir Oswald 79
*Mother Earth News Handbook of
Homemade Power* 223
Museum of Modern Art, New York
153

Nagasaki, Japan 297, 325, 347
Napoleon 86, 159, 334, 402
NASA 161, 169, 187, 212, 396
NASA Lunar Excursion Capsule 142
National Gallery, Berlin 291
National Gallery, London 253–
256, 260
National Service 49
National Socialist Germany 202–204
NATO 272, 374
NATO magazine 272
Nautilus 61, 64, 66, 86
Nazi Germany 187, 200, 203
Nazis 19, 142, 200, 400
Nervi, Pier Luigi 53
Neuschwanstein Castle 154–155
Neutra, Richard 163
New Brutalism 99–100, 175
New Towns 79, 274
Newby, Frank 175–178
Nikkei Index 358
Nine Chains to the Moon 162
Nissan Sunny 211
Nixon, David 169–170, 177
Nixon, President Richard 77
Nobel Peace Prize 208
Northgate Hall, Oxford 54, 60
NSU project 12, 368

Oates, Tom 223
Ohl, Herbert 82
Oldenburg, Claes 278, 344
Olivetti typewriter 292
Olsen, Fred 93
Olympia and York 247, 377
Olympia typewriter 16, 292
Olympia Supertype Electronic

typewriter 382
One Canada Square, London 371
OPEC 225
Opium War, The 134
Oppositions 20
Otto, Frei 284
Outram, John 198, 239
Ove Arup & Partners 64, 173–175
Overtime tractor 241
Oxford Architectural Students
Society 52
Oxford College of Technology, Art
and Commerce 51
Oxford School of Architecture 13,
48–49, 55
Oxford School, the 52, 54

Pacific War 348
Palace of Versailles 367
Palumbo, Peter 160, 229
Paris 13, 48–51, 68, 85, 87, 103,
245, 274, 281, 364, 366, 402
Paris Commune 346
Paris Concorde crash 350, 362
Paris 1968 221
Parker's Car Price Guide 214
Parthenon 117, 293
Patek Phillippe 394
Peak, The 289–290
Pearce Structures, Los Angeles 252
Pearce, Peter 243, 252
Pearl Harbour 219, 350
Pearl River Delta, China 348
Pearman, Hugh 229, 231
Pelli, Cesar 276
Pereira, William 275
Perriand, Charlotte 255
Peters, Lorraine 95
Peugeot 210
Piano, Renzo 156, 175
Piccadilly Line 143, 149–153, 424
Pick, Frank 81
Pike, Alexander 224
Piper, John 96–97
Pitney Bowes 383
Plater-Zyberk, Elizabeth 255
Playboy magazine 154
Plymouth Arrow 269
Plymouth Winter School 147
Porsche 356 190, 367
Porsche 911 series 93, 366–369, 371
Porsche Design Department,
Stuttgart 366

Porsche Tatzelwurm 241
Porsche, Ferdinand 206, 368
Portsmouth Speed Week 115
Potteries Thinkbelt 144
Poundbury 283, 285–286
Presley, Elvis 143
Price, Cedric 37, 60, 143, 175, 261
Prince of Wales 19, 160, 198–205,
238, 244, 273, 276, 280, 283,
285, 289, 320, 352, 375
Progressive Architecture Movement
54–55
Prouvé, Jean 82
Pyke, Geoffrey 86

Quartz, Begnamino 372
Quatermass 272
Queen Elizabeth II 102, 274, 276

R34 airship 365
Radio Luxemburg Hit Pick 57
Ragon, Michael 64
Rand, Ayn 164, 336
Range Rover 72, 212
Reichmann, Paul 376–377
Reliance Controls 100, 174–175,
245, 262, 362–363
Remington typewriter 292
Renault 93–94, 263–264
Renault Distribution Centre 176, 263
Rensselaer Polytechnic Institute
17, 147
Restoration Architecture 159–160,
170–172
RIBA Building, Portland Place 54
RIBA Conference on New
Opportunities, 1981 79
RIBA external examiners 58, 272
RIBA Gold Medal Address, 1982 78
RIBA Journal, The 15, 68
Rice Francis Ritchie 173
Rice, Peter 168, 173–177
Richard Rogers Partnership 132
Richards, JM 13–14
Richmond Riverside 135, 212
Rickaby, Tony 60
Roark, Howard 164, 336
Roberts, Andrew 350
Robinson, Fitzroy 176, 212, 216
Rockwell, Norman 173
Rogers, Richard 128–132, 134, 136,
156, 167, 173–175, 245–246,
258, 262, 277, 282, 295, 362, 389

Rolls Royce 108
Romerstadt, Frankfurt 202
Ronan Point 213, 259, 336
Rosemeyer, Bernd 85
Rosenberg, Harold 25
Rothsay Castle 113
Rothschild, Jacob 254
Rousseau, Jean-Jacques 77
Rover Mini 18, 209
Rowe, Colin 126–127
Royal Air Force (RAF) 140, 362
Royal College of Art (RCA) 230, 366
Royal Fine Art Commission (RFAC)
    143–144, 180, 198, 204, 239, 244
Royal Institute of British Architects
    (RIBA) 67, 198–199
Royal Town Planning Institute 198
Royal Train Syndrome 233, 235
Russian Revolution 346

S Vitale, Ravenna 165
Saarinen, Eero 281, 289
Sadao, Shoji 221
Sainsbury Centre for Visual Arts 184
Saint Martin's Le Grand 176–177
Saint-Exupéry, Antoine de 309
Samuely, Felix 173
Sant'Elia, Antonio 166
Sarger, René 64
Sartre, Jean Paul 52
Sasaki, Hideo 275
Scharoun, Hans 60, 126, 142
Schlumberger Research
    Laboratories 176
Schoenberg, Arnold 52
Schon, Mila 164
School of Urban Planning (UCLA) 18
Schumacher, Fritz 220
Scientology 109
Scott-Brown, Denise 253–254
Scott Fitzgerald, F 51
Scott, Captain Robert Falcon 394
Scott, Sir Giles Gilbert 79, 258,
    293, 374
Scruton, Roger 76, 81, 84–85, 92
Sea Hawk 115–116
Seattle Art Museum, Seattle 256
Second Machine Age 180–183,
    238, 248
Second World War 14, 16, 27, 40,
    80, 107, 162, 181, 203, 220, 283,
    338, 346–347, 360, 366, 382,
    387, 390–391, 400–401

Shaw, George Bernard 253
Siedlung Torten 117
Sikorsky sky crane helicopter 211
Simondon, Gilbert 366–368
Simpson, Bart 283
SITE 256
Skeletor 118
Skidmore Owings Merrill (SOM)
    212, 255
Skoda 208
Smiles, Samuel 231
Smith, Peter 77
Smithson, Alison and Peter 99,
    102, 105, 158
Smithsonian Institution 385
Soleri, Paolo 224
Sony Corporation 397
Soviet Five Year Plans 182
Soviet Union 186, 271, 346, 361
Spanish American War, 1898 350
Speer, Albert 126, 201, 283–284
Spence, Basil 336–337
Spengler, Tilman 349
Spitfire 86, 257, 278
Spithead Review 364
Spon 148
St Paul's Cathedral, London 108,
    201–203, 343, 353, 376
Staatsgalerie, Stuttgart 117,
    125–126
Stalin, Josef 182
Stamp, Gavin 124, 194, 293, 330
Stansted Airport 261, 263
Starfighter 178
STATIC Studio 372
Stern, Robert 76
Stewart, James 35
Stirling, James 117, 124, 127, 129,
    135, 175, 258, 285
Stockhausen, Karlheinz 52
Storm Bird 116
Strauss, Richard 60
Strehlow, TGH 29
Suez Canal 219
Sunday Express 202–203
Sutherland, Graham 90, 98
Suzuki, Dr David 397
Sydney Opera House 173, 289, 302
Synergetics 252
Synergia Ranch 252
Tafuri, Manfredo 117, 126
Talbot, Fox 140
Taleban 346

Tange, Kenzo 64
Tate Gallery, London 125
Taurus System, Stock Exchange
    239, 376
Taut, Bruno and Max 60, 407
Team 4 174
Technical University of Munich 284
Technical University of Stuttgart 284
Technische Hogeschool,
    Eindhoven 147
technology transfer 18, 21, 82–83,
    158–59, 161–171, 241, 280–282
Tecton 174
Teflon 83, 108, 161, 163, 171
Terminal Architecture 20, 322
Terry, Quinlan 30, 92, 119–121, 127
    135, 198, 260
Tessenow, Heinrich 126, 284, 337
Thatcher, Margaret 182
The Daily Telegraph 15
The Futurist 223
The Ghost Dance Times 14
The Glenn Miller Story 35
The Guardian 15, 19, 143, 320
The Language of Post-Modern
    Architecture 109
The Late Show 15
The Observer 15
The Politics of Mass Housing in
    Britain 1945–75 80
The Private Future 16, 23
The Time House 16, 20, 22, 24, 58, 13
The Times 82, 362
Theme Pavilion 64
Theory and Design in the First
    Machine Age 162
Theory and Design in the Second
    Machine Age 16, 19, 180, 280
Third Millennium 117, 119, 136
Third Reich 205
Thompson, Hunter S 15
Thorndike, Edward 74
Thornton, John 148, 176
Time magazine 208, 292
Titanic 140, 350, 362, 398
Toker, Biltin 52–56
Town and Landscape Planning in
    Soviet Russia 78
Trabant 15, 207–210, 212
Trade Union Council 145
Treaty of Versailles 400
Trench Type telephone 41
Tribble Harris Li 253

Trotsky, Leon 271
Troy, Battle of 346
Turbinia 364
Turin Shroud 116

Ulysse Nardin 395
Unidad Popular government 17, 210
United Nations Department of
    Housing Building and Planning
    17
United States Air Force (USAF) 263
United States War Department 385
University of California,
    Los Angeles (UCLA) 88, 147, 276
Ur of the Chaldees 398
Urban Task Force 389
USSR 54, 187

V-2 Rocket 187
Vago, Pierre 64
van der Rohe, Ludwig Mies 83, 99,
    153, 163, 202, 245, 260, 291, 404
Venice Biennale, 1990 284
Venturi, Robert 126, 239, 253–256,
    280
Venturi, Scott-Brown and
    Associates 253
Verizon Communications Inc. 375
Verne, Jules 25, 61
Victoria and Albert Museum,
    London 200
Vietnam War 221
Ville Radieuse 179
Vitra Factory 288
Vitra Fire Station 290–291
VJ Day 219
Vogue magazine 272
Volkische housing 197
Volkischer Beobachter 202
Volkswagen Beetle 268, 368
Volvo 226, 268
von Braun, Werner 187, 220, 223,
    283
von Daniken, Erich 141
von Linde, Karl 400
von Senger, Alexander 78
von Stroheim, Erich 271
VSS Project 1978 177

Wachsmann, Konrad 252
Warnock Report 101
Waterhouse, Keith 76, 258
Webb, Mike 60, 62

Webb, Sam 148
Webber, Andrew Lloyd 271
Webern, Anton 52
Weimar Republic 203-204
Weissenhofsiedlung, Stuttgart 196
Welch, Raquel 292
Wells, HG 61, 388–389
West Berlin 154, 348
Westminster City Council 145, 234
Whittle, Frank 140
Whole Earth Catalog, The 222
Wichita House 38, 106, 108
Willis Faber & Dumas 93, 175
Wittelsbach 154
Wolf Rock Lighthouse 212
Wolfe, Tom 76
Wolin, Sheldon 220–221
Woodcock, Kevin 76
Woodstock Typewriter Company
    382
Woodstock, New York State 221
World Architecture magazine 15
World Trade Center, New York City
    305, 350–351, 365
Wren, Christopher 41, 143, 201,
    258
Wright Brothers 364, 384–385
Wright 'Flyer' 384
Wright, Frank Lloyd 94, 141, 256,
    299–300, 396
Wright, Orville and Wilbur 187, 384

X-Files 297

Yacht House 168, 282
Yamasaki, Minoru 350
York, Peter 272
Young, Jimmy 76, 96
Young, John 128
YRM 173

architecture art design
fashion history photography
theory and things

www.bdpworld.com

Editor: David Jenkins
Designer: Thomas Manss & Company: Thomas Manss, Joana Niemeyer
Archival Research: Oliver Pawley; Matthew Foreman

Black Dog Publishing Limited
Unit 4.4 Tea Building
56 Shoreditch High Street
London
E1 6JJ

Tel: +44 (0)20 7613 1922
Fax: +44 (0)20 7613 1944
Email: info@blackdogonline.com
www.blackdogonline.com

All opinions expressed within this publication are those of the
authors and not necessarily of the publisher.

British Library Cataloguing-in-Publication Data.

A CIP record for this book is available from the British Library.

ISBN: 978 1 906155 19 3

Every effort has been made to trace the copyright holders, but if any have been inadvertently overlooked the
publishers will be pleased to make the necessary arrangements at the first opportunity.

Black Dog Publishing is an environmentally responsible company. The Strange Death Of Architectural Criticism:
Martin Pawley Collected Writings is printed on Amber Graphic, a chlorine free (ECF) woodfree offset paper
manufactured from woodpulp sourced from sustainable forests.